Aquarium Fish Keeping

Aquarium Fish Keeping

George Hadwin

RANDOM

RANDOM PUBLICATIONS

NEW DELHI (INDIA)

Aquarium Fish Keeping

ISBN 978-93-5111-928-9

Published in 2016 in India by

Reprint 2019

RANDOM PUBLICATIONS

4376-A/4B, Gali Murari Lal, Ansari Road
New Delhi-110 002
Phone : +9111-43580356, 011-23289044, 011-43142548
e-mail: sales@randompublications.com,
info@randompublications.com, randomexports@gmail.com

Type Setting by : Friends Media, Delhi-110089
Printed at : Mehra Printers, Delhi-110 092

Preface

Fishkeeping is a popular hobby concerned with keeping fish in a home aquarium or garden pond. There is also a piscicultural fishkeeping industry, as a branch of agriculture.

When fish are living under good conditions with favourable water quality, nutritious food, and optimal temperatures, disease generally occurs only when new bacteria, viruses, or parasites are introduced into the fish's habitat. When fish are living under less than optimal conditions, their resistance to disease is reduced, and they may be infected by common diseases that are often present in the environment at low levels. For this reason, it is very important to make sure that we do all that we can to ensure a good environment for our aquatic animals and protect them from the introduction of exotic diseases.

Fishkeepers are often known as "aquarists", since many of them are not solely interested in keeping fish. The hobby can be broadly divided into three specific disciplines according to the type of water the fish originate: freshwater, brackish, and marine (also called saltwater) fishkeeping.

Freshwater fishkeeping is by far the most popular branch of the hobby, with even small pet stores often selling a variety of freshwater fish, such as goldfish, guppies, and angelfish. While most freshwater aquaria are community tanks containing a variety of compatible species, single-species breeding aquaria are also popular. Livebearing fish such as mollies and guppies are among those most easily raised in captivity, but aquarists also regularly breed many types of cichlid, catfish, characins cyprinids, and killifish. The book will be of invaluable help to teachers, students, researchers and all those who are interested in this subject.

– Author

Contents

1

Aquatic Fish

When fish are living under good conditions with favourable water quality, nutritious food, and optimal temperatures, disease generally occurs only when new bacteria, viruses, or parasites are introduced into the fish's habitat. When fish are living under less than optimal conditions, their resistance to disease is reduced, and they may be infected by common diseases that are often present in the environment at low levels. For this reason, it is very important to make sure that we do all that we can to ensure a good environment for our aquatic animals and protect them from the introduction of exotic diseases.

GOOD ENVIRONMENT

For private ponds that are managed for recreational fishing or ornamental fish, the most important environmental considerations are these:

- Water quality
  - *Oxygen*: A problem when there are excessive nutrients, dense growths of plants or algae, when herbicides have been used, when fish are stocked and fed at high levels, and when the weather is hot and cloudy.
  - *pH*: Some kinds of soil chemistry can make your water very acidic or very alkaline.
  - *Alkalinity*: This is a measure of minerals in the pond that help keep the pH at the right level.
- Food availability
  - Proper stocking, liming, and fertilization ensure that there is adequate natural food.
  - Supplemental feeding of quality fish feeds helps too.
- Pond balance
  - Proper stocking not only ensures good growth but also may include fish that control aquatic plants and snails that carry fish parasites.

For commercial aquaculture ponds, tanks, and raceways, the most important environmental considerations are these:

- Water quality
  - Dissolved gasses including oxygen and carbon dioxide
  - Waste products like ammonia and nitrite
  - Alkalinity for pH control
  - Calcium and magnesium (hardness) and salt levels
  - Temperature appropriate for the species
- Food quality
  - Appropriate protein and fat levels
  - Quality ingredients
  - Correct pellet size and form
- Stocking
  - The right species
  - The right stocking density

PREVENTING EXOTIC DISEASES

For private fishing ponds, the primary consideration is the health of the fish that you put in the pond. For sportfish, this means that the fish should come from a reputable farm and that the fish should look healthy and free of disease when you purchase and stock them. It may even be worthwhile to ask the supplier about their fish health inspection programme. Many sportfish farms have very rigourous disease prevention programme, and they will be happy to share that information with you. You should never stock fish that you have caught in the wild. The wild fish may carry diseases that you do not want in your pond. For ornamental fish ponds, the most important consideration is to buy healthy fish that come with some assurances about their disease status. Of special concern are koi. There are some very serious exotic koi diseases that you must avoid. If you buy healthy–looking fish produced in the United States by a reputable breeder, the chance of having problems with koi ulcer disease or koi herpes virus (KHV) are fairly low; however, new ornamental fish should always be quarantined for several weeks (preferably at water temperatures in the 70s) before they are put in your pond. It would also be a good idea to ask the breeder about their koi herpes virus prevention programme. Good koi breeders will be happy to tell you about their disease prevention measures.

For commercial aquaculture, preventing the introduction of exotic diseases is of critical importance. All farms that produce aquatic animals should have plans to prevent the introduction of exotic diseases. The main routes of introduction are (in order of importance) infected animals, contaminated water, contaminated equipment, and wild animals that visit the farm facility.

To avoid disease problems, farms must produce their own stock or buy stock only from sources with good fish disease testing programmes and good disease prevention plans. If possible, the farm should use water supplies that do not harbour exotic diseases (wells and springs are very safe; run-off water is good; surface water from lakes and rivers may carry significant risks). Equipment returning to the farm from other places should be cleaned and disinfected before entering. Visits to the farm by wild animals that may carry diseases must be discouraged.

RECOGNIZING FISH HEALTH PROBLEMS

It can be difficult to monitor aquatic animals for health problems, especially when the animals live in large ponds or in water that is not crystal clear.

The list below describes some of the clues that may suggest that your aquatic animals are sick:

- A reduction in feed consumption not clearly related to low oxygen or temperature changes
- Any change in behaviour including:
  - Fish congregating at the surface or at the water's edge
  - Fish congregating around fresh water inflows or aerators
  - Fish swimming slowly or in circles
  - Fish "flashing" (rubbing against the bottom or other hard surfaces)
- Damage to skin and fins including:
  - Fin erosion
  - Skin ulcers
  - Skin discolouration (darker, lighter, reddening)
  - White or tan fuzzy patches
  - White spots
  - Bumps on the skin
  - Open sores
  - Cloudy or swollen eyes
- Dead and dying fish (the obvious one!)

SICKNESS OF AQUATIC ANIMALS

The first step whenever any aquatic animal health problem is suspected is to look at the water quality. Commercial fish producers usually have some water quality testing equipment. All producers should be able to test for oxygen levels, ammonia, pH, and nitrite and should recognize optimal and acceptable levels of these chemicals. Sportfish farm pond owners and ornamental fish owners will often need to seek out professional assistance with their water quality testing. When water quality problems are ruled out, the next step is to consider parasites and other diseases. Many aquatic animal diseases produce symptoms that are very similar. A correct diagnosis usually requires an aquatic animal health laboratory with the expertise to recognize fish parasites by microscopy and the ability to culture and identify bacteria, fungi, and viruses. When a disease problem is suspected, the first thing to do is to contact a fish health professional or fish disease diagnostic laboratory for assistance.

FISH DISEASE DIAGNOSTIC LABORATORY

Finding help with a fish health problem can often be quite challenging. Assistance might come from state or university fish health laboratories, veterinary schools, extension programmes, wildlife agencies, or veterinarians who include aquatic animals in their practice. For commercial fish farmers, the best way to find fish health assistance is to consult your state aquaculture coordinator, your state aquaculture extension staff, your state veterinarian, other local fish and shellfish producers, or the American Veterinary Medical Association at www.aquavetmed.info.

For private sportfish ponds, you may find help at the same places as the fish farmers, but it is also likely that your state wildlife agency will be able to guide you. Ornamental fish owners may find assistance at the same sources as fish farmers, but they may want access to services like X rays, ultrasound, blood chemistry, and surgery that are only available through veterinarians.

Once you have identified a fish health professional, the next step is to call that professional and ask what kinds of information and samples will be needed.

The information needed will often include answers to the following questions:

- How big is the pond/tank?
- What species of animals are dying?
- How many fish are dying?
- How long have they been dying?
- Are there sick fish swimming around right now?
- How are those sick fish behaving?
- What do they look like (sores, spots, and the like)?
- Are they eating?
- Have you used any treatments?
- Have you treated weeds or algae recently?
- Have there been any recent changes in the colour or clarity of the water?
- What has the weather been like (temperatures, wind, and rain)?
- When did you last stock new fish?
- When did you last harvest fish?

In some cases, help may come to your farm or pond, but often you will be asked to send samples to a laboratory. These samples may include water, live fish, fish on ice, or other materials needed for testing. Only the laboratory can provide you with detailed directions. It is very important to always call the lab prior to sending any samples for testing.

TREATING FISH DISEASES

Drugs and chemicals to treat diseases in aquatic animals are highly regulated by the FDA and EPA. There are very few legal drugs, especially for food animals, and very strict limitations on their use.

All drugs and chemicals must be used exactly according to their labels or under direct veterinary supervision. Any violation is punishable by state and federal law, and any product treated with an illegal drug or chemical is "adulterated" and would be ordered destroyed.

When treating an aquatic animal disease:

- Be sure that the disease has been correctly diagnosed (often this requires assistance from a fish health professional).
- Be sure that the chemical or drug to be used is appropriate for the disease, the fish species, and the water quality (including the temperature).
- Be sure that the chemical or drug is legal for the use.
- Be sure that the chemical or drug is used exactly according to the label or according to guidance from your veterinarian.
- For food animals, be sure that the required withdrawal period (time elapsed between the last treatment and sale of the animals as food) is followed.

For commercial fish production, there are also several legal vaccines that can be used to prevent fish diseases. As with drugs, these vaccines must be used according to their labels.

FISH HEALTH INSPECTION AND CERTIFICATION

Commercial fish farms that ship fish alive, especially interstate or internationally, are often required to conduct inspections for fish diseases. Each state, federal, and international jurisdiction may write and enforce its own unique fish health regulations.

Before shipping any live product anywhere, it is imperative that you make sure that you understand the regulations of all the legal jurisdictions involved, that you have complied with all of the requirements and obtained all of the needed permits, and that your shipment (number, species, dates, etc.) is exactly according to those permits and regulations. Any interstate violation of fish health regulations can put you and your farm at risk for severe penalties (including felony convictions) and fines under state laws and the Federal Lacey Act.

Importation of fish into the United States is under the jurisdiction of the U.S. Fish and Wildlife Service (USFWS) (salmon, trout, and other salmonid fish species), the U.S. Department of Agriculture-Animal and Plant Health Inspection Service (USDA–APHIS), and the destination state. Federal and state permits may be required prior to shipment into the United States. Fish are often restricted to entry through certain ports where federal inspectors are available. Before importing fish, consult with the USDA-APHIS-National Center for Import and Export (NCIE) for advice and with the agriculture and wildlife agencies of the destination state. The NCIE can also assist you with exports to other countries. For other shipments of live animals, sometimes even within your state, be sure that you have complied with all state aquatic animal health regulations. The regulatory agency with jurisdiction over aquatic animals varies from state to state, and you may need to consult both the state agriculture agency and the state wildlife agency.

Extension fish health experts, other farmers, regional aquaculture centers, state aquaculture coordinators, and fish health testing laboratories may be valuable sources of information and assistance; however, penalties for errors can be severe, so careful shippers always confirm their regulatory knowledge with an official representative of the regulatory agency.

AQUATIC SYSTEMS OF THE BASIN

The aquatic systems of the Basin are diverse and productive. Already the resources are under pressure from human intervention and this is likely to increase in future. The current population of the Basin is around 500 million, which by 2031 could increase to over a billion, almost half of which could be below the poverty line. Perhaps the greatest single impact at present is for the diversion and storage of water from the river for irrigation. The annual run-off into the Ganges Basin is approximately 469 billion m^3. Of this, an estimated 85 billion m^3 is diverted by barrages, either into canal systems for irrigation and storage or for hydroelectric schemes. Of this diverted water, 60 percent is accounted for by canal projects. Every major tributary has at least one barrage across it. On each northern tributary from Nepal there are barrages at the border region with India. Near Hardwar, the water of the main stem of the Ganges is diverted by a major barrage into the Upper Ganga Canal that was built in 1854 and is largely used to irrigate 3.7 million ha of land with some electricity is also being generated. The main stem, below the barrage is reduced to a very low flow through much of the year.

This system of barrages greatly compartmentalises the ecosystem and certainly presents major barriers to migrations of fish, which may have a general effect on fish distribution as described elsewhere. They represent an artificial demarcation between the upland and lowland systems of the Ganges and, to some extent; they must act as sediment traps. In other cases, the presence of barrages can accentuate problems of pollution by reducing downstream flows for effluent disposal, particularly in the dry season, which can produce chemical barriers to fish distribution. There will be continued pressure to increase the area of croplands under irrigation within the lowland areas, as it is a principal means whereby crop production can keep up with population increases in future. A significant proportion of water diverted for irrigation is returned to the river although at a lower quality. The influence of micro-pollutants, which are related to the extent of the use of agro-chemicals, is uncertain but is likely to increase as the pressure to intensify agricultural production proceeds. In the Indian sector alone, more than 150 000 km^2 of the Ganges Basin is irrigated using some 85

000 m^3 of river water and 49 500 m^3 of groundwater but this, as in most irrigation systems, has led to extensive problems of soil salinisation. As a result the salt load of the returning irrigation water over 6.3 million tonnes of salt are estimated to be added to the water annually. However, observations on conductivity levels in the main river suggest this has yet to have major effects on the salt concentration of the river as a whole.

The largest barrage of all is Farakka. This was completed in 1975 and was built without consultation with the downstream user state, Bangladesh (or East Pakistan as it was until 1972), the border of which is 17 km downstream. The barrage is designed to regulate river water discharge and to divert a major part of the dry season flow along the Hooghly Canal towards the Bhagirathi-Hooghly and Calcutta rivers. There are also other barriers beyond the canal on the Baghirati itself. In 1995 a formal water sharing agreement was made between India and Bangladesh that agreed to minimum downstream flows and ensures annual meetings to discuss issues between the states. The impact of the Farakka Barrage complex upon the system would seem to include a progressive reduction in the significance of the hilsa fishery upstream of the Barrage as the route from the estuary via the Bhagirathi arm has been impeded. A further possible effect is that the reduction in flow down the Ganges (Padma) below Farakka allows greater incursions of tidal saline water into the southwestern region of Bangladesh, thereby reducing suitable land and water for agriculture.

It is, however, difficult to substantiate in this dynamic fluctuating tidal environment with great annual variations, mainly because of a lack of historical, baseline data. This indicates the importance of good pre and post implementation studies around such structures. As it is, the estuarine hilsa fishery of the Bangladesh delta seems to be maintained.

Within the delta of Bangladesh the principal process of compartmentalisation is not of the river itself but of the floodplains to facilitate the cultivation of rice. Some 40 percent of the floodplain has been modified by empolderment for flood control and irrigation. This has led to a compartmentalisation of distribution of fish particularly the migratory "white fishes" which includes all the major carps. As elsewhere in the Ganges Basin the catches of major carp have declined markedly in Bangladesh, for example, the major carp portion of the catch on Seimanganj floodplain declined from 66.4 percent in 1967 to 13 percent by 1984.

The compartmentalisation of the floodplains may well have contributed to this. A systematic investigation of the impacts of flood control and irrigation schemes on fisheries showed that under conditions of complete flood control reductions could be 81 percent. Under controlled flooding or partial empolderment there is no significant difference in catch with averages of 100-110 kg ha^{-1} inside and out. What does happen, however, is that there is a reduction in bio-diversity within polders of 19-25 percent but, most significantly, a reduction in migratory species up to 95 percent with the main emphasis being on the small floodplain resident species or black fishes. Given the fishing effort that can be deployed on these species in compartments during the dry season, their regular resurgence indicates very resilient life cycle strategies. Up to 59 percent of annual variance in catches can be due to effort under these circumstances.

To contrast this loss of species and valuable elements of the catch as well as to boost recruitment into local populations, major interventions are being undertaken on the floodplains of Bangladesh to redress the situation, either by direct stock enhancement with fry or juveniles or through habitat improvement and restoration. In the largest scale intervention, 60 000 ha were stocked with 50 million carp fingerlings, a mixture of indigenous major carps, Chinese and common carps, over five years which resulted in an incremental fish production of 20 811 tonnes. There is also evidence that recruitment has been augmented in the wider river populations. Stocking interventions, however, may be accompanied by undesirable social consequences including the further exclusion of poor and vulnerable groups from participation in a fishery that has increased in value. As well as enhancement, recruitment may be increased by such processes as habitat restoration.

An exercise in habitat restoration which focussed on the clearing of silted channels connecting floodplains to the main river channel increased the proportion of migratory species caught subsequently, including major carp from 2 percent of the catch to 24 percent, and increased the yield 6-fold, from 1860 kg to 11 384 kg per year throughout the study area. In these ways, some of the impacts of compartmentalisation of the floodplains are being addressed in the delta in a continuing fashion but many problems remain, particularly regarding management and governance issues.

In the upland areas of the basin in Nepal, the greatest impacts are said to be due to erosion and increased sediment load from deforestation and from the need to impound water for hydropower generation. The extent of forest removal and increased erosion, however, is difficult to assess. There is evidence that deforestation is a long-term, historical process that may not have accelerated greatly in recent times. It has also been shown that for a basin the size of the Ganges, the sediment delivery ratio is less than 10 percent and that consequently the main channel carries only a modest amount of sediment from the mountains and that, consequently, anthropogenic influences in the mountains have only a limited impact on the plains. It is possible that most of the sediment in the main river comes from storage places and channel erosion.

The other feature of upper basin use is the harnessing of the rivers for hydropower. Nepal has a great potential for hydropower but as yet only 0.27 percent of its assessed potential is being employed. The rather scattered nature of its own population renders micro projects and run-of-the river schemes good options for domestic generation but the export potential of electricity to northern India and beyond is a commercial imperative. Generating electricity on this scale seems to involve large storage dams which have a number of negative impacts including, as a barrier to fish distribution, possible resettlement of displaced people, disturbance of fragile environments both at the site and downstream and the need to provide roads and services.

The upland rivers certainly have a significance in the rural economies, which has been under-estimated, and it is, therefore, essential that proper evaluations be carried out on the advantages and disadvantages. Under ideal circumstances run-of-the-river projects can avoid many of the environmental disadvantages of storage dams but cases can be seen in Nepal where all the water of the river passes down the adduction tunnel with negligible flow remaining between inlet and outlet. This can provide as much a barrier to fish and navigation as a dam wall. Proper planning and management is required.

Other anthropogenic effects in the basin include pollution. At present, it is of local significance and largely a feature of the Lower Basin where urbanisation and industrialisation are proceeding. The Ganges Basin is reported to carry some 200 tonnes of biological oxygen demand (BOD) per day gross pollution.

However, it is still relatively localised and focussed on urban centres including Hardwar, Kanpur, Varanasi and Diamond Harbour near Calcutta. In addition, the national capitals of New Dehli and Dhaka both have significant impacts. The dry, low water season poses the greatest problems of dilution and dispersal of pollutants. Probably the worst section is between Kanpur and Allahabad largely due to discharges from the industries of Kanpur, which include tanneries, metalworking and dairies. This appears to be related to the decline in catch of fisherfolk from 30-40 kg to 15 kg per day downstream of the town. Elsewhere, although loads can be quite high, the river disperses them quite rapidly. Even at Varanassi, the main effluent plume is confined to near the city and the river recovers some 20 km downstream. Nevertheless, national governments are concerned and the government of India has been implementing the Ganga Action Plan to start cleaning up the river and preventing it from becoming worse whilst in Bangladesh, the Global Environment Fund is promoting pollution protection. At least at Patna, general water quality has recently improved with, for example, BOD being cut by 75 percent over a decade.

In general, the status of the Ganges Basin reflects the transitional nature of the economies of the constituent states. In developed countries, the greatest problems are commonly gross domestic and industrial pollution and abstraction whilst in developing countries it is frequently degradation of the basin through inappropriate land use, erosion and habitat loss. All of these processes are occurring in the Ganges and probably provides a number of case studies and lessons to learn for basins currently occupied by poorer states as their economic condition improves with development. There is, however, no overall management concept for the international basin as a whole. There is no international basin management authority such as exists on the Mekong with the Mekong River Commission and no regular fora for making basin-wide management decisions or for regularly sharing information. Critical information on hydrology and satellite imagery can often be classified for security reasons. Using basin-wide data can add dimensions to predictability and management options. For example, using upstream Indian rainfall data in relation to time series of Bangladesh catch data can help predict the likely impact on fish yields three years later. Taking into account all data on the fishes, the fishing communities and development needs it is possible to plan for fisheries management across Asian river basins including the Ganges. A basin-wide approach to management is essential for the economic and environmental sustainability of such large river systems.

AQUATIC GENETIC RESOURCES

Patent applications have caused no end of controversy in the use of plant genetic resources. Naturally, a seed company that develops a genetically modified strain of millet resistant to a fungal infection, for example, considers it a top priority to protect its invention so that competitors don't copy it and flood the market with a cheaper version. But what if the company came up with the idea by modelling its invention on another strain developed by farmers in a traditional agricultural community? The last few years have seen a succession of international disputes – a notable example being the outcry that arose when a US company attempted to patent Basmati rice despite its long history in south Asia. What if a pharmaceutical company succeeds in developing and patenting a pain-killing drug after hiring a researcher to visit shamans in the Amazon, learn about their healing practices, and bring back samples of their medicinal plants for analysis in the US?

Obviously, the ownership of ideas (whether scientific inventions or traditional knowledge) has been the source of far more wealth than the ownership of genetic resources in their physical state. The global trade in plant genetic resources is big business, estimated by ten Kate and Laird to be several billion dollars annually, so it's hardly surprising that the scramble to get legal protection for products and processes has had some significant impacts on developments in intellectual property law – developments that have been almost entirely shaped by plant genetic resources issues.

As we mentioned in the previous chapter, the number of genetically modified fish strains developed in the past couple of decades is infinitesimal compared to the number of plant strains. Pharmaceutical companies are struggling to find powerful cures based on marine organisms, but the vast majority of drugs inspired by compounds existing in nature are based on plants

– by 1996, only two of the top selling 150 pharmaceuticals were derived from marine organisms. Nevertheless, there may be sufficient parallels between some uses of plant and aquatic genetic resources – for example, between plant and marine bioprospecting and between farmed fish and crop enhancement – that patent law agreements can safely accommodate both types of activity.

Where the intellectual property comparisons between the two fields diverge most dramatically is in the area of traditional knowledge. There is simply no parallel in traditional fishing villages to traditional farmers' knowledge of crop breeding and to other communities' knowledge of medicinal plants. This might seem a matter of no great note were it not for the fact that several emerging national biodiversity laws, based loosely on the CBD guidelines, spell out the rights of traditional communities in terms of the knowledge they contribute to the use of aquatic genetic resources. There is no doubt that traditional fishing communities have a wealth of knowledge that comes from the importance of fish as food or ceremonial object – including knowledge of fish life cycles, migration habits, habitat preferences and of techniques for catching fish – yet it is likely to be largely irrelevant to uses for breeding. As we'll show in this and the following chapters, a too rigid interpretation of laws tying community rights to traditional knowledge could mean significant future conflicts (as the trade in aquatic genetic resources becomes more common) and run counter to the CBD's objectives of promoting conservation, sustainable use and equitable sharing of benefits.

GENES AND GENETIC INVENTIONS

By protecting the ideas of inventors from unauthorized use by others, intellectual property law (including patents, copyright, trademarks, industrial designs and trade secrets) protects an inventor's economic interests and the interest of society in encouraging new inventions that may benefit the public. A patent is a legal certificate that gives an inventor exclusive rights to produce, use, sell or import an invention for a fixed period, usually 17 to 20 years. A patent application must demonstrate that an invention is useful (have industrial application), novel (recent, original and not already publicly known), not obvious to a person skilled in the technology and more inventive than mere discovery of what already exists in nature. Patents can be granted for products, specific uses of products (eg use of a drug to cure cancer but not for purposes yet to be discovered), and processes used to create a product.

The law of patents was developed in 19th-century Europe to protect inventions of factory machinery and excluded the protection of living materials, foods and medicines. However, demands for protection of inventions related to commercial uses of genetic resources have revolutionized patent criteria, and the state of the law remains in flux in the wake of new scientific advances and amid controversies about the patenting of life and the role of traditional knowledge in invention. In the 1960s, the US legislated the right of plant breeders to patent seeds, preventing others from selling the same variety, and in 1980 the US Supreme Court accepted the first patent on a genetically altered micro-organism. By 1997, the US had granted 69 patents on animals.

Keeping track of the current state of the law is further complicated by the fact that different countries take different approaches to patent law. The European Patent Convention provides that microbiological processes are patentable but 'essentially biological processes' are not, thereby excluding plant varieties obtained by conventional breeding. No such restriction exists in the US. Decisions by the US Patent and Trademark Office to grant monopoly rights over plant, animal and human genetic materials have sparked a rush to collect, map and patent genes, based largely on their potential.

Developing countries have been under pressure to recognize US patents, although many developing countries exclude patent protection for plant varieties and animal races. Both the scope of protection and the rights of patent holders continue to be expanded as the law continues to evolve in industrial countries. By contrast, developing countries such as Argentina, Brazil and India have set limits by allowing patents on processes but not products and by requiring patent holders to make socially useful products available in the domestic market.

Genetic modification of animal life (the 'Harvard mouse' is a controversial example) has drawn attention to the need to address demands to allow patents on living creatures. Pharmaceutical companies and bioprospectors collecting on their behalf have been actively patenting processes to develop drugs and cosmetics derived from research based on aquatic genetic resources that range from marine invertebrates to algae. Patenting of new fish varieties (such as the Super Salmon and Arctic char varieties) and of processes used in their development has been more limited but can be expected to increase significantly as the aquaculture industry expands. The US Patent and Trademark Office led the way by approving a patent protecting a method of increasing the growth rate of a transgenic salmon.

The adaptation of patent laws to cover genetic resources is still controversial. A cotton gin is a very different type of invention from a cotton (or catfish) gene. Patenting of living materials not only raises ethical questions, it also frequently raises concerns about the novelty of 'inventions', especially when an inventor may have relied for inspiration on traditional knowledge. Historically, while technology exporting countries have been quick to develop patent legislation to promote new development, technology importers have had little reason to develop their own patent laws. Developing countries have been understandably reluctant to embrace universal patent laws relating to uses of genetic resources (as TRIPS proposes) because applicants from industrialized countries are the primary beneficiaries. As Halewood notes, the net effect of globalization of intellectual property laws through agreements such as TRIPS and the North American Free Trade Agreement has been primarily to benefit developed countries in the use of genetic resources. Plant breeders have pushed for an extension of intellectual property rights to include new varieties produced by breeders. There are no equivalent mechanisms for aquatic genetic resources, but these are likely to develop, albeit with modifications that reflect the fact that few aquatic animals have been domesticated.

CONTROLLING ACCESS TO GENETIC INVENTIONS

All countries that are members of the World Trade Organization (WTO) are obliged to implement TRIPS. The agreement focuses on the importance of intellectual property rights in promoting trade liberalization. The emphasis on intellectual property in WTO agreements is a response to the explosive growth in information technology and biotechnology in international trade as well as the desire of some industrial countries to protect products from intellectual 'piracy' in foreign markets.

TRIPS requires all member states to set minimum standards of intellectual property protection, thereby ensuring a far higher degree of global uniformity than previously existed. Patents must be available for inventions in all fields of technology without discrimination, whether products are imported or locally produced. Article 27 requires member states to adopt national level intellectual property systems for all products and processes, including pharmaceuticals, modified micro-organisms and microbiological processes. Unlike the earlier international undertaking, TRIPS clearly applies to inventions derived from aquatic genetic resources.

Negotiations on the passage of TRIPS highlighted the very different viewpoints of industrial and developing countries on the extent to which patenting of biological diversity-related inventions should be permitted. The most controversial section of TRIPS has been Article 27.3(b). While it allows countries to exclude plants and animals as well as essentially biological processes from patentability, WTO members must provide protection for plant varieties either by patents and/or by an effective *sui generis* system – that is, a unique system of rights for a specific item or technology. The exemption for plants and animals remains a controversial issue, with some developed countries facing strong pressure from industry to push for the removal of the exemption. Some critics of TRIPS argue that doing so would undermine the CBD by depriving countries of the right to prohibit IPRs on life forms and by diminishing their ability to negotiate a fair share of benefits arising from the use of genetic resources. During a 1999 review of TRIPS, a group of least-developed countries proposed, unsuccessfully, that TRIPS should contain a provision that patents must not be granted without the prior informed consent of the country where the genetic resources originated. In 1998, an Organization of African Unity (OAU) model law proposed a prohibition against patents on inventions derived from biological resources obtained from member countries. In essence, developing countries were pressured into accepting TRIPS in return for the promise of the economic advantage created by improved opportunities for trade. Some developing countries objected to the imposition of Western notions of 'inventions' in parts of the world where many important innovations had occurred in an evolutionary and informal manner in farming and other local communities. Indigenous groups have condemned TRIPS as flying in the face of indigenous traditions of treating community knowledge as a shared resource and as essentially forcing indigenous peoples to adopt Western patent laws in order to prevent the commercial appropriation of their own knowledge. In the opinion of one group, TRIPS pushes indigenous peoples to 'play in a game in which the rules are defined by the opponents'.

PLAIN DEALING OR PATENT THEFT

The urgency of addressing the question of community rights over genetic resources has been heightened in recent years by a flurry of complaints about biopiracy. The Crucible Group defines 'biopiracy' as the taking of genetic or biological resources without the prior informed consent of local people or a competent state authority for access and benefit sharing under mutually agreed terms. Most frequently, charges of biopiracy are related to the use of plant genetic resources and often are spurred by patents of discoveries that are in some way related to the use of traditional knowledge of farmers or of indigenous communities. One much publicized example was the attempt by a US company to patent Basmati rice. Another was the dispute between the pharmaceutical company researcher and the Wapishana people.

Had there been an access and benefit-sharing law in place, the Wapishana might have negotiated an agreement with the biochemist to share in the profits from any future royalties or obtain some other more immediate reward, or they might simply have denied him permission to make collections or refused to give him any information about their traditional uses. They might also have demanded benefits that he felt unable to provide without knowing whether his research might lead to a deal with a pharmaceutical company or the development of a marketable product. Article 8(j) of the CBD is intended to deal with exactly this type of situation. Situations like the one involving the Wapishana have occurred many times in different parts of the world, as traditional communities attempt to earn recognition for the value of their plant knowledge, and examples of benefit-sharing agreements are beginning to occur with more and more frequency.

Biopiracy and Aquatic Genetic Resources

It's hard to imagine aquatic resources parallels for the biopiracy. One might have occurred if Aqua Bounty had developed and patented the 'Super Salmon' after learning from indigenous people about the anti-freeze properties of the ocean pout, which were used to create the new strain. Even then, the company might have argued that the desirable characteristics of the pout were obvious to any observer. Traditional knowledge of aquatic biodiversity may be abundant but is not necessarily relevant to uses of aquatic genetic resources such as aquaculture and the development of pharmaceutical products from animals that live in areas that are inaccessible to local people.

Nevertheless, complaints about biopiracy of marine organisms are not uncommon. Indeed, one of the main catalysts for the passage of access legislation in the Philippines in 1995 was a series of newspaper articles on biopiracy of marine invertebrates (and of plants) by foreign collectors. After the law came into effect, the complaints continued, and communities began targeting the government for not properly enforcing the law and for its lax requirements for obtaining community consent.

When the US-based pharmaceutical company Neurex Inc isolated and patented the toxin SNX-111, produced by the Philippine sea snail *Conus magnus*, civil society organizations took both the company and government to task. The stakes were large: sales of the pain-killing drug derived from the toxin reportedly earned Neurex more than US$80 million during the first year of marketing. Critics charged that the government supported biopiracy by funding research by scientists at the Marine Science Institute (MSI) who collaborated with the University of Utah in collecting specimens, isolating the toxin and forming a private company to capitalize on the snail.

Previously, collectors for the MSI would purchase specimens from fishermen in several areas of the country, who gather different varieties of cone snail for their ornamental value and have no use for the meat. Philippines law now requires foreign collectors to partner with Philippines research institutions, which must get community consent for collections (whether or not traditional knowledge is needed by collectors). To comply with regulations under the law, MSI holds public information sessions in communities where collections of marine organisms are proposed and must also obtain permission from local government representatives. Critics of the process note low turnouts at information sessions and suggest that local people may not even be aware that marine bioprospecting is taking place in their communities.

Making informed consent requirements both fair and feasible is a tough challenge. If the consent process is too cumbersome and expensive, collectors may simply go to other, more 'friendly' countries if the organisms they're looking for can be obtained elsewhere. For both countries and communities, it's a question of how to develop effective regulations without killing the goose that might lay a golden egg.

The Philippines law distinguishes between collections for academic and commercial purposes. Getting a fair share of whatever profits may arise from research by foreign collectors continues to be an issue for countries that have not yet passed laws regulating access. In the Bahamas, University of California researchers obtained a permit for the collection of soft coral, without charge and with only the condition that they file reports on their work. The university subsequently obtained a patent on a production process that was in turn sold to a company that marketed it to the cosmetic company Estée Lauder, which used it in the development of beauty products. The Bahamian government unsuccessfully attempted to negotiate royalty payments from the extracting company, which responded that it might simply move its collection activities to more accommodating Caribbean countries where the same species is abundant. The Bahamian government is now in the process of developing legislation to govern access to genetic resources.

University of California researchers have also been criticized for patenting the anti-inflammatory agent pseudopterosin, a compound found in sea whips in the Caribbean and subsequently incorporated in a skin cream also marketed by Estée Lauder. The average annual royalty income received by the university for patented pseudopterosins is reported to be more than US$750,000.

While bioprospecting for marine invertebrates gets most of the attention, biopiracy concerns sometimes extend to fish as well. The Amazon region has been hard hit by illegal trade in wildlife, and the Brazilian government attempts to be vigilant in stemming its flow. However, given the size and remoteness of the region, enforcement of environmental law is a stupendous task. In another example of suspected aquatic biopiracy, a German aquarist who planned to breed ornamental cichlid varieties (cichlids include important food fish such as tilapias and tiny ornamentals prized for their bright colours) travelled to Brazil to collect wild specimens in the middle Rio Negro. When apprehended by a representative of IBAMA, the Brazilian Institute responsible for enforcement of protected species laws, the collector was examining the viscera of cichlids to determine their natural diet. He had apparently obtained written permission from the nearest municipality but had not sought the necessary approvals from IBAMA. He was deported and ordered not to return.

Biopiracy Debates in Brazil

The chief prosecutor for the Brazilian State of Amazonas, who opened an enquiry into biopiracy in 1997, estimates that about 20,000 individual plant samples are illegally removed from the country every year. Scientific laboratories generally receive the samples and information from third parties who don't say where they came from.

How is the information obtained? A representative from IBAMA notes: 'The scientists congregate in small frontier towns. Then they ask the Indians what they would do if they had a headache, muscle pains or a bad stomach. The local people then take them into the jungle and show them which plant they would use to cure those symptoms. The scientists pay the Indians a little money, then take the plant back to their labs. There, they discover the principle by which the plant works and sell their preliminary research on to the pharmaceutical companies for development'. VRobert Smeraldi, director of the Friends of the Earth Amazon programme, notes: 'There is widespread smuggling of genetic material by unauthorized companies. I'm not talking about respectable pharmaceutical companies being directly involved, but I do believe they could benefit from illegal research'. A Brazilian cancer specialist was sharply criticized by the media after receiving close to US$1 million from the American National Cancer Institute to analyse a number of Amazonian plants. His critics argued that if information taken from indigenous peoples is used to develop the world's first anti-cancer drug, the Indian tribes might lose out even if the cancer specialist himself does not profit. In his defence, the researcher noted: 'While we continue to talk and worry about biopiracy, fewer people are out there actually studying the Amazon, which is a serious form of scientific neglect. Of course biopiracy happens, but we have to balance this against not researching the rainforest at all. Ultimately that is much more damaging to mankind'. The money that changes hands in the collection of ornamental fish can stymie the most determined efforts at enforcement, especially in areas like the Amazon – the largest and perhaps most ungovernable river basin in the world. Rohter reports that zebra fish from the Xingu River are so valuable that specimens are used as local currency and that dealers' profit margins are comparable to those in the cocaine trade, with a particularly rare specimen bringing as much as US$600 from a Japanese collector.

Although Brazil has attempted to control sales to prevent rare species from being wiped out, black market dealers continue to thrive. Rohter quotes a regional IBAMA representative as stating that, with only five agents to monitor all wildlife in an area twice the size of New Jersey, little can be done to protect illegal traffic. A tropical fish expert at the Emilio Goeldi Museum in Belem notes that tropical fish dealers routinely file false customs declarations and shipping waybills to get around restrictions, yet that there is little public interest in the problem. Stopping unauthorized collection of aquatic genetic resources is a challenge at the best of times. Access laws are unlikely to work unless government has the political will and provides the necessary funds for enforcement. This support may be absent in both developed and developing countries depending on the degree of cooperation among different levels of bureaucracy and of coordination among policy structures. Bribery of officials may create an additional impediment in countries where it is a common tradition.

Opposing Views on Biopiracy

Even when the approval of national agencies and indigenous communities is received, charges of biopiracy may still arise. Indigenous communities may grant permission for collections to occur without understanding (or in some cases being adequately informed of) the true purpose of the collection, as in the case of the Wapishana and the cunani plant. Collectors may take unfair advantage of communities that lack the capacity or the necessary information to negotiate fair deals. Even if the purpose of collection is fully understood, agreements may be perceived to be grossly unfair. Indigenous people may receive a pittance for the right to collect or may be offered royalties that never come to pass or are minuscule in relation to profits. A 1998 estimate placed annual global sales of pharmaceuticals at US$300 billion, of which between 25 and 50 per cent are derived from genetic resources. With almost 70 per cent of the total number of ethnolinguistic groups in the world living in 225 regions of the highest biological importance (WWF, 2000), it may be assumed that indigenous communities have been and will continue to be primary sources of the genetic resources needed for pharmaceutical development.

As the Wapishana example illustrates, biopiracy applies both to physical resources and the knowledge that makes their value immediately evident to collectors. Communities face challenges on both fronts: protecting their knowledge against misuse or appropriation under foreign intellectual property laws; and protecting resources over which they may have no legal authority. Very often, in the eyes of communities, the greatest perpetrators of biopiracy are not foreign interests but levels of government in their own countries that exercise authority over 'public' resources nationwide and deny indigenous and other communities a say in who collects plants, fish and animals in community territories. In several countries, struggles for the right to self-determination are fuelled in large part by frustration over lack of access to traditional resources and exploitation by outside interests who have no obligation to seek community consent once having received the consent of governments. Corporations may face accusations of biopiracy even when they have conscientiously complied with all government regulations or have negotiated with communities in what they believe to be good faith. So may collectors from scientific institutions who depend on access to genetic resources for basic research, and whose findings are freely published.

Accusations of biopiracy may relate to activities ranging from the collection of individual animals (eg rare Brazilian ornamental fish) to the entire system of collection of biological and genetic resources – what Shiva describes as the sequel to colonization of countries, in which 'colonies have now been extended to the interior spaces, the 'genetic codes' of life forms from microbes and plants and animals, including humans'. As Dutfield (n.d.) points out, noting that exploitation of genetic resources has even been called 'the slavery of the new millennium', such rhetoric may in fact undermine legitimate efforts to gain fairer treatment for countries and communities that seek a more level playing field. While the term 'biopiracy' may sound inflammatory to some, the issue raises legitimate questions about fair play for countries and communities that provide aquatic genetic resources.

TRADITIONAL KNOWLEDGE

What happens if, without a community's permission, a company patents a product or process made possible by the use of the community's traditional knowledge? While it is true that many indigenous communities have a history of freely sharing their knowledge about wild plants and animals, they may have concerns about the unauthorized use of their knowledge that have nothing to do with compensation but a lot to do with issues such as a lack of respect for a living creature or deceitful dealings with a community, etc. Patent offices rarely require applicants to disclose whether an idea has been appropriated from a traditional community. Even if a traditional community wanted to seek recourse, using the avenues of Western legal systems might be both contrary to its beliefs and unaffordable.

Interest in access to traditional knowledge about plant genetic resources has grown by leaps and bounds as the gene rush seeks out new sources of potentially valuable information – like the gold rushes of earlier centuries, making a valuable find may be a long shot, but the potential rewards may be so high that it's worth the effort and the risk. That's why the question of who owns traditional knowledge and how communities can control its use has become such a big issue in recent years. It's also why international agreements like the CBD have placed so much emphasis on using the demand for traditional knowledge as a rationale for the expansion of community rights.

APPROACHES TO THE RECOGNITION OF INDIGENOUS RIGHTS

Countries take many approaches to the recognition of indigenous rights of ownership and control over aquatic genetic resources. Canada has been actively involved in the negotiation of treaties with indigenous peoples. The Inuit, a people along the Arctic coast, recently completed an agreement that recognizes both land and resource rights. The Canadian DFO retains a role in the management of sea-going fish, but communities have the right to prior informed consent to collection of fish broodstock.

Arctic charr, the northernmost species in the family Salmonidae, has long been a staple in the diet of Inuit peoples on the coast of the Arctic Ocean in Canada. While some charr inhabit landlocked lakes, most are anadromous, migrating in late summer from the ocean to rivers and lakes to spawn, and reaching a weight of up to 11.3 kg. During recent years the popularity of the fish in urban markets has increased, creating an additional source of income for Inuit fishers in northern Canada. But charr are slow growing, and the genetically unique subpopulations or stocks of charr are extremely sensitive to overfishing. Consequently, Inuit communities developing sustainable management plans have had to grapple with how best to conserve a diminishing resource while supporting local fishing economies (eg Holman Hunters and

Trappers et al, 1994). The Northwest Territories Scientists' Act requires consent of local communities before any scientific research is undertaken in the Territory. Enacted in 1974, the Act was one of the earliest examples in a developed country of legislation that reflects emerging international principles for respecting indigenous knowledge and returning benefits to knowledge holders and their communities. In 1993, Canadian Inuit concluded negotiations of a land claim agreement with the government of Canada. The Nunavut Land Claims Agreement established principles of Inuit priority in the harvesting of marine resources and of ownership over the resources in Inuit-owned land and marine areas.

Soon after the 1993 land agreement came into effect, Canada's DFO began refusing fish harvesting, research and farming permits in the Nunavut region unless the prior consent of local communities had been obtained. Icy Waters, the major charr farming company in the Arctic, proposed a joint venture with Inuit communities and an Ontario university research group to set up a new company, Suvaaq Inc., to improve the company's existing broodstock that were based on previous DFO collections. Under the proposal, each of seven participating Inuit communities would receive a 5 per cent equity stake in the new company in exchange for sperm from six male Arctic charr from two separate stocks found in waters near the communities. Icy Waters suggested that Inuit communities would also benefit through education and practical experience in fish farming and access to genetically improved stocks as these were developed. The business proposal provided that each community would own its original fish contribution but that hybrid lines resulting from cross breeding would be owned by Suvaaq. The proposed project would result in Icy Waters gaining access to a total of 14 genetically distinct charr stocks through local communities. Final approval of the proposed project required consent from the communities (through local Hunters and Trappers Associations), DFO and the Nunavut Wildlife Management Board. The latter body, established under the land claims agreement to oversee the protection and wise use of wildlife and wildlife habitat for the benefit of the Inuit and other residents, advises the governments of Nunavut and Canada, which maintain decision-making authority. The nine-member board includes four Inuit representatives and four from the Canadian and Nunavut governments.

Several difficult issues emerged during negotiations on the proposal. Local fishermen worried that the sale of genetically improved farmed fish would have a negative effect on markets and prices for wild caught fish (Nunavut Wildlife Management Board, 1998). Icy Waters attempted to allay this fear by suggesting that successful farming could benefit local fisheries by reducing commercial harvesting pressure on wild stocks, ensuring a valuable sport fishery, and increasing consumer awareness of charr. Ownership issues added a further complication. These included not only concerns about Suvaaq ownership of successive generations of charr hybrids but also the possibility that the university research group might try to obtain a process patent based on genetic mapping of charr. Mapping would accompany the collection of genetic resources and was necessary in order to ascertain whether the genetic differences between the collected populations were significant. Finally, some Inuit expressed concern that the project showed a lack of respect for charr and that the spirit of the charr might take revenge on the Inuit people if the project went ahead, a not unusual sentiment among native people who may accept technologies as a necessary evil yet still feel uncomfortable with the spiritual implications of altering nature.

Ultimately, communities withheld their consent and the Wildlife Management Board turned down the proposal. Icy Waters was later able to obtain broodstock from two charr stocks from one community that had consented to their collection prior to the land claims agreement, and the company still pays royalties to that community. These broodstock were subsequently cross-bred with the company's base stock.

Icy Waters described the failed negotiations as expensive and time-consuming, complicated by the difficulty of dealing with several different levels of authority, the need to negotiate with several communities over a vast land area, a high level of confusion about the implications of fish farming, and a long history of local suspicion of southern interests.

Some of the issues that characterized the Icy Waters negotiations – such as the patenting of products and processes – surface frequently in negotiations of agreements for access to genetic resources. However, the Icy Waters example also illustrates that collectors of aquatic genetic resources may face extra complications that are unlikely to occur in negotiations for access to plant genetic resources. For example, the need for genetic diversity of broodstock may necessitate negotiations with several communities over a wide area (because genetic differences, at least in salmonids, usually reflect geographic separation), and in different government jurisdictions, adding to the cost and complexity of negotiations.

Indigenous communities may also hold spiritual beliefs that create significant concerns about the movement of fish from their natural habitat – in addition to potential environmental concerns about introduction of fish into areas where they are not indigenous. Suspicion or confusion about possible effects of fish farming on local fishing economies is common, and will also hamper negotiations. And because government policies for fish conservation and use are still at the stage where the genetic fine structure of fish populations is poorly represented (and, in fairness, usually not even known), the ground-rules are often less clear than in the plant world. The Icy Waters case is typical in that genetic mapping of the collected stocks would have taken place as they were collected. In other words, the genetic distinctness of the resources in question was not even known. What chiefly distinguishes the communities involved in the Icy Waters negotiations from many others in the world is that they have substantial degree of control over the of use their genetic resources and the clearly recognized authority to withhold consent.

Most indigenous and local communities around the world (and in Canada, for that matter) have no such authority. This is one among many factors complicating the efforts of countries to develop access laws and policies that acknowledge in a meaningful way the importance of involving local and indigenous communities in decisions regarding applications for access.

Fish and shellfish are nutritious foods that constitute desirable components of a healthy diet. Most seafoods available to the U.S. public are wholesome and unlikely to cause illness in the consumer. Nevertheless, there are areas of risk. The major risk of acute disease is associated with the consumption of raw shellfish, particularly bivalve molluscs. For persons living in areas in which reef fish are consumed (Hawaii, Puerto Rico, the Virgin Islands), there is a risk of ciguatera; other natural toxins (paralytic shellfish poisoning, neurotoxic shellfish poisoning, etc.) have been associated with shellfish from endemic areas. Finally, there are less well-defined risks of acute and chronic disease related to environmental contamination of aquatic food animals. Dealing with such risks on a short-term basis requires improvements in the present system of regulatory control. In the long term, amelioration and eventual elimination of some hazards require strengthening and more effective application of control measures to prevent the disposal of human and industrial waste into offshore marine and fresh waters. Because of the strong public interest in seafood safety and the declared intention at the congressional level to develop a new inspection system, a clear opportunity exists to introduce innovative methodologies for control that address directly the important health issues associated with seafood consumption.

This report reviews the nature and extent of public health risks associated with seafood, and examines the scope and adequacy of current seafood safety programmes. The conclusions and recommendations arrived at are summarized in the following material:

- Most current health risks associated with seafood safety originate in the environment and should be dealt with by control of harvest or at the point of capture. With minor exceptions, risks cannot be identified by an organoleptic inspection system.
- Inspection at the processing level is important to maintain safety of seafoods, but there is little evidence that increased inspection activities at this level would effectively reduce the incidence of seafood-borne disease.

With currently available data, it is possible to identify the source of much of the acute illness associated with seafood consumption, though the dimensions of the problems are not always known; these data, in turn, can form the basis for national control programmes.

- Chronic illness resulting from seafood consumption is associated primarily with environmental contamination; thus, control depends on improved understanding of the occurrence and distribution of the chemical agents involved, the exclusion of contaminated seafood from the market, and increased action to prevent additional pollution of the waters.
- Because well over half the nation's seafood supply is imported and environmental contamination is globally pervasive, it is important that the safety of imported seafood be ensured through equivalent control measures in exporting countries.
- One-fifth of the fish and shellfish eaten in the United States is derived from recreational or subsistence fishing, and these products are not subject to health-based control; there is need to improve protection for consumers of these products by regulation of harvest and by education concerning risks associated with their consumption.
- Because the problems are largely regional, the primary effective control – except for imports – is at the state level, and this effort should be strengthened. However, there is need for federal oversight, general rule setting, and support to ensure the effectiveness of state-based programmes and to provide expert assistance and specialized facilities.
- There is a lack of understanding of the nature of seafood hazards in the food service sectors and by the consuming public and health professionals; a vigourous campaign for information dissemination and education in these matters is needed, particularly for high-risk consumers and high-risk products such as raw shellfish.
- An improved national surveillance system should be developed to provide more reliable and comprehensive information on seafood-borne disease incidence. Data will then permit meaningful risk identification and risk assessment as a basis for effective regulation of seafoods (current data on disease occurrence in seafood consumption are too fragmentary to allow reliable risk assessment of microbiological and natural toxin hazards).

A summary of hazards, risks, and their control for the major groups of hazardous seafoods. They are arranged in order of importance. Among seafood consumers, the group at greatest risk appears to be consumers of raw molluscs because of environmental contamination and naturally occurring vibrios. Consumers of recreational and subsistence fishery products are the second largest constituency at risk, both from natural toxins and from environmental contaminants. Inhabitants of islands in the Caribbean and tropical Pacific Ocean, and to a lesser extent of the Gulf of Mexico States, are uniquely at risk from ciguatera due to consumption of fish that feed on or near tropical reefs and prey upon reef fish. Although U.S. mainland inhabitants have developed the disease from imported fish, ciguatera is a highly regional problem that greatly skews disease reporting because of its geographical concentration and its high visibility in affected regions. There is a more general risk to consumers from certain fresh and frozen fish due to a milder toxic disease, scombroid poisoning.

There is generally a low risk to seafood consumers of food-borne disease due to control failures during processing or at the food service level. Fish do not normally carry microorganisms such as *Salmonella* or *Campylobacter*, which are commonly found in land animal carcasses and are the major causes of reported food-borne disease (though fish may acquire bacteria from contaminated water). Some ethnic practices in the preparation of fish for eating, place a small number of people at high risk from botulism, but this is not a significant hazard for most consumers of fish.

Thus, the health risks associated with seafood – although diverse – are identifiable and, to a significant extent, controllable by innovative measures aimed at geographically restricted or species-specific problems. Some risks, particularly those associated with environmental contamination, may be increasing; their elimination will require a major commitment on the part of both government and industry to change methods of waste disposal in our society. These and the more visible hazards mentioned can be greatly mitigated by a regulatory system specifically aimed at the causes, be they natural toxins, microorganisms, or contaminants. However, this will require something other than organoleptically based inspection systems, which may be useful for quality control and grading but are essentially worthless for detecting and controlling health risks.

2

Aquatic Macrophytes

WATER QUALITY

Water bodies with medium and dense macrophyte cover are characterised by a low concentration of suspended sediments, hence high water transparency. Where aquatic macrophytes disappear, such as under the impact of eutrophication, water transparency is reduced. In lakes where macrophytes reappear after a period of absence, water transparency gradually improves with the increasing vegetation cover. The success of prey capture by fish which locate their prey visually, such as pike, depends on good water transparency. Pikeperch tolerates a lower water transparency than pike.

Several of the chemical parameters influenced by plants that have been observed to reach lethal limits for common freshwater fish are dissolved oxygen, acidity and ammonia. Frodge *et al.* (1987, 1995) measured dissolved oxygen and pH values in patches of Brasina scherberi in the northwest of the USA and found their values ranging from above (in open water) to below (in the patches of the macrophyte) lethal limits for rainbow trout (Oncorhynchus mykiss) within 10 m of each other in the same lake.

Rainbow trout in cages positioned at 1 m depth below Nymphaea odorata, where dissolved oxygen concentration was consistently less than 4 mg L^{-1}, were found dead within 12 hours. Significant mortalities of largemouth bass occurred at both the surface and at 1 m depth in dense beds of the floating leaved macrophyte Brasenia schreberi, and in the bottom water of 2 m or more depth of both floating leafed and submersed species, where dissolved oxygen concentrations were less than 2 mg L^{-1}.

The authors suggested that high densities of aquatic plants can have significant detrimental localised effects on fish and reduce the amount of habitat available to fish within the system. Perna and Demilio (1986) found that dissolved oxygen concentrations in the Ticino River, Italy, with submersed aquatic plants, changed by up to 4.0 mg L^{-1} between day and night. A trout farm, receiving water fom this river, experienced difficulties as a result of the temporary low oxygen concentrations.

Dissolved oxygen content in water may substantially change between day and night when large stands of aquatic macrophytes are present. This may result in substantial diel movement of fish within the plant bed to avoid low dissolved oxygen concentrations in the morning and high pH in the afternoon (Killgore *et al.*, 1991). In many Amazonian floodplain lakes dissolved oxygen concentrations are often very low and anoxia is frequent at least in deeper waters. Lago Camaleao in Brazil is situated about 15 km above the confluence of the Amazon River with Rio Negro.

During low water, the lake is dry, apart from a small, muddy pool of 1-2 ha of 50-80 cm depth and the dry lake bottom is covered by terrestrial and semi-aquatic herbaceous plants, which produce considerable amount of organic material. When the water level rises, the lake becomes flooded, the terrestrial plants die and decompose, while aquatic plants develop in great quantities, with grasses being the most abundant among them.

When some of the aquatic plants start dying, about 60 per cent of the lake is still covered by the grass Echinochloa polystachia, and floating plants Eichhornia crassipes and Salvinia auriculata become abundant. The highest levels of dissolved oxygen have been recorded in the lake when there are still large open water spaces, but a heavy oxygen deficit is present when there is a large-scale plant decomposition in progress. This may reduce the values at the water surface to 0.5 mg L^{-1}. An increase in dissolved oxygen concentration is noticed with the reduction in the macrophyte cover. Junk *et al.* (1983) describe the consequences of the low dissolved oxygen concentrations in this lake: the fish is forced to expend much energy and time in the search for oxygen, for instance coming to the surface to swallow air, or staying near the surface to use the oxygen-rich surface layer.

This may increase the danger of being caught by predators. Food diversity is considerably reduced because phytoplankton and zooplankton become scarce. The bottom fauna is lacking because of the lack of oxygen. The authors also list the advantages of the low dissolved oxygen concentrations among aquatic macrophytes of Lake Camaleao: interspecific competition for food is reduced, as only a small number of fish species utilises the existing food sources; and there is a reduction in predators.

The presence of many juvenile fish under hypoxic conditions may be related to this factor. In Lake Camaleao, about 40 species of fish were able to live under extremely low oxygen conditions, 12 of which were air breathers, and 8 possessed other adaptations to the oxygen deficiency. For example, Colossoma macropomum, is known to be able to increase its haemoglobin content and erythrocyte counts associated with seasonal hypoxia. This species initiates aquatic surface respiration when dissolved oxygen level falls below 0.5 mg L^{-1}. Jedicke *et al.* (1989), who recorded diurnal changes in dissolved oxygen concentration beneath floating macrophytes in a varzea lake, showed that while the maximum concentrations exceed 12 mg L^{-1} in the afternoon hours, in the early morning hours the water is virtually deoxygenated.

Junk (1973) measured vertical oxygen profiles in stands of Leersia hexandra in Lago dos Passarinhos (25 km from Manaus, Brasil). The profile was similar to that measured in dense stands of Paspalum repens of varzea: high dissolved oxygen concentrations at the surface, rapid decrease into the roots, and a slight increase at the lower margin caused by an inflow of oxygenated water from open areas. Within 20 cm depth the dissolved oxygen concentration dropped to less than 0.5 mg L^{-1}, and H2S sometimes formed at a depth of 30 to 140 cm. In a dense, floating island in Lago Paru, 10 m inside the mat of Paspalum repens, the dissolved oxygen concentration dropped from 6-8 mg L^{-1} at the surface to almost nil in a depth of 20 cm, to increase to about 3 mg L^{-1} at 30 cm and deeper. Junk (1973) also noted that low conductivity of water is not a limiting factor for faunal abundance in the floating meadows of the varzea, until it falls below 30 ìS20. In the reservoir Bung Borapet in Thailand, Junk (1977) recorded dissolved oxygen profiles underneath stands of several aquatic macrophytes. The lowest concentrations were measured 10 m inside the stand of Coix aquatica, where there was no oxygen present already at 10 cm depth. Very low concentrations were also measured underneath Leersia hexandra and Ischne globosa, while underneath water hyacinth the lowest dissolved oxygen concentration, measured above the bottom, was 2.5 mg L^{-1}. All four plants form floating islands which drift around the reservoir.

WIDESPREAD IN TROPICAL FRESH WATERS

Hypoxia is widespread in tropical fresh waters, particularly in floodplain pools and permanent swamps. It is prevalent in extensive papyrus swamplands, underneath sudd in deeper waters of the newly established reservoirs, and it may pose a formidable barrier to the dispersion of many fish groups. While some non-air breathing fish may occasionally penetrate in the almost deoxygenated papyrus swamps of East Africa, the fish inhabitants there are primarily air breathers such as Protopterus aethiopicus, Polypterus bichir, Clarias lazera, Ctenopoma muriei. In a small cyprinid Barbus neumayeri, not an air-breathing fish, the respiratory mode affected its dispersal through hypoxic papyrus swamps.

This fish, which feeds on insect larvae and aquatic plants, was found to inhabit swamp waters with dissolved oxygen concentrations between 0.34 and 1.24 mg L^{-1}, but always in places with at least 0.6 m^2 of open water surface where it has access to the water surface and higher oxygen. In response to severe hypoxia it uses aquatic surface respiration at the air-water interface, where diffusion produces a very thin layer of well oxygenated water, despite oxygen scarcity in the rest of the water column. Chapman and Liem (op. cit.) also found significant differences in the gill morphology between B. neumayeri from the papyrus swamp and those from the main river, thus affirming the need for a morphological adaptation, as well as having access to the open water within the swamp. But high water quality is not a necessary prerequisite for optimal fish production, unless fishery managers are to satisfy a demand for fish species that can exist only in oligotrophic waters, such as salmonids and coregonids. With most cyprinids, the higher the trophic level, the higher fish production - to a certain level. This approach has been used in common carp ponds in Europe and Asia. On the other hand, where sport fishery targets fish species in clean rivers, any deterioration of water quality results in the reduction or loss of such species.

EUTROPHICATION AND AQUATIC MACROPHYTES

Eutrophication has become a problem in many countries. De Nie (1987) has briefly reviewed long-term changes in aquatic macrophytes of selected water bodies under the impact of eutrophication in Finland, Germany, the Netherlands, Poland, Switzerland, UK, and the USA. For example in some small water bodies in the Netherlands, the area covered by submersed vegetation declined by a factor 6. In the polish lake Mikolajskie (460 ha) over the period 1963-1980 the decline in the biomass of aquatic macrophytes was 16.6 per cent per year, which equalled to 94 per cent over the entire period. In five eutrophicated lakes of Finland the submersed vegetation had greatly decreased or became restricted to small areas.

Also in Germany the eutrophication influenced especially the submersed macrophytes, and in Lake Constance the depth of occurrence of the Characeae changed from a maximum of 25 m in the 1950s to 5-7 m in 1978. In shallow lakes of the Norfolk Broadlands, palaeolimnological study has shown that starting with the 19th century Strumpshaw Broad was rich in Characeae and epiphytes, with productive fisheries and rich in wildlife. In the beginning of the 20th century the Characeae were replaced by taller macrophytes, such as Potamogeton pectinatus, Myriophyllum spicatum and Ceratophyllum demersum. During that period the eutrophication started by sewage effluents from the nearby city and cultivation and fertilisation of the surrounding land. The fisheries was still productive. This was followed by changes towards the middle of the 20th century, and especially afterwards: by the early 1970s aquatic macrophytes disappeared and phytoplankton started to predominate. The fisheries became less productive and there was an increase in the erosion of the banks and in sedimentation.

Inputs of nitrogen and phosphorus especially in shallow freshwater bodies have led to considerable changes in the aquatic community structure, enhancing phytoplankton production, which in turn has caused suppression or complete disappearance of aquatic submersed macrophytes. Such changes have also meant changes in aquatic invertebrate and fish species composition and biomass. Based on their experiments inducing artificially eutrophication using high nitrate treatment, Daldorphy and Thomas (1991) identified three possible mechanisms which may be responsible for the rapid transition to phytoplankton dominance:

- Competition by phytoplankton for resources such as light and nutrients, where high phytoplankton density attenuates the photosynthetically active radiation impinging on macrophytes;
- Inhibition of macrophyte growth by toxic factors of algal and bacterial origin. During algal blooms, considerable quantities of organic matter may accumulate in the sediment. The addition of such material greatly reduces the growth of submersed macrophytes, possibly due to the phytotoxic organic acids released during decomposition;
- Inhibition of macrophytes by epiphytic algae.

Biomanipulation

The term "biomanipulation" was used by Shapiro *et al.* (1975) to include lake improvement procedures that alter the food web to favour grazing on algae by zooplankton, or that eliminate fish species that recycle nutrients. Cooke *et al.* (1988) expanded this term to the elimination of certain species or restructuring of the fish community to favour the dominance of piscivorous instead of planktivorous fish. In broad terms, biomanipulation is the management of aquatic communities by controlling natural populations of organisms to produce desired conditions. Lazzaro (1997) refers to biomanipulation as a set of deliberate modifications of certain key communities, and/or their habitats, to improve water quality/clarity and/or (less often) fisheries characteristics. Van Donk (1998) uses this term in a sense of man-made modification of fish populations.

The principal objective of biomanipulation in shallow lakes is to generate a period of clear water of sufficient length to allow macrophytes to establish. Both a relative increase in the piscivorous fish stock and a reduction in nutrient levels are thought to be important in stabilising the system in the long term. With increase in lake trophy, the area occupied by and biomass of submersed macrophytes decreases, and in hypertrophic lakes aquatic plants are scarce or absent. Disappearance of macrophytes leads to other changes in the aquatic communities.

Highly eutrophic to hypertrophic lakes have a characteristically high phytoplankton production and in Europe large stocks of plankton-feeding fish, such as bream (Abramis brama) and roach (Rutilus rutilus). To improve the water quality, as well as to establish a higher fish species diversity, including fish of fishery significance, a technique of biomanipulation has been developed. Biomanipulation aims at decreasing the phytoplankton biomass, therefore increasing water transparency, which in turn leads to re-establishment of aquatic macrophytes.

The macrophytes provide then a substrate for periphytic fauna and lead also to an increase in bottom-dwelling invertebrates, both of which diversify the source of food for fish. In a shallow and small Lake Zwemlust in the Netherlands, biomanipulation involved complete removal of all planktivorous and benthivorous fish species (ca. 1000 kg ha^{-1}), introduction of a new simple fish community (pike and rudd) as well as of "seedlings" of Chara globularis and roots of Nuphar lutea. While before the manipulation no submersed vegetation was present in the lake, the second year after the manipulation about 50 per cent of the lake bottom was covered by macrophytes dominated by Elodea nuttallii, increasing to 80 per cent in the third year.

The expansion of macrophytes was possible due to the drastic reduction in phytoplankton, especially cyanobacteria. Other changes resulting from the biomanipulation was development of strong populations of zooplankton and benthic/epiphytic macrofauna, especially snails Lymnaea peregra, and a pike/ rudd fish community.

In summer and autumn the abundance of macrophytes and filamentous algae led to nitrogen limitation of the phytoplankton. The persistence of clear water in the summer after the biomanipulation was believed to be caused by macrophytes, rather then by zooplankton grazing on algae.

Van Donk (1998) followed the changes in Lake Zwemlust for 10 years and noted that after the initial biomanipulation the lake shifted several times between the turbid and the clearwater state. In years 4-5 Ceratophyllum demersum became the dominant macrophyte. Both Elodea and Ceratophyllum compete strongly with phytoplankton for nutrients, especially nitrogen. In the next three years, these plants became nearly absent, and Potamogeton berchtoldii became the dominant species in spring. However, periphyton growth on this plant led to its early collapse, which was followed by an increase in phytoplankton and the lake became turbid during late summer and autumn. In 1995 E. nuttallii reappeared and became again the dominant macrophyte. Next year, it became scarce and Potamogeton abounded, and the lake shifted again to the turbid state.

PRESENCE OF SUBMERSED MACROPHYTES

She concluded that the presence of submersed macrophytes seems to be essential in keeping this lake clear. However, she added that herbivory, especially by coots, and to a lesser extent by rudd, was probably an important factor in triggering the shift from perennials to non-perennials. The number of larger rudd (only larger rudd are herbivorous) was quite low until 1990 but increased in 1991 to 297 kg ha-1, to stabilise at 200-300 kg ha^{-1} during 1992-1996. As rudd feeds only when water temperature exceed 16°C, and avoids Ceratophyllum, suggested that it had much lower impact on total macrophyte biomass than coot.

The biomanipulation of Lake Zwemlust by re-establishment of macrophytes and filamentous algae has created a habitat for periphytic fauna and changed the environmental and trophic conditions for fauna inhabiting the bottom sediments. This was achieved mainly by changing the physical properties of bottom sediments and the water, especially water transparency and the dissolved oxygen concentration. Zoobenthos achieved a higher biomass than phytofauna, except in submersed plants, especially Elodea nuttallii, which occupied the majority of the bottom surface. Filamentous algae were readily eaten live by chironomid larvae and during the algal decay in autumn, when sedimenting, also by the benthic Lymnaea peregra, Asellus meridianus and Gammarus pulex.

In order to improve lake water quality in Lake Vaeng in Denmark, a total of 2.5 tons of bream and roach were removed, reducing the biomass of planktivorous/benthivorous fish by approximately 50 per cent. Again, there was a change from cyanobacteria and small diatoms to a dominance of large diatoms, larger greens and cryptophytes, change in zooplankton from the dominance of rotifers to large cladocerans, and increase in water transparency and dissolved oxygen content. Submersed macrophytes, mainly Potamogeton crispus and Elodea canadensis, increased in abundance. In the following years, Elodea coverage fluctuated. This was paralleled by the fluctuation of aquatic birds coot and mute swans, with their high numbers recorded only in years with high macrophyte density.

A similar parallel between the density of aquatic macrophytes and coot were also observed on another Danish lake Stigsholm. The grazing intensity in Lake Vaeng is suspected to inhibit colonisation of the lake by aquatic plants. In both Danish lakes the results of the studies suggest that waterfowl may suppress macrophyte biomass and development in shallow lakes, and thus have a negative impact on some lake fish.

In a large eutrophic lake in Minnesota, USA the water was highly turbid prior to biomanipulation (summer transparency less than 30 cm), virtually devoid of macrophytes, with large stocks of planktivorous fish bluegill, small yellow perch, and big-mouth buffalo. Benthivorous black bullheads were also abundant. The zooplankton community was typical of those subjected to intense planktivory by fish, being dominated by small-bodied species of cladocerans, by Cyclops bicuspidatus thomasi, and several rotifers. The fish removal by rotenoning, which led to virtually all fish being killed, followed by restocking, resulted in a much improved water transparency and dramatic changes in zooplankton, phytoplankton, and in submersed vegetation revival. Unlike other lakes, in Lake Christina the post-manipulation increases in water clarity and submersed macrophytes were caused by the increases in zooplankton grazing, with the peak daphnid abundance in late May-June. These months are the critical growth period for submersed macrophytes.

SUPPRESS THE SMALL ZOOPLANKTIVOROUS FISH

In Europe, pike and pikeperch have been used to suppress the small zooplanktivorous fish such as bream, roach and perch. In fully overgrown lakes, a high cyprinid (<15 cm) production as high as ca. 300 kg ha^{-1} can be consumed by a high pike biomass (100 kg ha^{-1}). Such a high production of planktivorous cyprinids is associated with a total phosphorus concentration of ca 400 ìg P L^{-1}. At a higher biomass of cyprinids the large-bodied zooplankton disappears, phytoplankton increases, causing a decrease in the macrophytes area, and leading to the dominance of Potamogeton pectinatus and plants with floating leaves. This in turn leads to changes in fish stocks, with the pike-tench associations being replaced by bream-pikeperch populations. There is an increase in benthic-feeding fish, which in turn increases the internal loading and turbidity. Concluded that in shallow eutrophic lakes of northern Europe aquatic vegetation and northern pike are effective tools to maintain water quality, but these are limited by the maximum nutrient concentration aquatic vegetation can sustain.

Pikeperch is more efficient then pike in turbid water, therefore, in a more eutrophicated environment. Addition of piscivores, however, will not have a lasting effect unless they are stocked every year. Therefore, removal of the fish stocks and maintaining them at very low levels for a number of years gives better effect. The available data suggest that in phytoplankton-dominated lakes, the total fish biomass will be between 200 and 500 kg ha^{-1}. Where only half, or somewhat more of thek biomass has been removed, there has been no real improvement.

Highlighted the indirect effects of the fish community on submersed vegetation in shallow eutrophicated lakes: eutrophication and the accompanying phytoplankton and periphyton dominance shade off the macrophytes leading to their demise. This leads to decline of piscivorous fish species, and an increase in phytoplankton feeding fish. Return from the phytoplankton-dominated state depends on an increase in piscivore stocks, either through restocking or growth of the small surviving piscivores.

The resulting decrease in phytoplankton biomass and increase in light availability will promote the re-establishment of submersed macrophytes. In reality, this should be accompanied by substantial reduction of the planktivorous fish stocks, to achieve good results.

A study of lakes in Florida has shown that leaving a small fringe of vegetation around a lake for the purpose of water quality improvement will have little or no effect on the lake's trophic status. Significantly reducing macrophyte coverage of a lake, for example from 60 per cent to 20 per cent or from 40 per cent to 0 per cent will cause major and observable water quality (water clarity) changes. Conversely, the cover must be raised to 30 per cent to 50 per cent before significant improvement in water clarity will be observable.

The general contention of biomanipulation is that removal of fish from shallow lakes may invoke "cascading impacts" that enhance water clarity, stimulate macrophytes, and establish a new steady state. Recent, large-scale biomanipulations have made it possible to update earlier recommendations regarding when, where, and how biomanipulation should be performed. Formulated more applicable recommendations as follows:

- The reduction in the biomass of planktivorous fish should be 75 per cent or more;
- The fish reduction should be performed efficiently and rapidly (within 1-3 years);
- Efforts should be made to reduce the number of benthic feeding fish;
- The recruitment of young-of-the-year fish should be reduced;
- The conditions for establishment of submersed macrophytes should be improved; and
- The external input of nutrients (phosphorus and nitrogen) should be reduced as much as possible before the biomanipulation.

Recent biomanipulations have shown that, correctly performed, the method also achieves results in large, relatively deep and eutrophic lakes, at least within 5 years. Provide decision trees for biomanipulation and for aquatic macrophytes establishment.

The question whether trophic cascades and 'classical' biomanipulation apply to the tropics. The 'trophic cascade hypothesis', developed for temperate systems, does not seem to be a good candidate for tropical lakes, for several reasons, among which is its typical linear structure from piscivores → zooplanktivores → zooplankton → phytoplankton, which disregards the widespread omnivory over size-selective zooplanktivory *per se*. In direct reference to fish Lazarro mentions the seasonality of spawning in temperate waters compared to the spawning of tropical fish, which may spawn at different times, therefore juvenile fish maintaining a permanent pressure on zooplankton.

Filtering omnivores (not visual zooplanktivores) often dominate the planktivore community in tropical waters, without being limited by the presence/ absence of zooplankton, nor controlled by fish predators as because of their fast growth they soon reach size larger than the predator's mouth gape.

Tropical waters have smaller, 'sedentary' carnivorous fish, unlike temperate waters where large-sised piscivores dominate. Macrophytes in tropical waters grow faster and all the year. They can provide serious management problems, as their proliferation is not controlled in eutrophic systems, and they represent a highly variable and unstable sink or source of nutrients. Concluding, Lazzaro says that the above characteristics of tropical lakes and reservoirs weaken the top-down links between piscivores and planktivores, and between zooplankton and phytoplankton. Because of their weakness, there is little chance for a successful biomanipulation.

VERTEBRATES OF FISHERY SIGNIFICANCE THAT FEED ON AQUATIC MACROPHYTES

Opuszynski (1992) and Opuszynski and Shireman (1995) classify herbivorous fish as those in which food constitutes more than 50 per cent plant material by weight or volume, at least in some period of their life. Most species are opportunistic, changing their diet to whatever food items are abundant or available. Food habits also change with the age of fish and seasons, which may determine food availability. A generalised conceptual model gives major reasons why a herbivorous fish selects its food. Opuszynski and Shireman (1995) mention that 24 families of fish contain freshwater herbivorous representatives. In total 37 species are listed as feeding on macrophytes, and two on "plants material". Twenty of the macrophyte-feeding species belong to the family Cyprinidae, eight to the family Cichlidae. Among these, grass carp is the only fish used on a large scale for aquatic weed control. The authors do not indicate whether under macrophytes are meant aquatic macrophytes, or terrestrial macrophytes (such as flooded grass and other herbaceous plants of floodplains), or both.

Submersed, emergent and floating-leaved aquatic macrophytes are all subject to substantial grazing losses, which often alter relative abundance of macrophyte species and sometimes affect plant productivity. Prejs (1984) gives examples of intensive grazing on *Elodea canadensis* and *Ceratophyllum demersum* by rudd and tench in Polish lakes. Most fish are opportunistic, feeding on a wide variety of food items according to their availability. This is also true of herbivorous fish which frequently ingest aquatic invertebrates dwelling on aquatic plants.

The reason is that many aquatic grazers prefer bacteria and microscopic algae because these groups have higher protein and lower cellulose and lignin and ash contents.

FEEDS ON SUBMERSED, FLOATING AND EMERGENT PLANTS

This is valid for grass carp which feeds on submersed, floating and emergent plants, as well as, *e.g.* mahseer (*Tor tor*), which scrapes moss and algae from rocks in rivers of India and Pakistan, or feeds on aquatic macrophytes. Opuszynski (1992) pointed out the scarcity of information on the proportion of animal food in herbivorous fish, mentioning microorganisms as the most protein-rich food in nature, and easier to digest than plant cells. Juveniles of herbivorous fish depend on high-protein animal food to survive, shifting gradually to mixed animal-plant food as they develop and grow. Opuszynski mentioned that when grass carp were fed only lettuce in experiments, they were hardly able to grow, but considerable improvement in growth was achieved when the fish were fed earthworm diet.

Plant food is less digestible than animal food because of the cellulose, which is difficult to break down. Grass carp has a muscular gizzard stomach where plant material is ground together with sand grains. Other herbivorous fish use pharyngeal teeth (pharyngeal mill) situated in the throut, to cut, tear and grind the plant material Both methods assist in breaking down the plant cell walls. Herbivorous fish compensate for the shortage of protein in plants (duckweed contains 31 per cent, water hyacinth 24 per cent) as compared to animal food (up to 80 per cent protein) by ingesting higher quantities of food, the daily intake of which, in grass carp, may exceed their body weight.

Many aquatic macrophytes have secondary compounds that may reduce grazing. Lodge (1991) in a brief summary of the literature, listed the major groups of compounds: alkaloids, flavanoids, steroids, saponins, phenolics (including tannins), glucosinolates. The digestibility of protein in plants decreases with increasing concentrations of tannins. Plants containing more than 6 per cent to 7 per cent tannin (dry weight) would be so low in digestibility as to be of little food value; most higher aquatic plants contain less than 2 per cent to 3 per cent tannin when harvested before maturity, but tannin values tend to increase with age.

This chapter leans especially on the information contained in papers and publications by Schuytema (1977); Opuszynski and Shireman (1995); van der Zweerde (1990); Welcomme (1985); grass carp synopsis by Shireman and Smith (1983); special section on grass carp in the United States, as appeared in the Transactions of the American Society 1978, Vol. 107, No. 1; Proceedings of the Grass Carp Symposium. This is supplemented by material gleaned from a number of other papers. The section dealing with grass carp is not exhaustive, and the reader is advised to seek more information in the relevant publications listed above. Twelve other herbivorous fish species/genera.

Grass Carp

Adult grass carp eat exclusively plant material, but when young, grass carp are often considered facultative carnivores. When *Tubifex* worms were fed to fry and fingerlings of grass carp a large proportion of energy intake was retained. When fingerlings were fed lettuce they grew very little, due to poor digestion and absorption; and when fed pellets made from pondweed they did not grow and had low absorption efficiencies. In comparison, larger grass carp fed *Potamogeton crispus* also had a large faecal loss but retained 12 per cent of the consumed energy.

While the use of grass carp for biological control of aquatic plants has been found to be advantageous in many situations, especially where chemical or physical control for whatever reason cannot be applied, Schuytema (1977) pointed out at a number of negative impacts, the possibility of which should be assessed prior to the introduction of grass carp. Among them are: uncertainty of the effect on native fish, possibility that removal of plants may eliminate endemic fish food and cover and waterfowl food; lack of knowledge of proper stocking rates; difficulty of live capture; possibility of natural spawning; possibility of introducing a disease vector, lack of knowledge of local plant preferences; and nutrients released into the water by excretion leading to increased primary productivity.

Whatever the negative aspects of using grass carp for aquatic macrophyte control, given existing problems associated with eutrophication and exotic plant species, large-scale aquatic vegetation control programmes using grass carp are likely to increase in the future. In the Netherlands the introduction of grass carp has been considered a success, regarding its control of aquatic weeds. The area stocked with grass carp has steadily increased since 1977. In 1987 there were 1092 sites with grass carp and 820 users (a total of 270 tons in 2300 ha). Water Boards are the major users of grass carp, with other users having a larger number of relatively small sites.

FEEDING PREFERENCES OF GRASS CARP

Numerous studies have dealt with the aquatic plant preferences of grass carp. Because of food selectivity, the grass carp occasionally increases some stands of plant species by preferential feeding on one or more favoured plants. This situation may continue until the preferred food supply is exhausted, and then it usually starts to feed on less palatable species. Small-sized grass carp utilise soft vegetation while older fish can utilise harder, more fibrous plant material. Water hyacinth is usually avoided, as is the cattail (*Typha*). In some water bodies grass carp may prefer to feed on filamentous algae such as *Cladophora* and *Spirogyra*. Elsewhere, *Nitella* may be avoided. In total, however, grass carp have been reported to consume over 170 different species of aquatic macrophytes. They also reported that grass carp consumed more softer and succulent submersed aquatic macrophytes when water temperatures were below 12–15°C. Prabhavathy and Sreenivasan (1976) reported that in India grass carp is known to ignore all aquatic vegetation in the presence of *Hydrilla*. Bhukasvan *et al.* (1981) reported that grass carp preferred submersed macrophytes such as *Najas graminae* and *Hydrilla* and the floating macrophytes (*e.g. Azolla pinnata*).

Vincent and Sibbing (1992), who fed grass carp various aquatic plants, followed how the fish chooses and chews its food. Given that leaf toughness, availability of particular leaves, and spacial availability of each particular species of macrophytes are characteristics that affect the energy costs of ingestion, the amount obtained by bite and the potential nutritive value are factors affecting the benefit derived from ingestion. Vincent and Sibbing (1992) detected a clear selection for some plants because of the type of chewing mechanism of grass carp, *i.e.* pharyngeal teeth. *Elodea canadensis*, grass *Glyceria fluitans*, and filamentous alga *Zygnema* sp. were readily taken. *Lemna minor, Potamogeton lucens* and leaves of *Typha latifolia* were not acceptable. The authors suggested the possible limiting factors: *Potamogeton* and *Elodea* were probably avoided as the fish has difficulty in extracting a single, manageable stem. Grass cannot be swallowed quickly enough, and chewing is limiting with *Typha* as the leaves are too tough. *Lemna* is rejected perhaps because it has an unpleasant taste.

Grass carp was introduced into India in 1959, and since then it has been used in composite culture of carps, particularly in ponds infested with aquatic weeds (Nandeesha et al, 1989). It controls there *Hydrilla, Najas, Ceratophyllum, Wolffia, Lemna, Spirodela, Ottelia, Vallisneria, Potamogeton, Utricularia, Trapa, Myriophyllum, Limnophila, Nechamandra*, and algae *Nitella, Spirogyra, Pithophora*. It has been found ineffective in controlling the floating plants *Eichhornia, Pistia, Salvinia* and *Nymphaea*. However, *Eichhornia, Hydrilla* and *Najas* are used by grass carp for attachment of its eggs. Due to the conversion to excreta of aquatic macrophytes using grass carp in composite fish culture reduces the cost of fish production. In India, grass carp has also been used for control of aquatic macrophytes with limited success in the Chambal irrigation system. In Egypt, experiments with grass carp were carried out in a small drainage canal in the Province of Giza near Cairo, with favourable results: submersed weeds were effectively controlled. Further experiments and management measures covered several other canals in the country. Grass carp also found a ready use as human food, with poaching of fish from the canals on a large scale at night. The use of grass carp in one of the Egypt's main irrigation canals improved irrigation conveyance efficiency through decreasing the percentage of submersed aquatic weeds from 35 per cent to 6 per cent, although not affecting the floating water hyacinth.

In pond experiments in Alabama, grass carp reduced water hyacinth plant size by eating the roots. When stocked at 16 per 0.04-hectare pond water hyacinth was eliminated within 30 days after the fish were stocked. In the USA, *Chara* and *Hydrilla* seem to be the favourite submersed plants of grass carp, in Europe it is the exotic *Elodea canadensis*. For more information on plant preferences as food of grass carp see Schuytema (1977) and Shireman and Smith (1993).

The selective feeding of grass carp may lead eventually to the establishment of an unwanted aquatic plant, such as *Ranunculus* in the Karakum canal in Turkmenistan. Triploid grass carp is a functionally sterile strain of grass carp that have proved to be effective in controlling aquatic plants in southern California. Pine *et al.* (1990) followed the impact of grass carp on aquatic macrophytes in static and flowing water in canals in northern California in winter, spring and summer. *Potamogeton pectinatus, Myriophyllum spicatum* and *Potamogeton nodosus* produced longer shoots in canals with flowing water than with static water. During spring and summer, triploid grass carp showed a distinct variation in the preference of aquatic weed types in flowing and static water. Accessibility and ease of mastication were found to be more important in determining preference than nutritional quality of the plants.

Van der Zweerde (1990) enumerated and briefly commented on the factors which influence successful aquatic weed management with grass carp: water depth, regularity of previous control measures, water temperature, grass carp density, size of the grass carp, predation, selectivity of aquatic plants by the grass carp, surface area of grass carp stocking in a channel network, and proper integration of the use of grass carp in the overall management programme of a water body. A successful control of submersed aquatic macrophytes also requires a certain level of dissolved oxygen concentration, with the lethal point for grass carp being 0.5 mg L^{-1}, a level which may be reached for example in dense growth of *Hydrilla*.

GRASS CARP ON ENVIRONMENT, ON OTHER FISH AND WATERFOWL

When grass carp (stocking rate 74 fish ha^{-1}) eliminated aquatic vegetation over 3 600 ha in the 8 100 ha Conroe reservoir in Texas, this resulted in an increase in nutrient (phosphorus and nitrogen) concentrations, and a decline in water transparency by 40 per cent as a result of a build up of phytoplankton. Once the vegetation was removed, autotrophic production switched from macrophytes to phytoplankton, resulting in a nearly twofold increase in algal biomass as measured by chlorophyll *a*. Zooplankton was relatively unaffected by plant control for a year and a half, which was followed by a decline in cladocerans as a result of an increase in planktivorous fish.

Vegetation removal by grass carp in Lake Conroe system represented the single largest reduction in aquatic vegetation by any means in North America. Prior to the biological control using grass carp, the dominant submersed plants were *Hydrilla verticillata, Myriophyllum spicatum* and *Ceratophyllum demersum*. The most notable declines were observed for several small, phytophillic *Lepomis* spp, for bluegill *Lepomis macrochirus*, and for crappie *Pomoxis* spp. Biomass of largemouth bass *Micropterus salmoides* did not decline but the density of age-1 and older fish did decline. Density of threadfin shad *Dorosoma petenense* increased nearly fivefold.

There was a collapse in the stocks of three cyprinodont species and two other species, *i.e.* bantam sunfish *Lepomis symmetricus*, and brook silversides *Labidesthes sicculus*, while catches of inland silversides *Menidia beryllina* and threadfin shad increased significantly. The original largemouth bass - crappie - hybrid striped bass (*Morone chrysops* × *M. saxatilis*) fishery was replaced by a channel catfish -white bass - hybrid striped bass - largemouth bass - black crappie fishery after vegetation removal. Hence, the structure of the sport fish community changed. Several changes were likely linked to changes in structural complexity and primary production resulting from vegetation removal. The littoral fish community shifted from a sunfish and shad community to one that also included sizeable numbers of cyprinids, inland silversides, and channel catfish. The total number of species declined over the 7-year study period.

Available prey:predator ratio remained similar after vegetation removal for large predators but increased an order of magnitude for small predators. The responses of some species to complete vegetation removal in Lake Conroe are consistent with known life history requirements.

Numerous studies exist on the feeding impacts of grass carp on other fish species. Grass carp consumes phytoplankton and infusoria during the first 2–4 days of life, changing to zooplankton after 5 days. The fish do not become phytophagous until they are about one month old and 2.5–5 cm in length. Aquatic macrophytes become a regular constituent of the diet when the fingerlings reach 55 mm TL.

In experiments it was found that 7 to 11 months old grass carp would eat aquatic invertebrates and trout fry in the presence of palatable plants when there was no cover for the prey. Elimination of aquatic vegetation may have disastrous consequences on native aquatic invertebrates, fish and aquatic birds, as the balance between plants and the regular local fauna dependent on them is disturbed. Kilgen (1978), referring to the work of other authors, mentions that grass carp increased bluegill (*Lepomis macrochirus*) reproduction, reduced largemouth bass (*Micropterus salmoides*) populations, and reduced bluegill production in ponds.

A study on more of 100 lakes in Arkansas, where grass carp was introduced as a biological weed control agent, showed that plant removal by grass carp did appear to improve the condition factor of largemouth bass, bluegill and redear sunfish (*Lepomis microlophus*), and Bailey (1978) suggested that the introduction of grass carp will not always improve or harm fish populations. This has also been confirmed in the study of 8 lakes in Florida, which have experienced the long-term removal of all aquatic vegetation with grass carp (10 to 15 years): there was no consistent trend with aquatic macrophyte removal. Some grass carp lakes supported excellent fish populations, and some did not. From this study Canfield and Hoyer (1992) concluded that the long-term loss of aquatic macrophytes from a lake ecosystem will not necessarily lead to a decrease in a lake's total or sport fish population, but there exists a potential for such a decrease. Reviewing the management of aquatic vegetation with grass carp in Iowa over the period 1973–1993, Mitzner (1994) pointed out that in the 2 000 private waters that have been stocked with grass carp, partial control of vegetation is rarely attained: normally there is an all-or-none response. In lakes with 100 per cent control of vegetation there are only minor changes in sport fish populations. According to Mitzner, sport fishing is not adversely impacted by grass carp introductions and in most cases catch has increased because of more available access to shore by anglers fishing for bluegill and crappie.

The beneficial influence of grass carp on tench in the Lancaster Canal, England, is described by Petridis (1990). Grass carp, through moderate consumption of aquatic plants (dominant species *Elodea nuttallii*) produced better conditions for the exploitation of benthic organisms by the benthophagous tench (*Tinca tinca*), because tench (>35 cm fork length) were able to search for food in the open areas created. This also enabled the fish to make use of zooplankton, mainly the large species *Eurycercus lamellatus* whose restricted phytophilic habitat made it vulnerable to predation.

MODERATE CONTROL OF VEGETATION IN TEMPERATE CLIMATES

Epibenthic animals, in particular gastropods and *Asellus aquaticus*, suffered from the predation, which caused severe reduction of them in the site totally depleted of vegetation. In this site, tench utilized a diet in which red chironomids were the dominant prey group together with a large amount of fine detritus. Petridis (1995) suggested that a moderate control of vegetation in temperate climates, using the grass carp, could be a satisfactory management technique for the improvement of aquatic habitats. Reviewing literature, the same author mentions an increase in the growth rate of bream (*Abramis brama*) when stocked with grass carp.

Benthivorous species are generally considered to increase their production and growth, benefiting chiefly from the direct utilization and nutrient release of the undigested grass carp faeces. In England, tench can be stocked with grass carp at high densities, because both species occupy different ecological niches, and both species benefit each other through feeding activities. The changes in the natural habitat of some Arkansas lakes (USA) stocked with grass carp resulted in replacement of *Lepomis microlophus* and *Esox niger* by largemouth bass (*Micropterus salmoides*), bluegill (*Lepomis macrochirus*) and the gizzard shad (*Dorosoma cepedianum*). Grass carp stocking also led to a decrease in crayfish (*Procambarus clarkii*) production in small ponds. The interference seemed to arise from the competition for plant food. The grass carp affects other fish through interference with their reproduction, broadening or narrowing their food base, and decreasing refugia. In the former Soviet Union grass carp introductions have adversely affected pike, perch, crucian carp (*Carassius carassius*), and roach (*Rutilus rutilus*).

In a USA reservoir, the stocked grass carp through the subsequent elimination of vegetation disrupted the macroinvertebrate food base and this resulted in a 50 per cent reduction of centrarchid biomass. In the Austrian lake Neusiedler grass carp was introduced alongside six other alien species to enhance the fisheries. Its presence has resulted in almost the complete disappearance of submersed macrophytes, an important spawning habitat for a number of fish species. While it is not possible to separate the impact of this fish from other impacts, such as water level regulatory measures, which led to a loss of habitats within the reed belt due to drying out, and eutrophication, it is believed that its presence contributed to the disappearance of some of the indigenous fish species from Neusiedler Lake. In Lake Marion, South Carolina (USA), removal of *Hydrilla verticillata* by triploid grass carp led to an increase in littoral fish, especially Centrarchidae, as hydrilla decreased from a maximum of 4 700 ha (approximately 50 per cent of the surface area) to less than 100 ha. The mean lengths of most littoral species were similar during the study period, during which, in spite of a substantial decline in hydrilla, other forms persisted. This provided an intermediate level of structural complexity, preventing any detectable negative effects on the littoral fish.

In reservoirs, aquatic vegetation may conflict with other reservoir uses, such as boating, swimming, and electric power generation. Some reservoirs are important habitats for migrating and wintering waterfowl which is foraging on aquatic vegetation. The use of grass carp to control aquatic vegetation in some reservoirs may reduce habitat quality for waterfowl because plants preferred by grass carp are also important as waterfowl food and as habitat for invertebrate food items. In Guntersville Reservoir in Alabama, introduced grass carp reduced the presence of native aquatic macrophytes by 44 per cent, but at the same time the invasive exotic milfoil (*Myriophyllum spicatum*) increased by 15 per cent, as grass carp finds this plant less palatable. Although milfoil is eaten by American coots (*Fulica americana*) and some ducks during autumn and winter, a mixture of native plants and milfoil is more desirable. Native aquatic plants provide better habitat than does milfoil for aquatic invertebrates, which are important dietary components for a variety of waterfowl species. Milfoil also is higher in fibre than are native aquatic species typically eaten by waterfowl in southeastern USA and most ducks and geese are limited in their ability to digest and assimilate fibre. Use of grass carp to control aquatic vegetation in Guntersville Reservoir reduced the quality of waterfowl habitat by reducing the biomass of the native aquatic plants.

In Florida Lake in South Africa, which for a number of years experienced a major invasion of *Potamogeton pectinatus*, *Lagarosiphon muscoides* and *L. major*, triploid carp was introduced to control these aquatic plants. Within a period of one year the mean wet mass standing crop of the weeds in the lake was reduced to one sixth of the initial value.

Reduction in the weed cover coincided with changes in the populations of aquatic plant-eating birds, such as coot (*Fulica cristata*), Egyptian goose (*Alopochen aegyptiacus*), and yellowbilled duck (*Anas undulata*). Owing to the reduction in plant presence by grass carp, small fish became more exposed to fish-eating birds such as reed cormorant (*Phalacrocorax africana*) and whitebreasted cormorant (*P. carbo*), which have both increased in numbers at the lake following the clearing of aquatic macrophytes from the surface.

Stocking Rates

Stocking rates of grass carp and the age/size of the stocked fish differ from water body to water body and would be determined by many factors, including the amount and species of aquatic plants present, water temperature, and the objective of the use of grass carp as biological control agent. In Russia the stocking rates could be 79 kg ha^{-1} of one-year fish to clear ponds of vegetation, and 254 kg ha^{-1} to keep canals clear of aquatic plants. In India, effective stocking rates ranged from 654 to 5200 ha^{-1} for fish of various weights. In fish culture ponds in the USA a rate of 247–1235 fingerlings ha^{-1} efficiently cleared aquatic weeds from ponds, and in lakes twenty-five of 20–25 cm fingerlings ha^{-1} were sufficient. Stocking rates for grass carp for the control of aquatic macrophytes are usually estimated from the surface area of macrophyte coverage. But this reduces the predictability of the outcome because this approach does not account for plant biomass, which can vary with plant depth and the plant species in question. Osborne *et al.* (1982) determined the stocking rate based on whole-lake plant biomass: 14–20 grass carp per metric ton (wet weight) of plants would eliminate *Hydrilla verticillata*, and the 20 grass carp per metric ton would do this in less than 4 months.

For the lakes in the Pacific Northwest of the USA, where water temperatures are lower than in Florida, Bonar (1990) estimated grass carp stocking rates of 4.7–15.1 fish per metric ton. Cassani *et al.* (1995) tested in eight small warm-water impoundments (0.8–45.3 ha) of Florida various stocking rates for triploid grass carp to identify a threshold rate at which macrophytes were suppressed but not eliminated. Stocking rates of 4–8.4 grass carp per metric ton of vegetation (wet weight) resulted in gradual reduction to zero macrophyte biomass in 8–17 months. The plants in question were *Najas guadalupensis, Hydrilla verticillata, Ruppia* sp., *Chara* sp. All these plants are readily consumed or preferred by grass carp, but slight differences in chemical composition of different populations of the same plant species can potentially affect preference and consequently consumption rates. According to Bonar *et al.* (1993) grass carp consumption was positively correlated with the concentration of calcium and lignin and negatively correlated with the concentrations of iron and cellulose.

EXPERIMENTS SHIFTS IN MACROPHYTE SPECIES COMPOSITION

In the Cassani *et al.* (1995) experiments shifts in macrophyte species composition took place at sites where macrophytes were suppressed or began to regrow after a period of zero macrophyte biomass. However, the number of species present and composing at least 4 per cent by weight of the total macrophyte biomass did not decline. Osborne and Sassic (1981) who studied the impact of grass carp on hydrilla infestation in a central Florida lake concluded that only small grass carp should be stocked, and that one can expect the fish become ineffective as a means of weed control as they approach a body weight of 14 kg, due to their reduction in the absolute, as well as the relative weight of vegetation consumed with increasing size.

In New Zealand incremental stocking of 60 grass carp (total 218 kg live weight ha^{-1}) in a small 1.9 ha eutrophic sand dune Lake Parkinson led to the apparent eradication of *Egeria densa*, and to a more than 99 per cent reduction in the cover and biomass of other macrophytes. Grass carp numbers were then gradually reduced by trammel netting and seining, with the last fish being removed using rotenone. Five years after the removal of grass carp predominantly native macrophytes re-established themselves in the lake. The emergent *Eleocharis sphaceolata* returned to the margins, and the submersed communities dominated by *Potamogeton ochreatus* and *Nitella hookeri* grew to a maximum depth of 5 m.

In most water bodies outside its area of natural distribution spawning of grass carp must be induced artificially. However, a number of countries reported natural spawning where the fish has been transferred. In the Tone River in Japan grass carp has spawned since 1947, in a reservoir in Taiwan the escape of fingerlings from a pond resulted in its establisment and natural reproduction. Natural reproduction has taken place in a river and lake system in Mexico after the fish were released following water hyacinth control experiments. In Turkmenistan, grass carp reproduces in irrigation canals. Some countries (*e.g.* New Zealand) have regulated the introduction of grass carp, and some states of the USA have banned its use.

In some countries the ban on the use of grass carp has been eased under condition that a sterile diploid or triploid form of the grass carp is used. In New Zealand, only sterile fish are released for weed control. In the laboratory, triploid grass carp is known to exhibit a slight reduction (10 per cent) in ingestion rate. A number of fish diseases has been introduced with the introduction of grass carp into Europe.

Environmental impact of grass carp on the aquatic ecosystem cannot be disputed: by suppressing some species of macrophytes other species may increase; by grazing off some plants the spawning substrata of important fish may disappear; without a counterbalance of phytoplankton-feeding fish, water quality deteriorates. Aquatic systems function best with a moderate abundance of aquatic macrophytes and introduction of grass carp could assist in reaching such equilibrium. When using grass carp in a multi-use lake (in North America) Leslie *et al.* (1987) made the following recommendations:

i. only sterile triploid fish should be used and they should be used only in lakes with a legitimate aquatic plant problem;
ii. the relative value of different lake uses should be taken into consideration; grass carp are not good candidates for locations where they negatively impact valuable lake resources like waterfowl habitat;

iii. the kind and quantity of vegetation should be surveyed; grass carp may be used where the target species is abundant and highly palatable to grass carp;

iv. grass carp movement should be restricted to target areas;

v. a low stocking rate of grass carp should be integrated with other plant control methods. The best approach is to first reduce the biomass of target plants with other methods and then use a low stocking rate of grass carp to browse regrowth. If stocking rates are too low, additional fish can be stocked.

A grass carp symposium in Florida, USA met to discuss the effects of stocking grass carp for aquatic plant control in the USA. Even after 25 years since stocking grass carp for the purpose of plant control, some management concerns remain open and require better answers. Grass carp has been used especially to suppress the invasive hydrilla, which has rapidly established itself in many water bodies of the USA. Only in Florida, well over 2000 water bodies have been stocked with grass carp. Haller (1994) gave two possible scenarios on the use of grass carp to suppress hydrilla in a landlocked prime sportfishing lake of 2000 ha area. In the first scenario, by the end of the second year, grass carp, after consuming hydrilla, including the regrowth of the second year, starts feeding on native plants, and in the fifth year there are no aquatic macrophytes left in the lake. The lake remains plant free for 20 years, and revegetation is attempted to improve sport fishing, but is unsuccessful because there is a residual grass carp population still in the lake. In the second scenario, Haller shows a combination of application of herbicide and grass carp stocking, but also shows the presence of adverse conditions such as heavy predation on the stocked fish, low water level promoting regrowth of hydrilla, poor impact of herbicide in repeated treatments in the following years.

With further stocking inputs of grass carp to make control more effective, accompanied by rising water level, the result is as in the scenario one. In both situations one ends with a lake with very little emergent vegetation, and no submersed vegetation for 15–20–25 years. According to Haller, at present, there are no clear-cut guidelines for stocking rates of grass carp which could be applied to all the water bodies, and little is known on the long-term effects of grass carp on the ecosystem of such water bodies. At the same symposium Brakhage (1994) pointed out that at present every system will have to be treated separately with a commitment to monitor the effects of the control programme and modify the approach.

STRUCTURAL COMPLEXITY OF AQUATIC MACROPHYTES FOR FISH

A thorough study by Killgore *et al.* (1991) addressed the habitat value of aquatic plants for fishes in North American water bodies, but more specifically in the Potomac River. Their general conclusions can be widely accepted for numerous water bodies in temperate regions of the northern hemisphere. They followed the seasonal change in density and species composition of aquatic plants in relation to the spatial and temporal distribution of fishes. In their discussion, they included references to findings of other authors, supporting their conclusions.

During the spring when plant density is relatively low in the Potomac River, fish abundance is highest in areas without plants because of the occurrence of anadromous, pelagic-oriented species, or in areas with mature stands of *Myriophyllum*, rather than emerging short stands of *Hydrilla*. During the spring, fish tend to associate with aquatic plants that overwinter or emerge early from the substrate for food and cover and disperse to the more established macrophyte beds in the summer and fall.

Once the plant community reached its maximum density in the summer, plants capable of establishing dense stands, such as hydrilla, can occupy the entire water column. This slows down fish movement and foraging efficiency of fish. Therefore, more fish are often found in areas of intermediate levels of structural complexity, particularly for piscivorous species. In late summer through autumn immediate densities of submersed aquatic plants usually contained more species and numbers of fish than areas having dense growths. Some fish species such as pumpkinseed fish (*Lepomis gibbosus*), however, prefer high plant densities.

The piscivorous largemouth bass (*Micropterus salmoides*) and yellow perch (*Perca flavescens*) were commonly observed occupying small spaces devoid of plants in dense vegetation, ready to ambush their prey. Banded killifish were found at the water surface immediately above the plants, at the periphery of the dense stands, in spaces ("holes") formed in the plant beds, or the bottom directly below dense canopy formations to utilise both open and structurally complex areas for foraging and predator avoidance. The presence of largely small fish in dense stands of aquatic plants, and larger, piscivorous fish being more common at the periphery of the plant beds, as reported in the literature, was not confirmed from the Potomac River.

Cailteux *et al.* (1994), who compared the growth of largemouth bass in vegetated versus non-vegetated lakes in central Florida observed that bass from lakes without aquatic macrophytes became piscivorous at the size of 60 mm which resulted in significantly faster first year growth than bass from vegetated lakes which did not become piscivorous until when larger than 120 mm. Although largemouth bass from unvegetated lakes grew faster than in vegetated lakes, survival to recruitment appeared to be much lower.

Studies of European fish species have shown that differences in stem densities of aquatic macrophytes result in different foraging rate: the foraging rate of rudd (*Scardinius erythrophthalmus*) on *Daphnia* decreased at stem densities greater than 200 m^{-2} and that of juvenile perch (*Perca fluviatilis*) did not decrease even at the highest stem density of 600 stems m^{-2}. The foraging efficiency of roach (*Rutilus rutilus*) decreased substantially even at the lowest stem density. Similar results were obtained by Diehl (1988) in a study of the foraging efficiencies of roach, bream (*Abramis brama*), and perch feeding on chironomids: the foraging performances of roach and bream decreased strongly in the presence of vegetation whereas the foraging performance of perch was only slightly affected by vegetation.

Because perch and roach make up most of the total fish biomass in many European lakes, the effects of vegetation structure on the interactions between these two species will have ramifications for overall community and lake ecosystem dynamics. Roach as a competitor with juvenile perch may severely limit the recruitment of perch to large piscivorous stages in the absence of vegetated habitats. In other experiments, when simultaneously offered perch and rudd in field enclosures, pike captured more rudd than perch in environments lacking vegetation, whereas the opposite was the case in environments with vegetation. Pike has been found to be a more efficient predator than perch and pikeperch (*Stizostedion lucioperca*) in vegetation.

Crowder and Cooper (1982) who, in experimental ponds in the state of Michigan, USA, investigated the relationship between macrophyte density (dominated by *Ceratophyllum demersum*) and the interaction between bluegills (*Lepomis macrochirus*) and their invertebrate prey noted that at high macrophyte densities fish captured less prey and grew more slowly despite the presence of a higher biomass of invertebrates. Fish diets at high macrophyte density did not broaden; the fish simply consumed less (but larger prey, than at low macrophyte densities) and grew more poorly as a result. At low macrophyte density fish diets tended to be narrower. The authors concluded that in the long term, intermediate macrophyte density may be the best habitat both in terms of foraging and growth of the predator and stability of the fish-prey interaction. However, they also stressed the importance of considering multiple variables (food, habitat structure, temperature, predators) and assessing resource availability, if we are to better understand resource use in spatially complex environments.

Randall *et al.* (1996) who studied the density of fish in relation to the density of macrophytes in the Great Lakes of North America, found fish production significantly higher in littoral habitats with abundant submersed macrophytes, as measured by percent bottom cover, than in adjacent areas with low macrophyte abundance. Vegetated sites had higher densities of fish, smaller fish, and greater species richness than unvegetated sites. The authors recommended that conservation should be directed at protecting not only the productive vegetated littoral habitat but also adjacent areas which benefit from the high productivity as well.

AN IMPORTANT IMPACT ON FISH FREQUENTING AQUATIC MACROPHYTE STANDS

The architecture or spatial arrangement of plant species has an important impact on fish frequenting aquatic macrophyte stands. Structural characteristics unique to aquatic plants create spatial complexity in aquatic habitats which are important to growth and survival of freshwater fishes. The littoral of lakes and ponds with aquatic macrophytes is physically complex and spatially patchy. Dibble and Killgore (1994), using literature information, listed the following salient points showing the significance of plant structural complexity, *i.e.* habitat at the microlevel, for freshwater fish:

(i) It deters predation by altering the outcome of predator-prey interactions;
(ii) Serves as critical refuge sites for smaller fishes;
(iii) Is important for successful spawning of fish;
(iv) Increases survival and recruitment of juvenile fishes;
(v) Growth rates of young fish increase in these habitats because plant leaves and stems offer a habitat rich in food resources for fish by providing attachment substrate and protection for many microinvertebrates.

Caffrey (1993) summarized the significance of aquatic plant complexity as follows: broad and dissected leaves provide abundant cover and concealment for adult fish and nursery habitats for fry. They also provide a wide range of microhabitats for fish food invertebrates and periphyton, and spawning substrates for fish and invertebrates. Coarse fish which deposit their adhesive eggs on most plant species prefer submersed plants with broader or complex forms. Floating-leaved plants offer minimal cover, direct or indirect food supply or spawning substrates for fish or invertebrates. This is reflected in the low mean fish standing crop. Filamentous algae do not provide cover, but harbour a large number of invertebrates. This probably explains the good fish crops in Irish canals with a moderate algal growth.

Plants with a year-round presence, such as submersed *Hippuris vulgaris, Myriophyllum spicatum* and charophytes, all broad or complex-leaved, provide favourable conditions for fish and have a high standing crop. However, plants which in a temperate climate die down for the winter months and initiate their growth cycle late in the spring, provide poor habitat for fish.

Habitat that is spatially complex may incorporate a variety of microhabitats and thereby support a more diverse community. But special complexity may also restrict access to preferred habitat and thereby limit species distribution. Thus, patchy distribution of habitat is important in structuring and stabilizing communities. Even macrophyte beds that are evenly distributed around a lake often are locally patchy, consisting of patches or bands of vegetation that are separated by open areas. Weaver *et al.* (1997) examined how the patchy distribution of submersed macrophytes affects the distribution of littoral fishes within Lake Mendota, Wisconsin (USA). When patchiness in the structure of macrophyte beds was considered along with macrophyte abundance, the distribution response of fish to habitat complexity was better explained.

Patchiness within vegetation provides prey fish with a habitat in which shelter is in close proximity to open spaces that harbour zooplankton, the preferred prey of many age 0+ fishes. Reduced density within the macrophyte patches increases the manoeuverability of prey fish, and the visibility of macroinvertebrates, and thereby improves their capture success on their prey (Dionne and Folt, 1991). In Lake Mendota decline in the abundance of native plants and small fish and in the growth rate of prey and piscivorous fish coincided with the invasion of *Myriophyllum spicatum* in the mid-1960s. During the decline of *Myriophyllum* in the late 1970s native plants have recolonized, and with them the fish community has been recovering.

The plant structure complexity also determines the invertebrate biomass in plant stands. In Lake Krankesjon in Sweden *Chara tomentosa*, which grows there in dense beds and constitutes a more complex structure than *Potamogeton pectinatus*, another common plant in this lake, has a higher invertebrate biomass. The complex structure also offers a more efficient shelter against predation from fish. *Chara* overwinters with green parts and thus offers a more permanent habitat beneficial for the aquatic invertebrates, and consequently also more beneficial for fish than *P. pectinatus*, which enters senescence during the long winter period.

The predation by fish on in-benthos (*i.e.* tubificids and chironomid larvae) is also affected by the density of vegetation. In experiments in enclosures with various densities of floating-leaved macrophytes (nymphaeids) the abundance of chironomids in the upper sediment layer was negatively affected by perch at low and medium *Nuphar* densities. Densities of Tubificidae were similar in the surficial sediments in the presence and absence of perch, but in the deeper layers were about twice as high in the presence of fish than in the controls. At high vegetation density perch had no impact on chironomid larvae in the benthos. The authors concluded that the behavioural responses of chironomid larvae and tubificid worms to perch differ, and that a high density of floating-leaved macrophytes protects the chironomid prey from fish.

STRUCTURAL BENEFITS PROVIDED BY AQUATIC MACROPHYTES FOR FISH

In addition to the structural benefits provided by aquatic macrophytes for fish, the shade that is created by plants also attracts and may benefit fish. Availability of aquatic plant species that provide appropriate shade may increase both foraging efficiency and predator avoidance by offering a microhabitat that improves detection of food items and predators, which ultimately increases growth and survival. Substrate type and submersed vegetation are important factors in cichlid habitat preferences. The American cichlid species occupy a great variety of habitats but prefer muddy bottom areas with abundant aquatic vegetation (Resendez-Medina, 1981). In Lake Bacalar in the Yucatan Peninsula, Mexico, cichlids were found exactly in such a habitat, probably because of the abundance of prey and shelter.

Feeding Habitat

While herbivores may directly feed on aquatic macrophytes, to other fish aquatic vegetation provides a high density invertebrate prey and periphyton (epiphytic algae) associated with the macrophytes. Fish have feedback effects on vegetation by their direct consumption of vegetation and indirectly via other trophic components or abiotic routes such as sediment-feeding induced turbidity. Fish may therefore also affect habitat structure.

Artificial, macrophyte-like structures were found to impair the foraging of juvenile roach), but were no obstacle to feeding on cladocerans by young rudd and perch. In a study in a hypereutrophic pond in England, Venugopal and Winfield (1993) found that juvenile cyprinids (roach, rudd) and perch were found both among dense, peripheral macrophytes, represented largely by water lilies (*Nuphar lutea*), and in the open water of the pond, although the cyprinids were apparently more abundant among the macrophytes. The higher abundance of cyprinids was confirmed by a significantly higher CPUE within the macrophytes, indicating that they were more abundant or more active in this highly structured habitat. Winfield (1986) found that a dense stand of artificial *Nuphar* sp. had no effect on the feeding rate of zooplanktivorous roach and actually increased the performance of rudd and perch relative to those in open water, possibly due to the reduced predation. Perch feed effectively on cladocerans in weed beds, and the fish also find a refuge among the plants. Some submersed aquatic plants, such as *Potamogeton berchtoldii*, provide some refuge for zooplankton against predation but this is not the case with the nymphaeid *Numphar lutea*. Further studies of Moss *et al.* (1998) have shown that predation of perch on *Daphnia* increases with less dense stands of the water lilies.

Numbers of other small crustaceans and rotifers were mostly unaffected by fish predation. Moss *et al.* (1998) suggested that the refuge will operate even more effectively with cyprinids such as roach and bream who are not as effective hunters among plants structures as perch. Perch may also find alternative food among the plants, such as benthic/epiphytic invertebrates. If these animals are easier to catch than mobile ones in dense vegetation, then this may give an additional refuge mechanism for forms such as *Daphnia*.

A prolonged aquatic macrophyte senescence may have a negative impact through the removal of shelter and food base for fish. It can be compared to a management measure using mechanical control of aquatic vegetation. In the warm temperate coastal lake Swartvlei, South Africa, a littoral plant community dominated by *Potamogeton pectinatus* and two charophyte species underwent a marked seasonal regression in winter months. This resulted in a 60 per cent decline in primary production, 74 per cent slump in littoral invertebrate biomass, and a 54 per cent decline in the abundance of two fish species associated with macrophytes, for which invertebrates and filamentous algae from the littoral zone were of major importance as food source. The disappearance of the macrophytes resulted in a decrease in the condition of *Monodactylus falciformis* and *Rhabdosargus holubi*. The virtual disappearance of aquatic macrophytes also had an impact on the physico-chemical features of the aquatic environment.

Spawning and Nesting in Macrophytes

It is not the purpose of this publication to give a detailed account of all freshwater fish species which use aquatic macrophytes for attaching their eggs or making nests. Therefore, only some examples are given here. Obligatory and non-obligatory plant spawners (phytophils) stick adhesive egg envelopes to submersed live or dead plants. Among these are many cyprinids such as *Labeo* and small *Barbus*, characin and siluroid fish species, *Puntius (=Barbodes)* spp, *Polypterus* spp, *Clarias batrachus*.

Gymnarchus niloticus make floating flask or raft shape masses of aquatic weeds in which they lay their eggs. The siluroids *Callichthys callichthys* and *Hoplosternum littorale* both make a raft constructed of bubbles and aquatic plants. Many cyprinids lay their adhesive eggs on floodplains on flooded terrestrial vegetation. In Africa, *Heterotis niloticus* builds nests in flooded plants at the margins of floodplains. Catfish *Pangasius sutchi* scatters its eggs among submersed weeds and bushes in the shallow inundated margins of the klongs or canals of Indochina. The following European fish release their eggs among submersed macrophytes where they adhere to the plants: *Tinca tinca* and *Scardinius erythrophthalmus* spawn for example among *Myriophyllum* beds, carp *Cyprinus carpio* utilises a range of plants, including *Carex, Glyceria,* fresh shoots of *Phragmites* and *Salix* roots. Other species include: *Blicca bjoerkna, Carassius carassius, C. auratus gibelio, Rutilus rubilio* and *R. arcasi*. Some other fish stick their eggs to submersed plants but other substrata are utilized in their absence: *Rutilus rutilus, Leuciscus idus, L. leuciscus, L. souffia, Alburnus* alburnus, *Rutilus frisii, R. lemmingi*. *R. rutilus* spawns on *Fontinalis* and *Elodea* beds, *Scirpus, Salix* roots, stones and submersed logs. *Abramis brama* may spawn on stones in lakes, in rivers it utilizes only areas with a weak current and macrophyte substrata, *e.g. Rorippa, Botumus, Sagittaria, Glyceria* and *Nuphar*. Pike (*Esox lucius*) spawns among aquatic plants, such as *Equisetum, Phragmites, Carex* and littoral Poaceae in Finland.

Many North American fish are obligatory plant spawners: these include members of Amiidae (*e.g. Amia*), Esocidae (*e.g. Esox*), Cyprinidae (*e.g. Cyprinus,*

Cyprinella, Notemigonus), Catostomidae (*e.g. Ictiobus*), Cyprinodontidae (*e.g. Fundulus*), Atherinidae (*e.g. Labidesthes*), Umbridae (*e.g. Umbra*), Centrarchidae (*e.g. Elassoma*), and Percidae (*e.g. Perca,* some *Etheosoma*). Most data on spawning success relative to structural complexity and plants come from studies of adult sport fish that construct nests (*i.e.* largemouth bass and bluegill).

Although nest spawners successfully spawn in areas devoid of vegetation, they prefer sites with aquatic plants or some other type of structure nearby for refugia. Sunfish of the USA (Perciformes, *e.g. Micropterus salmoides, M. dolomieu*, and *Lepomis gibbosus*) form nesting sites among the macrophytes. Aquatic vegetation is used as nursery habitat for larvaė by at least 12 families of the North American fish. Some species exhibit ontogenetic shifts in habitat use. For example, prolarvae of yellow perch prefer shallow, dense macrophyte areas, while postlarvae prefer deep, low density macrophyte zones.

Many phytophils and phytolithophils lay eggs on substrates just below the water substrate where they are vulnerable to sudden falls in water level. Removal of instream vegetation during the spawning period can have a dramatic effect on spawning success. Mechanical control of aquatic plants in streams can also directly remove the eggs of phytophilous fish species and food organisms for the fish. In Lake Ontario fish which lay eggs in submersed stands include northern pike (*Esox lucius*), perch (*Perca flavescens*), and largemouth bass (*Micropterus salmoides*). In five marshes near Toronto, Stephenson (1989) found over 20 fish species using the wetland during the breeding season.

The nesting of the American Perciformes may lead to changes in the aquatic macrophyte species set up. After clearing *Myriophyllum* for their nests and the nesting period, the nests of *Lepomis gibosus, Micropterus salmoides* and *M. dolomieu* have been gradually invaded by diaspore-propagated plant species, including *Isoetes*, which do not spread vegetatively. Every following spawning season about 20 per cent of the original nest sites are not occupied, and the result is a mix of *Myriophyllum* and the other species of aquatic plants which occupy the abandoned nests. The nesting contributes to the formation of a mosaic of different aquatic plant species.

In South America, *Serrasalmus spilopleura* spawn on floating vegetation including *Eichhornia crassipes*, for example in southeastern Brazil. *Serrasalmus* is an important food fish for riverine people in several places in central and northeastern Brazil.

AQUATIC MACROPHYTES AS A FISH HABITAT

The term "aquatic macrophytes" includes largely flowering plants (angiosperms), some ferns and mosses (pteridophytes) and macroscopic algae (stoneworts, *e.g. Chara*, and the alga *Cladophora*). De Nie (1987) used the following division for aquatic macrophytes, which, expanded by the major tropical and subtropical plants, is also applied in this publication:

A. Aquatic macrophytes rooting in sediment
   i. Emergent aquatic macrophytes: these include angiosperms *Typha, Phragmites, Scirpus, Carex, Acorus, Butomus, Sagittaria Paspalum, Echinochloa, Vossia* etc.
   ii. Floating-leaved aquatic macrophytes: these include *Nymphaea, Nuphar, Nymphoides, Potamogeton, Polygonum, Hydrilla, Cyperus papyrus* etc.
   iii. Submersed macrophytes: these include the algae *Chara* and *Nitella*, moss *Fontinalis*, and angiosperms *Myriophyllum, Elodea, Potamogeton* etc.

B. Freely floating macrophytes: These include: ferns *Azolla* and *Salvinia*, angiosperms *Lemna, Eichhornia, Pistia, Ceratophyllum, Hydrocharis*,, etc.

   Cowx and Welcomme (1998) listed a number of characteristics of aquatic plants which make them important to fish:

   - water purification - a. direct: for example, by oxygenation and conversion of toxic ammonia to usable nitrates; b. indirect: provision of huge surface area for microbes to do the same tasks
   - nutrient recycling - removal during growth season, return during senescence
   - physical link between water and air for many invertebrates, *e.g.* larvae and nymphs of caddis flies, mayflies, chironomids, which are food for fish and have aquatic larval stages and aerial adults
   - refugia for zooplankton which graze phytoplankton and keep water clear
   - cover for huge range of invertebrates, many of which are food for fish
   - cover for fish - value and type varies with age/species of fish as well as type of vegetation
   - spawning areas and sites of oviposition for many cyprinid and percid fish, *e.g.* tench, roach, rudd, perch, and also for pike (all fish of the temperate waters of the western Eurasia)
   - food source (living and dying) - direct source of vegetarian fish, *e.g.* grass carp; indirect source via other animals
   - affect flow patterns - accrete sediments and deflect flow thus providing quieter waters and faster shallows
   - create discrete habitat which is as functional as physical structure.

Aquatic macrophytes are essential if a healthy fish stocks are to be maintained in natural water body. Opuszynski and Shireman (1995) pointed out that some plants or combination of plant species seem to be better fish habitats than others. Plant density is of importance, and the trophic state of the water body also plays an important role in determining what species and what biomass of fish will be present. The more research results become available, the more complicated the aquatic macrophyte-fish interrelationships appear to be. The shallow marginal littoral with aquatic macrophytes contains a greater diversity of aquatic animals than the offshore open water areas. For example, in Lake George in Uganda, the vegetated littoral contained 19 fish species compared to around 10 species in the mid-lake.

Submersed macrophytes have major effects on productivity and biogeochemical cycles in fresh water because they occupy key interfaces in stream and lake ecosystems. Changes in aquatic macrophytes can have major consequences for commercially important fish species. Most macrophytes are rooted, and constitute a living link between sediments and the overlying water. Carpenter and Lodge (op.cit.) found by 1985 seventy-two papers on the effects of environmental factors on macrophytes, but only 22 papers which emphasized the effects of macrophytes on the environment. Since their publication there have been a number of detailed field studies, and an increasing number of field experimental studies on the function of macrophytes in aquatic environment and their impact on the environment.

In the northern temperate lakes fish community structure and stability have been associated with the presence, abundance, species composition, growth form, and structural heterogeneity of macrophytes in various studies. The mechanisms that maintain or alter community structure, and their relative importance, differ among communities and vary with spatial and temporal scale. Aquatic and marginal plants may be a key factor determining whether or not there is any fishery interest in the highly modified urban watercourses which are most accessible to the majority of people.

Aquatic macrophytes have great effect on physical environment, especially light penetration through the water column, water temperature, water flow and substrate. Within stands of aquatic vegetation the light intensity quickly decreases with depth, although great differences exist in the degree of light attenuation betwen species. The vertical temperature gradient within macrophyte stands is as steep as 10°C m^{-1}, compared to gradients of less than 0.2°C m^{-1} in neighbouring unvegetated areas.

Diel oxygen changes as large as 8 mg L^{-1} occur in the waters of dense submersed macrophyte stands. Oxygen may be released into water by some floating plants, such as water hyacinth from rootlets of which oxygen actively diffuses into water.

Submersed macrophytes oxygenate the water more effectively than floating-leaved macrophytes, as solid cover of the latter prevents effective reoxygenation from the air. Decaying macrophytes consume large amounts of oxygen and macrophyte leachate stimulates oxygen consumption by suspended bacteria. Large mats of floating aquatic plants, such as *Salvinia molesta*, *Eichhornia crassipes* and *Cyperus papyrus* will produce almost totally deoxygenated conditions underneath these plants, because they reduce the light penetration and prevent oxygenation of water blocking the water-air interface.

Macrophytes have positive effect on water clarity through a number of mechanisms. These include provision of habitat for plant-associated macroinvertebrates and a refuge for cladocerans, both of which graze on phytoplankton and epiphytes.

While food and habitat provided by plant beds support diverse fish populations, piscivores among them reduce numbers of small planktivorous fish, thereby reducing predation pressure on zooplankton. Macrophytes may also suppress phytoplankton growth through the release of alleopathic substances, and through luxury nutrient uptake and enhanced denitrification. Phosphorus may be reduced by certain plant species that oxidize the sediment. In addition, reduced water movement in plant beds can lead to increased sedimentation rates and reduced turbidity. Where light conditions are deteriorating, mechanisms such as the shedding of epiphyte-burdened leaves, and a shift from low-growing species to taller ones may stabilize the plant state.

OTHER HERBIVOROUS AQUATIC VERTEBRATES

Activities of some other aquatic or semi-aquatic vertebrates, such as turtles, birds, manatee, nutria, muscrat and cattle, through their grazing activity on aquatic macrophytes, may influence fish species composition, abundance and production.

HERBIVOROUS TURTLES

The herbivorous turtles *Kachuga tectum* and *Hardella thurgi* feed on aquatic plants in India and Bangladesh, with the first species found to feed in India on the following: *Lemna, Ceratophyllum, Eichhornia, Hydrilla*, and *Ipomea*. The species can be easily bred under controlled conditions and there is a good scope for their utilisation in the biological control of aquatic weeds. In Florida, the turtle *Pseudoemys floridiana* is also herbivorous. In Delaware waters (USA) Townsend (1979) estimated that fresh aquatic macrophytes formed about 13 per cent of the diet of the snapping turtle (*Chelydra serpentina*).

Birds

Many ducks and geese, domesticated or not, as well as swans and coots, are consumers of aquatic plants. The smaller species of ducks are rather selective, giving preference to duckweeds and other small plants with soft tissues. Among aquatic birds, only geese and swans are strict herbivores, and apart from aquatic macrophytes both consume a certain amount of terrestrial plants. Other aquatic birds consume seeds and/or fruits of aquatic plants, thus reducing their reproduction. McAtee (1939) found that a number of waterfowl species feed on Potamogetonaceae, Cyperaceae and Polygonaceae,

Potamogetonaceae being the preferred food source. Grazing affects both the biomass and the growth of submersed macrophytes significantly. In the colonization phase waterfowl may prevent growth of submersed macrophytes.

Waterfowl often consume significant portions of annual aquatic macrophyte production: 40 per cent peak standing crop of *Potamogeton pectinatus* in Delta Marsh, Manitoba, Canada ; 30 per cent peak standing crop of *P. filiformis* in Loch Leven, Scotland (Jupp and Spence, 1977); and about 50 per cent peak standing crop of an assemblage of submersed macrophytes in Tipper Grund, Denmark.

SIGNIFICANT FOR THE HERBIVOROUS COOT

Shifts from high density in aquatic macrophytes to phytoplankton and back to macrophytes may occur naturally or under human influence. Such shifts may also lead to changes in species composition, biomass and migrations of aquatic birds. When a storm destroyed macrophyte beds in Lake Ellesmere in New Zealand, the population of black swans declined from 40 000–80 000 to 4 000, over a period of about 20 years.

In southern Sweden in Lake Krankesjon, *Potamogeton pectinatus* and *Chara tomentosa* expanded spatially after more than a decade of phytoplankton blooms and sparse submersed vegetation. During the expansion of submersed plants the number of resting and breeding waterfowl increased. The increase was significant for the herbivorous coot (*Fulica atra*) and mute swan (*Cygnus olor*), and for omnivorous dabbling ducks. Submersed plants, and especially their green parts, form the main food item of swans and coots, and the increase in abundance of these birds indicates that shortage of suitable food was limiting during the previous state of phytoplankton dominance.

The increased abundance of dabbling duck was related to the increase in both plants and invertebrates. Further changes occurred, such as decrease in the density of planktonic Cladocera, increase in the species diversity of benthic invertebrates and the change in their dominant species. The increase in the mean size of perch (*Perca fluviatilis*) could be the result of a better food supply in form of invertebrates associated with the aquatic plants.

Invasion of Currituck Sound, North Carolina, by *Myriophyllum spicatum* increased the total biomass of submersed macrophytes, and this in turn led to an increase in numbers of dabbling ducks (*Anas rubripes, A. platyrhynchos, A. acuta, A. americana, A. crecca*), ring-necked ducks (*Athya collaris*), and American coot (*Fulica americana*).

The above examples suggest that population densities of water birds are often closely related to the abundance of aquatic macrophytes. But it is also true that an increase in macrophytes that results in more food for some water bird species may represent a decrease in available habitat or feeding opportunity for other species. A negative relationship between macrophyte cover and bird abundance has been recorded for several species of birds associated with Florida lakes. Nelson and Kadlec (1984), in their review paper describe the interactions occurring among macrophytes, macroinvertebrates, and waterfowl in freshwater wetlands as a complex interdependency in which dynamic changes in the abundance and distributional pattern of macrophytes resulting from climatological fluctuations influence functional processes in litter decomposition and macroinvertebrate communities that, in turn, affect reproductive effort and success of waterfowl.

Lilie and Evrard (1994) found that large, dense stands of submersed vegetation of Wisconsin wetlands offered greater shelter for macroinvertebrates from predation by birds, hence also had a higher biomass of invertebrates compared to less dense stands. Less dense macrophyte stands provide only limited refuge for macroinvertebrates, hence better opportunities for feeding by birds and fish on them. They found that macroinvertebrate densities below 5000 individuals m^{-2} resulted in low densities of breeding pairs of blue-winged teal (*Anas discors*), but this had no effect on mallard (*Anas platyrhynchos*) pair densities.

A number of studies has shown a direct effect of fish on benthic invertebrates, and in this way competition between fish and waterfowl. Winfield and Winfield (1994) provided further evidence in their study of interactions between fish populations and overwintering tufted duck (*Aythya fuligula*) of Lough Neagh, Northern Ireland.

They leaned on previous studies, which found that such competitive interactions occur especially during the waterfowl breeding season when their protein requirements are high. Breeding hens utilise invertebrates as a source of proteins for egg-laying, and ducklings depend heavily on the consumption of invertebrates as a source of protein during their first few weeks of life.

During such periods in life of the water birds, competition for food by fish may determine whether some water birds will select a particular water body for nesting and breeding. Erikson (1979) found that the distribution of fledged goldeneye (*Bucepala clangula*) was negatively associated with the presence of fish, mainly roach and perch. Giles *et al.* (1990) suggested that significant diet overlap exists between perch and ducklings of mallard (*Anas platyrhynchos*) and tufted duck.

In the above interactions, the observed or postulated competition resulted in waterfowl being out-competed by fish. In Lough Neagh, the largest lake in the UK, molluscs (especially *Lymnaea peregra* and *Valvata piscinalis*) were the dominant prey in the diet of tufted duck, followed by chironomid larvae. Molluscs also formed a major component of the diet of roach, while the diet of eel was overwhelmingly dominated by chironomid larvae. Tufted ducks are primarily carnivorous with molluscs dominating the diet and chironomid larvae typically assuming primary importance only when the former are unavailable.

Interestingly, in other localities, roach often feed predominantly on macrophytes or filamentous algae and such a plant-dominated diet was found by Giles *et al.* (1990) to minimise the overlap between roach and waterfowl in a macrophyte-rich lake. The same authors also found that consumption of cladoceran zooplankton by adult roach minimised diet overflap between roach and waterfowl in a macrophyte-poor lake. In Lough Neagh it is likely that the benthivorous roach population increase during the winter may result in a decline in the overwintering numbers of tufted duck. This further reconfirms the observations by Andersson (1981) on increasingly eutrophic lakes in southern Sweden, where declines in waterfowl were probably caused by competition for benthic food resources with increasing cyprinid populations, principally roach and bream (*Abramis brama*).

Food competition between a freshwater fish community and tufted duck was further confirmed through an experimental removal fish from a quarry lake (17 ha) in England. The fish community was dominated by adult bream and roach, with numerous small perch and abundant pike (*Esox lucius*).

The fish employed several mechanisms in the suppression of macrophyte growth including uprooting by benthivorous species (bream, carp), browsing of germinating seedlings (roach), and probably increasing nutrient cycling favouring an algal dominated open water plant community. Prior to the fish removal this lake had very little submersed aquatic vegetation. After the fish removal, dense beds of several species of submersed macrophytes grew over the whole lake bed.

The post fish-removal increases in snail biomass have probably been central to the increased brood size at fledging recorded in this lake. The numbers of herbivorous wintering wildfowl (mute swan, *Cygnus olor*, coot, *Fulica atra*, and gadwall, *Anas strepera*) using the lake have increased dramatically following fish removal and the consequent surges in submersed aquatic plants.

In Florida lakes, Hoyer and Canfield (1994) found that birds do not significantly impact the trophic status of the lakes under natural conditions, but lake trophic status is a major factor influencing bird abundance and species richness on lakes. They found no significant correlation between annual average abundance and species richness and macrophyte abundance. Bird abundance and species richness remain relatively stable as macrophyte abundance increases, but birds that use open-water habitats (*e.g.* cormorant *Phalacrocorax auritus*) are replaced by species that use macrophyte communities (*e.g.* duck *Aythya collaris*).

On the other hand, Lodge (1991), referring to literature data, pointed out that waterfowl influence submersed and emergent plants locally and seasonally: snow geese (*Chen caerulescens*) substantially reduce macrophyte (predominantly emergent and wetland plants) biomass on their summer breeding grounds, at migration stop-over sites, and on their wintering grounds. Less gregarious waterfowl, *e.g.* breeding ducks and swans during the macrophyte growing season, also substantially reduce plants, perhaps over larger areas than colonially nesting geese.

The presence of black swans (*Cygnus atratus*) is closely bound with the presence of aquatic macrophytes. Black swans, introduced to New Zealand from Australia, are exclusively herbivorous. A shallow lake (Hawksbury Lagoon) benthic vegetation was for some time fully dominated by thick mats of filamentous green algae *Spirogyra, Rhizoclonium* and *Enteromorpha intestinalis,* with charophyte *Nitella hookeri* also dominating the biomass at times. The only angiosperm recorded was *Ruppia*. After a 2–3 year period of macrophyte and benthic filamentous algal dominance, the lake switched to phytoplankton dominance. The reason for this was not, however, the impact of swans through direct feeding on benthic algae, but rather the change in the depth penetration of light, which occurred as a combination of phytoplankton and other suspended matter increase. Under such conditions, the additional effect of black swans grazing might well be critical and lead to the decline in aquatic macrophytes.

The same authors also assessed the impact of the faecal loading rates to nutrient dynamics. The data suggest that waterfowl faeces have low ratios of nitrogen to phosphorus, so that in lakes where their contribution is large, the phytoplankton will tend to be dominated by cyanobacteria. However, in Hawksbury Lagoon black swans faecal contribution to nutrient dynamics was slight, less than half of that estimated for Canada geese on a small Michigan lake. Geese feed on pasture, thus bringing into water nutrients from external source, rather than recycling material like black swans, feeding on benthic algae. Mitchell and Wass (1996) constructed a conceptual model for the roles of black swans and other non-seasonal factors in decline in macrophyte biomass in shallow lakes.

In lakes where for whatever reason submersed aquatic macrophytes have disappeared, *e.g.* in eutrophicated water bodies, the regrowth of macrophytes may be delayed by waterfowl grazing. Kiorboe (1980) stated that grazing by coots has only a minimal effect on macrophyte growth because grazing often takes place outside the growing season of the plants. Coots, however, pull out whole plants and may influence the macrophyte composition and succession by removing especially plants still present during autumn and winter. In experiments, under the impact of waterfowl grazing, especially coot (*Fulica atra*), plants growing on mud were found to have been pulled out of the sediment and most of them had disappeared.

A high number of of coots appeared on the Dutch Lake Zwemlust when perennial macrophytes became dominant after biomanipulation. Van Donk (1998) suggested that high grazing pressure by coots on *Elodea* and *Ceratophyllum* during the first years after biomanipulation probably promoted the rise of *Potamogeton berchtoldii*. This plant was not negatively affected by coots because this species forms nongrazable overwintering structures. The impact of sequential grazing on aquatic macrophytes by rudd and coots in Lake Zwemlust, as reflected in changes in the total biomass of macrophytes.

Information on the consumption of aquatic macrophytes by herbivorous birds is sparse: in Lake Zwemlust, Netherlands, the estimated annual consumption by coots was calculated as being between 30 and 1 200 kg. This compares with the consumption of 170 to 360 kg by the fish rudd (*Scardinius erythrophthalmus*). Mitchell and Perrow (1998) suggested that birds may have a major impact on the dynamics of plant biomass in temperate waters only during a low macrophyte production - either early in the growth phase of seasonal species, when biomass is low, or in autumn, when seasonal plant growth has slowed or ceased. Arrival of migratory flocks may dramatically increase the grazing impact and lead to a substantial decline in plant biomass after seasonal growth has ended.

Olofson (1991) found significantly higher growth of fenced-in macrophytes (*Potamogeton crispus*) than of unfenced macrophytes in Lake Stigholm, Denmark. The fish grazing was of minor importance as most herbivorous fish were prior to that removed. He concluded this was the result of grazing on water plants by waterfowl. Jupp and Spence (1977) found that plants of *Potamogeton filiformis*, protected from waterfowl grazing, became up to 5.3 times larger than unprotected plants.

Lauridsen *et al.* (1993) concluded that waterfowl will be able to delay the re-establishment of submersed macrophytes, especially in shallow parts, where waterfowl are able to reach the bottom when feeding. This might delay the recovery of eutrophic lakes.

Concluding, one can say that birds typically consume only a small fraction of the annual aquatic macrophyte production. Their major influence appears to derive not from what they consume but from the loss of the future growth potential of plants, compounded through the growth period. The macrophyte biomass parameters that are relevant to zooplankton or fish may not always be so for birds, as birds are highly mobile and sampling in - say - two or four weeks interval is quite inappropriate. Birds mobility means that the option of emigration to seek a better habitat is always available. Where large generalist herbivores such as aquatic birds continue to increase, they may become an impediment to managing lakes for the clearwater state: a small increase in herbivory by such birds could tip the balance towards the turbid phytoplankton state, and in turn this would impact on fish.

Manatee (*Trichechus spp*)

In Florida and Guyana, *Trichechus manatus* is known to consume 36 genera of macrophytes, but not water hyacinth when other plants are available. It was reported that they efficiently clear canals when present in sufficient density. Various ponds and canals in Guyana have been kept clear of aquatic weeds by *Trichechus inunguis* for many years. This species, which inhabits the tropical rivers of south America, feeds at any level from bottom to surface and is able to feed also on the floating vegetation. Their preference is for succulent aquatic macrophytes, but they will consume almost any aquatic plant. They prefer submersed to floating, and floating to rooted-emergent plants. In the Chagres River in Panama weed control using the manatee was unsuccessful. Some authors pointed out some of the limitations and difficulties in attempting to utilize this species. While it is a voracious feeder it tends to graze selectively and, except in situations where it can be confined to a small area and thus forced to feed on all plants, it will bypass thick stands of one species to feed on another which it prefers. This

factor, coupled with its scarcity, its low reproductive rate and the high cost of managing it, suggests that it is unlikely to be widely used in weed-control programmes.

Estimates for wet weight food consumption by captive manatees (*T. manatus*) range from 5 to 11 per cent of body weight per day. Etheridge *et al.* (1985) made a detailed field study of manatees of the Crystal River, Florida, where they determined that the longest animal feeding in a 24 hour period was 6 hours and 10 minutes, with an average of 5 hours per day, an equivalent of approximately 7.1 per cent of their own body weight. The introduced hydrilla was the principal food of manatees there.

The authors, using Haller and Shireman (1982) data on aquatic plant biomass for Kings Bay, where the plant covered 165 ha, concluded that 18 manatees per ha would be required just to maintain the hydrilla at a constant biomass by consuming daily productivity. This is nearly ten times as many manatees than are present in the area. They argue that previous assessments of efficiency of manatees in controlling aquatic plants might have been exagerated, unless the local plant productivity was much lower than that in Kings Bay, and conclude that manatees cannot be considered efficient control agents for aquatic macrophytes.

Trichechus senegalensis inhabits the west coast from Senegal to Angola in Africa, but nothing is known about its plant-feeding habits.

Nutria (*Myocaster coypus*)

Schuytema (1977) reviewed the impact of nutria on aquatic plants. This animal, often introduced for its pelt and meat, is able to control the emergent *Typha angustata* and *Phragmites australis* in ponds in Europe and Israel, and water grass (*Echinochloa*) in Africa (Cameroon). This it does quite efficiently, and where nutria is present close to common carp ponds it can significantly increase fish production by destroying the emergent vegetation. The burrowing habit of nutria is a negative aspect of its presence as it may lead to damage to pond embankments, canal banks and dams. In Kenya nutria (coypu), which was imported for fur-farming in 1950, escaped and arrived at Lake Naivasha from 1965 onwards, where, by the early 1970s, there was a large population. Coypu are generally blamed for the disappearance of water-lilies (*Nymphaea caerulea*) from Lake Naivasha, on which individuals were widely observed to be feeding. Water-lily shoots make up a major part of the coypu's diet. Water-lilies began to disappear in the eastern part of the lake at around the same time that the crayfish *Procambarus clarkii* populations were high (4 ind. m^{-2}). The crayfish had a substantial effect upon the submersed vegetation, which was reported to be abundant in 1979 but had completely disappeared from the lake by 1983, the last year in which crayfish harvest exceeded 100 tons. It is likely that water-lilies disappeared under the combined grazing pressure of coypu and crayfish.

In the Norfolk Broads, UK, the highest rate of decrease in young reed shoots was found when the population of coypu was very high.

Muskrat (*Ondatra zibethicus*)

In the Czech Republic muskrat consumed or used in lodge construction 9–14 per cent of the annual net biomass production of *Typha latifolia*. In a lake in northern Germany a population of muskrats consumed or damaged 0.27 ha of *Typha*, 0.15 ha *Phragmites australis*, 0.86 ha *Glyceria*, and 1.58 *Scirpus*. The damaged area of *Scirpus* and *Phragmites* did not recover even when the muskrats significantly decreased in number. In the USA muskrat in the Atchafalaya Bay, Louisiana, graze on submersed swards, for example *Eleocharis*.

AQUATIC MACROPHYTES AS A LINK IN THE FOOD CHAIN

EFFECT OF FISH GRAZING ON NUTRIENT RELEASE

Herbivorous fish have a limited ability to convert plant material into animal tissue and to remove excess nutrients from the system. But being relatively efficient grazers and inefficient assimilators, they may play a significant part in initiating the internal, biologically mobilized nutrient source, or accelerate their recirculation. Thus, if with advancing eutrophication, the rate of macrophyte consumption increases due to the increase in number of herbivores, a new part of their biomass may finally be converted into additional algal biomass - the main troublemaker in lakes of the temperate zone. Considerable information is available on the impact of grass carp grazing on water quality.

Grass carp partially digests its food and the faeces are a large source of nutrients. Nutrients are readily utilised by phytoplankton, resulting in elevated algal biomass, and in some situations leading to algal blooms. Bettoli *et al.* monitored the changes in chlorophyll *a* concentration prior to and after the introduction of grass carp in Lake Conroe. Not always the primary production changes under the impact of grass carp grazing on macrophytes. In Red Haw

Lake, Iowa, where within three years the introduced grass carp reduced aquatic macrophytes from 2 438 g m^{-2} to 211 g m^{-2}, mean nitrites, nitrates, biological oxygen demand, and turbidity showed significant decreases, while alkalinity increased significantly. Mean concentrations of organic and inorganic phosphates gradually increased, but were not statistically different. During the first two years the average primary production was nearly identical, followed by a decrease in the third year.

Grass carp consumed all major plant groups, with preference for *Najas* and *Potamogeton*. Lembi *et al.* found that as much as 54 per cent of the phosphorus and 42 per cent of the nitrogen released by consumption of plants by grass carp in Indiana ponds were incorporated into new fish tissue. Most of the phosphorus not taken up by the fish was sequestered into components other than water or phytoplankton. The same authors also noted that potassium concentrations in water appeared to be an excellent indicator of vegetation consumption by grass carp. The authors suggested that the impact of the grass carp on water quality should be minimal in temperate zone small water bodies if the fish is stocked early in the season when vegetation biomass is low. Leslie *et al.* detected a significant increase in nitrate-nitrite concentrations in two Florida lakes following macrophyte removal by grass carp.

Increased alkalinity may have been related to decreased photosynthetic activity and the resulting release of carbonate ions following the elimination of macrophytes. Mitzner reported a significant increase in alkalinity following a 91 per cent reduction of aquatic macrophytes by grass carp in a lake in Iowa. Elimination of macrophytes in a cooling reservoir in North Carolina using *Tilapia zillii* also resulted in an increase in nitrate/nitrite and alkalinity concentrations. An intensive decomposition of macrophytes of their residues may result in an increase in ammonia, the concentration of which, if exceeding 1.0 mg L^{-1}, would stop grass carp to feed (Kracko and Noble, 1993). In experiments in aquaria the macrophyte *Anacharis canadensis* was eliminated by the grazing activity of rudd.

The grazing resulted in an increase in phosphorus concentration in water. In ponds this caused an increase in the biomass of epiphytic algae but no increase in phytoplankton. Common carp reworking and digestion of bottom sediments may lead to a substantial increase in phosphorus in water. Lamarra suggested that a carp population of 200 kg ha^{-1} could internally load a lake with orthophosphate at 0.52 mg P m^{-2} day^{-1}. This might result in an increase in phytoplankton where plant control using common carp is proposed.

Aquatic Macrophytes versus Phytoplankton

In southwestern Finland, the small and shallow Lake Littoistenjarvi alternates between two alternative states: mesotrophic, characterised by well-developed stands of aquatic macrophytes, and eutrophic, when the macrophytes decline. The high abundance of submersed macrophytes and clear water in the early 1990s, was followed in 1992 by high nutrient and chlorophyll levels, high turbidity and reduced stands of macrophytes. The situation changed again during 1993–1996 when the lake water was clear, chlorophyll levels low relative to total phosphorus, and aquatic macrophytes moderately abundant.

The roach stock was moderately strong (71 kg ha^{-1}) after the high abundance of submersed macrophytes in the early 1990s, declining to about 28 kg ha^{-1} by 1996. Perch biomass was notable, but consisted mainly of large (>20 cm) individuals that were probably piscivorous. In 1994–1996 the total fish biomass did not decrease, but there was a clear shift in the size distribution towards larger fish; especially small roach were almost absent in 1995–1996. This size shift probably led to a lowered predation pressure on zooplankton, and the cladoceran biomass showed some increase in 1994–1996.

In this Finnish lake cladoceran zooplankton was thus controlled by fish predation, but water quality was not dependent on zooplankton. Phytoplankton abundance was more tightly linked to long-term fluctuations of submersed plants. The abundance of large crustaceans in 1993 (and an almost absence of *Daphnia*) and in later years of the littoral cladocerans *Sida* and *Simocephalus*, probably originated from the submersed vegetation, which may also have offered a refuge from fish predation for other fish. Interestingly, during 1993–1996, phytoplankton biomass remained low in spite of very low crustacean zooplankton biomass during most of the summer. Similar role of submersed aquatic plants has been also reported for some other lake ecosystems.

Periphyton Function

Sand-Jensen and Borum and Sand-Jensen and Sondergaard belong to a number of workers who pointed out the importance of epiphytic (synonym: periphytic) algae coating submersed macrophytes as a factor which leads to the suppression of aquatic plants. Excessive growth of epiphytes is harmful to the macrophyte, because insufficient quantities of light and inorganic carbon (HCO_3 and CO_2) can reach the plant and consequently the macrophyte photosynthesis is hampered (Sand-Jensen and Sondergaard, 1981). Epiphytic algae are more efficient at obtaining nutrients and light due to their large surface area to volume ratio, high biotic potential and closer proximity to the water column. They may also have more efficient nutrient uptake mechanism.

Periphyton provides more nutritious substrates than sediments or vascular plant tissues, and consequently it is an important energy source for both detritus and grazing food chains. Epiphytic algae benefit from inorganic nutrients and dissolved organic compounds leaking from the host macrophytes, and these may be readily used and beneficial to algal and bacterial communities of the epiphyton, especially in oligotrophic waters. Difference in algal communities on different species of macrophytes under low nutrient availability has been suggested to be due to host-specific composition of the released organic and inorganic compounds. Periphyton is grazed by a diversity of both invertebrate and vertebrate aquatic organisms.

The invertebrates include molluscs, nematodes, microcrustaceans (Cladocera, Copepoda, Ostracoda), amphipod and isopod crustaceans, crayfish, mysids, chironomid larvae, caddisfly and mayfly larvae. Invertebrate grazers may play an extremely important role in controlling periphyton. Grazing snails benefit macrophytes by removing the epiphytic cover, as shown in experiments by Bronmark : the growth rate of *Ceratophyllum demersum* increased in the presence of snails by almost 30 per cent due to the removal of epiphytic cover. Similar results were obtained by Martin *et al.* in Bays Mountain Lake where the biomass of submersed macrophytes (*Najas flexilis* and *Potamogeton diversifolius*) increased 60x in cages where snail-feeding redear sunfish and small sunfish (*Lepomis macrochirus* and *L. microlophus*) were excluded.

The results suggested a chain of strong interactions (*i.e.* from fish to snails to periphyton to macrophytes) that may be important in lake littoral system. This contrasts sharply with earlier predictions based on cascading trophic interactions that propose that fish predation on snails would enhance macrophyte biomass. In an experimental study on a small pond in southern Sweden, with dense submersed vegetation dominated by *Elodea canadensis*, with much less abundant *Potamogeton pectinatus, P. obtusifolius, P. crispus, Ranunculus trichophyllus*, and *Chara* sp., the presence of tench indirectly increased the biomass of periphyton through a reduction of grazing pressure by snails, on which the fish fed.

A similar study carried out on two North American lakes showed that the highly specialized moluscivorous fish *Lepomis gibbosus* dramatically reduced the density and biomass of snails, which in turn resulted in an increased biomass of epiphyton. These studies showed strong cascading interactions between fish, snails, algae and submersed macrophytes. Given the difference in shade tolerance between plant species, cascading trophic interactions initiated by a predatory fish may well influence distribution patterns and species composition of submersed macrophyte communities in lake littoral zones. With an increasing density of predators feeding on snails the most shade-intolerant macrophytes are predicted to disappear first, and at high levels of predation, possibly coupled with increased nutrient enrichment, the entire submersed macrophyte community may disappear.

Intermediate-sized herbivores - fish and crayfish - reduce macrophytes and periphyton similarly, with the literature suggesting that the periphyton consumed by these species is primarily filamentous macroalgae that may be intentionally ingested by the herbivores. But Scott and Crossman pointed out that many American fish are algivorous or use filamentous algae as a substantial food source, particularly in late summer. In the slow-flowing rivers of southeast

England young-of-the-year roach (*Rutilus rutilus*) and chubb (*Leuciscus cephalus*) switch to feeding on periphyton when preferred zooplankton is not available, either due to low numbers or at night when visual feeding is precluded. This switch coincides with a decline in the growth rate of these fish. By contrast, the smallest herbivores- snails and insects - have little (insects) or no impact (snails) on macrophytes but do substantially reduce periphyton, especially microalgae. The seasonal timing of the presence of different grazers may differ substantially. Chironomid larvae often dominate in spring, and graze until their pupation and emergence. Snails are present all year around and may remain active even at low temperatures. In some water bodies oligochaetes appear to be the most important herbivores in terms of overall grazing impact. But seasonality may be weakly expressed, or completely lacking in tropical waters. Thus, the consequences of grazing may differ in subtropical and tropical lakes from those in temperate water bodies. Botts and Cowell found that abundance of epiphytic algae and invertebrate grazers were only weakly correlated in a subtropical lake, whereas in temperate lakes they usually show strong temporal correlation. In Argentina, the three rivers, Uruguay, Paraguay and Parana, form Rio de la Plata.

The characid fish *Prochladius lineatus* is the dominant species among the some 300 species that inhabit Rio de la Plata. It represents around 60 per cent of the biomass and over 70 per cent of fish catches. It has been suggested that one of the causes of the extraordinary success of this detritivorous fish is its capacity to selectively feed on nutritionally superior detritus, *i.e.* epiphytic detritus, rich in total amino acids. Also, it has been suggested that it might obtain periphyton associated with roots and shoots of aquatic macrophytes. As water hyacinth covers 80 per cent of lakes and ponds of the middle Parana floodplain, Planas and Neiff investigated this plant, collected from the Parana River floodplain, for periphyton. They found that mats of water hyacinth let through insufficient light to allow full development of periphyton. Weisner *et al.* investigated a combined impact of epiphytes and waterfowl grazing on submersed vegetation on three Swedish eutrophic shallow lakes in the clear-water state.

They found that mechanisms hampering submersed vegetation were strongest at shallow and/or sheltered locations. The growth of *Myriophyllum spicatum*, planted in the same substrate and at the same water depth, was compared between sheltered and wave exposed sites in two lakes. After 6 weeks the plants were significantly smaller at the sheltered sites, where periphyton production was about 5 times higher than at the exposed sites. Enclosure experiments were conducted to evaluate the effects of waterfowl (mainly coot *Fulica atra* and mute swan *Cygnus olor*) grazing on macrophyte biomass. *Potamogeton pectinatus* growth was decreased by grazing, whereas *M. spicatum* was not affected. The effects were greater at a sheltered than at a wave-exposed site. The results suggest that competition from epiphytes and waterfowl grazing hamper the development of submersed vegetation at sheltered and/or shallow locations.

Zooplankton

Aquatic macrophytes provide shelter or refuge to zooplankton, and the presence of especially large zooplankton controls small phytoplankton. If the larger zooplankton becomes scarce, the phytoplankton community will change to slow-growing bigger, mainly inedible blue-green species. These bigger, often colonial algae compete more successfully with the small algae for nutrients and establish high-density populations, sometimes leading to algal blooms. In turn, this restricts light penetration into deeper water and leads to the death of submersed macrophytes. In the English lake Little Mere experiments were conducted to investigate the relative importance of top-down (zooplankton grazing) and bottom-up (nitrogen-limitation) control in limiting algal growth, and the role of aquatic macrophytes in this process.

It is generally recognized that submersed macrophytes provide a refuge for cladocerans and a habitat for plant-associated macroinvertebrates, both of which graze on phytoplankton and epiphytes. However, in experiments with a high stickleback (*Gasterosteus aculeatus*) density the fish controlled the zooplankton associated with the macrophytes. The same conclusion was reached by Jeppesen *et al.*, who found that the refuge effect of submersed macrophytes almost disappeared - even for small-sized cladocerans - if fish density exceeded ca. 4 fish m^{-2}. However, if plant density is high and fish are not forced into the vegetation, pelagic zooplankton may aggregate in the submersed macrophytes during the daytime.

Floating-leaved plants and reed belts have a comparatively low refuge effect due to low stem density. The efficiency of plant beds as refuge for zooplankton is often high in eutrophic lakes. In less eutrophic and mesotrophic lakes, the impact of predatory fish increases. In Europe, in such lakes perch predation becomes more important, and the foraging conditions for predatory fish improve, due to, for instance, increased transparency. Young planktivorous prey fish thus seek refuge in the vegetation, which does not provide effective refuge from the predator. In mesotrophic-oligotrophic lakes the predatory pressure on planktivores becomes even stronger. In some other English lakes (Cromes Broad, Hoveton Little Broad/Pound End, and Upton Broad) *Daphnia* spp exhibited an early summer peak of abundance but had declined rapidly by July, probably as a result of predation by fish.

In dense macrophyte stands *Daphnia* spp persisted after their elimination in open water, indicating some refuge effect. At sites with macrophyte cover and/or low fish predation pressure, *Daphnia* was replaced by *Ceriodaphnia*, both with or without *Simocephalus*, thus maintaining large populations of grazing

Cladocera, apparently exerting a high grazing pressure on phytoplankton. This occurred even under high predation pressure by fish. The authors have suggested that dense macrophytes offer the most suitable refuge for cladocerans through provision of predator-free space. Cascading trophic interactions are known to play an important role in the transfer of fish predation effects via zooplankton to the phytoplankton community, and this may affect also the structure and function of the microbial community. Jurgens and Jeppesen followed the cascading effects on microbial food web structure in a dense macrophyte bed (mainly *Potamogeton pectinatus*) under experimental conditions. As a result of differing fish predation pressure (strong where no macrophytes present, low where macrophytes present), there was a high density of different cladocerans and cyclopoid copepods in the enclosure system with macrophytes, whereas ciliates, rotifers, and cyclopoid copepods dominated in the enclosures without macrophytes. In the macrophytes the abundance of phytoplankton, protozoans and bacteria was very low, whereas with no macrophytes a diverse assemblage of pico-, nano- and microplankton coexisted with the metazooplankton community. Ciliate density was approximately two orders of magnitude higher in the enclosures without macrophytes.

The protozoans there probably exerted considerable grazing pressure on the bacterial and algal communities. Bacterial concentrations were four- to fivefold higher in enclosures without macrophytes than those with macrophytes. The experiments have shown that fish predation impact can cascade from fish to the bacterial level, and that this is probably a general feature of more eutrophic systems, such as shallow eutrophic lakes in the temperate climate of the northern hemisphere.

Aquatic Macroinvertebrates

Aquatic macrophytes are an important habitat for aquatic macroinvertebrates. The plants provide protection from predators and current, and are a direct and indirect source of food of fish and aquatic birds. In plant beds, benthic invertebrates are generally more numerous and more diverse than in open water. Diehl and Kornijow showed the increase in epiphytic macroinvertebrates with increasing macrophyte densities, and how this is paralleled by an increase in fish biomass. Species composition and biomass of macroinvertebrates usually differ from plant species to species, depending on the structural complexity of the plant, changes in the morphology of macrophytes during the growing season, amount of the periphyton and detritus on plants, changes in water level, life cycle of the individual macroinvertebrate species, and some other factors. Differences in invertebrate richness, biomass and distribution will have a direct effect on the fish populations depending on aquatic macroinvertebrates as source of food. Indirectly, macrophytes are also important for the benthic macroinvertebrates, for which they provide protection against foraging by fish and aquatic birds, as well as providing the invertebrates with a supply of organic matter from the decomposing plants.

Kornijow and Gulati investigated aquatic macroinvertebrates associated with aquatic vegetation about 18 months after the biomanipulation of Zwemlust, a small Dutch lake. They found that the macrofauna did not differ notably from that in non-manipulated lakes. The species diversity differed on the different species of aquatic plants. The greatest diversity was on *Chara* sp., moderate on other two submersed plants *Elodea nuttallii* and *Ceratophyllum demersum*, and on *Phragmites australis*, and the lowest on filamentous green algae, primarily *Mougeotia* sp. Some taxa were restricted to certain plants, *e.g.* the mollusc *Acroloxus lacustris* found solely on reed, while the molluscs *Armiger crista, Planorbis corneus, Valvata piscinalis* and leeches, except *Erpobdella* sp., were recorded only on the submersed plants. Larvae of Tipulidae and Ephydridae occurred exclusively on filamentous algae.

DENSITY AND BIOMASS OF THE FAUNA

The density and biomass of the fauna per 100 g of plant wet weight on different plant species markedly differed, with the lowest values on reed and among *Mougeotia*. Much higher density and biomass occurred on submersed plants, especially on *Chara* sp. Generally, the densities of the phytomacrofauna were relatively low but the biomass values high, compared with many other lakes. Gastropoda, larvae of Chironomidae and Trichoptera were the main quantitative components of the phytomacrofauna. It was noted that the greater the fragmentation of macrophyte leaves the greater the faunal density, and usually higher the taxonomical variability of the associated animal populations. In this respect, Lake Zwemlust aquatic vegetation confirmed findings from some other lakes. There was a high degree of similarity between the fauna associated with *Ceratophyllum* and algal mats, with a high dominance of the chironomid *Cricotopus* larvae. The larvae feed primarily on the algae constituting mats and those covering the macrophyte.

During strong stratification, aquatic macrophytes provide a diversity of microhabitats and refugia for aquatic macroinvertebrates which are temporarily or permanently excluded from the lake bottom by low dissolved oxygen concentrations. Differences in the habitats provided by the floating *Pistia stratiotes* and submersed *Ceratophyllum demersum* in Volta Lake (Ghana, West Africa) were reflected in species composition, dominance and standing crops of their associated aquatic macroinvertebrates. While grazers and filter-feeders, such as zygopteran nymphs and chironomid larvae, dominated *Ceratophyllum*, submersed *Pistia* roots were utilised by predatory anisopterans, the hemipteran *Diplonychus*, and the grazing molluscs *Bulinus forskali* and *B. truncatus rohlfsi*.

The density of macroinvertebrates in *Pistia* roots reached a maximum of about 16,000 individuals m^{-2}, which is close to the density of 18 620 individuals m^{-2} collected by Pelli and Barbosa from *Salvinia molesta* roots in a lake in Brazil. The dry mass of macroorganisms on *Pistia* at 12 g m^{-2} was higher than that reported in the literature for floating plant associated invertebrates from African, Asian or South American lakes. The association of *Ceratophyllum* with shallows was found to represent a protective mechanism for the associated macroinvertebrate fauna: wind-blown *Ceratophyllum*, carried off-shore and found stranded in the crowns of drowned trees several hundred metres from the shore, supported considerably lower animal densities than those in the shallow littoral.

Ceratophyllum Demersum

The free-floating submersed *Ceratophyllum demersum* is a common plant in tropical African waters. While it can be a nuisance plant as it provides a habitat for host snails of the parasite *Schistosoma haematobium*, it is considered to be beneficial for fish as it serves as a substrate for aquatic invertebrates and periphyton, on which many fish feed. Due to the vertical distribution of this plant, which may reach several metres of length, Petr, rather than making an attempt of expressing the number and biomass per square meter, which would be irrelevant because a different length/depth of the individual plants, expressed the abundance and biomass of invertebrates associated with *Ceratophyllum* as per 1 000 g of dried plant.

During three months of observations, the inshore *Ceratophyllum* contained 16 502, 39 020, and 92 156 organisms, respectively (corresponding to 34, 40 and 76 g wet weight), as compared to 12 095, 6 891, and 6 234 organisms (corresponding to 7.6, 5.9 and 5.2 g wet weight) in off-shore *Ceratophyllum* plants, stranded on drowned trees. The off-shore, usually isolated individual plants, are exposed to heavy fish predation, and their recolonisation appears to be minimal. If using conservatively the biomass per 1 000 g of dried plant as a biomass per m^2 for the inshore habitat, the biomass exceeds twice the maximum biomass of invertebrates found on *Pistia* roots in the same lake, *i.e.* 35 g m^{-2}. The rich aquatic invertebrates of aquatic plants in Volta Lake must play an important role in the high fish production in this reservoir.

High densities of macroinvertebrates associated with aquatic macrophytes have been recorded from the borders of macrophyte beds on floodplains of Orinoco (Venezuela) and Parana (Argentina), and there was considerable difference between the 'isolation' phase, *i.e.* when the floodplains were not connected with the river, flooding phase, and the inundation period. In Orinoco floodplain lakes, where macrophytes develop only during the rainy season, there is only one density peak. The peak densities there were: for water hyacinth 38 000 org. m^{-2}, 68 000 org. m^{-2} for *Paspalum repens*, and up to 600 000 org. m^{-2} for *Nymphaea*. Such high densities represent lucrative feeding grounds for numerous fish. In a review on herbivory on aquatic macrophytes Lodge pointed out that while a majority of herbivorous invertebrates eat periphyton, many do eat macrophytes. Those who eat macrophytes may be functionally important in food webs and nutrient fluxes. As a trophic link they are significant in community and ecosystem functions.

Some caddisfly larvae are known to be among the few aquatic invertebrates directly feeding on aquatic macrophytes. High densities of herbivorous insects, such as a caddisfly, several moths, several weevils, and one or more chironomid species, are known to accompany the decline in *Myriophyllum*. *Myriophyllum spicatum* and *Hydrilla verticillata* have become serious aquatic weeds in many parts of continental USA, and a search is going on for effective insect biological control agents. Balciunas and Balciunas *et al.* reported on their search for such agents in China and Australia, which followed Balciunas previous search in Africa.

In Lake Tanganyika, *Polypedilum* chironomid larvae damage apical meristem of *Hydrilla*, and together with grazing by fish, are the two factors mainly responsible for containing *Hydrilla*. Whether the emphemeropteran nymphs of *Povilla adusta*, which burrow in *Polygonum* stems in Volta Lake and in rootlets of *Pistia stratiotes* in Lake Chad cause a serious damage to their host plants, is not known. They do not feed on them and use them as shelter from which these larvae filter phytoplankton from the surrounding water, or graze on the periphyton. The nymphs are known to burrow into bark and wood of trees, which speeds up the destruction of trees inundated in some African tropical reservoirs.

In Lake Victoria and Lake George (both in Uganda), where the nymphs burrow into papyrus plants, they also attack wooded canoes of fishermen, or even boats made of fibreglass. The nymphs require for their existence a relatively high dissolved oxygen concentration in the surrounding water, which limits their lateral distribution within the fringing papyrus swamp to only about 1.5 m distance from the edge.

In laboratory conditions the trichopteran *Anabolia nervosa* larvae were found to show a preference for young leaves of *Potamogeton perfoliatus*, which were richer in nitrogen than leaves of terrestrial trees *Alnus glutinosa* and *Fagus sylvatica*. The larvae consumed 3 times more fresh *Potamogeton* than *Alnus* leaves, but the same amount in terms of dry mass. Larvae grown on *Alnus* accumulated more fat than larvae grown on *Potamogeton*, while the reverse was true for protein accumulation. The study demonstrated that fresh tissue of *Potamogeton perfoliatus* provided a valuable source to this caddisfly larva. In the field, *i.e.* a Danish stream, however, the plant constituted only 1–5 per cent of the food intake by this trichopteran. The highest plant consumption was from early May to mid-June, but the invertebrate herbivores harvested only 1.3 to 1.8 per cent of the total annual plant production. Otto and Svensson discovered in experiments that the caddisfly larvae of *Sericostoma personatum* (Spence), found in Swedish waters, consumed significantly less leaves with high nitrogen content than leaves with low nitrogen content, and suggested that the low palatability of aquatic macrophytes may be due to chemical defence mechanisms. Larvae of the trichopteran *Potamophylax cingulatus* were also tested and confirmed that aquatic plants produce secondary plant substances, which reduce the attacks by aquatic herbivores.

A study of invertebrates associated with three macrophytes in the Macquarie River, Tasmania (Australia) showed major differences in the invertebrate assemblage in any one month, and also a large turnover of taxa associated with the species of macrophyte species from one month to the next. The three macrophytes sampled were *Myriophyllum simulans/variifolium, Triglochin procera* and *Eleocharis sphacelata*, each one differing in the structural complexity and its location in the littoral zone. The greatest abundance of macroinvertebrates was found associated in all months (and at all water levels) in the structurally complex and shallowest *Myriophyllum*. However, this plant had a much lower number of taxa than the structurally simpler and deeper water *Triglochin* and *Eleocharis*. The invertebrate abundance and *Myriophyllum* biomass were found to initially increase together, but as the plant biomass became very high, *i.e.* the plant became dense, the invertebrate abundance declined. This may have an implication for fish feeding, which in such a case is limited by the plant density and the availability of the prey. A similar situation was also found on *Myriophyllum*-associated mosquito *Anopheles*, with the density of the mosquitoes decreasing with an increase in the stem density.

Cebrian and Duarte found that consumption of freshwater macrophytes, seegrasses and terrestrial grasses by invertebrates and vertebrates ranged fom 1 to 80 per cent of plant production. In two studies of floating-leaved freshwater macrophytes the invertebrate consumption of plant production was less than 10 per cent for *Nymphoides peltata*, and 3–6 per cent for *Nuphar lutea*. A number of authors as quoted in Jacobsen and Sand-Jensen have observed a heavy damage of submersed and floating-leaved macrophytes by invertebrate herbivores.

Presence of Vegetation Serves

cachlan found an increase in the number of pulmonates and bivalves in the mud of Lake Kariba, a reservoir in eastern tropical Africa, following an invasion of aquatic macrophytes. But Killgore *et al.* found that dense monospecific beds of *Myriophyllum spicatum* contained few benthos and could support less diverse fish community. In the USA, on the other hand, in ponds without vegetation, common carp and bluegill greatly reduced the abundance of oligochaetes and nematodes.

Availability of aquatic invertebrates as fish food depends on the effectiveness of the shelter provided to them by aquatic macrophytes, and their productivity. Their productivity will depend on the food availability. Epiphyton, the source of food of the majority of macrophyte dwelling macroinvertebrates, is at its optimal development when the surrounding water has intermediate nutrient concentrations.

The most important aspects of the periphyton-invertebrate grazer-fish interaction in lakes is that herbivorous invertebrates provide an alternative food source for fish and hence reduce the pressure on zooplankton. Without such invertebrates, the ontogenetic shifts seen in feeding adult fish would not occur and all fish would compete for the same food resource, a situation seen in plantless eutrophic lakes. Such feeding on invertebrates by fish will result to some extent in an increase in periphyton, but the overall cost to the plants may be outweighed by gains resulting from increased zooplankton abundance.

Insects, which are used for biological control of nuisance aquatic plants, may also become food for fish, thus negating their impact. To control *Myriophyllum spicatum*, the aquatic weevil *Euhrychiopsis lecontei* was released in Lake Auburn. Fish stomach analysis of the sunfish (*Lepomis macrochirus*) and pumpkinseed (*Lepomis gibbosus*) has shown a frequency occurrence for the weevil larvae and adults of 10.3 per cent to 28.6 per cent. The findings suggest that sunfish and pumpkinseed predation may decrease the effectiveness of the biological control of *Myriophyllum* using *E. lecontei*. Additional information on herbivore and detritivory on freshwater macrophytes by invertebrates is given in a review by Newman.

PROPORTION OF AQUATIC MACROPHYTE

Crayfish

The proportion of aquatic macrophyte in crayfish food may represent up to 75 per cent of their total food intake as documented by a number of workers since the 1980s. Crayfish can also substantially reduce or eliminate submersed vegetation, as documented, for example, from lakes and ponds in the northern USA and from Lake Naivasha, Kenya. In New Mexico the crayfish *Orconectes causeyi* successfully cleared several lakes of *Potamogeton*, *Elodea*, *Ranunculus* and *Myriophyllum*, but avoided *Polygonum*, *Scripus* and *Typha*. In Arizona's Parker Lake, when the crayfish (*Orconectes causeyi*) population increased, their intensive grazing on submersed plants reduced the protective cover, which in turn increased the crayfish vulnerability to the predatory largemouth bass. As the predation by largemouth bass increased, the population of crayfish decreased, which led to the recovery of *Myriophyllum* and an increase of crayfish. Investigations of prey capture rates of trout (*Oncorhynchus mykiss*) feeding on two species of amphipods in an environment also rich in crayfish (*Orconectes propinquus*) and smallmouth bass (*Micropterus dolomieu*) have shown that prey capture rates of trout fell drastically with increasing cover. Capture rates of crayfish by smallmouth bass also declined.

In England, the introduced signal crayfish *Pacifastacus leniusculus* fed on the following five main diets, in order of their importance: vascular detritus, filamentous green alga *Cladophora*, crayfish fragments, chironomid larvae, and mayfly nymphs. The larger the crayfish, the more vascular detritus was ingested. The frequency of occurrence of *Cladophora* was increased with crayfish size in the winter. Reductions of macrophyte root or shoot biomass by grazers range up to 100 per cent, with reductions exceeding 50 per cent reported for crayfish, insect larvae, snails, fish, and waterfowl. In laboratory experiments, non-consumptive destruction by *Orconectes rusticus* comprised 30–95 per cent of cut macrophyte biomass, with the percentage differing among macrophyte species. *O. rusticus* is known to feed selectively, as tested on 14 different plants species by Lodge. Evergreen aquatic plants are not preferred, while those preferred are usually perennial. Avoidance of evergreens by grazers is also a common pattern among terrestrial grazers. This appears to result from secondary chemical defences.

Chambers *et al.* (1990, 1991) studied the impact of crayfish introduction on submersed plant communities and associated aquatic macroinvertebrates. In feeding preference trials with *O. virilis*, out of ten submersed aquatic plant species *Chara* sp. and *Lemna trisulca* were the preferred food, followed by *Myriophyllum exalbescens* or *Utricularia vulgaris*. Chemical analysis of the plants have suggested that the feeding preference of this crayfish is given by the ease of handling small, short, bottom-dwelling plants (*Chara* and *Lemna*), and not by the plant chemistry. The same species of crayfish had a significant impact on both the aquatic macrophytes and macroinvertebrate community, even at a low biomass of less than 20 g m^{-2}.

Tests carried out under semi-natural conditions in plastic pools containing *Potamogeton richardsonii*, *Myriophyllum exalbescens*, *Nuphar variegatum* and *Sparganium eurycarpum* have shown that there was a major difference between the impact of the females and the males on the vegetation. While the authors described the effect of female crayfish as generally stimulatory, leading to an increase in the biomass of *Myriophyllum* and *Potamogeton*, and to an increase in *Myriophyllum* length, the plant growth was negatively impacted by male crayfish. The experiments have also shown the feeding selectivity of the crayfish: of the four macrophytes only *Myriophyllum* was consumed, while the crayfish just clipped the shoots of the other three plants which were left to float on the water surface. Female crayfish *O. virilis* were found to virtually eliminate snails from the surfaces of the macrophytes.

Thus, the observed increase in the biomass of *Potamogeton* and *Myriophyllum* seemed to be related, at least in part, to the reduction in herbivorous snail abundance. Crayfish thus seems to indirectly alter the macroinvertebrates by changing the abundance and species composition of the aquatic macrophyte community.

Cronin followed the feeding choices of the Louisiana crayfish *Procambarus clarkii*, a commercially valuable species now cultivated in a number of other countries. When plants were offered as fresh tissue, *Procambarus* consumed large amounts of *Chara*, *Ceratophyllum* and *Spirogyra*; intermediate amounts of *Typha*; and little (if any) *Potamogeton*, *Batrachospermum*, *Nuphar*, *Carex*, or *Iris*. The three preferred species are finely branched or filamentous suggesting that plant structural properties are important determinant of *Procambarus* feeding decision. Cronin also tested crude extracts from plants: those from *Ceratophyllum*, *Nuphar* and *Iris* significantly reduced consumption, while extract from *Typha* significantly stimulated feeding. But according to Bolser *et al.*, while lipophylic crude extract from *Typha* significantly deterred feeding of this species of crayfish, when offered it in an agar-based diet lacking structural defences, the crayfish showed great preference for it. According to Cronin among plants without chemical defence mechanisms *Procambarus* will target those with high nitrogen content. Cronin concluded that generalist herbivores such as *Procambarus*, base their feeding decisions on multiple plant traits such as morphology, structure, chemical defences, and nutritional value. *Procambarus* will eat only plants that they can handle, shred, and digest.

In experiments, crayfish *Pacifastacus leniusculus* had a strong impact on snail mortality. Their study suggested that crayfish can structure the abundance and size distribution of thin-shelled snails (*Lymnaea stagnalis*) through size-selective predation and reduction of macrophytes. Hanson *et al.* observed a decrease in the density of amphipods and the total biomass of non-molluscan invertebrates at male crayfish biomasses of 5 and 10 g m^{-2} and suggested that this may be directly related to crayfish predation or indirectly to reduction in macrophyte biomass and species richness. In laboratory experiments with *O. rusticus* and *O. virilis* Olsen *et al.* observed that *O. rusticus* damaged more snails than *O. virilis*, and *O. rusticus* had a greater weight-specific ingestion rate than *O. virilis* on snails but not macrophytes.

Feeding beef liver to *O. rusticus* significantly reduced consumption and non-consumptive destruction of macrophyte *Vallisneria*. Lodge and Lorman suggested that the presence of snails probably reduces macrophyte consumption by *O. rusticus* in the littoral zone of northern Wisconsin lakes. In Australia in experiments carried out by Whisson, *Vallisneria* sp. was found to have a protective function for juvenile and adult crayfish marron (*Cherax tenuimanus*), reducing the predatory impact on them of silver perch (*Bidyanus bidyanus*). The author suggested that there could be a useful role for this plant in commercial marron production.

Changes in macrophyte communities due to both the direct and indirect effects of crayfish grazing may, in turn, affect fish communities, through the loss of the opportunity of some fish to hide from predators, change in or shortage of suitable spawning grounds, changes in or loss of food organisms such as periphyton, macroinvertebrates, zooplankton. In Wisconsin lakes, the introduction of *O. virilis* has been linked to detrimental changes in the fish community. Carpenter and Lodge summarized the impacts of omnivorous crayfish on a lake ecosystem. Rickett warned of the possibility of excessive vegetation elimination in lakes or ponds by uncontrolled crayfish populations. In northern Wisconsin lakes, the probably inadvertent introduction of the crayfish *Orconectes rusticus* and the subsequent increase in its numbers went in parallel with a decline in submersed macrophytes. In Lake Metonga, the disappearance of macrophytes stopped the recruitment of the fish walleye (*Stizostedion vitreum*), and in some other northern Wisconsin lakes the indigenous crayfish *Orconectes virilis* and *O. propinquus* were displaced by the intruder. Where the population of crayfish crashed, as in Lake Naivasha, Kenya, due most probably to overfishing of the introduced *Procambarus clarkii*, this was followed by the recovery of rooted aquatics.

Crowder *et al.* constructed a simplified generalized food web for submersed macrophyte system. Boxes contain the major types of interactors. Lines ending in arrows indicate positive effects to the upper trophic level of energy flow up the web. Lines ending in closed circles indicate negative effects on the lower trophic level due to the level above. These may include the potential for predators to "control" prey densities. Dashed lines indicate potential interaction such as leaking of nutrients from macrophytes to epiphytes or indirect effects of cover on predator-prey interactions. Dotted lines indicate possible routes of nutrient recycling from consumers. The authors point out that individual systems will diverge from this diagramme, and many species shift from one role to another through ontogeny. In many systems, the herbivores include both mesograzers (primarily oriented towards epiphytic algae) and macrograzers (primarily oriented towards macrophytes). In systems dominated by macrograzers, the hypothetical effects of reduction of large predators would be an increase in macrograzers, which could lead directly to losses of macrophytes along with their associated epiphytes and fauna.

3

Fishery: Aquatic Species

A fishery is an organized effort by humans to catch fish or other aquatic species, an activity known as fishing. Generally, a fishery exists for the purpose of providing human food, although other aims are possible (such as sport or recreational fishing), or obtaining ornamental fish or fish products such as fish oil. Industrial fisheries are fisheries where the catch is not intended for direct human consumption.

Regardless of purpose, however, the term fishery generally refers to a fishing effort centered on either a particular ecoregion or a particular species or type of fish or aquatic animal, and usually fisheries are differentiated by both criteria. Examples would be the salmon fishery of Alaska, the cod fishery off the Lofoten islands or the tuna fishery of the Eastern Pacific. Most fisheries are marine, rather than freshwater; most marine fisheries are based near the coast. This is not only because harvesting from relatively shallow waters is easier than in the open ocean, but also because fish are much more abundant near the coastal shelf, due to coastal upwelling and the abundance of nutrients available there.

Nearly all the fish species connected with littoral zone of European lakes consume some aquatic plant material during their lives. Prejs (1984) listed 15 species, of which *ide (Leuciscus idus*), roach (*Rutilus rutilus*), and rudd (*Scardinius erythrophthalmus*) had a high content of plants in their food; bream (*Abramis brama*), white bream (*Blicca bjerkna*), chub (*Leuciscus cephalus*), crucian carp (*Carassius carassius*), gudgeon (*Gobio gobio*), stickleback (*Gasterosteus aculeatus*), tench (*Tinca tinca*), and carp (*Cyprinus carpio*) had small amounts, and bitterling (*Rhodeus sericeus amarus*), bleak (*Alburnus alburnus*), perch (*Perca fluviatilis*), and juvenile pike (*Esox lucius*) had sporadic occurrence. The main plant consumers, roach and rudd, use the majority of the species of submersed macrophytes which occur in sufficiently high densities, but they prefer soft submersed plants. The absence of some plant species in the food, even common species, is due primarily to their physical properties or to their odd taste or toxic properties, *e.g.* Ranunculaceae. Several indigenous Euroasian fish species inhabit aquatic macrophytes as adults: tench, rudd and pike. The submersed macrophytes form important feeding habitats for perch, roach, bleak, and eel (*Anguilla anguilla*), while the ruff (*Gymnocephalus cernua*) prefers the *Chara* beds.

In the southern USA, the fish *Enneacanthus gloriosus, Lucania goodei, Lepomis macrochirus, Heterandria formosa*, among others, are substantially more abundant in vegetation than other fish species. In the South African lake Swartvlei the fish species *Monodactylus falciformis* and *Rhabdosargus holubi* directly depend on periphyton and associated macroinvertebrates of submersed aquatic plants. The Australian tropical lungfish *neo-ceratodus forsteri* feeds on *Hydrilla verticillata, Vallisneria spiralis* and some other aquatic plants (Kemp *et al.*, 1981). Among the important freshwater culturable fish species of India, Jhingran (1977) named *Barbus carnaticus* and *Etroplus suratensis* as partially feeding on aquatic macrophytes. In plant beds rich food supply in form of periphyton, its associated invertebrates and bottom fauna, is generally more numerous and more diverse than in open waters. Within the diverse aquatic plants, the habitat-specific differences in invertebrate composition directly influence habitat selection by fish and foraging behaviour of individual fish. Many young fish need aquatic macrophytes as shelter and protection from predation or to avoid cannibalism. Aquatic macrophytes also serve some fish as a spawning habitat, for the attachment of eggs, and some fish form nesting sites among the macrophytes.

Recent habitat restoration programmes conducted in the Great Lakes Basin of northern America have focused on the importance of aquatic macrophytes for the production of northern pike. It was found that macrophytes are of a greater significance as nursery rather than spawning environment. Adult fish abundance was found to be related to the extent of macrophyte cover, which was found optimal from 35 to 80 per cent but inversely related to body size, this resulting in a lower fish biomass in the stands of heavy density.

FISHERIES HISTORICALLY

Fisheries have been important parts of human life and food production throughout history. Fish acts as one main food in people's everyday life as well as food security of the nation. Fisheries have become a part of human cultures and mythologies, providing a community identity and a subject for artists throughout the ages. Partially, this is because fisheries are irretrievably wrapped up in humanity's perpetual fascination with the sea, and partially, because they have been a major source of food and income for many communities throughout the ages. One of the world's longest lasting trade histories is the trade of dry cod from the Lofoten area to the southern parts of Europe, Italy, Spain and Portugal. The trade in cod started during the viking period or before, has been going on for more than 1000 years and is still important.

In India, the Pandyas, a classical Dravidian Tamil kingdom, were known for the pearl fishery as early as the 1st century BC. Their seaport Tuticorin was known for deep sea pearl fishing. The paravas, a Tamil caste centred in Tuticorin, developed a rich community because of their pearl trade, navigation knowledge and fisheries.

Fisheries in the Present Day

Today, fisheries are estimated to provide 16 per cent of the world population's protein, and that figure is considerably elevated in some developing nations and in regions that depend heavily on the sea. Fisheries are a huge global business and provide income for millions of people. Fisheries have been and continue to be culturally important for many communities as well.

According to the Food and Agriculture Organization of the United Nations, total world capture fisheries production in 2000 was 86 million tons. The top producing countries were, in order, the People's Republic of China (excluding Hong Kong and Taiwan), Peru, Japan, the United States, Chile, Indonesia, Russia, India, Thailand, Norway and Iceland. Those countries accounted for more than half of the world's production; China alone accounted for a third of the world's production. Of that production, over 90 per cent was marine and less than 10 per cent was inland.

There are large and important fisheries worldwide for various species of fish, mollusks and crustaceans. However, a very small number of species support the majority of the world's fisheries. Some of these species are herring, cod, anchovy, tuna, flounder, mullet, squid, shrimp, salmon, crab, lobster, oyster and scallops. All except these last four provided a worldwide catch of well over a million tonnes in 1999, with herring and sardines together providing a catch of over 22 million metric tons in 1999. Many other species as well are fished in smaller numbers, both locally and globally.

Methods

Fishing methods vary according to the region, the species being fished for, and the amount of income and technology available to the fisher. A fishery can consist of one man with a small boat hand-casting nets, to a huge fleet of trawlers processing tons of fish per day. Some common commercial techniques today are trawling, seining, driftnetting, handlining, longlining, gillnetting, and diving.

Trawling

Trawling is a method of fishing that involves actively pulling a fishing net through the water behind one or more boats.

Structure of a Trawl Net

When two boats are used (pair trawling), the horizontal spread of the net is provided by the boats, with one warp attached to each boat. However, single-boat trawling is more common. Here, the horizontal spread of the net is provided by trawl doors (also known as "otter boards"). Trawl doors are available in various sizes and shapes and may be specialized to keep in contact with the sea bottom or to remain elevated in the water. In all cases, doors essentially act as wings, using a hydrodynamic shape to provide horizontal spread. As with all wings, the towing vessel must go at a certain speed for the doors to remain standing and functional. This speed varies, but is generally in the range of 2.5-4.0 knots. Nets for trawling in surface waters and for trawling in deep water and over the bottom. Note the "tangles" with all of the marine life caught up in them.

The vertical opening of a trawl net is created using flotation on the upper edge ("floatline") and weight on the lower edge ("footrope") of the net mouth. The configuration of the footrope varies based on the expected bottom shape. The more uneven the bottom, the more robust the footrope configuration must be to prevent net damage.

Environmental Impacts of Trawling

Although trawling today is heavily regulated in some nations, it remains the target of many protests by environmentalists. Environmental concerns related to trawling refer to two areas: a perceived lack of selectivity and the physical damage which the trawl does to the seabed.

Selectivity

Reports of the lack of selectivity of trawling have been present since it started (about the 1600's) and it became used more widely (about 1900). Trawl nets may be non-selective, sweeping up both marketable and undesirable fish and fish of both legal and illegal size. Any part of the catch which cannot bc used is considered as by-catch. Size selectivity is controlled by the mesh size of the "cod-end" - the part of the trawl where fish are retained. Fishermen complain that a mesh size which allows undersized fish to escape also allows a proportion of legal-landing sized fish to escape as well. There are a number of "fixes", such as tying a rope around the "cod-end" to prevent the mesh from opening fully, which have been developed to work around technical regulation of size selectivity. One problem is when the mesh gets pulled into narrow diamond shapes (rhombuses) instead of squares.

The capture of undesirable species is a recognized problem with all fishing methods and unites environmentalists, who do not want to see fish killed needlessly and fishermen, who do not want to waste their time sorting unsellable fish from their catch. A number of methods to minimize this have been developed for use in trawling. Bycatch reduction grills or square mesh panels of net can be fitted to parts of the trawl, allowing certain species to escape while retaining others. Trawling for shrimps has specifically been cited as having high levels of bycatch in various parts of the world.

Ecological Damage

Because bottom trawling involves towing heavy fishing gear over the seabed at a speed of several knots, it is destructive to the ocean bottom. The primary sources of impact are the doors, which can weigh several tonnes and create furrows when dragged along the bottom, and the footrope configuration, which usually remains in contact with the bottom across the entire lower edge of the net. Depending on the configuration, the footrope may turn over large rocks or boulders, disturb or damage sessile organisms or rework bottom sediments. Published research has shown that benthic trawling destroys the cold-water coral *Lophelia pertusa*, an important habitat for many deep-sea organisms. The primary focus of dispute over the impact of trawl gear is on the magnitude and duration of these impacts. Opponents of trawl gear argue that the impact of trawl nets is widespread, intense and long-lasting. Defenders of trawl gear maintain that impact is mostly limited and of low intensity compared to natural events.

Pelagic trawling is a much "cleaner" method of fishing, in that the catch usually consists of just one species. However, some cases of it have been attacked for depleting resources which are important sources of food for certain sea birds. An instance of this was the RSPB linking a population crash of sea birds in the North Sea to pelagic fishing for sand eels, which are food for many seabird species. This led to political pressure for the closure of this fishery; the seabird populations subsequently improved. However, a second population crash of seabirds which occurred with no effect on the stocks of sand eel, cast doubt on this link.

Other uses of the Word "Trawl"

The noun "trawl" has many possibly confusing meanings in commercial fisheries. For example, two or more lobster pots that are fished together may be referred to as a trawl. In some older usages "trawling" meant "long-line fishing"; that usage occurs in Rudyard Kipling's book *Captains Courageous*. (This use is perhaps confused with trolling, where a baited line is trailed behind a boat)

The word "trawling" has come to be used in a number of non-fishing contexts, usually meaning indiscriminate collection with the intent of picking out the useful bits. For instance, in law enforcement it may refer to collecting large records of telephone calls hoping to find calls made by suspects. The word "trawling" occurs frequently in general literature and is used to mean searching through literature for information more often than it means catching fish.

Hand-line Fishing

Handlining is one of the oldest forms of fishing and is still common. The method consists of a single fishing line with a weight and one or more lure-like hooks are attached. The line is jigged or moved up and down in a series of short movements, most often close to the sea floor. The motion attracts the fish, which are normally caught while trying to eat the lure but also as they move close to jigged the lure. The line is then hauled onboard and the fish removed. Handlining are most often used to catch groundfish and squid but also other species are sometimes caught, including pelagic species.

Long-line fishing

Long-line fishing is a commercial fishing technique that uses hundreds or even thousands of baited hooks hanging from a single line. Swordfish, tuna and Patagonian toothfish are commonly caught by this method. It is also practiced on a smaller scale in New Zealand, where a twenty five hook maximum is prescribed by law.

Longlines can be set to hang near the surface, for instance in tuna fisheries, or on the sea bottom, such as in the Patagonian toothfish fishery.

Long-line fishing is controversial because the lines can lead to significant bycatch, often of endangered species such as sea turtles, petrels and albatrosses. Methods to mitigate such incidental mortality have been developed and successfully implemented in some fisheries. These include the use of weights to ensure the lines sink quickly, the deployment of streamer lines to scare birds away from the baited hooks as they are deployed, setting lines only at night with ship lighting kept low (to avoid attracting birds), limiting fishing seasons to the southern winter (when most seabirds are not feeding young), and not discharging offal while setting lines.

GILLNET

Gillnetting is a common fishing method used by commercial fishermen of all the oceans. Because gillnets can be so effective their use is closely monitored and regulated by fisheries and enforcement agencies, such as the National Marine Fisheries Service in USA. Mesh size, twine strength, as well as net length and depth are all closely regulated to reduce bycatch of non-target species. Most salmon fisheries in particular have an extremely low incidence of catching non-target species.

History

Gillnetting began with First Nations fishermen using canoes and cedar fibre nets. They would attach stones to the bottom of the nets as weights, and pieces of wood to the top, to use as floats. This allowed the net to suspend straight up and down in the water. Each net would be suspended either from shore or between two boats. By around 1864, gillnetting had expanded to European, Japanese, and other international fisheries. The boats used by these fisherman were typically around 25 feet long and powered by oars. Many of these boats also had small sails and were called "row-sail" boats. At the beginning of the

1900s, steam powered ships would haul these smaller boats to their fishing grounds and retrieve them at the end of each day. However, at this time gas powered boats were beginning to make their appearance, and by the 1930s, the row-sail boat had virtually disappeared.

In 1931, the first powered drum was created by Laurie Jarelainen. The drum is a circular device that is set to the side of the boat and draws in the nets. The powered drum allowed the nets to be drawn in much faster and along with the faster gas powered boats, fisherman were able to fish in areas they had previously been unable to go into, thereby revolutionizing the fishing industry.

During World War II, navigation and communication devices, as well as many other forms of maritime equipment (ex. depth-sounding and radar) were improved and made more compact. These devices became much more accessible to the average fisherman, thus making their range and mobility increasingly larger. It also served to make the industry much more competitive, as the fisherman were forced to invest more into there boats and equipment in order to stay up to date with the current technology.

This type of net was heavily used by many Japanese, South Korean, and Taiwanese fishing fleets on the high seas in the 1980's. Because of their indiscriminate nature, catching near everything in their path, and lack of regulation as well as a growing concern for the plight of whales and dolphins, gillnets were banned by the United Nations in 1993 in international waters.

Types of Gillnets

Anchored Sink Gillnet -
Drift Floating Gillnet -
Drift Sink Gillnet -
Anchored Floating Gillnet.

Diving Activities

Type of diving	Classed as
Underwater archaeology (shipwrecks; harbours and houses sunk by storm or earth movements)	scientific
Aquarium maintenance in large public and commercial exhibition aquaria	commercial, scientific
Cave diving	technical, recreational
Civil engineering in harbours, water supply and drainage systems	commercial
Constructing,testing & maintaining equipment for the oil & offshore construction industries	commercial
Boat and ship inspection, cleaning and maintenance	commercial, naval
Demolition and salvage of ship wrecks	commercial, naval
Fish farm maintenance	commercial

Fishing, *e.g.* for pearls, scallops, abalones, crabs, lobsters, sea crayfish	commercial
Diver training for reward	professional
Media diving: making television programmes, etc	professional
Harbour clearance and maintenance	military
Stealthy infiltration	military
Manned torpedo,frogman	military
Mine clearance and bomb disposal, disposing of unexploded ordnance	military, naval
Search and recovery diving	commercial
Search and recovery by police for evidence and bodies	police
Rescue diving for underwater casualties	police
Diving to investigate or arrest unauthorized divers	police, military, naval
Surveying sea life and freshwater life, marine biology	scientific, recreational
Underwater tourism	recreational

Fisheries and Communities

For some communities, both currently and historically, fisheries provide not only a source of food and work but also a community and cultural identity.

This shows up in art, literature, and traditions. These communities are generally those that have been historically dependent on fishing as a source of income and food.

Fisheries Science

Fisheries science is the academic discipline of managing and understanding fisheries. It draws on the disciplines of biology, ecology, oceanography, economics and management to attempt to provide an integrated picture of fisheries. It is typically taught in a university setting, and can be the focus of an undergraduate, master's or Ph.D. programme. It is in universities worldwide, usually organised as multidisciplinary programmes involving parts of traditional university disciplines. In some cases new disciplines have emerged, as in the case of bioeconomics. A few universities also offer fully integrated programmes in fisheries science.

Important Issues and Topics in Fisheries

Considering the importance of fisheries, and that they depend on a natural resource, it is no surprise that there are many pressing environmental issues surrounding them. These can be classed into issues that involve the availability of fish to be caught, such as overfishing, sustainable fisheries, and fisheries management; and issues surrounding the impact of fishing on the environment, such by-catch. These fishery conservation issues are generally considered part of marine conservation, and many of these issues are addressed in fisheries science programmes. They are also, however, controversial. There is an apparent and growing disparity between the availability of fish to be caught and humanity's desire to catch them, a problem that is exacerbated by the rapidly growing world population. As with some other environmental issues, often the people engaged in the activity of fishing – the fishers – and the scientists who study fisheries science, who are often acting as fishery managers, are in conflict with each other, as the dictates of economics mean that fishers have to keep fishing for their livelihood, but the dictates of sustainable science mean that some fisheries must close or reduce to protect the health of the population of the fish themselves. It is starting to be realized, however, that these two camps must work together to ensure fishery health through the 21st century and beyond.

TYPES OF FISHES

Fish are a huge group of animals, represented by over 28000 different species. They are the oldest as well as the largest group of vertebrates. They are characterised by being almost exclusively aquatic throughout their lives. They are limbless, but have two sets of paired fins as well as a variety of single fins.

They breathe predominantly by using organs known as gills. They are cold - blooded (poikilothermic), which means their body temperature varies with that of their surroundings. Their skin is usually covered with scales.

Most temperate freshwater fish are called teleost (' true bone ') fish, which means that they have a bony skeleton. The only fish found in temperate freshwater that do not belong to this group are the sturgeons and the lampreys. Neither of these groups is found commonly in still - waters, although a few species of sturgeons have been introduced into still - waters in recent years.

Teleost fish are extremely successful and well adapted to their environment.

FISH SPECIES

There are around 50 species of fish found for at least part of their lives in the freshwaters of the British Isles. This is quite a small number of species considering the diversity of the aquatic habitats available to them and the number of species in similar waters in continental Europe. Although many of the species are native to the British Isles, there are also many that have been successfully introduced over the centuries. Some of these have settled and become well established and are now generally considered ' native ', for example the carp. Some, however, still raise concerns among conservationists about the potential impact they may have, should they become more widespread; the zander and wels catfish for example, are described as ' non - native ' and are subject to regulation.

Fish species have developed and evolved to make the best use of certain habitats. Many of the species present in the British Isles are especially developed to live in rivers. These species are usually unsuited to living in still - waters as they are not adapted to this very different type of habitat. In this chapter we will concentrate on those species already adapted to the still - water, and those that are commonly stocked in still - waters with apparent success, such as the chub. The barbel has been included, as it is stocked commonly in still - waters, but it should be borne in mind that special conditions must be maintained for this species owing to its requirement for clear, oxygen - rich water.

This chapter sets out some detailed information about each species, which should allow fishery managers to understand better the species under their custody. The ecology of lakes, should allow the manager to establish the best conditions for the fish species and assess any other species for likely success in any given situation.

Cyprinidae

The barbel is a large river fish with a long, streamlined, slightly flattened body. The juveniles are an overall brown colour but as they get larger they develop a dark brown back with golden bronze flanks and a creamy white underbelly. Adults generally grow to around 70 cm, but can get up to 90 cm and weigh in excess of 6 kg (the British rod - caught record 2008 is 9.837 kg). The barbel is native to the southern UK and mainland Europe. It is widespread and relatively common.

The barbel will generally mature after 3 - 5 years. Spawning takes place once a year in the late spring, usually May - July. Barbel spawn in small groups among gravel and stones in fast - flowing rivers. The adhesive eggs stay within the gravel bed until they hatch 10 - 15 days later. The fry tend to congregate in slow flowing areas where they feed on zooplank-ton. As they mature and get larger they tend to move out into the main flow of the river, feeding on invertebrates and even small fish in among clean gravel and associated vegetation.

The barbel is a very popular coarse fish, being one of the most sought - after river fish. They are a hard fighting fish that can grow very large, attracting specialist anglers. Barbel have increasingly been stocked in still - waters over several years.

They appear to grow and survive reasonably well, but there is little evidence that they can successfully spawn in most still - waters. It is vital that any stocking is with barbel obtained from a reputable fish farm. Barbel can sometimes be introduced from fish poached from the wild. Not only is this very harmful to the wild populations but evidence suggests that these fish find it very difficult to make the transition from rivers to still - waters. Generally barbel should not be stocked in shallow still - waters with a predominance of bottom feeders such as carp.

Common Bream (Abramis brama)

The common bream is a large, bottom - feeding species with a deep thin body. When young it is a very silvery fish, but as it matures it becomes darker and more golden brown to green. It can grow to nearly a metre in length and weigh up to 8 kg (the British rod - caught record 2008 is 8.329 kg). The common bream is native to the UK and central Europe where it is widespread and common. It is a popular food fish in eastern Europe.

Bream generally mature after 4 years. Spawning takes place in May and June in dense vegetation in shallow water. The males develop white bumps (tubercles) over the body surface and become territorial. The females spawn at night in large groups and their sticky eggs attach to the vegetation. After 5 – 10 days the eggs hatch. The fry start by feeding on zooplankton such as rotifers and then larger zooplankton such as daphnia. They quickly move on to their normal adult diet of benthic invertebrates, preferentially worms, molluscs and insect larvae such as chironomid midge larvae. The adults feed by using their extendable tubular mouth to root around in the pond bottom, taking large mouthfuls and ' winnowing ' out the food items. They are strongly shoaling fish from larval fry to late adulthood. Some of the very large individuals appear to be solitary or in small shoals.

The common bream is one of the most popular of the coarse fish. It responds well to anglers ' baits and is readily caught. It grows quickly to a good size and survives well in many different conditions. As a bottom feeder it will disturb the bottom of the pond, causing suspended solids to cloud the water column. They are good in a mixed silver - fish population. The common bream should not be mixed with large numbers of carp as the species compete for the same food source.

The silver bream is a small mid - water species, with a deep, compressed body. When young it is a very silvery fish but as it matures its back becomes a darker olive/grey, although it still retains a very silvery look. Its maximum size is around 20 – 25 cm in length (the British rod - caught record 2008 is 0.425 kg). The silver bream is native to England, central and northern Europe, where it widespread and reasonably common. In England it is generally restricted to the southeast but is becoming more widespread.

Silver bream mature at around 3 – 4 years old. Spawning takes place in May – July in dense vegetation in shallow water. They spawn in groups early in the morning, scattering their sticky eggs among the submerged weeds. The eggs hatch in 4 – 8 days and begin feeding on small planktonic invertebrates, moving to larger invertebrates and plant material as they grow. Silver bream form strong shoals with individuals of a similar size and age throughout their lives. The silver bream is not a popular species for anglers, largely because it is commonly mistaken for a small common bream. Indeed it is very similar to a common bream of the same size, except the silver bream is slightly thicker in the body and has larger scales. They do make useful additions to a lake as they feed in a very different manner.

The carp is a large, bottom - feeding species with a thickset rounded body. They are usually a dark olive brown on the back, lightening to a light yellowish brown on the belly. It can grow to very large sizes, sometimes exceeding 1 m in length (the British rod - caught record 2008 is 26.9 kg). The carp is native to eastern Europe and Asia, but has now achieved worldwide distribution. It is very widespread and common in the UK, where it was first introduced in the nineteenth century.

Carp mature after 2 – 3 years. Spawning takes place in June to July in dense vegetation on the margins of the water body. The males develop small white lumps (tubercles) on the flanks and head. The females spawn at dawn and the sticky eggs attach to the weed. The eggs will hatch after 5 – 7 days and the fry start feeding on zooplankton, particularly rotifers. They quickly move to feeding on the bottom - dwelling invertebrates that make up the bulk of their diet. Their mouth is well designed for this feeding technique, being protrusible. However, carp are a very adaptable species and they can often be seen feeding on invertebrates on marginal vegetation and even off the surface. They tend to move around in small shoals of similar - sized individuals. The carp is probably the most popular species for anglers on still - waters. It grows quickly to very large sizes and responds well to a variety of anglers ' baits. It is a very adaptable species so can survive and thrive in many different conditions. As a bottom feeder, it will disturb the sediment on the bottom of the water body, causing suspended solids to cloud the water.

Carp have been bred for food over many centuries and it is one of the main global species for aquaculture in ponds. This has led to several different varieties of carp being commonly found. The most obvious of these varieties is the common carp, which is the fully scaled type. Mirror carp were bred to make it easier to remove the scales before cooking. Ornamental varieties are also common, from full - colour varieties, known as koi, to slightly gold - tinged cross breeds known as ghost carp. These are all the same species of fish, however.

The chub is a large, mid - water and surface - feeding fish with a rounded, streamlined body. When young it is a very silvery fish with an olive green back; as it gets larger its upper body darkens to a steel grey colour but retains the silvery flanks and belly. It is a large fish, attaining sizes of between 40 and 50 cm, rarely getting to up to 80 cm (the British rod - caught record 2008 is 3.9 kg). The chub is native to the UK and central Europe and is widespread and common. It is caught for food in some parts of Europe. Chub generally mature after 3 – 4 years. Spawning takes place during April – June among clean gravel and stones in flowing water. They spawn in the early morning in small groups of one female with several males in attendance. The eggs hatch within 6 – 8 days and start to feed on benthic invertebrates. As they grow older their diet changes to include larger invertebrates, fruit, vegetation and even small fish. When young, chub move around in shoals but as they mature they become much more solitary and even appear to be somewhat territorial. In rivers they migrate significant distances to feeding and spawning areas. Little is known about their activities in still - waters. The chub is a popular fish among anglers because it is a large, hard - fighting fish that responds well to anglers ' baits. It grows quickly to a good size and appears to do very well in still - waters. Current evidence suggests that it does not successfully spawn in most still -waters, although it does spawn in large, clear - water lakes.

The crucian carp is a medium - sized, deep - bodied fish with marked lateral compression. Young fish are a golden bronze colour, which turns darker as they get older, with mature specimens being olive brown on the back through deep bronze on the flanks to a golden yellow on the belly. Adults can attain 20 – 30 cm in length and 1.5 kg in weight, although many crucian carp populations remain ' stunted ' with the mature adults rarely getting more than 15 – 20 cm and 0.5 kg (the British rod - caught record 2008 is 2.01 kg). The crucian carp is native to the UK, Europe and central Asia. There is some argument about whether it is a native to the UK and western Europe, but there seems little evidence to suggest it is introduced into these areas, where it is widespread.

Crucian carp generally mature after 2 – 3 years. Spawning takes place in May – June in shallow water, in thick vegetation. The fish shed sticky eggs onto the vegetation where they take between 5 and 7 days to hatch, depending on the vegetation. Once hatched, and after the yolk sac has been used, the fry tend to form loose shoals and feed on small zooplankton. As they grow they start to feed mainly on invertebrates, such as molluscs and worms on the bottom of the pond, as well as plant material. Both the juveniles and the adults tend to live in loose shoals. They tend to occupy the mid - water and bottom of still - waters. Crucian carp prefer still - waters and particularly thrive in rich, lowland still - waters with abundant vegetation. Crucian carp have a remarkable ability to survive very low dissolved oxygen situations for long periods, leading to situations where they are often the only fish species to survive. Here they form healthy populations dominated by small ' stunted ' individuals. In larger waters they can grow much larger and seem to adopt a slightly different body shape.

This is a very popular angling species and is readily caught. It survives well in well -managed fisheries dominated by silver fish, but it is generally unsuitable for stocking in waters dominated by common carp. Crucians readily hybridise with goldfish and common carp. They are then displaced by the vigourous hybrid. They are also threatened by the non - native parasitic tapeworm *Bothriocephalus acheilognathi*. The goldfish is a medium – sized mid - water species with a relatively deep and laterally compressed body. Wild goldfish are a deep brown colour throughout their lives, although there are many colour variants from deep orange through to almost white. Adults can get to around 30 cm and 1 kg in size. The goldfish is native to Asia, but owing to its ornamental value it has achieved worldwide distribution, being found on most continents. It is an introduced species in the UK. Goldfish generally mature after 2 – 3 years. Spawning takes place during June and July in thick weed in the shallow margins. The eggs hatch in 4 – 7 days, depending on the water temperature, and the young feed on zooplankton. As they grow, the diet changes to small invertebrates and plant material. Goldfish tend to form loose shoals and prefer shallow, rich ponds with abundant vegetation. They are a hardy species, however, and appear to thrive in most still - water conditions.

The goldfish has become increasingly common in still - waters in the UK and Europe. It is apparently popular with some fishermen. Goldfish readily hybridise with common carp and crucian carp, producing vigourous offspring that can successfully outcompete the original parent stock. Stocking with goldfish or hybrid strains is advised against.

The grass carp is a large mid - water feeding species with a solid, rounded body. It has a dark blue - black back, shading to silver on the belly. It can grow quite large, with adults reaching up to 100 cm in length (the British rod - caught record 2008 is 20.185 kg). Grass carp are originally from Asia, but have been widely distributed around the world as a method of weed control. They were introduced into England in the 1960s to control weed growth in some still - waters. Since then they have become widely distributed, but because of their specialised breeding requirements there appear to be no breeding populations.

Grass carp mature after 3 – 4 years. Spawning takes place in fast - flowing water in the headwaters of large rivers. Temperatures must be around 23 – 25 ° C. The eggs are unusual in that they are pelagic, being carried down river in mid - water until they hatch in the slower flows downstream. The fry start by feeding on small invertebrates, but as they get older they begin to feed on aquatic plants. Grass carp form loose shoals throughout their lives. Grass carp are not particularly popular among anglers as they are generally difficult to catch and do not fight as hard as their size might suggest. They are not very effective in controlling weed growth as they do not feed until the waters are quite warm.

The gudgeon is a small, rounded, bottom - dwelling fish. Its back is a dark olive green to brown with lighter flanks and a silvery belly. It has dark markings along the flank and upper body. It is a very small fish, rarely reaching over 15 cm although it can grow to about 20 cm. (the British rod - caught record 2008 is 0.141 kg). Gudgeon are widely distributed throughout Europe and Asia and they are native to the UK. Gudgeon mature at between 2 and 3 years old. They will spawn on stony or gravely bottoms, or among weed, and prefer flowing water, although they will spawn successfully in still - waters. They spawn during May or June and the eggs hatch in around 15 days. They feed on insects, molluscs, crustaceans and occasionally plant material. They are generally a solitary fish, but sometimes form into small shoals of perhaps a dozen individuals. The gudgeon is not a popular target species for anglers, but it does do well in some still -waters where it probably makes an important contribution to the health of the lake.

The minnow is a small mid - water species with a long rounded body. It has a brown - gold body with numerous brown and black spots down the flanks usually joining to form an obvious black line along the body. It is a small fish, rarely exceeding 10 cm in length (the British rod - caught record 2008 is 0.135 kg). The minnow is a native to the UK, Europe and Asia where it is very widespread and common.

Minnows mature after 1 – 2 years. Spawning takes place in June or July, usually over clean stones or gravels. The males particularly become more colourful during spawning, with a scarlet belly and black throat. The eggs take 5 – 10 days to hatch and immediately start feeding on small invertebrates. As they grow they continue to feed on a variety of invertebrates. Minnows generally aggregate into small, loose shoals. The minnow is not a target fish for anglers, although it can be important as a bait fish. It does well in lakes and ponds and can be a very useful addition to the lake ecology, particularly if predatory fish are present.

The orfe is a large, mid - water and surface - feeding fish with a rounded, streamlined body. When young it is a very silvery fish, but as it gets larger its upper body darkens to a brownish grey colour. Coloured ornamental varieties are common, particularly golden and blue orfe. It is a medium - sized fish, attaining sizes of between 30 and 40 cm, although it can occasionally get up to 80 cm. (the British rod - caught record 2008 is 3.7 kg). The orfe is native to central and eastern Europe and parts of Asia, where it is widespread and common. It is caught for food in some parts of Russia. It was introduced into England and is now widespread and common.

Orfe generally mature after 3 – 4 years. Spawning takes place during April and May, among weeds and clean stones in shallow water. The eggs hatch within 15 – 20 days and start to feed on benthic invertebrates. As they grow older their diet changes to include larger invertebrates, although they will take fruit, vegetation and even small fish. Orfe move around in shoals of similar - sized and aged individuals. They are found equally in rivers and still - waters. The orfe is a popular fish among anglers because it is a good - sized, hard fighting fish that responds well to anglers ' baits. It grows quickly, to a good size and it appears to do very well in still - waters.

The roach is medium - sized, mid - water fish with a relatively deep body. The young fish are silvery, but they quickly develop a dark blue – green back and light underside. Adults generally get to 20 – 40 cm and between 1 and 2 kg (the British rod - caught record 2008 is 1.899 kg). The roach is native to the

UK and Europe, where it is very widespread and common throughout the lowland catchments. Roach generally mature after 2 or 3 years. Spawning takes place once a year in the middle of spring, usually April – June. The roach spawn at dawn, shedding their sticky eggs on dense, submerged vegetation in the shallow areas of the lake. The eggs will hatch in 5 – 10 days. Once the yolk sac is used, the fry will feed on zooplankton and other small invertebrates. The juveniles prefer to live in large shoals in the shallow, marginal areas with plenty of vegetation, which provide cover and food. As they mature and get larger they move out into open water, shoaling in smaller groups of similar - sized individuals. These larger individuals feed on larger benthic invertebrates and pondweed, particularly attached algae (periphyton). They tend to occupy the mid - water to bottom of the pond.

The roach is one of the most popular coarse fish in the UK. It responds well to anglers ' bait and is readily caught. It grows steadily and survives well in many different conditions. It is an excellent species in any mixed fishery as it is very adaptable. In the right conditions, it can quickly overpopulate with a very large population of small fish. The rudd is a medium - sized, top - feeding species, with a deep, laterally compressed body. It has a dark greenish - brown back, grading through to a silvery underside. The flanks are golden brown. The iris is a deep gold with a red fleck on the upper side. The fins are normally a bright red. It can grow to 20 – 25 cm and 0.5 – 1 kg (the British rod - caught record 2008 is 2.1 kg). The rudd is native to the UK and central Europe, where it is very widespread and common.

Rudd generally mature at 2 – 4 years and live to 10 – 14 years. They spawn in late spring, usually from April to July. Rudd spawn by shedding their eggs on submerged vegetation around the margins. The eggs hatch in around 5 – 10 days and the fry stay within the protection of the vegetation, feeding on small zooplankton. As they grow they form compact shoals, feeding on the surface and in midwater. They prefer zooplankton, weed - dwelling invertebrates and terrestrial insects on the surface. Rudd appear always to spend their time in fairly compact shoals, no matter how large they get.

The rudd is a popular fish to catch, being attractive and readily taking bait, which is particularly important if other species are more reluctant to feed on anglers ' bait. It grows steadily but rarely attains large sizes. It is a very good fish for a mixed fishery, as it does not compete directly with any other fish species. The tench is a large, bottom - feeding species, with a thickset, slightly laterally compressed body. The tench is a beautiful olive to dark green throughout its life, with small orange to red eyes. Adults generally grow slowly to a maximum length of 60 – 70 cm and can weigh up to 7 kg. (the British rod - caught record 2008 is 6.9 kg). The tench is native to the UK and Europe, although absent from the northern parts of both. The species has been widely introduced into Asia and North America.

Tench generally mature at 3 – 4 years old. Owing to their slow growth, they may only be 15 cm at this age. Spawning takes place once a year in spring, usually between May and July. They spawn among aquatic plants in shallow waters, to which their sticky eggs attach. The eggs will hatch in 4 – 5 days, and once the yolk sac is used the fry will feed on zooplank-ton, before switching to grazing among the bottom of water plants on a variety of aquatic invertebrates and attached algae. Tench prefer still - waters, or very slow flowing rivers with an abundance of macrophytes. The juveniles may form loose shoals, but as they mature they become more solitary, almost appearing to have preferred territories.

The tench is one of the most popular and easily recognisable of the coarse fish in the UK and Europe. Its popularity relates to its size and its beauty. It is generally a difficult fish to catch on rod and line. It is quite adaptable to a mixed fishery, but does not thrive in waters without good communities of aquatic macrophytes. The pike is a large predatory fish, with a slim streamlined body and a large head with an enormous mouth full of teeth. It has a dark green, mottled back, grading through light green flanks to a creamy yellow underbelly. It is a very large fish, routinely growing to 50 – 100 cm and occasionally 140 cm and 30 kg (the British rod - caught record 2008 is 21.2 kg). The pike is widespread and abundant throughout the Northern Hemisphere in Europe, Asia and North America. It is a popular food fish wherever it is found.

Pike generally mature after 3 – 4 years, the males earlier and smaller than the females. They spawn among weed during February – May. The eggs attach to the weed and hatch after 10 – 15 days. When they hatch they start by feeding on invertebrates but quickly turn to small fish and then onto larger prey, including other vertebrates such as ducks and water rats. They are very partial to other pike and are, unsurprisingly, very solitary and territorial. It appears that females grow much larger than males, and it is said that any pike over 5 kg will be a female. They are an ambush predator, laying in wait for their prey and only striking at the very last minute when the prey is within one to two body lengths. The pike is one of the most popular freshwater fish in the UK. It grows exceptionally quickly to a large size and is a ferocious fighter, particular in the first moments as it attacks the bait.

Percidae

The ruffe is a small fish with an obvious spiny dorsal fin, large eyes and mouth. Its back is a dark green - brown colour with irregular dark blotches, whereas its underside is pale yellow to cream in colour. It usually grows to around 15 cm but can exceptionally grow to 25 cm (the British rod - caught record 2008 is 0.142 kg). The ruffe is native to much of Europe but was confined to eastern England, although its range has spread considerably in recent decades. The ruffe matures after 1 to 2 years. They spawn in shallow water among stones and vegetation, mainly in April to May, although they probably spawn several times in a year. Initially the fry grow quickly on a diet of small invertebrates before moving on to larger invertebrates and other food such as fish eggs and young fry. The ruffe is a shoaling fish, moving around in groups throughout its life.

The ruffe is not a popular fish for anglers, being such a small size and attacking baits destined for other larger target species. It has numerous alternative common names such as pope, tommy and daddie.

Perch (Perca fluviatilis)

The perch is a beautiful, deep - bodied fish with four to six dark bands over olive - green flanks. The abdomen is creamy silver with prominent red pelvic and anal fins. It can grow to 20 – 40 cm and weigh 1 – 2.5 kg (the British rod - caught record 2008 is 2.523 kg). The perch is native to the UK and Europe and is now widespread and common in the UK, northern Europe and Asia. It is a popular food fish in many countries; in England it used to be canned and sold as ' perchines '. Perch generally mature after 3 – 4 years and live to around 10 years. They spawn in early spring, usually March to May. Perch tend to spawn in the margins, producing long strings of eggs which lie wrapped around submerged vegetation. The eggs hatch after 10 days and the juveniles feed on small invertebrates as well as fish fry, including other perch fry. As they get older they start to feed on larger invertebrates and begin to feed actively on other fish. Small perch shoal in groups but as they get bigger they do become more solitary, with large individuals tending to move around in small shoals of just a few individuals.

The perch is a popular fish for coarse fisherman, being one of the most attractive of the freshwater fish species. It responds well to anglers ' baits and is readily caught. As a predator it is a useful fish to control the populations of other fish species. However, they can mature at a very small size (10 – 15cm) and in certain circumstances they can create an abundance of small perch. It appears that perch only grow to a large size where there is a plentiful supply of small prey fish.

Zander (Sander lucioperca)

The zander is a large predatory species with a long, thick body. The back is a dark brown – green with obvious dark brown vertical stripes running to the middle of the body. It grows quite large, reaching average sizes of 50 – 70cm, occasionally much bigger to a maximum of 120 cm (the British rod - caught record 2008 is 8.7 kg). The zander is common throughout Europe. It was deliberately introduced into England (the River Great Ouse) in 1963 and has spread widely since. Zander generally mature after 3 – 5 years. Spawning takes place from April to June in among marginal vegetation. Pairs of fish spawn together at dawn and lay sticky eggs on vegetation and stones on the bottom. Unusually, both parents will guard the eggs until they hatch 5 – 10 days after spawning. The fry start on a diet of invertebrates but move quickly on to eat mainly of other fish. The zander is a hunter, patrolling open waters and chasing down small prey fish. Occasionally it appears to hunt as a group, although it mainly hunts as an individual. The zander is a very popular fish with anglers, being a fast - growing, large and aggressive fish. It survives well in larger, clear still - waters and may be a useful addition to a specimen water as it prefers small fish as prey. Licences are required to stock this species.

Gasterosteidae

Three - s pined s tickleback *(Gasterosteus aculeatus)*

The stickleback is one of the most common and recognisable species in freshwaters. It is a small, thin - bodied fish with an olive - brown back and silvery sides and underside. The body is covered in large bony plates and there are three obvious strong spines on the back. The stickleback is a very small fish that rarely exceeds 10 cm in length (the British rod -caught record 2008 is 7 g (0.007 kg)). Sticklebacks are widely distributed and common throughout Europe.

Sticklebacks mature after 1 – 2 years. Spawning takes place in March – June. They are unusual in that the male builds a nest of fibrous plant material and attracts females to spawn within it. The male also develops a vivid red throat to help attract a mate. The eggs take 10 – 20 days to hatch and are guarded constantly by the male. This guarding behaviour continues until the fry are a few weeks old. The fry feed on small invertebrates. As they get older they continue to feed on invertebrates but may extend their diet to include fish fry. Sticklebacks tend to aggregate into small shoals, only becoming solitary and territorial during spawning times.

The stickleback is not a target species for anglers. It is common in most still - waters and will almost certainly appear without help.

Nine - s pined s tickleback *(Pungitius p ungitius)*

This is a rare species. It is similar in most respects to the three - spined stickleback, except that it has 7 – 12 spines running along its back. It also goes dark with a black throat when in breeding condition.

FISH SPECIES SUITABILITY AND SELECTION

The main objective of manuring is to produce a good growth of plankton, mainly phytoplankton, but also zooplankton and bacteria which are protein-rich natural for fish. On this basis, the most appropriate species of fish for a manure-fed pond are therefore those species which are able to filter and feed on plankton (bacteria, phytoplankton and zooplankton) from the water. The most common filter feeders are carps and mixed feeder on algae-detritus are certain species of tilapia. The most commonly raised carp species are the bighead carp Aristichthys nobilis Richardson and the silver carp Hypophthalmychithys molitrix Valenciennes.

The carps are usually raised in polyculture with the grass carp Ctenopharyngodon idella and Indonesian carp Puntius gonionotus Linnaeus controls micro- and macro-vegetation at the water's edge, the Hoeven's slender carp Leptobarbus hoevenii Blk and the common carp Cyprinus carpio Linnaeus which is a bottom feeder. An important observation is that the detritus-feeding silver carp benefited most from the pond conditions, increasing its biomass share from an initial 5.8 per cent to 20.7 per cent from a series of investigation on the integrated farming systems in the Transkei, South Africa. The Indian carps, catla Catla catla Hamilton, mrigal, Cirrhinus mrigala Hamilton Buchanam and rohu, Labeo rohita Hamilton have also been used in experimental duck/ fish integrated farming systems in India.

Polycultures of carps have been widely assumed to be the most efficient way to obtain high fish yields but in Taiwan, the percentage of tilapia in the pond has increased markedly at the expense of the Chinese carps. The most commonly raised tilapia species are the blue tilapia Oreochromis aureus Steindachner, the grey tilapia Oreochromis mossambicus Peters, the Nile tilapia Oreochromis niloticus Linnaeus or their hybrids. Tilapia are more suitable than carp for manure-fed ponds since the former are more tolerant to low levels of dissolved oxygen than the latter. Air-breathing silver-striped catfish Clarias spp., are also integrated with pig farms. The detritusfeeding grey mullet Mugil cephalus L. may be excellent substitutes for the silver carp in integrated farming systems under saline conditions.

FISH YIELDS AND PRODUCTION RATES IN INTEGRATED FARMING SYSTEMS

There are few data on fish yields from ponds which received livestock manure (and spilled livestock feed). The fish yields in integrated livestock-fish farming systems reported in the literature vary greatly, with the actual and extrapolated equivalents ranging from 1.5 ton/ha/year to 18 ton/ha/yr. The variation in fish yield is due:

- The animal sub-system and its major manure input to the pond
- The fish species and stocking rates
- Intensification of culture management inputs *e.g.* addition of other off-farm feed

DIFFERENT TYPES AND AMOUNTS OF MANURE INPUTS

The rationale behind integrating fish with livestock is the large amount of nutrients (N-P-K) present in the feed that is recovered in the manure, with possible proportions of 72–79 per cent nitrogen, 61–87 per cent phosphorus, and 82–92 per cent potassium. These act as fertilizers in fish ponds to produce plankton which comprise high-protein natural food for certain species of fish.

Nitrogen and phosphorus are the nutrients most likely to be limiting for plankton growth in the pond but fish yield is probably more directly correlated to manure nitrogen content (Edwards, 1991) since nitrogen is more volatile than phosphorus.

Based on the nitrogen content of the different manures, it was possible to estimate the stocking density of different livestock (laying duck, dairy cow, pigs and buffalo) in order to produce the same fish yield of 174.7 kg/200 m^2/year in 13 family-level farms. Considering the livestock's manure characteristics (total live weight, age of livestock, feed characteristics of livestock, climate and management of livestock subsystem) and the varying N contents (per cent of the manure production/animal/year, *i.e.*, 2.6 per cent for laying duck manure, 1.9 per cent for pig, 2.2 per cent for dairy cow and 1.1 per cent for buffalo, the estimated number of laying duck, pig, dairy cow and buffalo required to the same fish yields are 1335, 410, 40, and 85 individuals respectively. Prinsloo and Schoonbee noted the comparative effectiveness of the manure on the development of organisms in the food web and promotion of biological activity in fish ponds are: duck manure > pig manure > raw chicken manure > cattle manure > sheep manure.

Manure may contain up to 25 per cent crude protein, but more than half of this is usually non-protein nitrogen (*e.g.*, uric acid) which is not assimilated by fish; therefore manure itself is a poor feed for fish. Manures also contain less energy than conventional pelleted feeds. Though many species of fish consume manure directly, it is a low quality feedstuff compared to conventional pelleted feed and natural plankton.

Another advantage of manure utilisation in fish ponds is that since carbon forms about 50 per cent of the biomass of plankton, the high organic content of the manure is an important source of carbon which is released by bacterial respiration. However, depending on the productivity and quality of water and soil, the effectiveness of livestock manure (enriched with cellulose-rich organic matter) in acting as nutrient sources for fish growth and in raising fish yield varies.

Two possibilities have been observed in Dor, Israel:

1. Manure would improve fish yields only under conditions of water and soil which are poor in essential nutrient minerals (*e.g.*, carbonates or organic matter), or of a low pH, fish ponds receiving very "soft" waters deficient in minerals, or ponds with a low primary production; and
2. Manure may be ineffective in raising fish yields above the rates achieved by daily applications of mineral (N-P-K) fertilizers, under

conditions when the fish pond is receiving daily applications of mineral fertilizers, or where fish ponds are highly productive with very fertile soil naturally-enriched with nutrient minerals and carbonates, or fish ponds with nutrient-rich waters resulting in a high concentration of algal-based detrital organic matter.

FISH SPECIES AND ANIMAL STOCKING RATES

Conservatively, 5 tons of tilapia/ha/year is attainable for integration with 150 pigs. Higher yields of about 15 tons/ha/yr of the air-breathing silver-striped catfish can be expected from integration with about 300 pigs. However, lower yields of carps (less than 5 t/ha year) should be expected and they should be integrated with fewer pigs since carps are more sensitive to low levels of dissolved oxygen than tilapia (Edwards, 1985).

INTENSIFICATION OF MANAGEMENT INPUTS

Yields of fish in integrated farming systems can be considerably increased through intensification involving an increase in stocking density of fish, supplementary energy-rich fish feed (cereal or rice bran and complete pelleted feed) and aeration of pond water.

A 5 tons of tilapia/ha/year is a conservative fish production figure for integration with 150 pigs in Thailand. Higher tilapia yields of 15 tons/ha/year have been reported for integrated systems with pigs but with the fish also fed soyabean cake and rice bran and pelleted feed for the last 2 months of growth, and the pond aerated with several paddle-wheels.

WAYS TO INTENSIFY FISH PRODUCTION IN INTEGRATED FARMING SYSTEM

It is possible to intensify fish production further by the addition of an energy-rich feed such as cereal or rice bran, and still further by adding complete pelleted feed. To ensure increased fish yields with increased levels of feed, it may be necessary to increase the number of fish stocked in the pond. Dissolved oxygen levels may fall to low levels with intensification, so it may be necessary to aerate the water with a mechanical aerator. Yields of 1.5 – 4.7 tons/ha/year were reported from commercial duck/fish integrated farms in Hong Kong; besides duck manure and spilled duck feed, the fish were fed corn meal, rice or wheat bran, oil cakes and bean fragments. Much higher yields were reported from commercial farms in Taiwan where the fish were fed rice bran and soybean cake: A moderately-low production of 7.4 –8.7 tons/ha/year were increased to 13.5–18.0 t/ha/year when the fish stocking density was increased, when the fish were fed pelleted feed during the last two months of the culture period, and when water was aerated by several sets of paddle wheels.

Another method of intensification of fish production is by stocking a higher initial fish biomass and by intermediate harvesting when the fish growth curve starts to slow down.

Such a management strategy should lead to a considerably higher cumulative fish yield. Some integrated duck/fish farms in Hong Kong produce two or more crops of fish each year by initially stocking fish of different sizes, followed by repeated harvesting and stocking.

Such method to intensify fish production is by manipulation of the fish stock to avoid both the initial slow rate of increase of the fish biomass (due to a low initial fish biomass) and the final slow rate of increase of fish biomass (due to the fish biomass approaching the carrying capacity or maximum biomass of fish that the pond can support under a given set of environmental conditions).

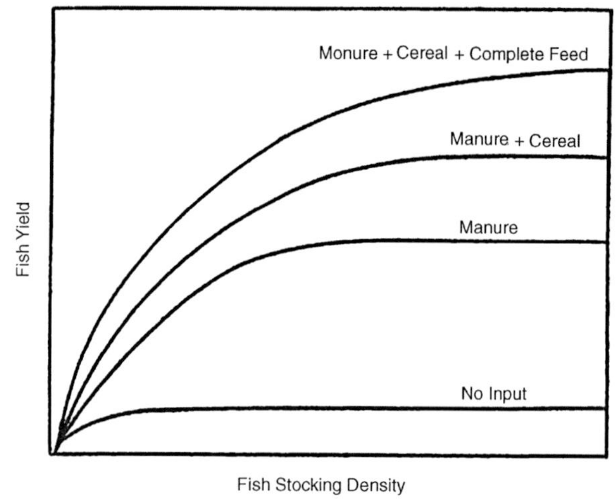

Fig. The Relationship Between Fish Stocking Density and Fish Yield as a Function of Various Types of Pond Nutritional Inputs.

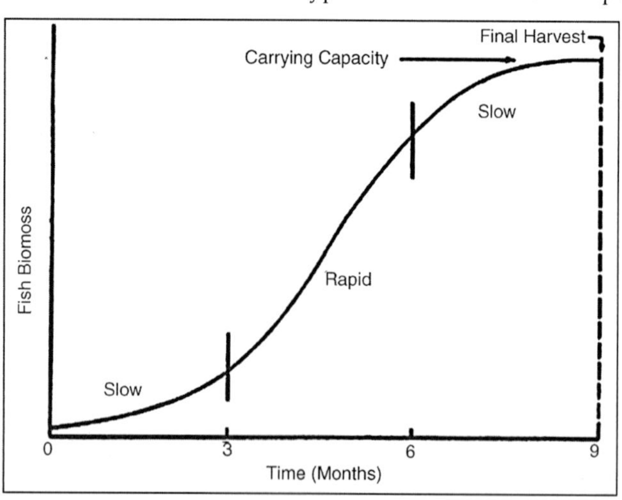

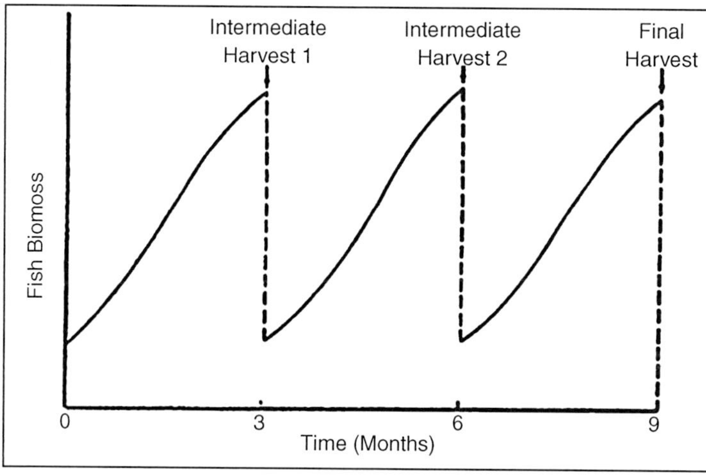

Fig. Upper Graph Normal Rate of Increase of a Fish Population. Lower Graph, a Higher Initial Stocking and Intermediate Harvesting to Avoid the Initial and Final Slow Periods of Increase in Weight, Respectively.

CONCLUSIONS

In integrated livestock-fish farming, the animal manure from the livestock properly applied could lead to a considerable increase in fish production. The use of animal manure to boost fish production is viable. The significant additional profit with the integration of livestock is especially due to reduced feed costs to the fish as well as extra revenue from the sale of birds/animals.

SPECIES GROW SUCCESSFULLY IN PONDS

Although a large number of fish species grow successfully in ponds, only a restricted number of species are usually cultivated on commercial scale. Reasons for this restricted choice is obvious. Commercial pond culture basically aims at achieving maximum possible rate of fish production and profit through optimum utilization of the natural food and the supplementary feed which drastically limits the choice of fish species for pond cultivation.

CRITERIA FOR SELECTION OFSUITABLE FISH SPECIES

- Adaptability to undrainable pond environment
- Faster growth rate
- Efficient utilizers of natural food resources of the pond
- Efficient converter of artificial feed
- Hardy and not easily susceptible to disease
- Easy to breed and rear the seed
- Prolonged breeding period or multiple breeding frequency
- Non-predaceous, planktophagous and preferably herbivorous and detritus feeder

- Compatability with other cultivable species of fish
- Palatable with high nutritive value
- High market demand and high price.

To find all these qualities in one fish species would be very unlikely. Therefore, the species having maximum required traits are considered to be desirable for cultivation in undrainable ponds. Carps fit well to these criteria and hence the most widely cultivated food fishes in South Asia are the quick-growing, non-predatory carps.

FISH SPECIES SUITABLE FOR CULTURE IN UNDRAINABLE PONDS

There are two major systems of carp culture in Asia: the Chinese polyculture system where Chinese carps are cultured together and the Indian composite fish culture system where the Indian major carps and Chinese carps are combined. In China, Chinese carps such as silver carp (Hypophthalmichthys molitrix), grass carp (Ctenopharyngodon idella), bighead carp (Aristichthys nobilis), mud carp (Cirrhinus molitorella), black carp (Mylopharyngodon piceus) and common carp (Cyprinus carpio) are cultured under polyculture system in ponds. Under the Indian system of composite fish culture in undrainable ponds, three Indian carps, *viz.* catla (Catla catla), rohu (Labeo rohita) and mrigal (Cirrhinus mrigala), two Chinese carps, *viz.* silver carp (Hypophthalmichthys molitrix) and grass carp (Ctenopharyngodon idella) and common carp (Cyprinus carpio) are extensively cultivated.

Catla

Fig. Anti-erosion Meaasures

Catla is the fastest growing Indian major carp species and widely distributed throughout India, Nepal, Pakistan, Burma and Bangladesh. It inhabits the surface layer of water and feeds upon plankton. Adult stages are predominantly zooplankton feeder, occasionally taking in decaying macrovegetation, phytoplankton and smaller molluscs. It attains maturity in the second year of life and carry over 70 000 eggs per kg body weight. It naturally breeds in rivers during monsoon season and under control conditions in bundhs as well. It does not breed in ponds.

However, it responds well to hypophysation techniques. Seeds are easily reared in undrainable ponds of relatively smaller size. Under composite fish culture in ponds it usually grows to over 1 kg in one year.

Rohu

Rohu is the natural inhabitant of river systems of India, Nepal, Pakistan, Bangladesh and Burma. In recent years it has been transplanted to many countries of the world including Sri Lanka, Mauritius, USSR, Japan, Philippines, Laos, Malaysia and Thailand. Normally it occupies the column region of the aquatic ecosystem and feeds mostly on vegetable matter including higher plants, detritus, etc. Like catla it naturally breeds in rivers and under special conditions in bundhs. Except by hypophysation to which it responds quickly, it never breeds in ponds. It attains sexual maturity during the second year. However, certain percentages of pond-reared specimens mature within one year. Fecundity varies from 226 000 to about 2 800 000 depending upon the size. Rohu spawns during the monsoon. Seeds collected from rivers or produced by bundh breeding or induced breeding are reared with ease in seasonal or perennial undrainable ponds. Under pond culture conditions it grows upto 900 g within one year.

Silver Carp

Silver carp is basically inhabitant of major river systems of South and Central China and in the Amur Basin of USSR from where it has been transplanted throughout the Indo-Pacific region including India. It is a surface dweller feeding mainly upon zooplankton during its early stages and gradually becomes predominantly a phytoplankton feeder.

Its relatively longer branchiospines provide a fine filter capable of retaining planktonic organisms. It readily accepts supplementary feed like oil cakes and rice bran mixture in pond culture systems. It does not breed in pond condition. However, through the technique of hypophysation they are induced to breed in ponds during the monsoon season. Fecundity varies greatly with the size and agroclimatic condition.

A fecundity range of 145 000 to 2 044 000 has been found from silver carp. It takes about 2–6 years to mature in China, whereas in India it matures very early, within 2 years. Males mature earlier than the females. In composite fish culture ponds it usually attains over 1.5 kg within one year of rearing. Seed rearing is done in smaller seasonal or perennial undrainable ponds with a high rate of survival.

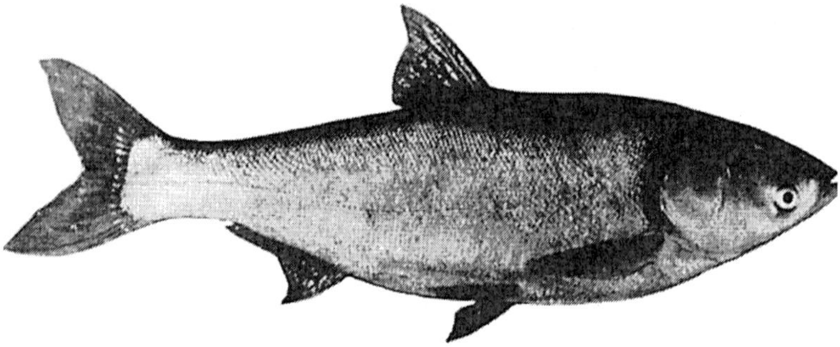

Fig. Silver Carp (Hypophthalmichthys Molitrix)

Grass Carp

Grass carp is a native of the river systems of South-Central and North China and the Amur river of USSR. Its suitability in aquaculture and biological control of aquatic weed infestation has resulted in wide-scale transplantation throughout the world. In early life it feeds on planktonic organisms and gradually switches over to macrophytes. They are voracious eaters and show distinct preference for vegetable food materials such as grass, leaves, weeds, etc.

Fig. Grass Carp (Ctenopharyngodon Idella)

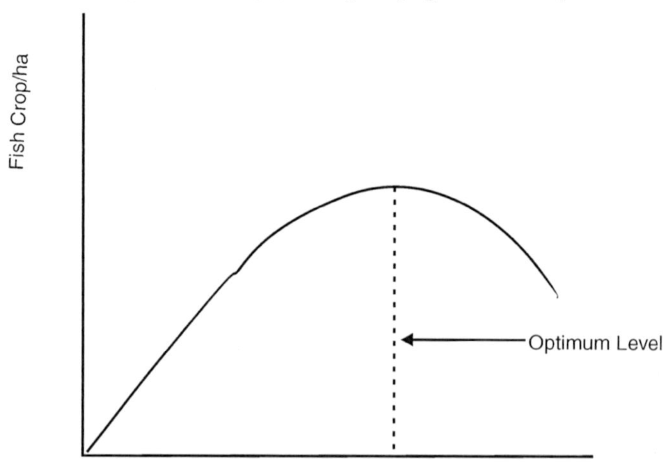

Fig. Grass Carp (Ctenopharyngodon Idella)

However, they also accept supplementary artificial feed materials. Usually only a portion of ingested food is digested and the rest is voided in semidigested or undigested form which, in turn, becomes choice food for the bottom dweller common carp In China it takes about 3–4 years to achieve maturity whereas in India it usually takes 2 years. The total number of eggs range between 308 800 and 618 100 from the fishes weighing between 4.7 kg to 7.0 kg. The fish does not breed under pond condition and hence seed production is achieved through hypophysation. Growth mainly depends on the rate of feeding. Under optimum feeding rate it can grow over 5 kg in one year Usually it grows to over 1.5 kg in composite fish culture ponds.

Mrigal

Mrigal inhabits all the major river systems of India, Pakistan, Bangladesh and Burma. The adult fish feeds upon filamentous green algae, diatoms, pieces of higher plants, decayed vegetable, mud and detritus. It is basically a bottom feeder and hence suitable for cultivation with column and surface feeder carps in ponds. Mrigal usually attains maturity within 1 or 2 years depending upon the agroclimatic conditions of the location.

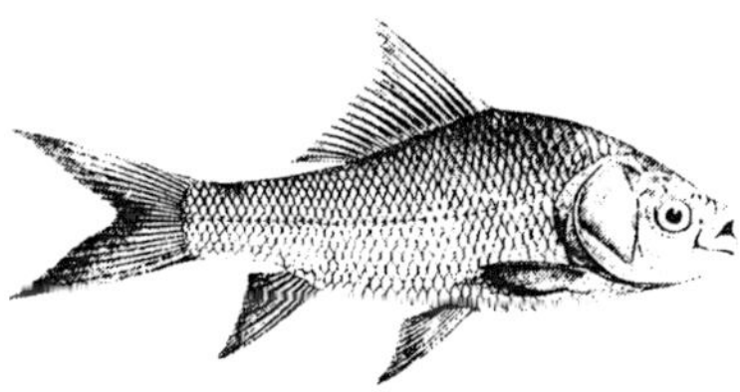

Fig. Catla (Catla Catla)

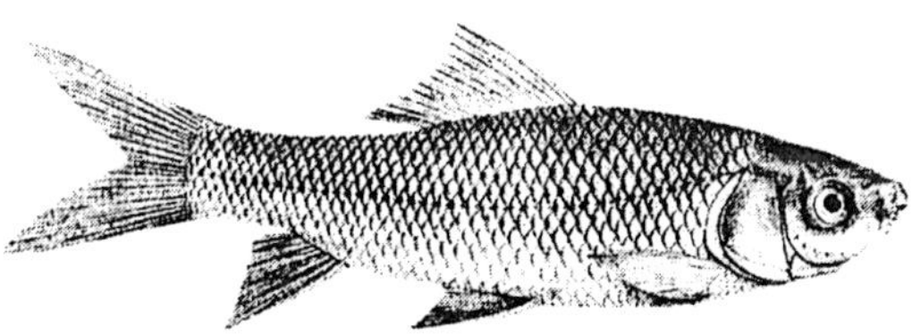

Fig. Rohu (Labeo Rohita)

Fig. Mrigal (Cirrhinus Mriqala)

Fecundity ranges between 124 000 to over 1 900 000 depending upon size. Spawning season is linked with the onset and duration of the southwest monsoon. It does not breed in ponds, but can be easily bred in bundhs and by hypophysation. It is now being induced to breed twice within the same spawning season. Rearing of seed is usually undertaken in seasonal or perennial undrainable ponds. Under pond culture conditions it grows to over 1 kg in one year.

Common Carp

Originally a native of temperate region of Asia, especially China, the common carp is now the most domesticated and cultivated carp species throughout the world. It is an omnivorous bottom dweller subsisting mainly on benthic fauna and decaying vegetable matter. It frequently burrows the pond bottom in search of food.

Fig. Common Carp (Cyprinus Carpio)

This habit of digging the pond bottom helps in maintaining the productivity of undrainable ponds and hence culture of common carp with other carp species is of great advantage. Moreover, it also feeds directly on the undigested excreta of grass carp. Growth mainly depends upon the bottom biota, stocking density and the rate of supplementary feed.

In composite fish culture ponds it grows to about 1 kg within one year. In a tropical climate it spawns throughout the year in the pond environment with two peak periods, one from January to March and the other during July and August. Eggs are small and adhesive in nature. In tropical conditions it attains maturity within 12 months

4

Food, Feed and Feeding

FISH PRODUCTS AND FOOD

FOOD

The flesh of many fish are primarily valued as a source of food; there are many edible species of fish as well as other sea food.

Shellfish include shelled molluscs and crustaceans used as food. Shelled molluscs include the clam, mussel, oyster, winkle and scallop; some crustaceans are the shrimp, lobster, crayfish, and crab.

Eggs, called roe, of various species may be eaten; roe comes from fish and certain marine invertebrates, such as sea urchins and shrimp. In some cultures, roe is considered a delicacy, for example caviar from the sturgeon. Squid and octopus are valued as food. Sea cucumber is considered a delicacy in Chinese cooking and is often served at New Year's feasts, usually in soups. In some cultures, for example China, Japan, and Vietnam, certain species of jellyfish. Fish oil is valued as a dietary supplement.

LIVE FISH

Live fish are collected for the international live food fish trade. Some seafood restaurants keep live fish in aquaria for display or for cultural beliefs. The majority of live fish kept at seafood restaurants, however, are desired for the freshness of the seafood, being killed only immediately before being cooked. Suiting customer preference, this practice makes the seafood higher in quality and better in taste. The prevalence of cultural beliefs and consumer standards helps to drive the demand for the live food fish trade. Hong Kong, for example, is estimated to have imported in excess of 15,000 tonnes of live food fish in 2000. This brought the value of their live food fish trade industry to US$400 million as reported by the World Resources Institute.

Fish can also be collected in ways that do not injure them such as in a seine net or by placing an electric current into the water. Such techniques are used most often by researchers for observation and study but are also used by those who collect fish for the aquarium trade. There are several organisations devoted to improving the methods of collecting, handling, transporting, exporting and farming of wild and domesticated live food fish, as well as freshwater and marine tropical fish destined for aquaria.

OTHER PRODUCTS

Pearls and mother-of-pearl are valued for their lustre. Traditional methods of pearl hunting are now virtually extinct. Sharkskin and rayskin which are covered with, in effect, tiny teeth (dermal denticles) were used for the purposes that sandpaper currently is. These skins are also used to make leather. Sharkskin leather is used in the manufacture of hilts of traditional Japanese swords. Sea horse, star fish, sea urchin and sea cucumber are used in traditional Chinese medicine. Tyrian purple is a pigment made from marine snails Murex brandaris and Murex trunculus.

Sepia is a pigment made from the inky secretions of cuttlefish. Fish glue is made by boiling the skin, bones and swim bladders of fish. Fish glue has long been valued for its use in all manner of products from illuminated manuscripts to the Mongolian war bow. Isinglass is a substance obtained from the swim bladders of fish (especially sturgeon), it is used for the clarification of wine and beer. Fish emulsion is a fertilizer emulsion that is produced from the fluid remains of fish processed for fish oil and fish meal industrially.

CULTURAL REFERENCES

Fishing is a widely used as a metaphor though as such it is possibly ambiguous. On the one hand, fishing with a net has nuances of gathering by honest effort. For example, in the New Testament, Jesus is reported to have said to his disciples: Follow me, and I will make you fishers of men. Matthew 4:19. On the other hand, fishing with bait or lure sometimes has nuances of catching by deception, possibly with an implication of greed on the part of the victim. For example, the expression "fishing expedition" (usually used to describe a line of questioning), describes a case where the questioner implies that he knows more than he actually does in order to trick the target into divulging more information than he wishes to reveal. Other examples of fishing terms that carry a negative connotation are: "fishing for compliments", "to be fooled hook, line and sinker" (to be fooled beyond merely "taking the bait"), and the internet scam of Phishing in which a third party will duplicate a web site where you would put sensitive information (such as ebay or a bank site) in order to obtain it.

OVERFISHING

The Traffic Light colour convention, showing the concept of Harvest Control Rule (HCR), specifying when a rebuilding plan is mandatory in terms of precautionary and limit reference points for spawning biomass and fishing mortality rate. Overfishing occurs when fishing activities reduce fish stocks below an acceptable level. This can occur in any body of water from a pond to the oceans. More precise biological and bioeconomic terms define 'acceptable level'. Biological overfishing occurs when fishing mortality has reached a level where the stock biomass has negative marginal growth (slowing down biomass growth), as indicated by the red area in the figure. (Fish are being taken out of the water so quickly that the replenishment of stock by breeding slows down. If the replenishment continues to slow down for long enough, replenishment will go into reverse and the population will decrease.)

Economic or bioeconomic overfishing additionally considers the cost of fishing and defines overfishing as a situation of negative marginal growth of resource rent. (Fish are being taken out of the water so quickly that the growth in the profitability of fishing slows down. If this continues for long enough, profitability will decrease.) A more dynamic definition of economic overfishing may also include a relevant discount rate and present value of flow of resource rent over all future catches.

Ultimately overfishing may lead to resource depletion in cases of subsidised fishing, low biological growth rates and critical low biomass levels (*e.g.*, by critical depensation growth properties). The ability of nature to restore the fisheries also depends on whether the ecosystems are still in a state to allow fish numbers to build again. Dramatic changes in species composition may establish other equilibrium energy flows that involve other species compositions than had been present before (ecosystem shift). (For example: remove nearly all the trout, the carp take over and make it near impossible for the trout to re-establish a breeding population.)

FISH PRODUCTION AND DEMAND

A major international scientific study released in November 2006 in the journal Science found that about one-third of all fishing stocks worldwide have collapsed (with a collapse being defined as a decline to less than 10 per cent of their maximum observed abundance), and that if current trends continue all fish stocks worldwide will collapse within fifty years. The FAO State of World Fisheries and Aquaculture 2004 report estimates that in 2003, of the main fish stocks or groups of resources for which assessment information is available, "approximately one-quarter were overexploited, depleted or recovering from depletion (16 per cent, 7 per cent and 1 per cent respectively) and needed rebuilding."

The threat of overfishing is not limited to the target species only. As trawlers resort to deeper and deeper waters to fill their nets, they have begun to threaten delicate deep-sea ecosystems and the fish that inhabit them, such as the coelacanth. In the May 15, 2003 issue of the journal Nature, it is estimated that 10 per cent of large predatory fish remain compared to levels before commercial fishing. Many fisheries experts, however, consider this claim to be exaggerated with respect to tuna populations. From 1950 (18 million tonnes) to 1969 (56 million tonnes) fishfood production grew by about 5 per cent each year; from 1969 onward production has raised 8 per cent annually. It is expected that this demand will continue to rise, and MariCulture Systems estimated in 2002 that, by 2010, seafood production would have to increase by over 15.5 million tonnes to meet the desire of Earth's growing population. This is likely to further aggravate the problem of overfishing, unless aquaculture technology expands to meet the needs of human population.

Overfishing has depleted fish populations to the point that large scale commercial fishing, on average around the world, is not economically viable without government assistance. By the 1980s, economists estimated that for every $1 earned fishing, $1.77 had to be spent in catching and marketing the fish. Some species' stocks are so depleted that consumers are often unlikely to get what they think they are purchasing, due to a phenomenon called "species substitutions," where less desirable species are labelled and marketed under the names of more expensive ones. For example, genetic analysis shows that approximately 70 per cent of fish sold as the highly-prized "red snapper" (Lutjanus campechanus) are other species.

MITIGATION

With present and forecast levels of the world population it is not possible to solve the overfishing issue; however, there are mitigation measures that can save selected fisheries and forestall the collapse of others.

In order to meet the problems of overfishing, a precautionary approach and Harvest Control Rule (HCR) management principles have been introduced in the main fisheries around the world. The Traffic Light colour convention introduces sets of rules based on predefined critical values, which could be adjusted as more information is gained.

The "United Nations Convention on the Law of the Sea" treaty deals with aspects of overfishing in articles 61, 62, and 65.

- Article 61 requires all coastal states to ensure that the maintenance of living resources in their exclusive economic zones is not endangered by over-exploitation. The same article addresses the maintenance or restoration of populations of species above levels at which their reproduction may become seriously threatened.
- Article 62 provides that coastal states: "shall promote the objective of optimum utilisation of the living resources in the exclusive economic zone without prejudice to Article 61"
- Article 65 provides generally for the rights of, *inter alia*, coastal states to prohibit, limit, or regulate the exploitation of marine mammals.

Overfishing can be viewed as a case of the tragedy of the commons; in that sense, solutions would promote property rights, such as privatisation and fish farming. Daniel K. Benjamin, in Fisheries are Classic Example of the "Tragedy of the Commons", cites research by Grafton, Squires, and Fox to support the idea that privatisation can solve the overfishing problem:

According to recent research on the British Columbia halibut fishery, where the commons has been at least partly privatized, substantial ecological and economic benefits have resulted. There is less damage to fish stocks, the fishing is safer, and fewer resources are needed to achieve a given harvest. Another possible solution, at least for some areas, is fishing quotas, so fishermen can only legally take a certain amount of fish. A more radical possibility is declaring certain areas of the sea "no-go zones" and make fishing there strictly illegal, so the fish in that area have time to recover and repopulate. Controlling consumer behaviour and demand is a key in mitigating action. Worldwide a number of initiatives emerged to provide consumers with information regarding the conservation status of the seafood available to them. The Guide to Good Fish Guides lists a number of these.

MARINE STEWARDSHIP COUNCIL

The Marine Stewardship Council (MSC) is an independent, global, non-profit organisation which was set up in 1997 to find a solution to the problem of overfishing. It has developed an environmental standard for sustainable and well-managed fisheries. Environmentally responsible fisheries management and practices are rewarded with the use of its blue product ecolabel.

Consumers concerned about overfishing and its consequences are increasingly able to choose seafood products which have been independently assessed against the MSC's environmental standard and labelled to prove it. This enables consumers to play a part in reversing the decline of fish stocks. As of January 2007, 22 fisheries around the world have been independently assessed and certified as meeting the MSC standard, and there are nearly 500 seafood products sold by retailers in 25 countries around the world. Their 'where to buy' page lists all currently available certified seafood. Fish and Kids is an MSC project to teach schoolchildren about marine environmental issues, including overfishing.

DEVELOPMENTS IN THE FOOD CROPS

Many major food crops upon which we depend originated and were first cultivated in Third World countries rather than in the industrialized countries where they are most productively exploited today and in which they have been improved by traditional plant breeding. The potato originated in South America, wheat in Ethiopia and the Near East, important maize varieties in South America, and rice in Asia. Moreover the so-called Vavilov centres, which contain the greatest variety of living species and which have been the source of much important gene material, are mainly in Third World countries.

The wealth of the industrial countries owes much to their past ability to exploit agriculturally crops and animals originating in other countries. In the colonial era the success of British scientists in smuggling rubber plants from Brazil to Sri Lanka, Singapore and Malaysia and the comparable more complex route by which coffee was introduced to Latin America from Ethiopia are instances of colonial powers obtaining significant wealth by exploiting plant material from the Third World. In one way or another the process by which institutions and firms in developed countries have continued to collect new plant and animal varieties from less-developed countries has continued. But what is still a major source of friction is the procedures by which legislative protection is developed to give companies in the richer countries commercial rights to exclusive exploitation of varieties developed from plants freely collected from other countries, and to extract high rates of profit from the sale of those varieties. Most extreme is the situation whereby under the USA Plant Patent Act of 1930, which covered asexually propagated plants such as certain fruits, flowers, ornamental shrubs and trees, it has been possible for plants discovered and smuggled out of other countries to be given patent protection in the USA.

The key to this is that the Act accepted the unfeasibility of requiring proof of an 'inventive-step' for the granting of a patent, and employed the criterion that as far as can be determined the plant variety is new. Since some novel variety found in the rain forests of South America may satisfy this criterion, and the source of the plant can be concealed from the authorities, the theft and smuggling of plants can be said to have been encouraged.

Seed companies in developed countries have successfully pressed their case for protection, and have progressively extended Plant Breeders' Rights (PBR) through both national legislation and the Union for the Protection of New Varieties of Plant (UPOV), which is an international agreement among signatory countries to honour a system of varietal rights. In the case of food crops, in the absence of patentability, PBR operates by registering distinct varieties. Pressure has been exerted upon less-developed countries to become signatories of UPOV and thus acknowledge the rights of breeders, most of whom are from developed countries. However, the majority have stalled or rejected membership, and have been fundamentally unhappy about accepting the principle of creating monopoly rights for others over plant material which in some cases originated in their own country.

The whole issue of intellectual property rights has been raised to a prominent political level by the USA's insistence that it be included as one of the thirteen areas for negotiation in the Uruguay Round of multilateral bargaining of the General Agreement on Trade and Tariffs. While the issue is a much broader one than that of plant and animal breeders' rights, it reflects a basic political conflict between the richer countries, determined to obtain secure returns on R and D expenditures by companies, and LDCs struggling to catch up and anxious to avoid having to pay royalties on products protected by PBR and patents. This conflict has broader moral and ethical dimensions when it relates to the issue of charging royalties for the seeds of food crops to countries where malnutrition is widespread.

Against the previous argument has to be balanced the need of those incurring R and D expenditure to capture enough of the returns to provide an incentive for R and D. At least that is certainly the case where R and D is to be undertaken by the private sector, which is politically the increasingly preferred solution in the UK, the USA and elsewhere. This, however, leads to another area of concern, which is that a small number of large multinational chemical and pharmaceutical firms have increasingly come to control the seed industry. Companies such as Shell, Sandoz, Dekallb-Pfizer, Ciba-Geigy and BP have become owners of most of what were small independent seed companies.

This linking between chemicals and seeds within firms has a strong commercial logic. It facilitates the marketing of packages consisting of seed varieties plus the appropri-ate fertilizers, insecticides, etc. It also allows the companies concerned to integrate their plant breeding, biotechnology and chemical research. One particular synergy for these companies will be to bioengineer varieties of major food crops to resist their own herbicides and weedkillers. This would permit chemical weed control to be extended to large-scale crops where this is not now possible, and is just one way in which the direction of biotechnolo-gical research may be influenced (biased) by the combination of forces giving a small number of companies extensive control over the basic means of agricultural production.

There are many other issues which could be touched on regarding corporate influence over the development of agricultural biotechnology. It is, however, understandable that the spokesmen for LDC countries, which are profoundly concerned about their dependence upon western technology and exercised by what is seen as colonial and post-colonial exploitation by the West, should be alarmed by the prospect of new rights being created over seeds and other biotechnological products. Certainly there are widespread fears that they will only gain access to the fruits of biotechnology on unfavourable terms and that their relative dependence on and subservience to western industry will be increased so that benefits to them will be small.

There are many western critics who would agree with this, and that the system by which agricultural biotechnology is delivered will favour the 'haves' rather than the 'have-nots'.

AGRICULTURAL BIOTECHNOLOGY: THEIR IMPACT

There are divergent views about the rate of uptake of new agricultural biotechnologies and their impact. Kalter and Tauer and the US Office of

Technology Assessment anticipate comparatively rapid take-up, while others (Buckwell and Moxey and Farrington do not foresee much impact until the next century, that is until ten to fifteen years have elapsed. The caution of the latter commentators is probably justified, for there are various hurdles to be jumped before biotechnologies can gain acceptance.

One hurdle to be overcome is the economic one. Self-evidently there must be some economic advantage to farmers or agro-industry from adopting the technology. Frequently what captures the scientific imagination turns out to be economically unviable in use, although it is only with use that efficiency can be improved and costs brought down.

A more demanding test still for biotechnologies will be to obtain legislative approval and public acceptance. These are intimately connected. In the case of machinery developments, provided safety standards are observed there are no legal impediments to developing new and improved machines, since there are no obvious problems of hazard to the public and therefore public acceptance. Chemical insecticide, fungicides and herbicides do, however, pose much greater problems because of concerns with toxicity, and elaborate testing and licensing procedures have evolved after a relatively haphazard set of procedures in the 1950s and 1960s, when widespread use was made of DDT and organo-phosphorous compounds without adequate recognition of their toxicity. In significant part, because of the problems which have been experienced with agro-chemicals, the licensing of biotechnologies will inevitably be based on testing at least as stringent as that which now exists for chemicals. Indeed the licensing procedures are likely to be more stringent because of public and scientific concerns.

Public acceptance of biotechnology in the food chain will be made more difficult by confusion about differences between biotechnologies. In the early 1980s there was a crescendo of concern about the use of steroids to promote faster liveweight gain in calves and cattle. The public outcry eventually led to the banning of such hormones for meat animals; but the legacy is a profound distrust of and hostility to new products such as synthetic Bovine Somatrophin (BST), which has the capacity to increase the milk yield of those dairy cows which are 'relatively' deficient in what is a naturally occurring hormone.

Although initial scientific results are favourable, and some minor doubts remain, the major influence leading the European Commission to impose a moratorium on the use of BST until the end of 1990 at least is concern about public perception; the Commission has stated 'It would be a serious setback to producers and to the Community's milk policy were present [positive] trends in consumption to be reversed as a result of adverse consumer reaction.

With newly bioengineered plants and animals scientific and public concerns are emerging which are of a different order from those associated with previous biotechnology. One relates to the possibility that crop failures may become more frequent if biotechnology leads to a reduction in genetic diversity in crops being grown; such a tendency has already been observed in relation to the Green Revolution technology for wheat.

There are also concerns about upsetting the balance of nature in unforseen ways, akin to the unanticipated consequence of introducing rabbits into Australia and then trying to control these by introducing myxomatosis. Thus questions arise such as what happens if herbicide resistance introduced into a commercial crop plant transfers itself by cross pollination into a closely related weed species, or indeed if the herbicide-resistant crop should colonize wild habitats. There are, of course, more lurid and absurd notions bandied about in the popular press which are similar in nature to the attacks made on Darwinism. The questions, both absurd and real, raised in relation to agricultural biotechnology will undoubtedly slow the rate at which it is adopted. Nevertheless instances of adoption are increasing: BST in the USA, a bioengineered baker's yeast in the UK, bioengineered sheep producing insulin, etc. As these become more widespread and increasingly affect lower-valued, bulk agricultural products, so the impacts of biotechnology on structural change will increase. The balance of economic power will switch increasingly to industry, to high-technology large farms and against smaller farmers in disadvantaged regions and countries. That, unfortunately, is a seemingly inevitable consequence of what we consider to be economic progress.

PLANT PESTS AGENTS

A pest is "a plant or animal detrimental to humans or human concerns (as agriculture or livestock production)"; alternative meanings include organisms that cause nuisance and epidemic disease associated with high mortality (specifically: plague). In its broadest sense, a pest is a competitor of humanity. 'Pest' is a generic word for other terms such as: insect pests (of agriculture or human disease vectors), vermin, weeds and plant pathogens. In the past, the term might have been used for detrimental animals only, thus for example, causing confusion where the generic term 'pesticide' meant 'insecticide' to some people.

A plant pest is any agent, substance or organism, or parts thereof, that may cause injury, disease or damage, either to plants or to the environment in which it is introduced. APHIS maintains a list of organisms considered to be plant pests, and therefore, subject to regulation under the FPPA. If an organism is not on the list, it may still be subject to regulation as a plant pest if there is reason to believe it is or will act as a plant pest. Organisms considered plant pests, or that exhibit the potential to be plant pests, are treated as 'regulated articles' under the FPPA. The regulations extend to the introduction of GM organisms meeting the definition of a plant pest or for which there is reason to believe they are plant pests. APHIS considers the environmental release of a

GM crop to be equivalent to the introduction of new organisms. Therefore, until proven otherwise, a GM crop is considered a 'regulated article' under the FPPA. The use of the term 'plant pest' in reference to GM plants means the 'non-pest' nature of the crop has yet to be determined. To date, all field tests conducted have demonstrated that GM crops exhibit no more 'pest-like' traits than their conventional counterparts. All GM plants developed to date have involved the use of at least one designated 'plant pest' as either promoters or vectors, and as a result, have been subject to regulatory review under the FPPA. APHIS takes the position that an entire plant can be designated as a regulated article, even if it was not developed using plant pests, if the plant is the product of genetic engineering, and the agency determines or has reason to believe it is a plant pest. Given this position, APHIS would likely challenge any attempt to introduce a GM plant into commerce unless the developer has first gone through the APHIS regulatory review process.

REQUIREMENTS FOR COMMERCIALIZATION

A number of years of field testing are required to evaluate the agronomic and product quality characteristics exhibited by new plant varieties developed within a laboratory or greenhouse. APHIS regulations outline procedures for obtaining a permit or providing notification prior to the importation, interstate movement or release of a regulated article, which of course, includes field testing. Prior to an introduction, a proponent must provide notification to APHIS of its intentions or submit an application to obtain a permit. The notification and permit requirements have evolved as an extension of the long-standing programm for the regulation of plant pests within the United States. Since 1987, APHIS has issued permits or acknowledged the receipt of notifications for the field release of more than 6500 new crop varieties.

Permits

For APHIS approval, developers must demonstrate that a new plant variety poses no significant risk to other plants in the environment or is at least as safe as similar crop varieties. APHIS review and approval are required for the shipment of seed and for the conduct of field trials involving new crop varieties. APHIS issues site-specific permits for field tests or releases into the environment.

Prior to field testing, APHIS may seek further clarification of study objectives, specify how, when or where research may be conducted, establish the data to be generated, collected and reported, stipulate additional requirements for the monitoring or securing of test sites, and specify methods for the disposal of crop residues that remain at the end of a study. The results of field trials are often used in making a determination as to whether a GM plant exhibits any effects on non-target species, or poses any unique plant pest problems. For field trials conducted under either notification or permit, developers of GM plant varieties are required to submit reports to APHIS that include: details regarding the methods of observation; the data collected; and interpretations concerning the effects on plants, non-target organisms, or the environment. In the event that a GM crop is likely to be the subject of a petition for a determination of non-regulated status, developers must provide a description of known and potential differences, and substantiate that the regulated article is not likely to pose a greater plant risk than the organism from which it was derived.

An environmental assessment is a requirement of the NEPA, Council on Environmental Quality regulations, and USDA procedures for issuing permits under the FPPA. Under the permit process, developers of GM plant varieties must disclose information concerning the plant, test facilities, and control measures in place for its transport and field testing. Based on this information, the USDA performs an assessment of the potential environmental impact following a release. If the agency reaches a 'Finding of No Significant Impact' (FONSI), a permit may then be issued.

Notifications

Depending on the plant species and intended introduction, applying for a permit from APHIS can be a complicated and time-consuming process. In the spring of 1993, APHIS introduced a simplified notification process as an alternative to applying for a permit, which in most instances applies to the introduction of GM plants. To qualify for notification, a GM plant must be introduced in accordance with the eligibility criteria.

Originally, six GM crops (corn, cotton, potatoes, soybean, tobacco and tomatoes) qualified for notification; however, the process was more recently expanded to include most other crop species not capable of becoming a noxious weed. The developers of new GM plant varieties are encouraged to contact APHIS when making a determination as to whether a GM plant would qualify for notification. If a particular GM plant does not qualify for notification, a more involved regular permit process must be followed.

For a GM plant to qualify for notification, it and its predecessor must not be a noxious weed, the introduced gene sequence(s) must be stably integrated within the host, not originate from a plant or animal pathogen, exhibit a known function that will contribute to plant disease, or encode for substances that could be potentially toxic or infective to non-target organisms, such as pharmaceuticals, or viral components other than those coat proteins already established as safe.

Performance standards also exist for the conduct of field trials to ensure that an adequate level of containment is provided for all introductions. It is the responsibility of the developer to ensure that an adequate level of containment is provided for field trials involving GM plants under notification. The performance standards utilized will vary according to the biology of the plant and the nature of the introduction. In general, this includes specifying methods for the proper handling, shipment, field monitoring and disposal of plant material at the end of the study.

As a part of the notification process, an applicant must provide information about the plant, identify the source of any genes used; the method of genetic modification; and the size, date and location of any proposed field test or introduction. Notification is required at least 10 days prior to the interstate movement or 30 days in advance of the field testing or importation of a regulated article that qualifies for notification with APHIS.

Determination of Non-regulated Status

Once sufficient data have accumulated through laboratory and field trials performed under permit or notification, a developer may petition APHIS for a determination of non-regulated status. A DONRS allows a GM plant to be grown, tested or used for crop breeding without further regulatory oversight by APHIS. APHIS will grant a DONRS if sufficient evidence can be provided to demonstrate that no plant pest potential exists (*i.e.* that the GM plant is not expected to become a pest, poses no significant risk to the environment, or is as safe as conventional plant varieties).

The developer is required to demonstrate a lack of change in disease or pest resistance status, an absence of any potential for contributing to development of a new plant pathogen or pest, as well as to address any questions relating to potential environmental consequences of the release.

APHIS examines several parameters when making a determination as to whether a GM crop should be considered a plant pest. Reporting requirements include submitting a detailed rationale for development; overview of the biology of the crop (competitiveness, survivability, dormancy); molecular characterization; protein expression; morphologi-cal/phenotypic characteristics; outcrossing/geneflow; weediness; insect and disease susceptibility; and, recombination potential (for viral genes).

Other considerations include assessing whether a GM crop could itself become a weed. In making this determination, factors that are considered include: how the seeds are dispersed in the environment; whether the seeds are capable of surviving over the winter; the potential for the development of volunteer plants; and whether these plants could reproduce into viable offspring. Another important consideration is whether the seeds or plants are capable of surviving outside of a managed agricultural environment (*e.g.* watering, fertilizer, etc.), and how the introduced traits could influence the viability of the crop under marginal conditions. APHIS also takes into consideration potential adverse effects on wildlife, including birds, beneficial insects and mammals, following the introduction of a GM crop. Some of this information comes from field trials that are conducted in multiple locations for several years. By observing crops growing under actual conditions of use in the field, scientists can compare insect populations existing within a field planted with GM crops to those coexisting in fields planted with a non-modified variety of the same plant. Field trials are also useful in identifying any changes in the plant physiology, such as height, colour, leaf placement, time of flowering, etc., that result from modifications in the genome of the plant.

Monitoring of these changes during field trials allows APHIS to evaluate how these changes might benefit or adversely impact the behaviour of wildlife in contact with these crops. Knowing that wildlife, such as deer, often feed on agricultural crops, APHIS also takes into consideration the nutritional content of the GM crop. Comparisons of the essential nutrient content are often made between the GM plant and its conventional counterpart. Other interests may include determining the impact of the modification on the levels of adverse factors (*e.g.* natural toxicants or anti-nutrients) present in the plant. APHIS maintains a list of all crops that have received a DONRS. At any time, APHIS retains the authority to prohibit the commercial planting of a GM crop if it is determined that it is becoming a plant pest.

PETITION PROCESS

Before a GM plant can be freely transported and commercialized, the developer must first petition the APHIS for a DONRS. A petition for a DONRS requires the submission of extensive data on the introduced gene construct, effects on plant biology and effects on the ecosystem, including the spread of the gene to other crops or wild relatives. Developing all data necessary to support a petition for a DONRS may take months or years depending upon the scientific issues that need to be addressed.

Based on the information provided within the petition, APHIS evaluates the potential impact (*e.g.* toxicological) that the introduced modifications will have on non-target organisms in the environment, including threatened or endangered species. A petition for a DONRS must provide a rationale for the development and introduction of the GM crop, starting with genotypic and phenotypic information on both the host and donor organism(s).

This includes a detailed description of the methods of transformation, identifying all gene sequences (*e.g.* promoters, leader sequences, introns, selectable markers, etc.), their function, and potential for plant risk following introduction. A combination of different analytical methods may be used to demonstrate the stable integration of an introduced gene sequence within the genome, its inheritance and expression in host plants. To the extent possible, the gene(s) of interest (*e.g.* resistance, marker genes), levels of expression, and im pacts on levels of inherent plant toxicants in plant tissues, under experimental and actual growth conditions in the field, must be characterized. Field performance studies (*e.g.* leaf morphology, pollen viability, seed germination, viability, insect susceptibilities, disease resistance, yield, etc.) are used to identify any differences or similarities in phenotypic characteristics exhibited by the GM and non-modified crop. The extent of field performance data required in support of a petition for non-regulated status depends not only on the nature of introduced gene sequences, but also on the physiology of the host plant. Less extensive field performance studies are required for plants that are: highly domesticated (*e.g.* corn); self-pollinating (*e.g.* soybean); male sterile; those with high seed germination rates (> 90 per cent); or unlikely to influence their potential weediness or fitness (*e.g.* delayed ripening, oil seed content). Whereas, GM crops exhibiting a tolerance or resistance to cold, salt, biotic (*e.g.* insects, pathogenic agents), or other abiotic (*e.g.* herbicide) stresses, are subject to more extensive field performance testing.

APHIS considers several parameters in reaching a DONRS, including whether the GM plant can cross-pollinate with other plants in the wild, and if it can, the ecological consequences (*e.g.* insect resistance, herbicide tolerance) that might result. Extensive databases are maintained on species capable of cross-pollinating with GM crops (*e.g.* corn, soybean, cotton, canola, etc.), based on the results of years of breeding experiments, biological surveys and research conducted by agricultural and weed specialists within APHIS. In instances where out-crossing might be expected to occur, APHIS may stipulate the planting of refuge areas to limit the potential for adverse ecological effects following commercial planting.

AGENCY RESPONSE

APHIS will grant a determination of non-regulated status if the developer can sufficiently demonstrate a lack of plant risk. In making a determination that a GM plant will no longer be regulated, APHIS prepares two documents, an environmental assessment and a DONRS to satisfy regulatory requirements under NEPA and FPPA, respectively.

Both documents are developed based on the review of data submitted as a part of the petition for a DONRS. Once the DONRS has been granted by APHIS, a GM crop no longer requires notification or permit prior to its movement or release within the United States. A review for DONRS is generally completed within 10 months of submitting a formal application to the APHIS, allowing sufficient time for publication in the Federal Register, and opportunity for public comment. Notices of all petitions for a DONRS are published in the Federal Register, and the public is given 60 days to comment for or against the petition, after which APHIS has up to an additional 180 days to either approve or deny it. APHIS provides access to a considerable amount of information relating to approved field trials and petitions received for GM crops. The petition for a

DONRS must include scientific details regarding the genetics of the plant, the nature and origin of the genetic material used, the potential for indirect effects on other plants, and any other information that could be considered unfavourable to the petition.

Extensions of Non-regulated Status

In certain instances, the non-regulated status of a GM crop may be extended to include other varieties of the same crop species, provided that changes in introduced gene sequences are insignificant, and no new plant pest issues would be expected. For an extension, developers must substantiate that the new regulated article poses no serious issues meriting review under separate petition, by providing a precise description of the genetic modifications to the regulated article and a detailed comparison to modifications made in the GM plant previously granted non-regulated status by APHIS. Field trials must be performed under notification or permit to demonstrate the similarities in the phenotypic properties. In support of multiple extensions, product identity standards may be submitted describing the genotypic and phenotypic properties exhibited by new plant varieties considered extensions of an existing DONRS for a GM crop.

Future Considerations

The USDA recently appointed an Advisory Committee for Agricultural Biotechnology that will work in conjunction with the NAS (Standing Committee on Biotechnology Food and Fibre Production, and the Environment) on the completion of a critical review of the regulations and policies used by APHIS in the commercial approval of GM crops. The committee comprises scientists, farmers and representatives of consumer groups and seed companies, and is anticipated to take two years to complete its assignment.

In addition to APHIS, other functional areas within the USDA are beginning to get more actively involved with the regulation of agricultural biotechnology. For example, the Grain Inspection Packers and Stockyards Administration (GIPSA) has made a commitment to work with farmers and industry groups in the development and validation of reliable test methods and quality assurance programms to differentiate GM from non-GM commodities.

As a part of this commitment, GIPSA intends to publish a proposed rule on the standardization of test methods and approaches for the detection and identity preservation of grains. GIPSA is also intending to offer accreditation services for laboratories testing grains for the presence of GM content, and to evaluate commercial test kits to ensure they can be considered accurate and reliable. It is expected that an administrative fee will apply to the accreditation services being offered by GIPSA. The USDA also has made continuous commitments to funding research that will assist federal regulatory agencies in making science-based decisions concerning the safe introduction of GM organisms into the environment. Active areas of research include assessing the potential risks associated with the environmental introduction of GM plants (*e.g.* gene flow), the cumulative effects of large-scale commercial plantings, the potential interactions between GM and non-GM crop species, programmed resistance, and the development of statistical methodology and quantitative approaches to measuring the risks associated with the field testing of GM plants, etc.

Environmental Protection Agency

The EPA has authority over the registration of chemical and biological pesticides under the Federal Insecticide, Fungicide and Rodenticide Act (FIFRA). A pesticide is any product 'intended for preventing, destroying, repelling, or mitigating any pest'. All pesticides require registration by the US EPA prior to their distribution. As a part of the registration process, an applicant is required to submit information and data in support of the safety of a pesticide in its intended use. In addition, US EPA is responsible for establishing acceptable tolerance levels for registered pesticides on or in raw agricultural food commodities under the FFDCA. At any point, US EPA has authority to amend or revoke a registration or residue tolerance, if an adverse effect is observed, or if the risks associated with the use of the pesticide are determined to be unacceptable.

Role

Under the Coordinated Framework, the US EPA was identified as being responsible for the review, assessment and registration of the products of rDNA technology that act as pesticides. Leading up to this publication, the US EPA had acquired considerable expertise in the registration of biological pesticides (*e.g.* microbial). The US EPA was first involved in discussions regarding the potential risks of pesticides developed using rDNA technology in the early 1980s, during a series of public meetings involving the FIFRA Scientific Advisory Panel (SAP) and the Biotechnology Scientific Advisory Committee (BSAC). It was recognized that the potential risks posed by plants modified to express pesticidal components through rDNA technology were unique and warranted additional consideration relative to conventional pesticides. For example, the potential for introduced genetic material to out-cross from a modified plant to a sexually compatible wild or weedy relative through pollen spread was one of the unique, theoretical risks posed by plant-pesticides.

As a result, the EPA proposed a plant-pesticide rule in 1994, outlining their interests in the regulation of products. A package of three proposed final rules was released early in 2001, redefining regulations for plant-incorporated protectants (PIPS), previously referred to as plant-pesticides. Essential elements of the proposed rules for the regulation of GM plants expressing pesticidal traits have been followed since 1994. The final rules provide further clarification of how PIPS will be regulated under FIFRA and FFDCA, including specific exemptions and became effective in September 2001.

Definition of Plant-incorporated Protectants (PIPS) or Plant-pesticides

US EPA's final rule clarifies the regulation of whole plants that contain PIPS. When plants are used intentionally for controlling pests in some way, such uses meet the definition of a pesticide under FIFRA. Nevertheless, the agency exempts the plants themselves from regulation, focussing instead on the substances they contain, previously referred to as plant-pesticides and now known as PIPS. A plant-incorporated protectant (PIP) includes the substance produced by the living plant, and all genetic material necessary for its production (including promoters, enhancers, etc.).

Thus, genes and substances (*e.g.* enzymes) responsible for the conversion of natural plant constituents into pesticidal substances would be considered PIPS. To date, PIPS registered by the US EPA have been proteins and the genes required to make these proteins within the plant. Crops involved include potatoes, cotton, field corn, sweet corn and popcorn.

Clearly, Bt toxins represent the most predominant class of PIPS that have been registered by the US EPA. Major reasons for this include the success of microbial products containing Bt and their long history of use for nearly 40 years. It has been estimated that combined, Bt corn, potato and cotton were cultivated on approximately 10 million acres in 1997, 20 million in 1998, and 29 million in 1999. As a result, less chemical insecticide has been applied, and there have been significantly higher crop yields. In addition, due to reduced opportunity for opportunistic fungal infections of insect-damaged corn, lower levels of mycotoxins have been produced, reducing the toxicological risk to both humans.

Exemptions

US EPA has concluded that living plants with pesticidal activity do not require a high level of regulatory scrutiny by the agency and thus, are exempt from regulation under FIFRA. The agency commented that focussing on the substance produced within the plant, *i.e.* the PIP eliminates any need for the US EPA to register plants, thus conserving agency resources and reducing potential overlap with other agencies, notably the USDA. For example, although whole plants that are used as biological control agents themselves, such as chrysanthemums, are exempt, substances that are extracted from plants, such as the insecticidal material pyrethrum, are not excluded from regulation under FIFRA. Further exemptions have been proposed, based on familiarity and presence of the pesticidal substances in the food supply. Only one of the additional proposed exemptions has been included in the final rule, and all others have been proposed for further public comment. Within the final rule, EPA has exempted PIPS and encoding genetic material originating from plants sexually compatible through conventional breeding but not through rDNA technology. The rationale for this exemption is that such substances could be bred, either naturally or through conventional plant breeding, from close plant relatives that share genetic material from a common gene pool.

On the other hand, genetic modifications that were never before possible can be made using rDNA technology, involving the genes from sexually incompatible plant species. Therefore, the exemption of plant-pesticides developed using rDNA technology, involving genes from sexually compatible plants has not been finalized as a part of the supplementary proposal to the final rules for PIPS. Other exemptions for further comment have also been identified within the supplemental proposal. The first group are PIPS that 'act primarily by affecting the plant'. The group have in common some sort of defence mechanism such that a pest would be less able to attach to, penetrate, or successfully invade a plant. Examples include:

- Some sort of structural barrier such as wax or plant hairs;
- Inactivation of or resistance to a pest or substance (*e.g.* toxin) produced by a pest;
- Creation of a deficiency in a nutrient or growth factor required by a pest;
- Hypersensitivity response that would contain or limit spread of the pest (*e.g.* necrosis of surrounding plant tissue, creating a functional barrier);
- Plant hormones that are naturally occurring but with change can affect a plant in a variety of ways with potentially dramatic results.

Herbicide-tolerant Crops

In the case of herbicide-tolerant crops, EPA determines whether the property of increased resistance may encourage higher rates or more extensive application of an agricultural chemical to food crops. The higher exposures to herbicides would be subject to evaluation through risk assessment, requiring the submission and review of detailed data. If the risk is determined to be acceptable, a herbicide product would require label extensions for the addition of new tolerant crop varieties.

Experimental Use Permit (EUP)

Small-scale research involving PIPS is covered under the permit and notification process that exists for new plant varieties administered by APHIS. The US EPA requires that an Experimental Use Permit (EUP) be obtained for all research and field testing involving greater than 10 acres of a plant modified to express a pesticidal substance. The EUP process allows a developer to gather the product use, performance, residue and other types of data, required in support of the registration of PIPS. All US EPA decisions concerning applications for EUPs are published within the Federal Register for comment.

Registration requirements

For the registration of a plant-incorporated protectant, the EPA evaluates the potential impact, on human health and the environment, of the pesticide substance and of the genetic material necessary for its expression within the modified plant. With this in mind, the EPA developed their guidance for evaluating the safety of PIPS based on data requirements that were established for microbial pesticides.

A number of modifications to the reporting requirements were required to focus the assessment on non-target toxicity rather than pathogenicity, as well as to evaluate the expression of the pesticide substance within the plant itself, rather than by spraying, etc. Although specific reporting requirements for the registration of PIPS are established on a case-by-case basis by the EPA, the general categories of information and data required in support of the registration of a plant-pesticide include:

- Product characterization
- Toxicology
- Environmental fate and exposure
- Non-target organism effects
- If necessary, plans for pest resistance management.

The EPA continues to hold meetings of their SAP to re-evaluate the reporting requirements that have been established for PIPS and to ensure that all potential human health and environmental concerns are being addressed as new scientific information becomes available. In addition, the developers of PIPS are encouraged to consult with US EPA during all phases of the research and development process, particularly when it concerns an environmental release.

Product Characterization

Product characterization allows for consideration of any potential hazard(s) that might be associated with anticipated exposure to a plant-incorporated protectant. This process includes a review of the source of introduced genetic material, including all regulatory sequences, the modifications that have been made, methods of transformation, inheritance, stability and expression in the host plant. For the introduced pesticidal substance, the anticipated modes of action, specificity and toxicity to both target and non-target organisms are evaluated. Target organisms may include weeds, insects and diseases (viral, bacterial, and fungal) affecting a crop. The crop itself, as a volunteer weed, may also be of concern following crop rotations. Once a PIP and any potential for exposure have been characterized, the data required in support of an environmental and human health risk assessment can be defined.

Ecological Effects

Environmental fate and exposure are important considerations when evaluating the potential impact of PIPS on the environment or on non-target organisms (*e.g.* wildlife, beneficial insects). Depending on the crop and introduced pesticide substance, data on the level of expression and rate of degradation may be required, first for the tissues of the modified plant, and secondly, the fate in soil, water, or any other environmental compartment. Such data allow the potential for exposure to the pesticide substance to be evaluated for non-target organisms via feeding on, or through decomposition of, the modified plants.

Studies are arranged in tiers, starting with Tier I, consisting of acute toxicology and basic characterization studies that help predict environmental fate. Depending on the results obtained in Tier I, and the level of concern, additional studies may be requested from higher tiers. It is expected that most PIPS will only undergo Tier I testing, since negative results are expected at relatively high exposure levels.

The 'maximum hazard approach' when used in Tier I provides a high level of assurance that adverse effects would not be expected to occur under actual conditions of use within the field. If the results of Tier I reveal a potential hazard at doses within the range of expected concentrations in the environment, additional studies would be requested in higher tiers to better characterize the potential for any kind of effect.

Data requirements may be satisfied by generating test data or by requests for data waivers with credible justification. The type and extent of dietary studies required will depend on properties of the crop and on the introduced pesticide substance. Dietary studies typically involve feeding plant tissues (*e.g.* grain, pollen) that express the PIP or that have been spiked with the pesticidal substance. However, when determined necessary, the pure pesticidal substance may be administered to non-target species at doses of up to 10 to 100 times the expected level of exposure in the field. Dependent upon the potential for exposure, additional studies may also be requested involving any number of other non-target organisms (*e.g.* honeybees, green lacewing, ladybird beetles, parasitic wasps, earthworms, etc.). When toxicity is observed, the potential for exposure becomes an important consideration when ascertaining whether an adverse effect might be expected under actual conditions of use in the field.

The requirement for provision of a resistance management plan is not routine practise for PIPS, but depends on an evaluation of the potential for resistance to develop and the threat to existing or functionally equivalent pest management practises.

To date, resistance management plans have only been placed on Bt PIPS. If considered appropriate, the EPA may request that a resistance management plan be submitted as a part of a condition for registration. A resistance management plan may require a commitment towards the generation of additional research data, to implement structured refuges, to perform annual resistance monitoring, to initiate remedial action plans, and to educate growers. The EPA has worked closely with academia, other federal agencies, public interest groups, industry, and growers, to establish resistance management plans based on the most current science.

Human Health Effects

For agricultural food crops, special consideration is given to evaluating the safety of the pesticidal substance introduced as a component of consumed foods. Rodents (often mice, to conserve test material) are orally administered the pesticide substance at doses of up to 100 000 times the levels of expected human consumption as a part of the diet.

Although the modified plant tissues would be considered the most appropriate vehicle for determining the acute toxicity of a PIP, it is not typically feasible, since only small amounts of the pesticidal substance are present in plant materials. Therefore, an alternative source (*e.g.* microbial) is often used to generate a sufficient amount of identical pesticide substance for testing purposes. In this case, the equivalency of the test substance obtained from an alternative source to the PIP (*e.g.* composition, identity, etc.) being expressed within the plant is an important consideration that must be well documented.

For pesticide substances that are proteins, the principal concern relates to the potential for the introduction of a new allergen or toxin into the food supply. Since most allergenic food proteins are stable to digestion, *in vitro* digestibility studies are used to predict how long a pesticidal substance may persist in digestive fluids (*e.g.* gastric, intestinal) following ingestion. In addition, heat stability studies are performed to provide an indication of the fate of the PIP during food processing.

Commonly, assays of amino acid sequence homology are performed to determine similarity to substances that are known to pose unique safety concerns (*e.g.* toxins, allergens). The EPA uses a 'decision tree' approach similar to that followed by the FDA in assessing the potential allergenicity of a new food protein. In many instances, US EPA and US FDA collaborate with each other when evaluating issues of safety for new pesticidal proteins being expressed in GM food crops.

Residue Tolerances for Plant-incorporated Protectants

Analogous to the consideration of tolerances for residues of conventional pesticides, the US EPA reviews data on the human, animal and environmental safety of PIPS to determine whether residue tolerances should be established for the amounts expected to be present in foods derived from the GM plant. Under Section 408 of the FFDCA, if the GM plant expressing a PIP is a food crop, the US EPA is obligated to establish the 'safe level' of pesticide residue allowed, or tolerance level.

The Food Quality Protection Act (FQPA) served to amend the FFDCA and FIFRA by outlining the process by which the safety of pesticide residues on raw or processed foods can be established. Under this process, in order for a pesticide residue to be considered safe, a 'reasonable certainty of no harm' must exist assuming aggregate exposure of the public, taking into consideration sensitive children within the population. To date, all pesticidal proteins that have been registered as PIPS have been determined to be non-toxic, and as a result, have been considered exempt from the requirement to establish a tolerance under the FFDCA.

Consistent with categorical exemptions as originally proposed for plant-pesticides under FIFRA, the US EPA also proposed that tolerances might not be required for pesticidal substances derived from sexually compatible plants, regardless of the process used to introduce the PIP, provided that the genetic material encoding the pesticidal substance was from a plant commonly used as food, and that the presence of the pesticidal substance in a host plant did not result in any new or significantly different dietary exposures. Final rules include exemptions from tolerances for the residues of PIPS, and their encoding nucleic acids, but only for PIPS derived through the conventional breeding of sexually compatible plants. US EPA is requesting further comment on the possible exemption from the requirement of a tolerance for:

- PIPS derived through rDNA technology;
- PIPS that act by affecting plant defences;
- PIPS developed based on viral coat proteins.

Future Considerations

The US EPA anticipates that the requirements for the registration of PIPS will continue to evolve as the science and policies relating to biotechnology continue to mature. In light of on-going criticisms that the plant-pesticide rule has received since its publication in 1994, a number of stakeholder workshops have been hosted by the US EPA. In March 1999, the House Agricultural Subcommittee hosted a congressional hearing to address a number of these concerns. One of the primary questions addressed was whether the definition of a pesticide under FIFRA provides the US EPA with the authority to regulate pest-protected plants that have been developed using rDNA technology.

Another concern was that the proposed rule was too broad in scope because all plants have natural defence mechanisms, and as such, would be classified as 'plant-pesticides'. In addition, an exemption from the plant-pesticide rule for those plants not developed using rDNA technology would serve to regulate the process used in the development of the GM plant, rather than on the pesticidal substance being produced within the plant. Further criticism related to the use of the term 'plant-pesticide' in relation to the products of the genes that had been introduced into GM crops.

As a part of its final rule, the US EPA recommended that plant-pesticides be renamed PIPS, an alternative name which distinguishes them from the other types of pesticide products requiring registration with the US EPA. A new FIFRA section has been added to the Code of Federal Regulations specific to the regulation of PIPS.

In doing so, the US EPA has acknowledged that the new final rule would be making a distinction between the products of conventional breeding and rDNA technology, *i.e.* regulating on the basis of process not product. One reason given for this divergence was that the use of this criterion would be expected to provide the public with increased confidence that an appropriate level of regulatory oversight was in place for assessing the risks of rDNA technology, which is a societal not scientific issue.

SAPs are charged with providing the Office of Pesticide Programms (OPP) of the US EPA with advice and guidance on human health and environmental issues relating to proposed regulatory decisions for pesticides, including PIPS, based on the latest scientific data. For example, the SAP for Bt Plant Pesticides met three times in the year 2000 to consider issues related to the safety of plants that had been genetically modified to express insect-specific Bt toxins.

The US EPA released a decision to temporarily extend registrations for all currently registered pest protected plants throughout the 2001 growing season. Additional provisions, such as the recently strengthened resistance management requirements for plant-pesticides, along with the original registration conditions, were considered to provide adequate protection during the extended time period. In addition, the reassessment process for these products has been designed to assure maximum transparency and opportunity for public comment in the regulatory decision-making process.

CONCLUDING COMMENTS

The US FDA has been praised for its science-based regulatory approach to evaluating the safety of products developed using rDNA technology based on the characteristics of the food product, and not the means by which it has been created. On the other hand, the regulatory approach of both the USDA and US EPA has been criticized for discriminating against the products of rDNA technology.

A consortium of 11 major international scientific societies and the Council on Agricultural Science and Technology (CAST), an organization representing 36 scientific and professional groups, have strongly criticized the US EPA for their proposed approach to regulating plant-pesticides on the basis of the process used in its development rather than the characteristics exhibited by the plant. More recently, the US Congressional Committee on Biotechnology released a report entitled 'Seeds of Opportunity' recommending revisions to the USDA and US EPA approaches to the regulation of GM plants. It was felt that the proposals by both agencies failed to take into consideration the current scientific consensus on the potential risks associated with agricultural biotechnology. Overall, the report was supportive of the science-based policy of regulation, based on the characteristics of a food product and not on the means by which it was created.

As a part of their role, each federal regulatory agency involved in assessing the human health and environmental safety of GM crops attempts to ensure that only the most current scientific data, information, and methods are referenced. The US FDA consults a Food Advisory Committee, the US EPA refers questions to Scientific Advisory Panels, and the USDA has recently established its own advisory panel. Aside from periodic reviews by credible independent research organizations such as NAS, the individual policies of each agency have been subject to regular review for harmonization with approaches recommended by international standard-setting bodies, such as OECD, WHO and FAO.

It is expected that many of the future food products of rDNA technology in agriculture may not be equivalent in composition to their conventional counterparts. However, the existing decision-tree approach to regulation anticipates these types of improved food products, and provides for the case-by-case assessment of their safety. Field testing and pre-market review for food safety provide the required level of assurance that the foods derived from the application of rDNA technology in agriculture are at least as safe as existing foods, and are consistent with all existing standards of food safety.

All new varieties of vegetables, fruit, corn and soybeans developed using rDNA technology have been subject to considerable scientific and regulatory review by the US FDA, the USDA and/or the US EPA. As such, the developers of new crop varieties have had to take into consideration not only the interests of farmers, food processors and consumers, but also the expectations of regulatory authorities.

Both regulators and consumers have had a number of opportunities to influence the acceptance of a new crop variety, and continue to have significant influence beyond final regulatory approval and commercial introduction. It is expected that the issues of human health and environmental safety will continue to be of major concern in the future as a greater number of GM food products reach later stages of commercial development. A recent trend has been observed towards the commercialization of products that offer more transparent benefits and value to consumers. The new products of rDNA technology will be expected to further challenge the flexibility that has been exhibited by the US regulatory process. As a result, both industry and regulatory authorities will need to be responsive to uphold the human health and safety record achieved for GM product introductions. The vast majority of the new products of rDNA technology are not expected to be commercially available until after 2005.

The crops and foods improved through rDNA technology have been developed with much more precision, and their human health and environmental safety has been assessed in more depth and detail than any other crops and foods developed using more conventional means. They are routinely evaluated for any potential impact on both the environment and food safety. Despite years of experience and research, no verifiable data implicating rDNA technology as a food safety or environmental hazard have presented themselves.

The research and development of GM crops have been performed under extremely controlled conditions and tight regulatory oversight from research and development within the laboratory through field trials and commercial planting for food-use. Based on evaluations conducted to date, no evidence exists to suggest that GM foods currently sold on the market pose any significant human health concerns or that they are in any way less safe than foods derived from crops developed through more conventional means.

Although the foods developed using rDNA technology have been subject to rigourous scientific review for safety, the US regulatory system has allowed for considerable advancement in the application of the technology, and significant product innovation. To continue to be successful, it is recognized that the US FDA, USDA and US EPA will need to cooperate: the approval process must be clear, timely and transparent; emphasis must be on science-based/risk-based regulatory assessments and decisions; the regulatory process must be flexible to adapt to new information; and, the agencies must be staffed by full-time, highly qualified scientists in many diverse fields.

Over the past 25 years, the approach to regulating the products of agricultural biotechnology has evolved in response to the experience gained during the research and development of applications for rDNA technology. In the future, as the number of products developed using rDNA technology continues to increase, additional research will be needed to better evaluate any potential effects on human health and the environment, and to further refine the scientific basis of making regulatory decisions.

Within the United States, the regulatory approach to evaluating the safety of products developed using rDNA technology continues to evolve as new applications continue to emerge and our understanding of the potential risks improves. To date, existing regulations have proven adequate to assure the safety of all new products developed using rDNA technology, and additional innovation has not been discouraged. Accordingly, the National Research Council has recommended that any new rules for the regulation of GM plants be sufficiently flexible enough to reflect improvements in scientific understanding. In the future, as rDNA technology finds broader application, and the new prospects for this technology become commercial realities, the regulatory approaches to evaluating the safety of GM food crops are expected to evolve accordingly.

APPLICATION OF SUPPLEMENTARY FEED

Supplementary feed is a very essential input in culture fisheries because natural food available in a pond is insufficient for rapid growth and higher production of fish.

The supplementary feed comprising rice polish, mustard oil cake, mishmeal agrimin, vitamin, mineral mixtures etc. are provided to the pond by placing in the four corners of the pond or provided in the tray mooring in a bamboo pole placed in the pond, to minimize wastage of feed which covers around 50 per cent of the recurring cost per annum. The feed is provided two times in equal amount in the morning and in the afternoon@ 2–3 per cent of their body weight. The feeding schedule to be practiced is as follows:

Feeding Schedule: (A)

- Single stocking single harvesting (SSSH):2–2.5 per cent of biomass–5000kg/ha/year
- Single stocking multiple harvesting (SSMH):2.5-3 per cent of biomass-8500kg/ha/yr
- Multiple stocking and multiple harvesting(MSMH): 2–2.5 per cent of biomass–6000kg/ha/year

Considering 10 per cent initial mortality ** Sale of 40 per cent fishes attaining a growth of around 400 gm in case of SSMH

Feeding Schedule: (B)

- Considering 10 per cent initial mortality *Sale of 40 per cent fishes attaining a growth of around 400 gm
- 35 per cent Harvesting = approx. 950 kg (1st phase) and Harvesting = 650 kg (2nd phase)

HEALTH CARE AND POND HYGIENE MAINTENANCE

Before releasing the fingerlings, a dip treatment for 1 minute should be given with 3 per cent KM_nO_4 (potassium permanganate) using water from the stocking pond. Alternatively 2 to 3 per cent common salt solution may also be used. In case of any parasitic infestation like Argulus sp, malathion @ 0.25–0.5 ppm 3–4 times at weekly interval can completely eliminate the parasite.

Test netting must be carried out periodically for ensuring growth and health status of the cultured fishes once in a month. CIFAX or WS Sukrena should be used at 0.01 ppm or @ 1 litre/ha- meter in water as prophylactic measure against Eqizootic Ulcerative Syndrome for reducing the stress factors by increasing pH, total alkalinity and total hardness of water. Therapeutic application of CaO @ 100 kg/ha depending upon the pH status of water is effective in checking the spread of disease when initial symptoms of EUS is seen. Application of CaO should follow only after one week of application of bleaching powder @ 1 mg/litre.

Application of 2 per cent solution of Common salt (NaCl) not only kills several disease organisms but may also have positive effects on the fish by stimulating appetite and increasing mucus secretion and improving resistance to handling. Excess levels, however, may stress the fish.

The three main causes of diseases are:

1. Improper and insufficient feeding.
2. Stress through extremes or toxic condition.
3. Attack by disease organisms.

The points to be considered for keeping the fish healthy are:

- Proper hygienic conditions should be maintained in the farm.
- Test netting should be done at monthly intervals for monitoring disease and growth.
- Behaviour of fish should be observed every morning.

Pond Bottom Raking

In order to remove toxic gasses from the pond bottom and overall improvement of pond environment, bottom raking should be done with a rope fixed with several sinks. When it is pulled, the sinks hit the surface of pond bottom and help emit toxic gases from the pond. The rope should be pulled 2–3 times a week.

Control of Algal Bloom

To control the bloom, following steps have to be taken to maintain hygiene of the pond:

- Suspension of fertilization.
- Suspension of supplementary feeding
- Prevention of light penetration: Light penetration into the pond is prevented in order to stop photosynthesis of phytoplankton by a temporary vegetative cover on the pond surface. Floating aquatic weeds such as water hyacinth, Pistia, etc., are used for this purpose.
- Reducing nutrients in pond water: Introduction of aquatic macrophytes such as water hyacinth, Pistia, etc., can reduce the nutrient level in pond water thus discouraging multiplication of phytoplankton.

YIELD

After farming 10–12 months based on the magnitude of the farming practices adopted a fish production of 3,000–6000 kg/ha/yr can be achieved.

It is established that the culture of fish is a highly profitable venture. The unemployed youth of our state may go for fish culture practices to earn their livelihood by adopting improved method of fish farming.

Fig. Scheme–Wise Expenditure, Production and Income

Sl	Culture Method	Input Cost (₹./ha/Year)	Production (Kg/ha/Year)	Income (₹.)	Net Profit (₹.)
1	Single Stocking Single Harvesting	79,000/-	4500	2,25,000/-	1,46,000/-
2	Single Stocking Multiple Harvesting	1,14,000/-	5500	2,75,000/-	1,61,000/-
3	Multiple Stocking Multiple Harvesting	1,13,000/-	6000	3,00,000/-	1,87,000/-

STEPS IN FEED FORMULATION

The first step in diet formulation is balancing the crude protein and energy levels. This can be accomplished by trial and error, by the square method for either crude protein level or energy level and then adjusting, or by solving simultaneous equations. At first, it is helpful to use at least three feeds tuffs during the initial balancing of protein and energy levels: one high in protein and high in ME, one low or intermediate in protein and high in ME and one low or intermediate in both protein and ME. Once practice makes one more proficient at diet formulation any number of feedstuffs can be used. One must remember to reserve room in the formulation for any feed additive, such as a vitamin or mineral pre-mix.

The second step in diet formulation is to check the levels of indispensable amino acids in the formulation to be sure the dietary levels meet the requirements of the animal to be fed. The requirements of fish for indispensable amino acids is expressed as the dietary level (as a per cent of the diet) or as a per cent of the dietary protein level.

To convert an amino acid level from the per cent of diet to per cent of protein, divide the dietary level of each amino acid by the dietary protein level. It might be of interest to calculate the dietary levels of all of the indispensable amino acids, but it is not practical to do it all of the time. If the levels of arginine, lysine, methionine and tryptophan meet the dietary requirements of the fish to be fed, the levels of the other six indispensable amino acids will most likely be above required levels. When using unconventional protein supplements, the levels of all ten indispensable amino acids should be checked. If the diet formulation is low in any amino acid, a feedstuff that contains high levels of that amino acid must be added to the diet at the expense of another ingredient. Once the amino acid requirements are met, the dietary protein and energy levels must be rechecked to, see if any substitution of ingredients has imbalanced the formulation.

A diet mixing sheet should be constructed to standardize diet formulation. The amino acids listed are for illustration purposes only and may be changed to suit different circumstances. In practical feed formulation, pellet quality and acceptability must be considered in addition to nutrient levels and cost. These considerations will vary from species to species and with the type of pellet being made and are dealt with in other sections of this manual.

BEST-BUY TECHNIQUES

The price of the feedstuffs used in diet formulations must be considered to formulate a cost-efficient diet. Feedstuffs can be compared with one another on the basis cost per unit of protein, energy, or amino acid.

For example, suppose one has wheat middlings and wheat millrun available for a fish diet, which feedstuff would be the least expensive source of energy?

Wheat millrun costs US $ 0.0858/kg and contains about 1200 kcal ME/kg.

$$\text{Cost/kcal} = \frac{.08758}{1200} = \text{US \$ 0.0000/15/kcal.}$$

Wheat middlings cost US $ 01883/kg and contain 1663 kcal ME/kg.

$$\text{Cost/kcal} = \frac{0.1883}{1663} = \text{US \$ 0.0001132/kcal.}$$

Thus, the wheat millrun which has a lower ME value for fish is the better buy because it costs less per kcal.

To compare oat groats and wheat middlings on a cost per unit ME basis one would do the following:

Wheat middlings = US$ 0.0001132/kcal and

Oat groats cost US $ 0.2652/kg and contain about 2450 kcal ME/kg.

$$\text{Cost/kcal} = \frac{0.2652}{2450} = \text{US \$ 0.001082/kcal.}$$

Oats groats, although costing more than wheat middlings, constitute a better buy on an energy basis.

The cost of protein is often the greatest part of the cost of a fish diet. Therefore, substantial savings can be made by using best-buy techniques to determinate least expensive protein supplement. To compare anchovy meal and herring meal, the following calculations are made:

Anchovy meal costs US \$ 0.5357/kg and contains 70.9 per cent protein.

$$\text{Cost per kg protein} = \frac{0.5357}{0.709} = \text{US \$ 0.7556/kg protein.}$$

Herring meal costs US \$ 0.4709/kg and contains 76.7 per cent protein.

$$\text{Cost per kg protein} = \frac{0.4709}{0.767} = \text{US \$ 0.61395/kg protein.}$$

On the basis of cost per unit protein, herring meal is less expensive as a dietary ingredient than is anchovy meal.

To compare feedstuffs on the basis of cost per unit of an amino acid, one can calculate the best buy in the same way as before. For example, sesame oil cake which has twice as much methionine content as does groundnut cake on a per unit protein basis would be a more attractive buy at comparable prices. These kinds of comparisons are only valid if the nutrient in one feedstuff is as valuable or available to the animal as the same nutrient in another feed. Such comparisons should be made whenever prices change.

FEEDING HABITS OF COMMON CARP AND CRUCIAN CARP

At the larval stage, feeding habits of the two are basically similar. They chiefly feed on rotifer, cladoceran, copepoda, chironomid larvae and other insects' larvae. Common carp and Crucian carp about 50 *mm* in body length tend to be omnivorous. Common carp are inclined to be more carnivorous, whereas Crucian carp more herbivorous. Both have feeding habits of phagotrophy. The pharyngeal teeth of Common carp are relatively developed, molarshaped in 3 rows, with transverse grooves on the rest of the inner row except the first tooth, which is smooth.

Common carp display a wide adaptation to foods. Their common natural foods are benthos such as snails, young clams, corbicula spp. cladocera, copepod, chironomid larvae, shrimps and insects' larvae. Also they take certain amount of detritus of higher aquatic plants and plant seeds. The nasal bone of Common carp is well developed so that their premaxilla and mandible could be projected out like a tube to dig the mud for organic detritus. Foods for Crucian carp are chiefly large amounts of detritus, diatom, filament algae, aquatic grasses and plant seeds, including a certain amount of cladocera, copepod, chironomid larvae and water earthworm etc. Under culture conditions, Common carp and Crucian carp also like to take commercial feeds such as oil seed cakes, brans, crops and silkworm pupae, etc.

FEEDING HABITS OF CHINESE BREAM WUCHANG FISH

At larval stage, Chinese bream feed mainly on zooplankton such as cladocera and copepod, whereas, at adult stage, mainly on aquatic grass such as Vallisneria spiralis, Hydrilla verticillata, and Potamogeton malainus and secondarily on Potamogeton crispus, Myriophyllum spicatum, Spirogyra and plant detritus. With a mouth small in size, and the pharyngeal teeth and callous pad small and weak, the ability and intensity of food intake of Wuchang fish fail to come up with Grass carp.

FEEDING HABITS OF MUD CARP

With a small mouth, transverse in inferior position, under the natural conditions, mud carp use the bony edges of upper and lower jaws to scrape diatom, green algae chlamydomonas and filament algae etc. attached to stones and something else. Not seldom, they take detritus of higher plants, bottom humus and a little zooplankton as feeds. Under culture conditions, they like to eat commercial feeds such as seedcakes, dregs, brans, and animal manures.

FEEDING HABITS OF TILAPIA

Tilapia are omnivorous fish, with a tendancy to be herbivorous. Tilapia feed mainly on zooplankton at larval stage. The scope of food enlarges with the growth. The usual common foods are all kinds of planktonic, benthic and epiphytic algae, tender higher aquatic plants, all organic detritus and a little animal feeds such as earthworms, small shrimps and aquatic insects.

Tilapia nilotica, possessing denser gill rakers, are more likely to feed on phytoplankton and could utilize the green algae Chlorophyta and blue algae Cyanophyceae which can not be digested by other fishes, but detritus occupies greater proportion among the natural feeds for Tilapia mossambica because they only have 14—19 gill rakers. Under culture conditions they can utilize all kinds of vegetable leaves tender grass, animal manures brans, seed cake and pelleted feeds if applied. At a proper temperature, they ability and intensity of their food intake are much higher.

GROWTH

The growth rate is an important criterion to evaluate production efficiency. Silver carp, Bighead, Grass carp, Black carp and Common carp, with the features of large size and speedy growth, have been taken as the dominant cultured species for polyculture in Chinese integrated fish farms, whereas Crucian carp, Wuchang fish and Mud carp, owing, to smaller size and slower growth are usually regarded as a secondary species for polyculture so as to raise per-unit fish yield. As a mass production, the latter are well-known species for high yields. The growth rate of every kind of fish involves genetics of species, besides, it's also closely related to water quality, water temperature, nourishment, stocking density and management. As a rule, the growth of body in length and weight is absolutely the fastest before the first sexual maturity, then it will slow down and even stop.

GROWTH OF SILVER CARP AND BIGHEAD

It is the second year that Silver carp grow the fastest. After the fourth year the growth rate decreases during th period of the 3rd—6th years, Silver carp gain the maximum weight. Bighead have the fastest growth during the period of the 2nd—3rd year, and gain the maximum growth in weight in the 3rd year.

GROWTH OF GRASS CARP AND BLACK CARP

Grass carp have the fastest increase in length during the period of the 1st—2nd years, and gain the maximum growth in weight during the period of the 2nd—3rd years. Black carp have the fastest increase in length during the period of the 1st—2nd years, and gain the maximum growth in weight during the period of the 3rd—4th years.

GROWTH OF COMMON CARP,

Crucian carp and Wuchang fish Common carp have the fastest increase in length during the period of the 1st—2nd years. The female fish grow faster than the male fish, and Common carp gain the maximum growth in weight during the period of the 4th—5th years. Crucian carp, have the fastest increase in length in the first year and gain the max growth in weight during the period of the 4th—5th years. Wuchang fish have the fastest growth during the period of 1st—2nd years, afterwards, the growth rate decreases gradually, and they gain the max growth in weight in the second year.

Table. Relationship Between the Age and the Growth of Main Cultured Fish

	Species	Silver Carp	Bighead	Grass Carp	Black Carp	Common Carp	Crucian Carp	Wuchang Fish
Age								
Item								
Max Increase in Length		2	2–3	1–2	1–2	1–2	1	1–1
Max Growth in Weight		3–6	3	2–3	3–4	4–5	4–5	2

GROWTH OF MUD CARP

Mud carp have the fastest increase in length but gain the minimum growth in weight in the 1st year. The increase in length will slow down gradually. Sexual maturity begins in the 3rd year with the continuation of gaining weight.

Table. Growth Rate of Mud Carp Reared in Ponds

Item	Age	1	2	3	4	5	6
Body Measurement	Absolute	14.5	23.4	26.1	29.2	33.6	36.5
Length (cm) Increase	Annual	14.5	8.9	2.7	3.1	4.4	2.9
Body	Absolute Measurement	70.9	257.9	354.5	499.1	739.3	969.5

Weight (g)	Annual Increase	70.9	187.0	96.6	144.6	240.2	230.2

NATURAL REPRODUCTION

Propagation of Silver Carp, Bighead, Grass Carp, Black Carp and Mud Carp

The natural spawning grounds of Silver carp, Grass carp and Black carp are vastly distributed in Pearl River, Qiantangjiang River, Changjiang River, Huaihc River, northwards up to Heilongjiang River systems, while those of Bighead mainly in Changjiang River, Huaihe River and Pearl River. Mud carp, as a subtropic species have the spawning-ground distribution in the southern part of China like Hainan Island, Guangdong, Guangxi, Fujian and Yunnan. Among all these river systems mentioned above, the spawning grounds of Changjiang River and Pearl River are the biggest. Quantities of fry of Silver carp, Bighead, Grass carp and Black carp proliferate in Changjiang River and Pearl River systems.

Chinese carps usually like to stay in the lower reaches of rivers, or river branches or lakes for fattening, where the water current is slow and the water is fertile with abundance of food.

When the spawning season is drawing near, the spawning schools begin to gather schooling and to migrate towards the middle and upper course spawning grounds. At that time, the gonads of thc broodfish have, in a great majority of cases, reached Stage *IV* while the gonads of the male fish have reached Stage *V*. If the ecological conditions in the spawning grounds are suitable for reproduction, they will proceed to spawn.

As for the main cultivated fishes in China, the spawning time in different river systems varies with the climatic conditions, but all in the summer. In Changjiang River drainage, Silver carp and Grass carp generally start spawning in late April to early May and Bighead in mid or late May, whereas in Pearl River Drainage, the spawning season begins in mid or late April, a little later for Bighead.

As a rule, the North is later than the South by 1—2 months. After July, the fry production is apparently reducing. During this period, the matured brood fish are ready to spawn in the spawning places when the water level of rivers rises and the temperature goes above 18°*C* below 30°*C*. Anyhow, the optimum temperature for spawning is 22°*C*—28°*C*.

As a subtropic species, Mud carp need a little higher temperature for spawning with the optimum temperature of 26°*C*—30°*C*, starting from late May through August and September.

Under the stimulation of proper ecological conditions (generally for about 20 hours). Spawning behaviours could be seen when the spawning schools of

Silver carp and Grass carp arrive in spawning grounds. There are two common forms—on water surface and under water.

Spawning on water surface is termed "floating spawning" and the latter "muffled spawning".

In "floating spawning", the estrus could be seen that males chase females excitedly, often bumping against the abdomen of the female with their head in swift swimming, jumping out of the water, then splashing in waves. Sometimes, the male and female would float on their backs with their pectoral fins vibrating violently.

When it reaches the climax of the estrus, the female and male discharge eggs and milt respectively. The eggs will be fertilized in the water. As for "muffled spawning", the action would take place under the water. Occasionally waves aroused by chasing could be seen on the surface. More often than not, the male fish are the overwelming majority in spawning schools. For Silver carp the male are 93.7 per cent on average and for Grass carp 77.5 per cent.

Table. Sex Composition of Silver Carp and Grass Carp in Spawning Schools

Drainage	Changjiang River			Xijiang River			Songhuajian River			Average	
Sex ratio Species	Number (ind.)	♂ (%)	♀ (%)	Number (ind.)	♂ (%)	♀ (%)	Number (ind.)	♂ (%)	♀ (%)	♂ (%)	♀ (%)
Silver carp	149	97.2	2.8	33	88	12	172	96	4	93.4	6.3
Grass carp	112	77.7	3.3	40	75	25		80*	20*	77.5*	22.5*

The age and body weight of spawning schools vary with regions: In Pearl River drainage, smaller in size; earlier in maturity, generally, one year earlier than in Changjiang River drainage. and in Heilongjiang River 1—2 years later than in Changjiang River.

Table. Age and Size of Spawning Schools of Silver Carp, Bighead, Grass Carp, Black Carp (in Changjiang) and Mud Carp (in Pearl River)

Species	Silver Carp		Bighead		Grass Carp		Black Carp		Mud Carp	
Sex	♀	♂	♀	♂	♀	♂	♀	♂	♀	♂
Item										
Age	4	3	3-10	3-7	4	3	4-15	3-10	3	2
Body weight (kg)	7-14	5-13	9-25	7-21	5-19	4-13	15-30	10-25	0.53	

The brood amount of Silver carp, Bighead, Grass carp and Black carp is great and the measurement is usually done by way of sampling. It consists of the absolute and the relative brood amounts. The former refers to the total quantity of eggs borne by a fish in one spawning season, while the latter means the quantity of eggs per gram of female body weight in one spawning season. There is no relation-ship between eggs/g of ovary and fish size.

Table Brood Amount of Silver Carp, Bighead, Grass Carp and Black Carp (Changjiang River)

Item / Species	Average Body Weight (g)	Average Ovary Weight (g)	Average Absolute Brood Amount (Piece)	Average Relative Brood Amount (Piece)	Eggs/ovary (g)	Average Maturity Coefficient (%)
Silver Carp	7,900	1,190	1,035,000	131.0	869.7	15.1
Bighead	19,900	2,710	1,925,000	96.7	710.3	13.6
Grass Carp	9,200	1,310	830,000	90.2	633.4	14.2
Black Carp	22,900	2,520	2,131,000	93.1	845.1	11.0

$$Note: Maturity\ coefficient = \frac{weight\ of\ gonad}{gross\ body\ weight} \times 100$$

The eggs of Silver carp, Bighead, Grass carp, Black carp and Mud carp are separated and non-adhesive, The discharged eggs expand by absorbing the water through egg membrane and become plump, transparent and elastic. With a bigger specific gravity than water, they will sink to the bottom in still water and yet, they are semibuoyant in the currents, floating in the water till the fry come into being.

Thc incubation of eggs requires about the same temperature as needed in the spawning of brooders, between 18°C and 30°C with the optimum temperature of 22°–28°C. The speed of embryonic development is in positive proportion with water temperature.

PROPAGATION OF COMMON CARP AND CRUCIAN CARP

With the wide distribution, Common carp and Crucian carp do not require strict environmental conditions in the development of gonads and in the process of reproduction; therefore, their natural propagation can be easily found in the still or running waters of the South and the North.

Their spawning season generally comes at the end of March to early April in the southern part of China, April-May in the northern part of China, and June in the northeast part of China; however, it begins as early as in late December in Pearl River basin. Although the spawning season makes its start at different times, the demand for water temperature is identical, 18°C above for Common carp and 20°C above for Crucian carp. As the eggs of Common carp and Crucian carp are adhesive, the fundamental condition for spawning is the materials (aquatic plants or resemblances) for the eggs to adhere to.

The spawning is in full flourish from midnight till dawn. But it's possible that they could spawn in the whole day if environmental conditions are favourable. In estrus, two to three, males chase one female, and the male will hit their head against the female's belly time and again so as to make the female lying on its side towards the aquatic plants. In a minute, the female spawns while the male discharges milt. The action of spawning repeats so many times, that the matured eggs could be discharged in large amounts. And then the eggs could stick to the aquatic plants in water.

The age of individual fish's sexual maturity and its body size vary with different environments and climates. In Changjiang and Yellow River basins, Common carp and Crucian carp generally reach maturity at the age of 2 full years. In northeastern part of China, it takes more than 2 years with bigger size. The brood amount is related with fish size. The average brood amount of Common carp, is 244,000 pieces for 3-year old fish of 44—48 cm in body length and 1.9—2.75 kg in body weight, 447,000 eggs for a 5-year old fish of 54 cm in body length and 3.5 kg in body weight. That of Crucian carp is 200,000—300,000 eggs for a fish of 0.5—1 kg in body weight.

At 20°C, the fertilized egg of Common carp takes 101—104 hour to incubate into fry; at 25°C, 49—53 hours; at 30°C, 47—50 hours.

WATER LAYER FOR HABITAT

Silver carp, Bighead, Grass carp, Black carp, Common carp, Crucian carp and Mud carp live in different water layers. It's due to their different feeding habits. Silver carp and Bighead chiefly feed on planktons. They dwell mostly in the upper layer where there is abundant plankton. Grass carp and Wuchang fish like to search for their food in the upper and middle layers, or near the river bank, lake side or pond dikes, Grass carp, Common carp, Crucian carp and Mud carp, like to stay in the bottom layer, because they are all benthos-feeders.

WATER TEMPERATURE

To a great extent, fish are poikilothermal or cold-blooded animals. The metabolism of fish is controlled by temperature. The appetite of the above mentioned fish is obviously diminishing when the temperature drops below 15°C and they stop eating below 5-7°C. As a whole, these fish except Mud carp have a wide-ranged adaptation to temperature. They can live in the temperature between 0.5°—38°C with the optimum of 25°— 32°C and yet, the optimum for food intake and growth is 25°—32°C (30°— 32°C for Mud carp). Silver carp, Bighead, Grass carp, Black carp and Wuchang fish begin to die when the temperature is below 0.5°C or above 40°C. Mud carp, *T*. nilotica and *T*. mossanbica will often freeze to death below 7°C, 8°C, 12°C respectively.

WATER QUALITY

Silver carp, Bighead, Mud carp and Tilapia, feed on plankton and habituate themselves to the fertile water where there is plenty of plankton. Grass carp and Wuchang fish feed on grasses. Since Black carp feed on molluscs they'd like to stay in sheer water. Common carp and Crucian carp can live in all kinds of waters with their strong adaptation.

PH VALUE AND DISSOLVED OXYGEN

The four main Chinese carp require certain amount of pH value in the water, generally 7.5—8.5 pH, with light alkalinity as optimum. Living in the water of 6.0—10.0 pH for a long time will retard the growth of a fish.

In addition, a fish must carry out normal gas exchange in water and demands a certain amount of dissolved oxygen in water. The higher the D.O, content the greater the feeding intensity. With D.O. above 4—5 mg/*L*, the feeding intensity of these fish is great, the growth fast, food conversion coefficient low. With D.O. below 2 mg/*L*, the fish lose their appetite, and below 1 mg/*L*, the fish will stop feeding and will gasp for air, and when the oxygen level drops further to below 0.5 mg/*L*, it will normally cause suffocation and death.

BIOLOGY OF ARTIFICIAL PROPAGATION

The artificial propagation means a series of processes from sexual maturity, ovulation, spawning upto incubation of fry under control by man. Gonads are also termed genital glands. The gonad of female fish is ovary, that of male fish testis. The eggs and sperms develop into maturity respectively in ovaries and testes when fish get to the age of sexual maturity.

The gonads have cyclic variance in development, and in the process of it, they are controlled by internal endocrine and nervous systems and external ecological conditions.

The two factors are associated and restricted each other.

1 Structure of ovary and ovum, stage division of ovary
2 Structure of ovary

The ovaries are in pairs, symmetric and sac-like. Their walls are formed by connective tissues and smooth muscles. The inner wall of ovary protrudes above septum, named as ovum-producing plate, where ova are turned out. Following maturity, the ova break follicular membranes and drop into the ovary cavity, the end of which adjoins a short oviduct with an opening to the exterior of body. There are blood vessels and nerve branches on the ovary tissue.

Structure of Ovum

Just like other animals' eggs, fish's ova possess the common features of body cells, consisting of cytoplasm (ovum cytoplasm), cell nucleus (ovum nucleus) and cell membrane (egg membrane).

At the initial stage of development, the sphere-shaped egg cells only have nucleus and cytoplasm. In further development, the egg will accumulate egg yolk materials by and by. The amount of egg yolk is much larger than that of egg cytoplasm. Polarization appears in their distribution, thus the egg is called polarized yolk egg thereby. The egg is topped by the so-called animal pole. Except for the yolk, most of the egg constituents such as cytoplasm and nucleus are concentrated near this pole. The yolk concentration increases towards the opposite, vegetal pole because of its larger granule and specific gravity. After fertilization, the first mitotic division of the cell cytoplasm and nucleus will take place and embryonic development will begin.

Egg yolk neither takes part in nor hinders the process of mitotic division. Egg yolk contains protein, fat, glycogen and vitamin etc., which are the nutritional materials for embryonic development. The nucleus consists of nuclear membrane, nucleole, nuclear fluid and chromosome. The nucleus is sphere-shaped but often leaf-shaped. Its function is to maintain genetic materials (DNA) and cell metabolism, passing the genetic material on to one generation after another.

The cell membrane is a membrane structure covering the exterior of egg cell, that can be divided into 3 kinds in accordance with the materials.

Primary cell membrane or yolk membrane is made of cell's own plasm, with lots of radiant duct-like pores, so-called radiant belt, which are helpful for the absorption of nutrients and the discharge of metabolic wastes.

Secondary cell membrane or chorion is secreted by follicle cells in ovary. The secondary cell membrane of fish is normally adhesive. It is very common in adhesive eggs of Common carp, Crucian carp and Wuchang fish etc..

Tertiary cell membrane is composed of the secretion from glands in oviduct, such as gummy cell membranes of frog and cuttlefish.

Fish do not have all the three above-mentioned membranes. Silver carp, Bighead, Grass carp and Black carp have just the primary cell membrane and Common carp, Crucian carp and Wuchang fish primary and secondary membranes.

THE DEVELOPMENT STAGES OF THE OVARY

The development stages of ovary maturity can be judged by visual observation or histologic survey. The development of fish gonad may be generally divided into six stages according to its appearance, colour, size, weight, and the distribution of blood vessels and the maturity of ova. Nowadays, the classification of the development stages of ovary adopted by each country is not identical. Five stages are admitted in India, Japan and the United Stages of America. Several countries prefer seven stages, whereas China does six. Set Silver carp as an example:

Stage I Ovary

By visual observation, the gonads are located at the lower part of air bladder, closely attached to the coelomic membrane, lineal in shape, transparent, flesh-white in colour and it's impossible to distinguish them into different sexes by the naked eye.

Tissue slice: cells tiny, diameter 12—22 um; nucleus rather big, occupying more than half of oocyte's diameter; very few nucleoli in the centre of the nucleus. By visual observation, ribbon-shaped, flesh-white in colour and emitransparent. It is impossible to distinguish ova one after another by the naked eye, and yet small eggs are visible when examined under a magnifyingglass; petaline-shaped when in fixation. It is possible to distinguish sexes. The maturity coefficient is about 1-2 per cent. Tissue slice: cell in multiangular shape or sphere-shape with a diameter of 90--300 um. A thin layer of ribbon-shaped follicles surrounds cell membrane surface. The nucleoli closely attach to the nuclear membrane.

Stage III Ovary

By visual observation, the capacity of the ovary has become conspicuously enlarged. It is due to the appearance of melanotic pigment so that it turns greenish grey in colour. Eggs are visible with the naked eye but not easily separable. The distribution of blood vessels is clear. The maturity coefficient of ovary is 3-6 per cent.

Tissue slice: The follicular membrane in oocyte is bilayer. The egg yolk begins to form. One or two layers of vacuoles appear on the edge of the cell. The cell is 250—500um in diameter. The nucleus in the centre is irregular or oval-shaped. Greater part of nucleoli are distributed on the edge of nuclear membrane and small part scattered in the centre.

The gonads of matured brooders are generally at stage III in winter.

Stage IV Ovary

By visual observation, it is long and sac-lake, occupying 1/3—1/2 of coelomic cavity. Ovary is fully distributed with blood vessels. The maturity coefficient is 12—22 per cent. Tissue slice: egg yolk granules fill almost all the space outside nucleus with only a little cytoplasm spreading around nucleus and near egg membrane. The egg is enlarged to 800—1580 um in diameter. Nucleus edge looks like waves in shape with a few nucleoli inserted in the troughs and most of nucleoli moving to the centre.

This stage can be further separated into 3 stages in the light of occyte's diameter and nucleus location. Early stage IV: egg diameter about 800 um, nucleus in the centre; middle stage IV: egg diameter about 1000 um nucleus in the centre or inclined to move to animal pole; late stage IV: egg diameter about 1580 um, nucleus having moved to animal pole, which is so-called polarized phenomenon.

Lots of experiments and practices have proved that no matured eggs can be obtained by inducement as the oocytes of silver carp, Bighead, Grass carp and Black carp are at early stage IV. Only in case of middle and late stage IV when the nucleus is eccentric or polarized, matured eggs can be acquired, and then the artificial estrualization will succeed. These stages could last as long as 1—2 months, even 3 months for some cases, providing that proper ecological conditions for spawning are not available during that period of time or no artificial propagation is performed.

Stage V Ovary

By visual ovservation quantities of oocytes come out from follicular membranes into ovary cavity, and eggs are in a state of flowing. The ovary and the belly are very soft. The eggs would flow out from cloacal opening by way of a slight pressure upon belly.

Tissue slice: the yolk granules start to fuse into a lump. The cytoplasm and the nucleus have already moved to animal pole. The nucleoli consenter in the centre of the nucleus, whereas the nuclear membrane has dissolved through perforation. The nucleus looks transparent.

When oocytes proceed to their maturity, the epithelial cells of follicles secrete a sort of substance which can dissolve and absorb tissues between the follicular and the egg membranes; thus the eggs can easily be released out from follicles thereby. The eggs are in a state of flowing in the saclike. ovary. This process is called ovulation.

The eggs, which are in a state of flowing, are released from the fish body, this process is termed spawning. The oocytes proceed very fast from stage IV to maturity (stage V). In nature, the process may be fulfilled in 20—40 hours after the rising of water in the rivers. Under artificial estrualization, it can generally be fulfilled within 10 to 20 hours or even in several hours. If the follicles discharged inmatured eggs ahead of time, the rate of fertilization would be affected. In another case, if the follicles could not release matured eggs in time, the eggs might be suffocated or degenerate by virtue of overripe and the rate of fertilization would be certainly affected too. Even if part of these eggs might become fertilized, the embryos could not develop normally. In other words, the success of either natural spawning or artificial insemination depends upon knowing exactly the maturity stage and the spawning time of a fish. If the matured eggs missed the chance of being released, the oocytes would degenerate and be absorbed.

Stage VI Ovary

By visual observation, the major portion of eggs has already been laid. There are still some phase-4 oocytes which have remained in the ovary. The ovary is slack and its size has been reduced conspicuously. Blood vessels have become enlarged with lump-shaped extravasated blood.

Tissue slice: After ovulation, there are lots of follicular membranes and undischarged mature eggs in ovary. The undischarged eggs will soon degenerate and be absorbed, forming a semi-transparent and irregular structure, orange yellow in colour. Besides there are still many interim oocytes

THE STRUCTURE OF THE TESTES AND SPERM AND THE DEVELOPMENT STAGE OF THE TESTES

The Structure of the Testes

The testes are paired and tubular. They are situated on both sides of the air bladder, attached to the ceolomic wall. Mature testes are white in colour. There are a lot of ampullae arranged irregularly inside. The spaces between ampullae are full of connective tissues.

The ampullae are composed of many spores or seminal vesicle sacs (spermatangium spermatogonia). Spore sacs are separated by a thin layer of follicular cells. In one spore sac there is plenty of synchronously-developing germ cells, and in different spores sacs, germ cells vary in developmental stages. The centre of the ampullae forms a hollow cavity. After the formation of sperms, spore sacs dissolve and the sperms enter the cavity of the ampullae. The terminal end of the testis is connected to a short seminal duct with an opening to the exterior of the body.

The Structure of Sperm

A sperm cell of Chinese carps consists of a head, a neck and a tail. The sperm head of Silver carp is almost spherical, 2.2—2.5 um in diameter, consisting of an apex and a nucleus.

The apex is situated at the front part of the head. It is also called penetrator for its function of penetrating into egg. The neck is very short and is situated between the head and the tail. The sperm neck of Silver carp is about 1.1 um in length. The tail, narrow and long, is many times more than the head in length. The sperm tail of Silver carp is about 35um in length. The tail is the metabolic centre and motor organ.

Mature sperms congregate in ampullae cavities because of the disintegration of spore sacs. Sperms will mix with the fluid secreted by the interstitial cells in sperms and the testis, forming so-called milt. The milt may be exuded or pressed out of body at the climax of brooders' estrus. 1 ml of Silver carp's milt holds approximately 48 million sperms.

The total amount of milt could reach 30–40 ml.

- Apex
- Nucleus
- Neck
- Middle part
- End-ring
- Spindle filament
- Plasm sheath
- Knots (front and rear)
- Flagellum

The Development Stages of the Testis

Just as the ovary, the development of the testes may be divided into six stages according to its appearance and tissue slice observation.

Stage I testes: Testes are lineal in shape, transparent, attached closely to ceolomic wall. It is impossible to distinguish sexes. On the tissue slice, scattered spermatogonia, 16um in diameter may be observed. The nucleus is big and round, 9 um in diameter. Ampulli and seminal vesicles are still under formation; therefore, there is no clear fixed arrangement of sperm cells. Stage II testes: Testes are lace-like, transparent or non-transparent. Blood vessels are not clear. Histologic characteristics of this stage are multiplication of spermatogonia, formation of seminal vesicles which are arrayed in bundles. At this stage, ampulli are solid and separated by connective tissues.

Stage III testes: Testes are rod-shaped, pink or yellowish, elastic on surface with clear distribution of blood vessels. On the tissue slice, a hollow cavity may appear in the middle of solid ampullae with one or several layers of seminal vesicles on ampullar walls.

Stage IV testes: Testes are milky white in colour with a clear distribution of blood vessels on the surface. It is impossible to squeeze out milt at early stage, but possible at late stage. On the tissue slice, some larger primary spermatocytes, some smaller secondary spermatocytes and the smallest spermation can be observed. All these above-mentioned cells congregate on the walls of seminal vesicles with a small number of sperms.

Stage V testes: Testes are white in colour and full of milt. The milt will flow out through cloacal opening if a male fish's head is taken up and its belly slightly pressed. A large number of sperms and sperm cells in different stages could be seen inside ampulli on tissue slice.

Stage VI testes: The capacity of the testis has greatly decreased after milt exudation, yellowish-white or pink in colour on tissue slice. Only spermatogo nia, a little primary spermatocytes and connective tissues remain in seminal vesicles. After exudation, the testies of the male fish is turning back to stage III and will develop on.

5

Breeding

BASIC PRINCIPLES OF BREEDING

Breeding is a complicated process which should be performed vary carefully. It also requires some knowledge of biology and especially the basics of genetics.

The principles that should be kept in mind are the genetic principles which may be summarised as follows:

- Genes are responsible for all the physiological characters for which we are breeding. Genes exists in pairs called alleles. At the time of formation of the sex cells in the females and males these alleles segregate and at the time of fertilization they combine to give rise to new genetic combinations which may express themselves in varied physiological characters.
- Genetic characters are expressed at varying degrees ranging from a maximum of expression to the minimum of expression. For example the character "size" can have a "maximum size" and" minimum size" expression. Similarly, the character "red colour" can have a "maximum expression" of "pure red" to a "minimum expression" of "very faint red" mixed with any other colour. However, in the applied sense the maximum and minimum expressions may not be true. It will be more correct to say that the characters are expressed in '.more" or "less" intensity. The "more" and the "less" of a character is expressed by anyone of the alleles of the same gene responsible for a single character like red, size, etc. The "maximum" or the "more" of the expression of a character is due to one of the alleles and it is called dominant gene and the allele responsible for the "minimum" or "less" of the expression is called recessive.
- At the time of segregation and combination the alleles form new combinations which result in the appearance or disappearance of a particular character. Thus, one character may disappear in one generation and may reappear in any of the subsequent generations

depending on the type of combinations of dominant and recessive allele/gene formed in each generation.

- The breeder's role and objective is to evolve such breeds in such a way that the desirable characters are kept expressed or retained and the undesirable characters are kept unexpressed or removed. For example, in gold fish one should retain its specific colour so that its value as gold fish can be maintained.
- The breeder should select the type of breeding suitable to achieve the above mentioned objective. The most common types of breeding are: inbreeding, out breeding and grading up. Inbreeding is breeding of related animals and out breeding is breeding of unrelated animals. Under inbreeding one can have close breeding (breeding between very closely related individuals such as between full brother and sister, father and daughter, mother and son, uncle and niece, auntie and nephew, etc., relations) and line breeding (breeding between individuals of the same breed which are far related other than those mentioned in the close inbreeding). Close inbreeding between father and daughter and mother and son and own brother and sister should be avoided by all means.
- Under out breeding one can have out crossing (crossing of umelated individuals of the same breed) and cross breeding (breeding of unrelated animals of different breeds). Under the cross breeding one can follow criss- cross breeding (breeding with two breeds alternatively), triple crossing (breeding with three breeds one after the other) and back crossing (breeding back to one of the pure parent races which were used to produce it). In grading up the local non-descript breeds are upgraded by successive breeding with selected pure breeds.
- Select the breeding stock according to the principle of selection. Only the good ones are selected for breeding. Fishes that are true to the desired characteristics, fast growing, active, agile, good feeders, good size and shape are selected for breeding. Needless to say that fishes with any defect or diseases should not be selected breeding.
- Breeding record should be maintained. The breeding record should contain the identification mark or number of the males and females, date of breeding and spawning, hatching, approximate number of hatchlings, fry and fingerlings, etc. The breeder should note any other relevant detail related to breeding.

These are some of the basic principles and practices one should follow in breeding and multiplying any type of animal for economic advantage. Basically the same principles and practices are also applied in the case of breeding of the ornamental fishes.

- Generally, while breeding, for every female fish two male fishes are placed inside the breeding tank. The same practice is followed in the case of ornamental fishes.

BREEDING TANKS

For breeding the ornamental fishes, first of all one should set up the necessary infrastructures.

A number of small tanks should be constructed and placed at a convenient place so that one can breed the desired number of fishes. In other words depending on the number of males and females used for breeding and the number of spawns one would like to have at a time or one year and the number of breeding activities performed in series the breeder has to build up a number of tanks.

ACTIVITIES IN BREEDING

There are a number of activities performed in a sequential order to raise the frys or fingerlings. Several tanks are required for carrying out a number of activities such as (1) stocking the male and female breeders, (2) spawning and breeding, (3) hatching, (4) fry raising, (5) raising of fingerlings and (6) rearing up to maturity. For the benefit of the reader these activities are explained briefly here.

Stocking

Stocking means to stock the selected mature males and females of ornamental fishes. The tanks used for this purpose are called stocking tanks. The stock also is called the breeder stock. The male and female breeder stocks of the same breed and different breeds are kept in separate tanks. The number of tanks required for stocking depends on the number and size of fishes of the same breed or different breeds.

Spawning and Breeding

Spawning means release of eggs by the female single or in a group. In the group they look like an egg-mass of jelly like substance. This egg-mass remain floating while being attached to some kind of fibrous material or plant parts. The single eggs either float around or sink deep to the bottom of the aquarium tank. Breeding usually means mating also.

But in the case of fishes the fertilization of the eggs takes place outside after the spawning is completed. At the time of spawning the male fishes release the milt (sperm excretions) on to the eggs and instantaneously the eggs get fertilized. In the case of fish breeding the term breeding signifies all these processes.

Hatching

Hatching is a biological process by which the developing embryo in the egg come out in the form of young fish called fry. Hatching can be done in the breeding tank or in another tank called hatching tank depending on the convenience of the breeder.

Fry Raising

The fishlings up to 15 days old are called fry. Ornamental fish sellers and growers buy or sell fishlings at fry stage. The fry rearing stage last for about 15 days. For the first few days the fishlings may not need any nutrition from out side since they have part of the yolk, from the egg from which each one came out, is attached to their body. This yolk reserve is slowly absorbed into the body providing the necessary nutrition. After two days they begin to eat very small particles of feed.

One of the best forms of feed is to powder the yolk of the boiled egg and tie it in a fine cloth tight and kept under pressure with the help of a clip fixed on the small bundle and hanging it in the tank water conveniently for the fry to pick at the particles of the yolk oozing out of the bundle under clip pressure. The most important thing to be remembered in fry raising is to avoid over crowding of fry in the fry raising tank.

Fingerlings Raising

Fishlings between 15 to 90 days old are called fingerlings. Among them those that between 15 to 60 days may be considered to be in primary fingerling stage and those 60 to 90 days to be fingerlings in secondary stage. Depending on the convenience one can have further categories of fingerlings such as one month old, two month old and three month old, etc.

SIZE AND NUMBER OF TANK

The size of the tank may be 45-90 cm long, 25-45 cm width and 25-45 cm height. Usually the width and height is maintained equal. Separate tanks are required for keeping the males and females. At the time of breeding one female and two males are placed together in one tank. After spawning and fertilization the males and the females are returned to their respective tanks. The number of fishes placed in a tank depends on the size or the length of the fish.

Generally one centimetre long (excluding the tail) fish require 75 sq cm tank area. Therefore, in a tank of 60x30 size we can keep 24 fishes (60x30/75 = 24) of one centimetre long or 4-5 fishes of five cm long (60x30/75x5 =4.8) or 2-3 fishes (60x30/75x10=2.4) of 10 cm long. Accordingly one has to estimate the number and size of the tanks he needs for breeding. Few stand-by tanks are also needed to cope up with any unforeseen demands during the breeding period.

It is advisable that the breeder stocks are kept in bigger tanks of at least 90x45x45 cm in size. Therefore, depending on the number of breeder stock and their size the breeder can estimate the number and size of the tanks required. Similarly the number and size of the tanks required for other breeding related activities can be estimated. Accordingly all the required number of tanks can be constructed and established.

ESTABLISHMENT OF BREEDING TANKS

The aquarium tanks are heavy and the tanks with water are heavier. Therefore, the tanks should be placed properly on a permanent place in the breeding shed farm and set in such a way that all the breeding operations can be carried out easily and efficiently. The movement of the labourer should be easier in the breeding shed or area.

Inside the breeding shed besides the tanks there should be place for production and storage of fish feed, place for equipments and instruments, medicines and chemical room, records and accounts keeping room, office or any other facilities required for the efficient and effective management of all the breeding operations.

The breeding tanks should be set up in the usual way with filters at the bottom, aquatic plants on the floor, aerator, light, etc. Try to set and adjust things in such a way that all the works can be done with least effort and energy expenditure. Ensure automatic free flow of fresh and well oxygenated water into each tank. For this permanently running water pipes should be fixed in the breeding area.

Normally, the quality of the water is neutral. However some of the fishes prefer water which is slightly acidic. To make acidic water take about half a cup of peat soil. Fill it with boiling water and allowed to stand for about 24 hours. The supernatant water is added to 50 litres of clean rain water, distilled water or boiled and stagnated tap water for a week. Everything should be arranged and constructed in such a way that the aquarium tanks and the shed can be easily cleaned whenever needed.

BREEDING PRACTICES

Selecting and conditioning of adult fish, observing the spawning and raising of the fry and fingerlings are the major activities that are related to breeding.

SELECTION AND CONDITIONING

Select only those fishes that are fulfilling certain standards in the breed characters. For this one should have a thorough knowledge about the various characteristics of the different breeds. Having these in the mind one can observe and judge the fishes (male and females) that are suitable for breeding. They are called the breeder stock.

After the selection the male and female breeders are kept separately till the breeding season. Each breeder should be provided at leas 75 sq cm area space per cm length excluding the tail. Needless to say that they should be provided with the best of the aquarium conditions in the quality water which should be clean, clear, chemically normal, well oxygenated and free flowing through an inlet and outlet at a constant rate.

While they are being prepared for breeding they should be fed with high protein feed so that they become physiologically fit for the reproduction. It is also to ensure the production of healthy larvae and young ones. All the worms and other minute organisms growing in organically rich water like sewage, sludge and drainage, etc., are high protein feed for the fish. Feeding of the very small thread like worms is best done by placing them in a cup like structure made of wire mesh. The worm wriggles out through the mesh swinging and swaying. Such movements of the worms will attract the fishes towards the feeder and they pick up the worms one by one and eat them. The breeding tank has to be prepared according to the breeding habits of fishes. Some breeds of fish may be carnivorous and even eat their own young ones. The breeder has to learn about the general habits as well as breeding habits of each species before he starts breeding the ornamental fishes for aquarium purposes. No single method is applicable to all the species of the fishes.

B. BREEDING HABITS

Breeding habit in fishes refers to the egg laying habits.

Fishes have three types of laying habits:

1. Egg scattering,
2. Egg depositing and
3. Bubble nest building.

There are some fishes that bear live fishlings. They are called "live-bearing" fish. The females of these fishes release the young ones after the eggs are fertilized and the hatchlings are nursed inside the mother.

Egg Scatterers

Eggs scatterers are those that scatter the eggs on the floor of the aquarium tank. The eggs remain freely scattered on the floor among the sand particles. There are others who release sticky eggs which adhere to the plant parts or some fibrous material placed in the aquarium tank. There are others which release the eggs mixed with a mass of jelly like sub- stance which swells up and floats on the surface of the water. All these come under egg scatterers category. Gold fish and all the other fishes belonging to the carp family are some of the examples of the egg scattered fishes. Some of the egg scatterers like Siamese fighters eat their own eggs. Hence, they are removed as soon as the spawning is over or the eggs are removed from the breeding tank. In the case of fishes that scatter and eat their own eggs one way to save the eggs is to keep the female and males in a small wire mesh cage inside the breeding tank. As the eggs are released they are fertilized by the milt from the male soon after fertilization the eggs sink to the bottom of the aquarium tank and remain safe. After the spawning and fertilization is over the breeder stock along with the wire mesh is removed.

Egg Depositors

Egg depositors are those fishes which deposit the eggs in a particular place in thc aquarium tank and leave them for hatching. Some of them guard their eggs while others leave them uncared. They make small dig ups on the ground of the tank at a convenient place and deposit the eggs. They do not eat their eggs as the egg scatterers but take care of the eggs. In some both male and females take care of the eggs and the hatchlings while in others only the female or the male may take care. Cicero fishes like *Hemichromis bimaculatus* and *Aequidens portalegrensis* are some of the examples of egg depositors.

Bubble Nest Builders

The bubble nest builders are those who make a kind of nest of bubbles which help the eggs floating and secure. The eggs remain floating as in the case of sticky and jelly mass. Bubbles are usually made under a leaf or attached to a leaf.

Anabantoids like gouraini arc somc of the examples of the bubble nest makers. The males among them make the bubble nest by frequently gulping atmospheric air and using the mucous from the mouth they make bubble out of the air they sucked in and deposit it under the leaf. A number of bubbles are placed together to form a bubble nest which acts like a raft or float. When the nest making is complete the males drive the female to the nest and encourages her to lay the eggs. As the eggs are released they are fertilized by the milt from the male. The fertilized eggs begin to sink to the bottom of the tank. Both male and the female pick up the sinking eggs one by one and place them on the bubble nest. The male guards the eggs till they are hatched. However as soon as the eggs are hatched the male should be removed otherwise it may eat up the entire lot.

The fertilization takes place soon after egg laying by the sprinkling of the milt by the male over the eggs and hatching occurs within one or two days after fertilization. Some fishes gather all the fishlings in the mouth whenever they sense some danger and release them as soon as the danger is over.

Fishes such as guppy, platy, molly and swordtail are some of the examples of livebearers. However, most of them are carnivores and eat up their own young ones. Hence, the breeders while releasing the young ones should be kept in small wire mesh cages inside the tank. As the young ones come out they escape out through the wire mesh and will grow safely in the tank. After all the young ones are released the breeders are transferred back to their own respective tanks. Therefore, at the time of setting the tanks this point should be kept in mind. From all these it is clear that a lot of variations are there in the general behaviour pattern and breeding habits of the various breeds of fish. Depending on the type of species the breeder has to study the breeding habits of each species.

BREEDING OF GOLD FISH

Gold fish is one of the most important ornamental fishes that are being reared by most of the aquarium keepers. Hence we shall explain the breeding of the gold fish in detail. The average life of a gold fish is about 10 years and they are highly e1irythermal (able to tolerate a wide range of temperature: 0 to 35°C). The male gold fish mature in one year while the female takes two years to mature. Select only those gold fishes from the lot that are fulfilling certain physiological standards. Place them in the tanks male and female separately and feed them properly to ensure adequate nutrition.

During the season of breeding the ovary of the female mature and swell up which can be noticed by the bulging on the abdomen. Further the gonadal opening of the female is large, round and protruding while in the male it is small oblong and slightly concave. During the breeding period two males and one female are kept placed together in a well prepared tank. To collect the eggs an artificial spawning nest made of some fibrous material fixed in the form of a ring. This ring is attached to the side of the aquarium tank wall or on to a plant which is being grown in the tank.

During the mating the males chase the female. This type of mating behaviour helps both male and female to release the eggs from female and milt (sperms with protective secretions) the eggs laid by the female is fertilized by the milt of the males. As the fertilized eggs are adhesive they stick to the fibrous material. The nests with the attached eggs are transferred to the hatching tank in case the hatching is done in a separate tank.

Hatching takes place within two or three days and larvae come out as tiny baby fishes. Initially they subsist on the part of the egg yolk which each one has inherited from the egg from which it is hatched. This egg yolk is attached to the abdomen of the larvae which is called yolk sac. Within two or three days the yolk sac is exhausted and the larvae are ready for ingesting feed. One of the best feeds that can be provided to the larvae at the initial stage is to feed the larvae with boiled poultry egg yolk tied up in a fine cloth into a small b1mdle tightly and kept under certain amount of pressure using a clip which will exert pressure on the bundle. The bundle along with the clip can be hung inside the aquarium tank at a convenient place. The larvae will pick at the bits of yolk oozing out from all sides of the bundles under the clip pressure.

After a few days powdered dry prawn mixed with boiled egg yolk is given as feed. The mix may be slightly wet and made into a ball and place in feeding cup. The frys will slowly pick on it and the small particles getting detached from the ball will be eaten by them.

Gradually other feeds like minute aquatic flora and fauna are being made available to them. *Moina, cyclops*, mosquito larvae, nauplius of *artemia, tubex* worms and chopped earth worms, etc., can be provided to them as they grow up. A mixture of any oil cake and rice bran or wheat bran in equal amount can be made into small balls after wetting can also be given to the fishes after one or two days. It is advisable that the change from the initial feed to the later one be done gradually by decreasing the former while increasing the latter simultaneously.

The first two or three days or till the yolk sac is exhausted the hatchlings can be considered to be in the larval stage. After the yolk sack is exhausted the hatchlings begin to take the feed and up to 15 days they are considered to be in fry stage. From 15 to 45 days they may be considered late fry stage. From 45 to 90 days they may be considered early fingerlings stage. Above 90 days up to about (not yet specified) 120 days they may be considered fingerlings stage. Most of the fishes mature between 1 to 2 years. Aquarium fishes can be sold at any stage between 15 to 120 days. Most people purchase frys for aquarium keeping. Only people who want to start a breeding unit or want to set up a ready made aquarium buy fingerlings and adults.

Depending on the demand they are multiplied and sold to the customers. According to the demand one can breed the required number of females and males. One can also time the breeding in such a way that he can get the fry and fingerlings ready at the peak season of demand.

BREEDING PLAN

Based on the genetic principles one should have a plan for breeding the ornamental fishes. Anyone or a combination of the standard methods of breeding plan may be followed in breeding and multiplying them. Depending on the quality of the progeny one has to select the breeding methodology.

If the breeder is planning to evolve a new cross breed of ornamental fish then he has to apply the method of cross breeding of unrelated animals of different breeds. He also has to employ a professional geneticist who can plan and do all the genetical analysis of the breeding data generated. By this the breeder produces the breeder and foundation stock for further breeding for maintaining genetic purity. The breeder stock is the fist few individuals of cross bred produced by cross breeding. The foundation stock is the multiplied number of the breeder stock which serve as a foundation for the newly evolved cross breed. If the expected result of the breeding plan is only to maintain the genetic purity of the breeding stock then he has to adopt double or triple crossing or at times close inbreeding. Commercial suppliers of ornamental fishes operate at this level of breeding.

If the breeder is planning to upgrade the local or non- descript fishes he can employ grading up method of breeding. Generally maintaining genetic purity between 60 to 70 per cent will be most advantageous to get better performance of the fishes. The breeder should plan his breeding in such a way that the resultant progeny has the genetic purity between 60 to 70 per cent. If the breeder is not having any basic knowledge about the genetic principles all that he can do is to select good male and female from the same species and breed and multiply them to sell to customers or grow them for oneself.

BIOTECHNOLOGY IN FISH BREEDING

Gonadotropin releasing hormone (GnRH) is now the best available biotechnological tool for the induced breeding of fish. GnRH is the key regulator and central initiator of reproductive cascade in all vertebrates.It is a decapeptide and was first isolated from pig and ship hypothalami with the ability to induce pituitary release of luteinising hormone (LH) and follicle stimulating hormone (FSH). Since then only one form of GnRH has been identified in most placental mammals including human beings as the sole neuropeptide causing the release of LH and FSH. However,in non mammalian species (except guinea pig) twelve GnRH variants have now been structurally elucidated, among them seven or eight different forms have been isolated from fish species. Depending on the structural variant and their biological activities, number of chemical analogues have seen prepared and one of them is salmon GnRH analogue profusely used now in fish breeding and marked commercially under the name of 'Ovaprim' throughout the world. The induced breeding of fish is now successfully achieved by development of GnRH technology.

TRANSGENESIS

Transgenesis or transgenics may be defined as the introduction of exogenous gene/ DNA into host genome resulting in its stable maintenance, transmission and expression. The technology offers an excellent opportunity for modifying or improving the genetic traits of commercially important fishers, mollusks and crustaceans for aquaculture. The idea of producting transgenic animals became popular when first produced transgenic mouse by introducing metallothionein human growth hormone fusion gene (mT-hGH) into mouse egg, resulting in dramatic increase in growth. This triggered a series of attemptson gene transfer in economically important animals including fish.

The first transgenic fish was produced in China, who claimed the transient expression n putative transgenics, although they gave no molecular evidence for the integration of the transgene. The technique has now seen successfully applied to a number of fish species. Dramatic growth enhancement has been shown using this technique especially in salmonids. Some studies have revealed enhancement of growth in adult salmon to an average of 3 P5 times the size of non P transgenic controls, with some individuals, especially during the first few months of growth, reaching as much as 10 P30 times the size of the controls.The introduction of transgenic technique has simultaneously put more emphasis on the need for production of sterile progeny in order to minimize the risk of transgenic stocks mixing in the wild populations.

The technical development has expanded the possibilities for producing either sterile fish or those whose reproductive activity can be specifically turned on or off using inducible promoters. This would clearly be of considerable value allowing both optimal growth and controlled reproduction of the transgenic stocks while ensuring that any escaped fish would be unable to breed. An increased resistance of fish to cold temperatures has been another subject of research in fish transgenics for the past several years. Coldwater temperatures pose a considerable stressor to many fish and few are able to survive water temperatures much below 0-1°C. this is often a major problem in aquaculture in cold climates. Interestingly, some marine teleosts have high levels (10 P25 mg/ml) of serum antifreeze proteins (AFP) or glycoproteins (AFGP) which effectively reduce the freesing temperature by preventing ice-crystal growth.

The isolation, characterisation and regulation of these antifreeze proteins particularly of the inter flounder Pleuronectas americanus has been the subject of research for a considerable period in Canada. Consequently, the gene encoding the liver AFP from winter flounder was successfully introduced into the genome of Atlantic salmon where it became integrated into the germ line and then passed onto the off P spring F3 where it was expressed specifically in the liver.The introduction of AFPs to gold fish also increased their cold tolerance, to temperatures at which all the control fish died (12 h at 0° C; Wang *et al.*, 1995). Similarly, injection or oral administration of AFP to juvenile milkfish or tilapia led to an increase in resistance to a 26 to 13° C. drop in temperature. The development of stocks harbouring this gene would be a major benefit in commercial aquaculture in counties where winter temperatures often border the physiological limits of these species.

The most promising tool for the future of transgenic fish production is undoubtedly in the development of the embryonic stem cell (ESC) technology. There cells are undifferentiated and remain totipotent so they can be manipulated *in vitro* and subsequently reintroduce into early embryos where they can contribute to the germ line of the host. This would facilitate the genes to be stably introduced or deleted.Although significant progress has been made in several laboratories around the world, there are numerous problems to be resolved before the successful commercialisation of the transgenic brood stock for aquaculture. To realise the full potential of the transgenic fish technology in aquaculture, several important scientific break P through are required.

There include:

- More efficient technologies for mass gene transfer
- Targeted gene transfer technologies such as embryonic stem cell gene transfer
- Suitable promoters to direct the expression of transgenes at optimal levels during the desired developmental stages
- Identified genes of desireable traits for aquaculture and other applications
- Informations on the physiological, nutritional, immunological and environmental factors that maximize the performance of the transgenics of the transgenics and
- Safety and environmental impacts of transgenic fish.

CHROMOSOME ENGINEERING

Chromosome sex manipulation techniques to induce polyploidy (triploidy and tetraploidy) and uniparental chromosome inheritance (gynogenesis and androgenesis) have been applied extensively in cultured fish species. These techniques are important in the improvement of fish breeding as they provide a rapid approach for gonadal sterilisation, sex control improvement of hybrid viability and clonation. Most vertebrates are diploid meaning that they possess two complete chromosome sets in their somatic cells. Polyploidy individuals possess on or more additional chromosome sets, bringing the total to three in triploids, four in tetraploids and so on.

Induced triploidy is widely accepted as the most effective method for producing sterile fish for aquaculture and fisheries management. The methods used to induce triploids and other types of chromosome set manipulations in fishes and the applications of these biotechnologies to aquaculture and fisheries management are well described. Tetraploid breeding lines are of potential benefit to aquaculture, by providing a convenient way to produce large numbers of sterile triploid fish through simple interploidy crosses between tetraploids and diploids. Although tetraploidy has been induced in many finfish species, the viability of tetraploids was low in most instances.

In teleosts, technique for inducing sterility include exogenous hormone treatment and triploidy induction. The use of hormone treatements, however could be limited by governmental regulation and a lack of consumer acceptance of hormone treated fish products. Triploidy can be induced by exposing eggs to physical or chemical treatment shortly after fertilization to inhibit extrusion of the second polar body triploid fish are expected to be sterile because of the failure of homologous chromosomes to synapse correctly during the first meiotic division. Methods of triploidy induction in clued exposing fertilized eggs to temperature shock (hot or cold), hydrostatic pressure shock or chemicals such an colchicines, cytochalasin-B or nitrous oxide.

Triploid can also be produced by crossing teraploids and diploids. Tetraploid induction involves fertilizing eggs with normal sperm and exposing the diploid sygote for physical or chemical treatment to suppress the first mitotic division. Gynogenesis is the process of animal development with exclusive maternal inheritance. The production of gynogenetic individuals is of particular interest to fish breeders because a high level of inbreeding can be induced in single generation.

Gynogenesis may also be used to produce all P female populations in species with female homogamety and to reveal the sex determination mechanisms in fish. It is convenient to use all female gynogenetic progenies (instead of normal bisexual progenies) for sex inversion experiments. Methodologies combining use of induced gynogenesis with hormonal sex inversion have been developed for several aquaculture species.

Androgenesis is the process by which would have commercial application in aquaculture. It can also be used in generating homozygous lines of fish and in the recovery of lost genotypes from the crypreserved sperms. Androgenetic individuals have been produced in a few species of cyprinids, cichlids and salmonids.

BIOTECHNOLOGY AND FISH HEALTH MANAGEMENT

Disease problem are a major constraint for development of aquaculture. Biotechnological tools such as molecular diagnostic methods, use of vaccines and immunostimulants are gaining popularity for improving the disease resistance in fish and shelfish species world over for viral diseases, avoidance of the pathogen is very important.

In this context there is a need to rapid method for detection of the pathogen. Biotechnological tools such as gene probes and polymerase chain reaction (PCR) are showing great potential in this area. Gene probes and PCR based diagnostic methods have developed for a number of pathogens affecting fish and shrimp. In case of finfish aquaculture, number of vaccine against bacteria and viruses have been developed. Some of these have been conventional vaccines consisting of killed microorgansism but new generation of vaccine consisting of protein subunit vaccine genetically engineered organism and DNA vaccine are currently under development.

In the vertebrate system, immunisation against disease is a common strategy. However the immune system of shrimp is rather poorly developed, biotechnological tools are helpful for development of molecule, which can stimulate this immune system of shrimp. Recent studies have shown that the non specific defence system can be stimulated using, microbial product such as lipopolysacharides, peptidoglycans or glucans. Among the immunostimulants known to be effective in fish glucan and levamisole enhance phagocytic activities and specific antibody responses.

CRYOPRESERVATION OF GAMETES OR GENE BANKING

Cryopreservation is a technique, which involve long-term preservation and storage of biological material at a very low temperature usually at -196 C, the temperature of liquid nitrogen. It is based on the principle that very low temperature tranquilise or immobilise the physiological and biochemical activities of cell, thereby making it possible to keep them viable for very long period. The technology of cryopreservation of fish spermatozoa (milt) has been adopted for animal husbandary. The first success in preserving fish sperm at low temperature was reported by Blaxter who fertilizes Herring eggs with frozen thawed semen.The spermatozoa of almost all cultivable fish species has now been cryopreserved. Cryopreservation overcomes problems of male maturing before female, allow selective breeding and stock improvement and enables the conservation.

One of the emerging requirement for that can be used by breeders for evolving new strains. Most of the plant varieties that has been produced are based on the gene bank collections. Aquatic gene bank however suffers from the fact that at present it is possible to cryopreserve only the male gametes of finfishes and there in no viable technique for finfish eggs and embryos. However, the recent report on the freezing of shrimp embryos. However, the recent report on the freesing of shrimps embryos by subramoniam and newton and Diwan and kandaswami look promising. Therefore, it is essential that gene banking of cultivated and cultivable aquatic species be undertaken expeditiously.

BREEDING MINOR CARPS

C. REBA (REBA)

C. reba is a bottom feeding omnivore although the young feed voraciously on zooplankton and grow very quickly, even faster than the young of catla and mrigal. C. reba does not spawn in ponds even though they attain full maturity there. Currently, C. reba is considered as 'vulnerable in natural waters' due to a decline in its abundance, extent of occurrence, area of occupancy and habitat.

Recently, C. reba has drawn attention as one of the potential new candidate species for aquaculture and captive breeding. C. reba is an annual breeder with a single spawning period restricted to south-west monsoons extending from May to July in Assam and Bangladesh, and June to August with a peak in June in West Bengal. The shallow waters affording the optimum range of temperature (approx. 28-30 C) may be a factor that induces the fish to spawn. The average fecundity was 420,000. The average diameter of eggs was 2.24 mm and average weight was 0.0042 mg.

LABEO BATA

Labeo bata, locally called as ilish bata, bhangon bata or bata, is one of them belonging to the Family Cyprinidae. It is a non-migratory fish and remains in one habitat throughout its life. The fish matures during monsoon season (April to July) in NE region and attends first maturity at 18.62 cm in total length.It breeds in floodplains during rainy season as Indian major carps. It spawns from May to July in at the range of water temperature 26.2–30.3°C.

LABEO GONIUS

Inhabits rivers. Spawns during the southwest monsoon. Does not normally breed in ponds. Artificial breeding done through hypophysation. Cultured in ponds along with other carp species.

BREEDING OF SARPUTI (PUNTIUS SARANA)

Puntius sarana locally known as Sar Punti is widely distributed fish found in India. P. sarana is a freshwater fish common in ponds and rivers, prefers shallow waters of floodplains for breeding, column-bottom dwelling nature and omnivorous in feeding habit, have good consumer demand as food fish for its high biological value. It is a profilic breeder and breeds during monsoon. In July and August it spawns in shallow water. However, poor survival of egg and larvae were noticed. Like many commercially important indigenous fish species P. sarana also needs urgent attention from conservation angles, as the population of this commercially important species is reported to be in drastic decline. Artificial propagation of seed of this commercially important fish species was done using Ovaprim @ 1 ml/kg weight of both male and female fish as an inducing agent with success. It was also found that a dose fish PG of 5 mg/kg to 6 mg/kg body weight of female was suitable for breeding.

INDUCED SPAWNING OF THAI PUTI (PUNTIUS GONIONOTUS)

Thai puti is an exotic species which breeds normally in streams and rivers like most tropical cyprinids. They can also breed in captivity like pond and tank water. Their breeding season starts from April and lasts till August. The natural source provides a negligible amount of fish seed because of higher mortality rate, mixture of cultivable and non- cultivable species and shrinkage of spawning ground which impede the extension and expansion of fish culture.

After the first attempt of induced spawning in early thirties this technique had been successfully tried in many countries of the world. The best ovulation, fertilization, hatching and survivability rates were achieved under higher dose of PG as used @2.00–5.00 mg/kg body weight 2 mg/kg weight of fish in first injection and 4 mg/kg in second injection) were found to be most effective for induced spawning of P. gonionotus. Slightly higher dose of hormone was required at the beginning and latter part of the spawning season and comparatively lower dose was required at the middle of the breeding season.

CAT/AIR BREATHING FISH BREEDING

Important cultured species are:

- Clarias batrachus
- Heteropneustes fossilis
- Anabas testudineus
- Pangasius sutchi
- Ompok spp.

ASIAN CATFISH (CLARIAS BATRACHUS)

Asian catfish, Clarias batrachus, is considered as a potential aquaculture species in Indian subcontinent. The Asian cat fish, locally known as Magur fish, is an important air-breathing cat fish with good markets especially in North-Eastern parts of India where it fetches a higher price than the major carps. The scarcity of marketable fish as well as seed from the natural ground has been felt in this catfish.

The potential to obtain magur seed from natural sources has become low due to the increasing use of pesticides in the paddy fields-which are the main breeding grounds of this fish. The breeding performance is an important parameter to evaluate the breeding success in captive condition, which depends on the type of hormone used and its potency, dose of hormone and maturity status of the fish Human chorionic gonadotropin (HCG) at 14–23 h latency in combination with 3000–4000 IU HCG dose is one among them and is reported successful in catfish during induced ovulation.

Appropriate combinations of the proper dose of inducing agent and stripping time always yield maximum egg output during induced breeding. A single injection of 0.6ml/kg body weight of ovaprim was the most effective. The males were given a single dose of 0.1–0.2 ml/kg body weight.

Again administration of fish PG of dosage varied from 12 to 30 mg/kg weight of fish given in two doses, a provocative dose of 5–10 mg /kg and a final dose of 8–20 mg/kg and 5–6 hours interval was found successful in spawning. In hapa nursing of magur, we achieved an average survival of 51 per cent while feeding with rice bran and mustard oil cake mixture at 1:1 ratio and termite twice daily. Before the female are stripped male fish with gravid testis are to be sacrificed, and testes are taken out and macerated in normal saline (0.9 per cent NaCl). The spermatozoa become inactive in this medium and this extract can be maintained for few hours in refrigerator.

After 16 hours of latency period female fish is stripped and ova are collected in to dry enamel tray. Before fertilization milt (spermatozoa) extract medium is activated by addition of fresh water. Sperms become active and motility of sperms can be confirmed in microscope. Sperm preparation thus obtained will be sufficient to fertilize the ova stripped from 2 females. Sperm extract is sprinkled over the ova and gametes are mixed gently with bird feathers and allowed to 2 to 3 minutes for fertilization. After repeated washing with fresh water fertilized eggs are transferred to hatching trays for incubation.

FLOW THROUGH SYSTEM OF MAGUR BREEDING

This is a simple device comprising a stand on which are placed a row of plastic tubs (12 cm dia, 6 cm high). Water supplied from the overhead tank through a common pipe to all the tubs with individual control tabs. Each tub is provided with an outlet at a height of 4 cm and connected to a common conduit to drain off water. In this model of flow through system the temperature monitoring system has not been used which seems to be necessary to increase the rate of survivality of magur larvae.

INNOVATIVE MODEL OF FLOW THROUGH SYSTEM

This is a modification in the CIFA flow through system by adding temperature monitoring system which is necessary to increase the rate of survivality of magur larvae. This innovative model device comprises a stand on which are placed a row of plastic tubs (12 cm diameter and 6 cm high). Water supplied from the overhead tank through a common pipe to all the tubs with individual control tabs. Each tub is provided with an outlet at a height of 4 cm and connected to a common conduit to drain off water. Lights are fixed over each tub for maintaining the temperature in the tubs during incubation. The wattage of bulbs is selected depending on the need of raise in temperature. Normally 100 Watt bulb is sufficient to maneuver the temperatures in Vidarbha Region where, during the monsoon the average minimum temperature is found to be 16 °C which may decline up to 6° C in extreme conditions. But the ideal water temperature required for the rearing of magur larvae is 22 ° C to 30 °C.

SINGHI (HETEROPNEUSTES FOSSILIS)

This is a common catfish found in freshwater swamps, ponds and tanks throughout the country. It is also suitable for pond culture. It reportedly attains a length of 200 mm at the end of the first year and a maximum length of about 450 mm. This fish breeds in ponds and confined waters almost throughout the year, peak season being monsoon. During rainy days, fishes move from wells to shallow inundated areas of paddy fields for breeding. The eggs are greenish in colour and are usually found attached to weeds. This fish has been successfully induced to breed in India by administering in one injection 75–100 IU of human chorionic gonadotrophin. It is also possible to induce this fish to breed 8 to 10 weeks ahead of peak spawning season by administering pituitary gland injections. By hypophysation these fishes can be induced to breed several times in the same season. Even the spawning season could be prolonged by 2–3 months when the fishes are kept exposed to light during this period for about 12 hours every day. The incubation period extends from 18–20 hours and the newly hatched larvae measure about 2–7 mm in length. At this stage, the larvae feed voraciously on zooplankton. Therefore, it is suggested that before stocking the larvae, the nursery ponds have to be prepared to have abundant zooplankton to get better survival of hatchlings.

BREEDING OF KAI (ANABAS TESTUDINEUS)

The adults are solitary and aggressive. It can gain weight up to 52gm in one year. Maturity occurs at the age of one when the fishes reach a size of 10–12cm in total length. The sexual dimorphism in A. testudineus is more apparent during breeding season. The mature male acquires a reddish hue on the body, particularly on the pectoral and ventral fins. The female shows only a faint reddish colour. Further in the male a distinct diamond shaped black spot appears in the caudal peduncle. In the female this black spot is oblong and somewhat diffused. Moreover, the female in contrast to the male, has a prominently bulging abdomen. The ventral distance between the bases of the two pectoral fins in the female is significantly greater than the male. In the breeding season, the female exhibits a prominent bulge at the vent, resembling the genital papillae while in the male this structure is absent. Mature males ooze out white milt and mature females ooze out ova even at a gentle pressure at the abdomen during breeding season.

In nature the eggs are scattered in open water at the onset of the rains without any nest. The male wraps itself in the female body, fertilizing the eggs as they are laid. Each time 200 colourless eggs are released until about 5000 nos are laid. The fecundity varies from 5000-35000 nos. The eggs rise to the surface and float. The eggs hatch in 24 hrs and the fry are about 2-3mm long. They are free swimming within two days of hatching.

While in artificial breeding with pituitary or synthetic hormone, a single dose of injection for both the male and female spawning actively and courtship behaviour starts after 6 hrs of injection. The water temperature to be maintained at 28° C + 1°C. Good spawning was reported with 8.0-12.0 mg/kg PG to female and 4.0 mg/kg of body weight to male admistration in hapa 7-8 hours after second injection in the temperature of 27-30°C. Fertilized eggs float on the surface of the water. It takes 18-19 hrs for hatching after spawning and newly hatched larvae measure 1.9-2.0 mm in length without any movement. Yolk sac completely absorbs on third day after hatching and settles at the bottom. Egg custard, plankton and Artemia are supplied as artificial feed for those frie up to 20-25 days. The survivability varies from 70-75 per cent.

BREEDING OF PANGAS (PANGASIUS SUTCHI)

Pangasiidae (order: Siluriformes) is a family of fresh water catfish common to southern and south-eastern Asia. Catfish of the genus Pangasius have been cultured in earthen ponds and other waters on the Indo-Chinese Peninsula since ancient times. The most important of these is Pangasius sutchi, which is commonly known as shark catfish or Thai pangas and reaches weights of 3 kg and lengths of 150 cm within 2 years of birth.

The fertilized eggs are adhesive and spherical with a yellowish or greenish-brown egg capsule. The yolk sac is yellowish-brown in colour and 1.20-1.80 mm in diameter. Nine hours post-fertilization, the first cleavage stage, embryonic shield, head, tail region, neural grooves and somites were evident. The incubation period ranges from 24-36 h at a temperature of 20-30°C.

The newly hatched larvae are quite transparent and light yellowish in colour with a body length of 2.98-3.10 mm. Eye pigments appear and the heart starts to work within 12-14 h of hatching. In 1-day-old pro-larvae, the mouth becomes well developed; barbules are elongated, prominent and look like tiny threads. The yolk sac is fairly well absorbed and the palatine teeth are fully developed during the 3 day pro-larval stage. At the end of 12 days of larval development, the stomach becomes functional and aerial respiration starts. After 2 weeks, the young fry is well-developed, and is of an adult appearance, that is, measuring up to 13.56 mm in length.

OMPOK (PABDA) SPP

Ompok pabda/bimaculatus (Ham.) popularly known as 'butter cat fish' or pabda is a freshwater species native to India specially in North East States of India. Open beels/mauns connected with rivers are common habitats. Pabda has fine flesh with a soft meat texture, good taste and high nutritional value. Presently Ompok spp has been listed as an endangered fish species in India due to its decrease in abundance and restricted distribution. Causes of the decline are likely to be indiscriminate fishing during the breeding season, wide use of pesticide and insecticides from agricultural fields causing pollution and siltation in habitat. The fish attained maturity at the end of the first year. Males matured earlier than females, which became mature at 30 -40 g in weight.

Fertilization is external and spawning occurs once a year during the monsoon season (June - August) with a peak in July. Fully ripe females and males were segregated and used in induced breeding. Females can be distinguished by a rounder, fuller abdomen, reddish vent colour and rounded genital papilla.

Males have an elongated and pointed genital papilla. Used Ovaprim to promote induction of spawning. Ovaprim was applied at 1 - 1.5 ml/kg body weight for females and 0.5-1.0ml/kg body weight for males, applied in a single injection. Females were stripped for spawning 8 - 10 hours after hormone injection and the eggs were collected in a tray. Milt was obtained from males by surgically removing the testes, which were macerated to produce a suspension to be mixed with the eggs for fertilisation. Eggs were subsequently washed thoroughly with clean water and transferred to a fibreglass/cement tank for hatching, with constant aeration.

EMBRYONIC DEVELOPMENT

30 minutes after fertilization the blastodisc begins to form over the yolk, following first, second and third cleavage. Sixty four cell stages were observed after 70 minutes postfertilisation followed by morula stage in two hours. Yolk plug stage appeared after five hours.

The cephalic and caudal end of the embryo had differentiated after 10 — 15 hours. After 16 —21 hours the gut had faintly appeared posterior to the yolk sac, leading to the anus, and movement of the embryo could be seen within the egg. After 22 hours movements of the embryo were observed. The eggs began to hatch after 23 hours.

LARVAL REARING

Newly hatched larva can be reared in fibre glass tanks and cement cisterns as well as in nurseries using pond water. Suitable water parameters are temperature 25±3° C, alkalinity 120-150 mg l^{-1} and dissolved oxygen in the range 3 - 5 mg l^{-1}. Initially the water level of containers was maintained.at 3 - 4 cm, and gradually increased to 15 - 20 cm after one week. Water levels were adjusted at different stages of rearing to minimize the stress to larva. Aquatic weeds such as Hydrilla can be provided to give cover for the larvae.

FEED

Yolk sacs were absorbed in around three days. Early spawn were cannibalistic, attacking and devour others. It was necessary to reduce the density of the stocked population to reduce cannibalism. Mixed zoo plankton, Tubifex worm, and egg custard were provided as larval feed.

Larvae accept zooplankton up to day 15. In fry stages and onwards the fish can be fed with compound feed (rice polish, silk worm pupae and boiled egg) at 100 per cent of body weight of the population. The average size of fry was 1.1 - 2.0 cm in length and 0.6 - 2.0 g in weight. Fry can also can be reared in fibre glass tanks and cement cisterns fed with both zooplanktons 2.0 - 3.0 Embyonic development at 1 hour and 10 minutes. Embryonic development at 1 hour and 42 minutes. Embryonic development at 11 hours and 40 minutes. Fry attained 5.0 - 6.0 cm and 3.0 -5.0 g after a rearing period of 40 days, which is a good size for stocking in grow out ponds.

BREEDING OF MURRELS

The important cultured species are:

- Channa marulius
- C. panctatus
- C. striatus

Among freshwater fish species, murrels (snakeheads) and catfishes secure the top rank economically. Murrels have long been commercially cultured in Thailand, Taiwan and Philippines. But fish farmers in India are not much familiar with murrel culture due to want of breeding, feeding and culture techniques. The common species are Therefore it is imperative to make murrel culture popular among fish farmers and unemployed youths for income generation.

Females with soft and swollen bellies are suitable for breeding. However a gentle pressure on the belly for oosing of eggs could check prime maturation. Males are selected by external examination of genital papilla since they do not ooze milt by pressure. The fecundity of Channa punctata ranges from 2,200 in a specimen of 12·1 cm TL to 33,873 in a specimen of 22·3 cm TL. Murrels are induced to spawn by injecting natural (pituitary, human chorionic gonadotropin) or synthetic (ovaprim, ovatide) hormones intramuscularly. Among the hormones tested a synthetic product of SGnRHa marketed by Glaxo Ltd. is recommended at a single dose of 0.5 ml/ Kg.

Each breeding set consists of one female and two males. Immediately after injection each breeding set is introduced into a breeding tank (6m x 5m x1m) having sides pasted with cement and bottom filled with clay. Aquatic weeds (*e.g.*, water hyacinth) are introduced into the breeding tank for hiding purposes. Spawning activities are observed after 6-10 hrs of hormone injection. Courtship behaviour continues till the complete release of eggs and milt (24-30 hrs). Fertilization is external and the fertilized eggs are usually floating. An egg mass of about 6-14 cm diameter consists of 5000-10,000 eggs (diameter 1.2mm - 1.5mm).

The rate of fertilization ranges between 70-90 per cent. Hatching takes place 24 30 hrs after fertilization and the hatchlings (2.8mm - 3.2mm in length) are guarded by the parents especially by the male parent. From a single spawning 4000-8000 hatchlings/female are obtained.

REARING OF SPAWN

The yolk sac is completely absorbed on the 3rd day and the mouth is fully formed. At that time the larvae start exogenous feeding especially on small plankton like rotifers. The young ones are allowed to stay with parents in the breeding tanks for one or two weeks. To avoid cannibalism the fry are removed from breeding tanks after two weeks. The fry are fed with boiled and finely ground chicken intestine or fish waste. After a month the fry (15mm length) attains red colour.

The fry are reared in cement tanks (3m × 1m × 1m) with a stocking density of 500/m^2. Whenever the young ones are reared, they should be of equal size to avoid cannibalism. Fry survival may be 65-80 per cent in the cement tanks. Water quality (29 ±°C, 0.06 - 6.52mgO2/l pH 7.5 - 8.2) and feeding are the deciding factors for the survival of the young ones. A flow through system is always preferred for better survival. The fry are reared in medium (3m × 1m

× 1m) or large cement (5m × 4m ×. 2m) tanks upto the fingerling stage. The fry reaches 4 to 5 cms after 2 months and the fingerlings are collected from the cement tanks for commercial culture.

Table. Effect of Different Doses of Two Hormones on Induced Spawning in C. punctatus and H. fossilis. The Low, Medium and High Dosages with Different Superscripts are Significantly Different (P<0.05)

Hormone	Fish mass (g)	Dosage Latency Fertilization Egg output kg/bw period (h) rate (%)		Hatching rate (%)		Survival rate of hatchlings (%)	
C. punctatus							
Ovaprim	65 – 80	0.1 ml	–	–	30 ± 8	–	–
	65 – 80	0.3 ml	28 – 34	73.5	3276 ± 75	65.0	30
	75 – 85	0.5 ml	28 – 34	75.0	198 ± 10	50.0	10
	60 – 70	1000 IU	–	–	102 ± 20	–	–
HCG	70 – 80	2000 IU	28 – 34	75.5	699 ± 78	65.5	50
	65 – 85	3000 IU	28 – 34	78.0	1253 ± 126	70.5	65
H. fossilis							
	100 – 105	0.3 ml	18 – 24	70.0	258 ± 85	50.5	10
Ovaprim	90 – 105	0.5 ml	18 – 24	75.0	1052 ± 220	60.0	30
	90 – 100	0.7 ml	18 – 24	70.0	6692 ± 790	50.0	15
	80 – 105	1000 IU	18 – 24	78.0	6336 ± 800	75.0	60
HCG	90 – 100	2000 IU	18 – 24	75.0	18376 ± 1020	60.5	50
	110 – 115	3000 IU	18 – 24	70.0	82922 ± 5432	60.0	55

SMALL INDIGENOUS FISHES (SIFS) AND THEIR BREEDING

Small indigenous fishes traditionally occupy an unenviable position and an inseparable link in the life, livelihood, health and the general well being of the rural mass, especially the poor. It has been reported that some species such as mola (A. mola), dhela (O. cotio cotio), darkina (E. danricus) and kaski (C. soborna) contain a high amount of vitamin A and other micronutrients and minerals.

Studies in Bangladesh and Cambodia showed that small fish species make up 50- 80 per cent of all fish eaten during the production season. Two species from the genus Esomus (E. danricus, E. longimanus) are rich in high iron content. Small scale aquaculture of A. mola, Puntius sophore, Osteobrama cotio, Cirrihinus reba, Labeo bata, Gudusia chapra, Notopterus nototerus, etc., along with Indian major carps have been reported in India.

Successful captive breeding of several SIF's have been reported under National Agricultural Technology Project (NATP) -NBFGR projects and also by several workers. Many of the SIF's are self breeders and need proper management practices to facilitate natural breeding mostly in monsoon.

INDUCED BREEDING METHOD

The technique of induced breeding consists of injecting fish pituitary gland into sexually mature carp fishes in their optimum physiological conditions under favourable water and climatic conditions during monsoon season. The optimum temperature of the water for the breeding ranges from 24 to 33 centigrade with cool and drizzling weather. Rain water is helpful in spawning and also ensures high rate of fertilization. Water temperature between 27 to 31°C results in better hatching. The normal breeding season ot' carps is during rainy season (during South-West monsoon, *i.e.*, between April to September). The induced breeding method is done in the following steps.

MAINTENANCE OF BREEDING STOCK

The most important aspect of induced breeding is the maintenance of the selected male and female fish belonging to a particular breed of carps, *i.e.*, catla, rohu, mrigal, silver carp or grass carp. The quality of the breeding stock is one of the major determining factors that contributes to the success of the fish farming. The breeding stock should be at least two years old and should be kept in ponds at the rate of 1000 to 2000 kg per hectare. The breeder should estimate the average weight of single fish in the pond by random sampling. He also should keep an account of the number of fish introduced into the pond and the number of fish dead by daily observation and recording. So from the average weight of single fish, the number of fish alive in the pond and the area of pond, one can estimate the total weight of the breeding fish per hectare. If the weight is more then reduce the weight by removing some fish that are poor among them. This is done by netting a large number of fish and then removing those having poor growth and physiological conditions.

The breeding stock should be introduced into the breeding pond at least six months before the breeding season. The breeder should therefore make proper calculations and planning of the time of breeding and introduction of the breeding stock into the pond depending on the arrival of the monsoon rains. In Assam and other parts of North East the rain starts in November onwards. In Kerala, the monsoon starts in the first week of June and moves upward and by first week of July covers all parts of the country. However, normally, the rainy season lasts till September, but in some areas it may extend till November.

There are some ratios and specifications to be kept in mind between the weight and number of various types of carps and between male and female. For example, if one wants to produce one crore fry or spawn (60 lakh Indian carps and 40 lakh Chinese carps) during a season one should keep 750 kg of breeding stock (450 kg in Indian carps and 300 kg of Chinese carps) comprising of males and females in an approximate ration of 1:1 by weight and 2:1 by number. The size of the pond required at the rate of 2000 kg per hectare will be 3750 square metre or 100×37.5 metre.

Similarly, if one wants to produce one million fry or spawn (6 lakh Indian carps and 4 lakh Chinese carps) during a season he should keep 75 kg of breeding stock (45 kg in Indian carps and 30 kg of Chinese carps) comprising of males and females in an approximate ration of 1:1 by weight and 2:1 by number. The size of the pond required at the rate of 2000 kg per hectare will be 375 square metre or 25×15 metre pond.

The pond should be free from weeds and predators, and should be enriched with manures and fertilizers (for more details consult Booklet No.524 on "Fish: Rearing of Carps") and should be provided with proper feed. (for details consult Booklet No.525 on Fish Feeding). A supplementary feed mixture of groundnut/ mustard oilcake and rice bran in 1:1 ratio by weight is fed at the rate of 1-2 per cent of the total body weight per day. In short the breeding stock should be maintained in the optimum physiological condition for breeding.

COLLECTION OF PITUITARY GLAND

The hormone responsible for the maturation of sex organs and the breeding tendencies in fish is secreted by the pituitary gland. This pituitary gland is situated just below the brain and immediately behind the optic chiasma in a concave space on the floor of the cranium. The pituitary glands may be collected from the fresh fish as well as from those which are well preserved provided the fish is weighing at least two kilograms. Pituitary glands of both males and females are taken; the glands could be from the same species or from the different species. Glands from induced bred fishes soon after spawning are also suitable for this purpose. Since mature common carps are available during most part of the year they also serve as a good source of gland material.

With a little practice anyone can learn to collect the pituitary gland from the fish. The glands are collected carefully during the premonsoon months depending on the places in India. They are preserved in absolute alcohol and kept in refrigeration.

METHOD OF COLLECTION

Select fishes of at least two kg weight and using a sharp knife open up the skull and expose the brain. The entire brain is lifted with the help of a forceps. Underneath the brain one can notice the pituitary gland covered with a membrane. Remove carefully the pituitary gland without rupture. In most of the fish markets heads are sold separately. Glands can be collected from these heads also provided they are from fishes of two kg and above.

SELECTION OF FISH FOR BREEDING

At the beginning of rainy season breeder fishes of two kg and above are netted out and selected for induced breeding. A male is easily distinguished by the roughness on the dorsal surface of the pectoral fin. The females possess soft, round, bulging belly and swollen, pinkish genital opening. When pressed gently on the belly of the mature male caw milt l (sperm containing secretion) oozes out freely at the belly near the vent. Similarly the mature female fish also can be gently pressed on its belly to extract the egg mass. This method of extraction of the milt and egg mass from the fish is called stripping. The fertilization takes place externally even in the nature too. In order to fertilize the milt from the male fish is poured over the egg mass collected into a basin or in the water inside the hapa (rectangular cloth container) fixed in a pond.

While the Indian major caws and males of Chinese carps are easy to select with the help of the above symptoms, a catheter alone may be useful in confirming the stage of maturity of female grass and silver carps. Insert a catheter through the genital opening and take out some oozytes and examine them in a petridish. The mature eggs of silver carp will be uniform in size and pale blue in colour whereas, that of the grass carp will be brownish or copper colour and uniform in size. Females with such eggs are selected for induced breeding. They are individually weighed and kept in hapas which is like an inverted mosquito net dipped in water.

DOSAGE OF INJECTION

The normal dosage is one injection of one ppm (one part for one million or one milligram of pituitary gland is injected into a kilogram of body weight of the recipient fish.) The females are given two injections at the interval of six hours. The males are given one injection at the time of the second injection given to the females. Depending on the maturity of fish and the climatic conditions the first dose vary from 2-4 mg/kg body weight and the second dose 5-10 mg/kg body weight. The males are given a single injection of 2-4 mg/kg body weight at the time of the second injection to the female. The silver carp and grass carp receive 3-4 mg/kg body weight as the dose of first injection and 8-10 mg/kg body weight as the dose of second injection. The males receive 3-4 mg/kg body weight at the time of second injection to the female.

Hydration of the gonads of the breeding is necessary for the successful spawning of carps. Hydration is induced by the injection of the pituitary gland and thereby the body weight of the breeding females increases. An increase of body weight by 3 per cent between the two injections is an indication of a better breeding success.

PREPARATION OF INJECTION MATERIAL

Select the fish for injection and detennine the weight and calculate the required pituitary gland for its injection. The pituitary gland is preserved in alcohol. For preparing the injection material, take out the gland from the alcohol and place it in a dish and allow the alcohol on the specimen to evaporate. The exact amount of pituitary gland is weighed out (with the help of sensitive balance which can weigh one hundredth of a milligram) and the rest is returned to the alcohol in the bottle. The weighed out gland is smashed thoroughly in a tissue homogeniser with a little distilled water or 0.3 per cent saline water. It is further diluted with the same liquid to a desired volume. The solution is centrifuged and only the supernatant solution is utilised for injection.

The extract can be prepared in bulk and preserved in glycerine (one part extract with two parts glycerine) and stored in refrigerator or ice for later use. It can be stored in ampules and transported to other places.

INJECTION TO BREEDING STOCK

The injection is prepared and kept ready before the fishes are caught for injecting. Depending on the weight of the fish the volume of extract may vary from 0.5 -2.0 ml/fish. One breeding stock means one female and two males. The combined weight of the two males should be more or less equal to one female. Catch the breeding female in a hand-net and place the fish in the net on a soft cushion and the injection is given intramuscularly near the tail of the body avoiding the lateral line (lines on both sides of the fish indicating the position of the line of nerves in the fish. This is noticed by the slight colour change on both sides in a line from head to tail). The first injection is given preferably late in the afternoon hours followed by the second injection after six hours. At the time of second injection to the females the males are also similarly injected with the required amount of pituitary extract.

Ordinary injection needles are used for injecting the pituitary gland. Necessary precautions should be taken to sterilise the needle and all the equipments used for the collection of milt and egg mass. The hands ot' the operators and the people helping him should be scrubbed and washed clean to avoid all possible infection. The injected sets of breeder fish (one female and two males) are then let into the breeding tank of metal or cement or plastic. The water temperature should be maintained between 27 to 31" centigrade for this any cooling device may be employed. A small flow of water should be maintained through the breeding tank.

If these arrangements are not possible then keep each set of breeders inside separate hapas fixed in ponds, marginal waters of canals, lakes or reservoirs. The breeding hapa is a rectangular cloth container (2.5×1.25×1.0 m) stitched with close meshed cloth, having an opening on one side with fastening arrangements to close the opening. The breeders are introduced and taken out through this opening.

6

Aquarium Fish Diseases

INTRODUCTION

There are literally hundreds of afflictions that can effect the health of your fish. The most common maladies seen in home aquaria are usually either bacterial or parasitic in origin. Fungal infections are also sometimes seen, and occasionally physical ailments.

Luckily, most fish ailments are easily diagnosed and can be treated with success. The most common of these afflictions are included here. How to prevent fish disease has steps you can take to reduce the possibility of disease and help to keep disease from spreading if it should occure. A table of contents is provided along with a diagnostic chart with links to appropriate medications.

Understanding how an aquarium and its filtration work to support aquatic life is vital in preventing fish ailments. The basics of life support are the same whether you have a freshwater aquarium, saltwater aquarium, or a mini reef.

FISH DISEASE

Fish ailments can be separated into 4 general types including bacterial infections, fungal infections, parasitic or protozoan infections, and physical ailments and wounds.

1. *Bacterial Diseases:* Bacterial diseases are usually characterized by red streaks or spots and/or swelling of the abdomen or eye. These are best treated by antibiotics such as penicillin, amoxicillin, or erythromycin.
2. *Fungal Diseases*: Comon fungal infections often look like gray or white fluffy patches. are
3. *Parasitic Diseases:* The most common parasitic disease called "Ich" can be treated most effectively with copper or malachite green in the right dosage. Most treatments will have copper as an ingredient. Many water treatments like "Aquari-Sol" will also contain copper as an ingredient. If the treatment you use is an anti-biotic or copper based, remember to remove all carbon from the filtration system.

4. *Physical Ailments:* Physical Ailments are often the result of the environment. Poor quality water conditions can lead to fish gasping, not eating, jumping out of the tank, and more. Tank mate problems can result in nipped fins and bite wounds.

HOW TO PREVENT FISH DISEASES

Some steps can be taken to reduce the possibility of your fish getting a disease.

Following these precautions can also help keep fish diseases from spreading if they do occur.

- Buy only good-quality, compatible fish.
- Quarantine new fish before adding them to the aquarium. (A hospital tank can be used for this).
- Avoid stressing the fish with rough handling, sudden changes in conditions, or "bully" tankmates.
- Don't overfeed your fish.
- Remove sick fish to a hospital tank for treatment.
- Disinfect nets used to move sick fish.
- Don't transfer water from the quarantine tank to the main aquarium.
- Don't let any metal come in contact with the aquarium water.
- *Anti-biotics:* When using any anti-biotic, make sure the biological filtration in your aquarium is not destroyed. You want to be certain the treatment does not kill the nitrifying bacteria in your system at the same time it attacks harmful bacteria on your fish. Although most of the treatments available at the store state that they will not harm your biological filter, sometimes they wil. It is best to either monitor your ammonia and nitrite levels, or use an ammonia remover such as "AmQuel" to be sure your levels of ammonia don't become a problem.
- *Copper Treatments:* When using any medication which has copper as an ingredient, be aware that most plants will not do as well. Invertebrates, such as snails, can also be killed if the amount of copper is sufficient. Indeed, most snail removers are copper based.

DIAGNOSTIC CHART

If you notice something is wrong with your fish, a proper diagnoses is usually all you need to worry about. In most cases, a proprietary treatment (fish medications) purchased at a pet store will work very well.

Steps to diagnosing and treating your fish:

- *Symptom*: Match the symptoms your fish is showing with those listed under the 'Symptom' column.
- *Possible Cause*: Learn about each disease by clicking on the link under 'Possible Cause'.

- *Medication:* Find the treatment for the disease under the 'Medication' column.
- *Product Link*: Use the 'Compare Prices' column to compare similar products and merchant's prices.

Red Pest

Symptoms: Bloody streaks on fins or body.

Red Pest is called such because of bloody streaks that appear on the body, fins and/or tail. These streaks could proceed to ulcerations and possibly lead to fin and tail rot with, in severe cases, the tail and/or fins falling off. As the disease is internal, external treatments are usually not effective, except in very slight cases. In slight cases, treat the aquarium with a disinfectant and clean the aquarium as best as possible. Do not feed a lot while the aquarium is being treated. To disinfect, use acriflavine (trypaflavine) or monacrin (monoaminoacridine) using a 0.2 per cent solution at the rate of 1 ml per litre. Both disinfectants will colour the water, but the colour disappears as the disinfectants dissipates. If the fish do not appear to respond favourably, discontinue disinfections. Then add an antibiotic to the food. With flake food, use about 1 per cent of antibiotic and carefully mix it in. If you keep the fish hungry they should eagerly eat the mixture before the antibiotic dissipates. Antibiotics usually come in 250 mg capsules.

MOUTH FUNGUS

Symptoms: White cottony patches around the mouth.

Mouth Fungus is so called because it looks like a fungus attack of the mouth. It is actually caused from the bacterium Chondrococcus columnaris. It shows up first as a gray or white line around the lips and later as short tufts sprouting from the mouth like fungus. The toxins produced and the inability to eat will be fatal unless treated at an early stage. This bacteria is often accompanied by a second infection of an Aeromonas bacteria. Penicillin at 10,000 units per litre is a very effective treatment. Treat with a second dose in two days. Or use chloromycetin, 10 to 20 mg per litre, with a second dose in two days. Other antibiotics can also be effective. Kanacyn (kanamycin) will treat both bacteria at once. Maracyn (erythromycin) is effective against C. columnaris, and using Maracyn 2 (minocycline) in conjuntion with it will treat the Aeromonas bacteria as well.

TUBERCULOS–MYCOBACTERIOSIS

Syn: fish tuberculosis, piscine tuberculosis, acid-fast disease, granuloma disease.

Symptoms: Emaciation, hollow belly, possibly sores.

Tuberculosis is caused by the bacterium Mycobacterium piscium. Fish infected with tuberculosis may become lethargic, hollow bellied, pale, show skin ulcers and frayed fins, have fin and scale loss, and loss of appetite. Yellowish or darker nodules may appear on the eyes or body and may deform the fish.

The main causes for this disease appears to be over crowding in unkempt conditions; *i.e.*, poor water quality. All fish species could be susceptible though some are more susceptible than others. Those most susceptible are the labyrinth air breathers like the Gouramis, Bettas, and Paradise Fish. Others include Neon Tetras, Discus, and the Ram Cichlid.

- There is no absolute treatment. However the most effective treatment known for this disease is to treat with Kanamycin and Vitamin B-6 for 30 days. Kanamycin can be purchased at your local fish store. Liquid baby vitamins work well as s Vitamin B-6 source. They are available at your local pharmacy. Add one drop per every 5 gallons of aquarium water during treatment.
- If the treatment is ineffective, the best thing to do is destroy the infected fish.
- If either unkempt conditions or over crowding are the suspected cause, correct the condition.

It is possible for humans to contract this disease so we recommend using caution when dealing with it. Humans are very rarely are at risk from aquariums though. It is more common to contract this disease from public swimming areas or as a food contaminant.

DROPSY

Symptoms: Bloating of the body, protruding scales.

Dropsy is caused from a bacterial infection of the kidneys, causing fluid accumulation or renal failure. The fluids in the body build up and cause the fish to bloat up and the scales to protrude. It appears to only cause trouble in weakened fish and possibly from unkempt aquarium conditions. An effective treatment is to add an antibiotic to the food. With flake food, use about 1 per cent of antibiotic and carefully mix it in. If you keep the fish hungry they should eagerly eat the mixture before the antibiotic dissipates. Antibiotics usually come in 250 mg capsules. If added to 25 grams of flake food, one capsule should be enough to treat dozens of fish. A good antibiotic is chloromycetin (chloramphenicol). Or use tetracycline. If you feed your fish frozen foods or chopped foods, try to use the same ratio with mixing. As a last resort add at most 10 mg per litre of water. Also, if unkempt conditions are the suspected cause, correct it.

TAIL ROT AND FIN ROT

Symptoms: Disintegrating fins that may be reduced to stumps, exposed fin rays, blood on edges of fins, reddened areas at base of fins, skin ulcers with gray or red margins, cloudy eyes. Tail and fin rot appears to be a bacterial infection of the tail and/or fins and may be caused by generally poor conditions, bully, or fin nipping tankmates. If aquarium conditions are not good an infection can be caused from a simple injury to the fins/tail. Tuberculosis can lead to tail and fin rot. Basically, the tail and/or fins become frayed or lose colour. Over time the affected area slowly breaks down. First, attempt to ascertain the cause. Then treat accordingly. Also, treat the water or fish with antibiotics.

If added to the water, use 20 - 30 mg per litre. If the fish is to be treated add an antibiotic to the food. With flake food, use about 1 per cent of antibiotic and carefully mix it in. If you keep the fish hungry they should eagerly eat the mixture before the antibiotic dissipates. Antibiotics usually come in 250 mg capsules. If added to 25 grams of flake food, one capsule should be enough to treat dozens of fish. A good antibiotic is chloromycetin (chloramphenicol) or tetracycline. If you feed your fish frozen foods or chopped foods, try to use the same ratio with mixing. As a last resort add at most 10 mg per litre of water. Also, if unkempt conditions are the suspected cause, correct it.

PARASITIC DISEASES

Argulus (Fish louse)

Symptoms: The fish scrapes itself against objects, clamped fins, visible parasites about 1/4 inch in diameter are visible on the body of the fish.

The fish louse is a flattened mite-like crustacean about 5 mm long that attaches itself to the body of fish. They irritate the host fish which may have clamped fins, become restless, and may show inflamed areas where the lice have been.

With larger fish and light infestations, the lice can be picked off with a pair of forceps. Other cases can best be done with a 10 to 30 minute bath in 10 mg per litre of potassium permanganate. Or treat the whole tank with 2 mg per litre, but this method is messy and dyes the water.

Anchor Worm (Lernaea)

Symptoms: The fish scrapes itself against objects, whitish-green threads hang out of the fish's skin with an inflamed area at the point of attachment.

Anchor worms are actually crustaceans. The young are free swimming and borrow into the skin, go into the muscles and develop for several months before showing. They release eggs and die. The holes left behind are ugly and may become infected. The anchor worm is too deeply imbedded to safely remove. Treatment can best be done with a 10 to 30 minute bath in 10 mg per litre of potassium permanganate. Or treat the whole tank with 2 mg per litre, but this method is messy and dyes the water.

Black Spot - Black Ick (Diplopstomiasis)

Symptoms: The fish, very irritated, scrapes itself against objects, appears as small black specks or smudges on the body and around the mouth, and if heavily infected may experience blood loss. Black Spot or Black Ick is rare in aquariums. It is generally seen in outdoor ponds, especially those with mud bottoms, but it can be introduced when adding new fish into the aquarium. Fish that are most readily susceptible are the Silver Dollar, Piranha, or other fish of these types. In general it does relatively little damage to the fish, even if they are heavily infested. The disease is caused by a parasite (larval trematode) that burrows into the skin of a fish where it forms a cyst that is about one millimeter in diameter. It has a complex lifecyle that in order to survive, requires fish eating birds or animals, snails, or fish at different stages infected with the disease. Black Spot is generally easy to cure. Either treat with salt baths or there are a number of commercially available treatments and preventatives.

Ergasilus

Symptoms: The fish scrapes itself against objects, whitish-green threads hang out of the fish's gills. This parasite is like the anchor worm, but is smaller and attacks the gills instead of the skin. Treatment can best be done with a 10 to 30 minute bath in 10 mg per litre of potassium permanganate. Or treat the whole tank with 2 mg per litre, but this method is messy and dyes the water.

Flukes

Symptoms: The fish scrapes itself against objects, rapid gill movement, mucus covering the gills or body, the gills or fins may be eaten away, the skin may become reddened.

There are many species of flukes, which are flatworms about 1 mm long, and several symptoms that are visible. They infest gills and skin much like ich, but the difference can be seen with a hand lens. You should be able to see movement and possibly eye spots, which is not found in ich. Gill flukes will eventually destroy the gills thus killing the fish. Symptoms of a heavy infestations are pale fish with drooping fins, rapid respiration, glancing off aquarium decor, and/or hollow bellies. Treatment can best be done with a 10 to 30 minute bath in 10 mg per litre of potassium permanganate. Or treat the whole tank with 2 mg per litre, but this method is messy and dyes the water.

Nematoda

Symptoms: Worms hanging from the anus.

Nematodes (threadworms) infect just about anywhere in the body but only shows itself when they hang out of the anus. A heavy infestation causes hollow bellies. Lighter infestations usually cause no problems with the fish. Short of destroying the fish, which is easier, two treatments have been suggested. First treatment; soak the food in parachlorometaxylenol and give the fish a bath or treat the aquarium with 10 ml per litre. The bath should last for several days. Second treatment; find special food containing thiabendazole as a nematode (threadworm) cure and hope the fish will eat it.

Leeches

Symptoms: Leeches are visible on the fish's skin.

Leeches are external parasites and affix themselves on the body, fins, or gills of the fish. Usually they appear as heart shaped worms (they are just curled up) attached to the fish. They are usually introduced to the aquarium via plants or snails. Since leeches are sucking and borrowing into the surface of the fish, removal with forceps can cause great damage, if not death, to the fish. If the fish is bathed in a 2.5 per cent solution of salt for 15 minutes, most of the leeches should just fall off. Those that do not will be affected enough to remove with forceps with minimal damage. Another treatment is to add Trichlorofon at 0.25 mg/l to the aquarium. Live plants should be removed and treated with potassium permanganate at 5 mg/l before replanting.

Uronema Marinum

Symptoms: Skin scraping, pale discolouration, loss of colour, weight loss, dehydration, flashing, and rapid breathing.

The saltwater parasite, *Uronema marinum*, is a free-living ciliated protozoa that can cause fatal infections in marine fish. It is an opportunistic feeder that normally eats on bacteria, but when the immunization of a fish is low it will attack, invading the fish's muscles and internal organs. This infestation is often the result of the introduction of a new fish, overcrowding, and poor water quality resulting from a high organic load in the aquarium.

This parasite is difficult to identify as the symptoms can also be indicative of other parasitic and bacterial problems. However, it can be debilitating and ultimately fatal to a variety of marine fish including Tangs, especially the Yellow Tang, Angelfish species especially those in the genus *Centropyge*s, Seahorses, many species of Butterflyfish, yellow headed Jawfish, and others.

The best way to avoid the problem is to keep your current tank free from infestation. Quarantine all new fish for a period of three weeks, improve the water quality of the tank, and reduce the stress level in the aquarium by reducing the number of fish and incorporating places for fish to hide and rest.

There are several types of medications that can be used to treat infected fish:

- Medications such as Malachite green, Copper Sulfate, or Methylene blue. Use caution and be sure to follow the manufacturers instructions.
- Freshwater bath—place infected fish in the freshwater bath for a period of three minutes or until the fish shows signs of stress.
- Low salinity (hypo salinity) treatment—lower the salinity in the quarantine tank to a specific gravity of 1.011 and maintain at this salinity for 21 days. Do not use this treatment with invertebrates or especially sensitive fish such as sharks and rays.
- *Nitrofurazone*: An antibiotic that has some antiparasitic action, and can be helpful when used along with formalin dips.

FUNGAL DISEASES

FUNGUS (SAPROLEGNIA)

Symptoms: Tufts of dirty, cotton-like growth on the skin, can cover large areas of the fish, fish eggs turn white.

Fungal attacks always follow some other health problem like parasitic attack, injury, or bacterial infection. The symptoms are a gray or whitish growth in and on the skin and/or fins of the fish. Eventually, if left untreated, these growths will become cottony looking. The fungus, if left untreated, will eventually eat away on the fish until it finally dies. After ascertaining the initial cause of the fungus and remedying that, use a solution of phenoxethol at 1 per cent in distilled water. Add 10 ml of this solution per litre of aquarium water. Repeat after a few days if needed, but only once more as three treatments could be dangerous to aquarium inhabitants. If the symptoms are severe the fish can be removed from the aquarium and swabbed with a cloth that has been treated with small amounts of povidone iodine or mercurochrome.

For attacks on fish eggs, most breeders will use a solution of methylene blue adding 3 to 5 mg/l as a preventative measure after the eggs are laid.

Ichthyosporidium

Symptoms: Sluggishness, loss of balance, hollow belly, external cysts and sores.

Ichthyosporidium is a fungus, but it manifests itself internally. It primarily attacks the liver and kidneys, but it spreads everywhere else. The symptoms vary. The fish may become sluggish, lose balance, show hollow bellies, and eventually show external cysts or sores. By then it is usually too late for the fish. Treatment is difficult. Phenoxethol added to food as a 1 per cent solution may be effective. Chloromycetin added to the food has also been effective. But both of these treatments, if not watched with caution, could pose a risk to your fish. It is best, if diagnosed soon enough, to destroy the affected fish before the disease can spread.

MISCELLANEOUS

Head and Lateral Line Erosion Disease (HLLD or HLLE)—Hole-in-the-Head Disease

Symptoms: Begins as small pits on the head and face, usually just above the eye. If untreated, these turn into large cavities and then the disease progresses along the lateral line.

Head and Lateral Line Disease is also known as Hole-in-the-Head Disease, Lateral Line Erosion (LLE), and Lateral Line Disease (LLD). It is attributed to a nutritional deficiency of one or more of: Vitamin C, Vitamin D, calcium, and phosphorus. Though its cause is not definitively determined, it is thought to be caused by a poor diet or lack of variety, lack of partial water changes, or over filtration with chemical media such as activated carbon.

HLLE has been reversed by one or more of the following treatments:

- Increase frequent water changes.
- Add vitamins to frozen foods.
- Add the addition of flake foods, as they are enriched with vitamins.
- Add greens, either frozen or in leaf form, to the diet.
- Decrease the amount of beef heart as it lacks many critical nutrients.
- Remove activated carbon filtration.

(This disease is often confused with another disease called 'Hexamita', because both these diseases are often seen simultaneously in the same fish. Hexamita is a protozoan disease that attacks the lower intestine. Discus and other large cichlids, especially Oscars, are especially prone to Hexamita.)

Eye Problems

Symptoms: Cloudy cornea, opaque lens, pop eye, swelling, blindness.

- Cloudy cornea can result from a bacterial invasion. Antibiotics may help.
- Opaqueness can result from poor nutrition or a metacercaria invasion (grubs). Try foods with added vitamins and changing the diet to include variety.
- Pop eye (exophtalmia) can result from rough handling, gas embolism, tumors, bacterial infection, or vitamin A deficiency. Gas bubble or bacterial infection can be treated successfully with penicillin or amoxicillin.
- Blindness can be caused by poor nutrition or excessive light. Lowering the light level and a change of diet to include lots of variety may help prevent it.

Swim-bladder Disease

Symptoms: Abnormal swimming pattern, difficulty maintaining equilibrium.

Swim bladder problems usually indicate another problem listed here.

If you suspect swim-bladder problems in a fish, first check and treat it for other diseases as listed below:

- Congenitally deformed bladder
- Cancer or tuberculosis in organs adjacent to the swim bladder
- Constipation
- Poor nutrition
- Chilling or rapid fluctuations in temperature
- Serious parasitic infestation
- Serious bacterial infestation

If you have eliminated other causes, make sure you are feeding the right food and make sure the fish is not constipated. Give it live food for awhile to ensure it is getting enough roughage. Also, check the temperature for your fish's requirements and keep the temperature stable.

NON-INFECTIOUS MALADIES

Physical Injuries

Even in the best of aquariums under the supervision of the most astute aquarists, injuries occur. Some times a bully fish is the culprit, or sharp decor. Sometimes there appears to be no explanation. As in the human world, accidents happen. If the cause of the injury is obvious, it should be remedied. Then the injury should be treated. The injury should be touched with 2 per cent Mercurochrome, which is supplied commercially. Also, depending on the fish's tolerance to water conditions, keeping the fish in slightly acid water should speed recovery (pH 6.6). Minor injuries, if the water conditions are good, should just heal themselves.

Constipation

Some fish are more susceptible to constipation than others. Usually fish with more compressed bodies like angelfish and silver dollars. Symptoms are loss of appetite and swelling of the body. The cause is almost always diet. Usually, with a change of diet, the condition rights itself. But in stubborn cases try dried food that has been soaked in medicinal paraffin oil. Glycerol or castor oil may also be used. If the diet is changed on a regular basis and live foods offered occasionally this condition may never occur.

Tumors

Tumors can be caused by a virus or a cancer, but most tumors are genetic. The genetic tumors may be caused from too much hybridization, common amongst professional breeders. Practically all tumors are untreatable. If the fish is in distress, it should be destroyed.

Congenital Abnormalities

Abnormalities usually occur when professional breeders are trying to acquire certain strains in breeds. Most are beneficial abnormalities like albinism or extra finnage. But undesirable abnormalities crop up and are usually culled out by the breeder. However, such abnormalities sometimes happen in the amateur aquarium. If the abnormality is not life threatening or degrades the quality of life, just leave it be and brag to your friends about the unusual inhabitant. Otherwise, the fish should be humanely destroyed.

VIRAL DISEASES

LYMPHOCYSTIS

Symptoms: Nodular white swellings (cauliflower) on fins or body.

Lymphocystis is a virus, and being a virus, it affects the cells of the fish. It usually manifests itself as abnormally large white lumps (cauliflower) on the fins or other parts of the body. It can be infectious, but is usually not fatal. Unfortunately there is no cure, but fortunately this is a rare disease.

There are two suggested treatments. One treatment is to remove and destroy the infected fish as soon as possible. The other treatment is to simply separate the infected fish for several months and hope for remission, which usually does occur.

PROTOZOAN DISEASES

VELVET OR RUST

Symptoms: Clamped fins, respiratory distress (breathing hard), yellow to light brown "dust" on body.

This disease has the appearance of a golden or brownish dust over the fins and body. The fish may show signs of irritation, like glancing off aquarium decor, shortage of breath (fish-wise), and clamping of the fins. The gills are usually the first thing affected. Velvet affects different species in different ways. Danios seem to be the most susceptible, but often show no discomfort. This disease is highly contagious and fatal.

The best treatment is with copper at 0.2 mg per litre (0.2 ppm) to be repeated once in a few days if necessary. Acriflavine (trypaflavine) may be used instead at 0.2 per cent solution (1 ml per litre). As acriflavine can possibly sterilize fish and copper can lead to poisoning, the water should be gradually changed after a cure has been effected.

Marine Velvet (Amyloodinium Ocellatum)

Symptoms: Respiratory distress (fast breathing - gills opening more than 80 times per minute); White, yellow to light brown, or grey "dusty" appearance on body, Loss of appetite, Rubbing or scratching against decor or substrate. Marine velvet is one of the most common maladies experienced in the marine aquarium, with the other being Marine Ich.

It is found in all the oceans of the world and often infects wild and newly caught marine fish. It is a fast moving disease that can cause mass casualties. Primarily it infects the gills of fish but can attach itself to the body as well, burrowing deep into the skin's subcutaneous layer. Deaths are generally a result of interference to the respiratory system.

This disease is highly contagious and fatal. Chemical treatments for this disease include using copper. Follow the instructions provided by the manufacturer. Natural methods include hyposalinity, a quarantine tank with a low salinity. A danger with with using low salinity is in re-acclimating the fish to a higher salinity. You must be able to accurately measure the salinity and must increase it very slowly.

COSTIA

Symptoms: Milky cloudiness on skin.

This is a rare protozoan disease that causes a cloudiness of the skin. The best treatment is with copper at 0.2 mg per litre (0.2 ppm) to be repeated once in a few days if necessary. Acriflavine (trypaflavine) may be used instead at 0.2 per cent solution (1 ml per litre). As acriflavine can possibly sterilize fish and copper can lead to poisoning, the water should be gradually changed after a cure has been effected. Raising the water temperature to 80°–83° F for a few days has also been effective.

HEXAMITA

Symptoms: The first symptom of slimy, white mucous feces, even while still eating and acting normal. Further signs are the fish hiding in the corner it's head down, head above the eyes gets thin, they blacken in colour, and swim backwards. Hexamita are intestinal flagellated protozoa that attack the lower intestine. Discus and other large cichlids, especially Oscars, are especially prone to Hexamita. As it is a disease of the digestive tract, a wasting away or loss of appetite may be experienced.An effective treatment is the drug metronidazole. A combined treatment in the food (1 per cent in any food the fish will eat) and in the water (12 mg per litre) is recommended. Repeat the water treatment every other day for three treatments. (This disease is often confused with another disease called Head and Lateral Line Erosion (HLLE), which use to be called "hole-in-the-head" disease, because both these diseases are often seen simultaneously in the same fish. Head and Lateral Line Erosion disease looks like cavities or pits on the head and face. It is not a protozoan disease, but is actually caused by environmental conditions.)

ICH, ICK, WHITE SPOT DISEASE (ICHTHYOPHTHIRIUS MULTIFILIIS)

Symptoms: Salt–like specks on the body/fins. Excessive slime. Problems breathing (ich invades the gills), clamped fins, loss of appetite. Ich, Ick, or White Spot Disease is the most common malady experienced in the home aquarium. Luckily, this disease is also easily cured if caught in time! Ich is actually a protozoa called Ichthyophthirius multifiliis. There are three phases to the life cycle of this protozoa. Normally, to the amateur aquarist, the life cycle is of no importance. However, since Ich is susceptible to treatment at only one stage of the life cycle, an awareness of the life cycle is important.

- *Adult Phase:* It is embedded in the skin or gills of the fish, causing irritation (with the fish showing signs of irritation) and the appearance of small white nodules. As the parasite grows it feeds on red blood cells and skin cells. After a few days it bores itself out of the fish and falls to the bottom of the aquarium.

- *Cyst Phase:* After falling to the bottom, the adult parasite forms into a cyst with rapid cell divisions occurring.
- *Free Swimming Phase*: After the cyst phase, about 1000 free swimming young swim upwards looking for a host. If a host is not found within 2 to 3 days, the parasite dies. Once a host is found the whole cycle begins anew.

These three phases take about 4 weeks at 70° F but only 5 days at 80° F. For this reason it is recommended that the aquarium water be raised to about 80° for the duration of the treatment. If the fish can stand it, raise the temperature even higher up to 85°.

The free swimming phase is the best time to treat with chemicals. Raising the aquarium temperature to 80° F will greatly shorten the time for the free swimming phase to occur. The drug of choice is quinine hydrochloride at 30 mg per litre (1 in 30,000). Quinine sulphate can be used if the hydrochloride is not available. The water may cloud but this will disappear. By reducing the time (with raised temperature) of the phases, you should be able to attack the free swimming phase effectively. Some aquarists like to use malachite green, but it tends to stain the plastic and silicone in the aquarium. Most commercial remedies contain malachite green and/or copper, which are both effective.

MARINE ICH (CRYPTOCARYON IRRITANS)

Symptoms: Salt-like specks on the body/fins. Rubbing or scratching against decor or substrate, Excessive slime. Problems breathing (ich invades the gills), Frayed fins, Loss of appetite, Cloudy eyes, Abnormal swimming.

Marine ich or white spot disease is one of the most common maladies experienced in the marine aquarium, with the other being Marine Velvet. This protozoa has four phases to its life, lasting up to 38 days depending on the temperature of the environment. This parasite affects marine and brackish fish. Aquarists are most familiar with the stage where the protozoa is infesting the host, the small white spots similar to a sprinkling of salt on the fish's body and fins. Unfortunately this visual clue is also the reason for difficulty in eradicating marine ich.

Once the parasite has left the host's body many aquarists believe their fish is cured and the problem is solved and so they cease treatment, only to have another larger reoccurrence. For eradication treatment must be carried through to completion, so understanding the parasite's life cycle will greatly increase your chances of success.

The life cycle is outlined here:

- *Trophont Phase*: When the parasite is growing in the skin or gills of the fish it appears as small white nodules, and the fish begins showing signs of irritation. It will spend 5 to 7 days (depending on the temperature) feeding on the fish. Once it reaches maturity it leaves the fish, reportedly after the lights go out. It is now called a protomont.

- *Protomont Phase*: The protomont will free swim or will crawl about the substrate for several hours (2 to 18 hours) producing a sticky wall around itself with which it is able to adhere to a surface. Once it adheres it begins to turn into a cyst and is now called a tomont.
- *Tomont Phase*: At this stage there is rapid cell divisions occurring, resulting in hundreds of daughter parasites that are called tomites. This stage can last anywhere from 3 to 28 days. Eventually the tomites hatch and begin swimming about looking for a host and are now called theronts.
- *Theront Phase*: newly hatched, they are swimming about looking for a host which they must find within 24 hours or they will die. Once a host is found they turn into trophonts and the whole cycle begins anew.

The life cycle of this parasite can vary dramatically and is dependent on temperature, they cycle faster in a warmer environment. Ideally the parasite would be eliminated while on the host or shortly after leaving the host. However, those that are buried in the gills are immune to treatment until they leave the fish. This along with the variability of the cycle makes it difficult to treat in a timely manner. So to rid the aquarium of this protozoa, it is recommended that you use a combination of water changes and chemical treatment, a multiple number of times.

- *Chemical*: Chemical treatments for this disease include using copper, formalin, or a combination of copper and formalin. Follow the instructions provided by the manufacturer.
- *Natural*: Natural methods include either a quarantine tank with a low salinity (hyposalinity) or large frequent water changes. For low salinity keep the specific gravity of the water at approximately 1.009-1.010 with temperatures of 78–80°F (25–27°C) for 14 days. A danger with with using low salinity is in re-acclimating the fish to a higher salinity. You must be able to accurately measure the salinity and must increase it very slowly. For the water change method, replace 50 per cent of the aquarium water daily for 14 days. This is perfectly safe method as long as temperature and salinity are the same, and this will remove the parasites while in a free swimming stage.

Reportably some healthy fish can develop a limited immunity. This immunity is short-lived lasting only about six months and may not be a total immunity, being a small amount of infestation rather than extensive infestation.

NEON TETRA DISEASE

Symptoms: Whitened areas deep into the fishes' flesh. Muscle degeneration leading to abnormal swimming movements.

So named for the fish it was first recognized on, the Neon Tetra. It is caused by the sporozoa Plistophora hyphesso-bryconis. Even though it is named after Neon Tetras, it can appear on other fish. Whitish patches appear as if just below the skin. In Neon Tetras it destroys the bright blue-green neon stripe. The organisms form cysts which burst and release spores.

The spores penetrate further and form more cysts. Eventually, the spores migrate to the water and are eaten by other fish in the food. These spores migrate into the digestive tract, then the muscles, and a new infection starts. There is no known cure. It is best to destroy the infected fish and clean the aquarium.

GLUGEA AND HENNEGUYA

Symptoms: Similar to Lymphocystis, the fish will have nodular white swellings on fins or body. Glugea and Henneguya are sporozoans that form large cysts on the fish's body and release spores. Luckily, these diseases are very rare. The fish bloat up, with tumor like protrusions, and eventually die. No cure, as of yet. It is best to destroy the infected fish before the spores can spread.

CHILODONELLA

Symptoms: Dulling of the colour due to excessive slime, fraying of the fins, weakness, gill damage.

This disease causes a blue white cloudiness on the skin and attacks the gills. Later the skin may be broken down and the gills destroyed. The fish may behave like they have irritations, by glancing off aquarium decor, they may have clamped fins and difficulty breathing. Acriflavine (trypaflavine) may be used at 1 per cent solution (5 ml per litre). As acriflavine can sterilize fish, the water should be gradually changed after a cure has been effected. It also helps to raise the temperature to about 80° F.

AFRICAN BLOAT OR "MALAWI BLOAT"

Symptoms: The first sign of 'bloat' is loss of appetite which is then followed by swelling of the abdomen, laboured breathing, listlessness, reclusiveness, possible red striations on the body, and stringy white feces.

There seems to be no explainable rationale as to its cause of bloat. Once a fish becomes afflicted it is often fatal. A fish that is not eating must be treated immediately or it can quickly become incurable and die.

Though It is not certain what this disease is, it is generally believed to be caused by a protozoal parasite complicated by bacterial infection. Bloat is a serious malady often associated with African cichlids especially those from Lake Malawi, thus the common name 'Malawi Bloat'. The *Tropheus* species from Lake Tanganyika are also very susceptible. The most common cause of this disease is stress and the first sign if illness is not eating. Stress can be caused by such things as transport, netting, poor water quality, insufficient diet, over feeding, and a lack of hiding places. Other causes, that are easily remedied, are an improper diet and adding too much salt to the water. Prevention is of utmost importance, and It is possibly to cure a fish if treated right away.

Following are some techniques aquarists use:

- Any new specimens you obtain can have bloat or will often soon develop it. When you first acquire them try to provide them with the same food that the dealer was feeding, and then wean them onto a good vegetable based diet; Spirulina flake and pellet.
- Some will soak the food in dissolved metronidazol and feed them that for the first few days when first obtained. Seachem makes a metronidazol that can be bound to food when used with their Focus product.
- A good vegetable based diet is important.
- A healthy group of fish will eat with gusto. But even though they can be very active feeders it is important to not overfeed them. Keep an eye on them, and if one is not eating with vigour some aquarists will then treat the tank with Clout.
- One author says that they will segregate an ailing fish the second they see signs of not eating, and then will do water changes every day for 5 days in the main aquarium.

Metronidazol is considered the most reliable cure and some use Clout as another cure, but do not use them together.

BACTERIAL DISEASES OF FISH

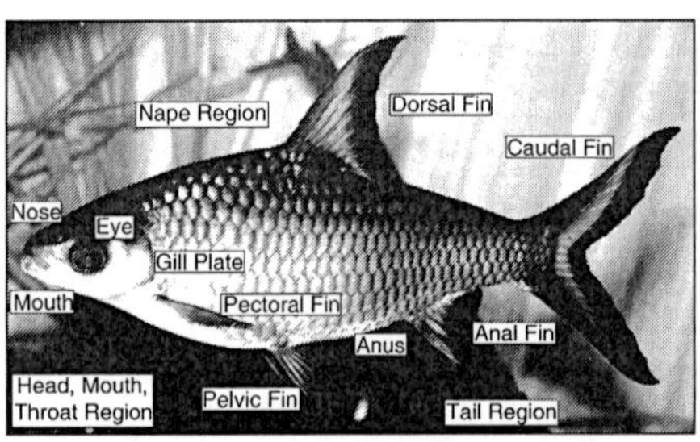

BACTERIAL HEMORRHAGIC SEPTICEMIA

- Gram negative motile rods
- Effects many freshwater species and usually is associated with stress and overcrowding.
- The clinical signs and lesions are variable. The most common finding is hemorrhage in skin, fins, oral cavity and muscles with superficial ulceration of the epidermis. Occasionally cavitary ulcers (similar to*A. salmonicida*) are observed.
- Exophthalmus and ascites are commonly observed. Splenomegaly and swollen kidneys are common. Histologically, multifocal areas of

necrosis in the spleen, liver, kidney and heart with numerous rod shaped bacteria are observed.

- Diagnosis is rendered by culturing the organism from affected animals: Remember this is a common water saprophyte with a great variation in virulence in serotypes.
- Disease is transmitted via contaminated water or diseased fish.

PSEUDOMONAS FLUORESCENS

- Short motile Gram-negative rods with polar flagella.
- Lesions similar to *Aeromonas hydrophila* with a hemorrhagic septicemia resulting in hemorrhage of the fins and tail and ulceration of the skin.
- *Pseudomonas anquilliseptica* causes a serious problem in Japanese eels with a septicemia resulting in petechial hemorrhage on fins and tail and ulceration of the skin.

VIBRIO

- Gram negative rod, lives primarily in a marine environment
- *Vibrio Septicemia: V. alginolyticus/V. anquillarum/V. salmonicida*
  - Septicemia has similar lesions to *Aeromonas hydrophila*.
  - See hemorrhage in the skin of the tail and fins, ulceration of the skin, hemorrhage in the muscles and serosal surfaces. The spleen may be enlarged and bright red. Histologically may see necrosis of the liver, kidney, spleen and occasionally the gut mucosa.
- Ulcer Disease of Damselfish: *V. damsela*
  - Deep skin ulcers and necrotizing myositis.
  - Lesions similar to *Aeromonas salmonicida*.
- *Vibrio Salmonicida*: Hitra disease or Cold water vibriosis

EDWARDSIELLA SEPTICEMIA

- Gram negative motile pleomorphic curved rod
- The disease affects primarily channel catfish but also observed in goldfish, golden shiners, largemouth bass, and the brown bullhead. This organism is the most serious disease involving the eel culture of Asia.
- The lesions are similar to *A. hydrophila* with small cutaneous ulcers and hemorrhage observed both in the skin and muscle. Muscle lesions often develop into large gas filled (malodorous) cavities. Diseased fish lose control over the posterior half of their body yet continue to feed.

EDWARDSIELLA ICTALURI (ENTERIC SEPTICEMIA OF CATFISH)

- Gram negative motile pleomorphic curved rod
- Disease affects primarily fingerlings and yearling catfish

- Clinical signs of enteric septicemia of catfish closely resembles those of other systemic bacterial infections. The most characteristic external lesion is the presence of a raised or open ulcer on the frontal bone of the skull between the eyes (Hole in the head disease).

AEROMONAS SALMONICIDA (FURUNCULOSIS, ULCERATIVE DISEASE OF GOLDFISH)

- Gram negative non-motile short rod
- Bacteria affects primarily salmonids but other freshwater fish can be affected.
- Clinically the disease may present as a septicemia with hemorrhage in the muscles and other sites. The major lesion is a subcutaneous swelling that often causes an ulcerative dermatitis. In chronic disease these lesions may cavitate into the adjacent musculature. In the septicemic disease, there is splenomegaly, ascites, and swelling of the kidneys. Histologically, there is necrosis of the affected tissue with abundant colonies of bacteria and few inflammatory cells due to the bacteria's leukocytolytic exotoxin.
- The disease is transmitted by contact with diseased fish, contaminated water, fomites, and infected eggs.

YERSINIA RUCKERI (ENTERIC RED MOUTH)

- Gram negative motile rod
- The bacteria affects salmonids; rainbow trout are the most susceptible.
- Clinically this disease manifest itself as a septicemia with exophthalmus, ascites, and hemorrhage and ulceration of the jaw, palate, gills and operculum. Hemorrhage of the musculature and serosal surfaces of the intestines, splenomegaly, and kidney swelling are common. Histologically numerous bacterial colonies admixed with inflammatory cells are observed in many areas of necrosis involving the liver, spleen and kidney.
- The disease is transmitted by contact with diseased or carrier fish, and contaminated water. Bacteria persist in asymptomatic non-salmonid fish and in some birds.

STREPTOCOCCUS INIAE

- Beta-hemolytic *Streptococcus* (Note: Beta hemolysin may not be present in culture media in all cases leading to the possible believe that this bacteria is a non-pathogen.)
- Disease of tilapia, hybrid striped bass and rainbow trout.
- Major problem in the tilapia industry. *Streptococcus iniae* presents either as an acute fulminating septicemia or in a chronic form limited primarily to the central nervous system. The septicemic form may

present with hemorrhage of the fins, skin, and serosal surfaces. Ulcers may appear. Microscopically, one observes a meningoencephalitis, polyserositis, epicarditis, myocarditis and/or cellulitis. Cocci/diplococci are present in the inflammation. In the chronic form, granulomas or granulomatous inflammation are evident in the liver, kidney, and brain (meningoe-ncephalitis). In the chronic disease, the brain is the best organ to culture.

- *Streptococcus iniae* is a problem primarily of closed recirculating culture system. Probably associated with overcrowding and poor water quality - high nitrates. Depopulation, disinfection and restocking with disease free fish are the best means of elimination of the organism.
- The bacteria is known to be a zoonotic agent. Individuals who have handled infected fish have developed cellulitis of the hands and endocarditis.

FLEXIBACTER COLUMNARIS

- Gram negative slender rods (3-8 microns)
- The disease is a serious disease of young salmonids, catfish and many other fish.
- This is a highly communicable disease. Lesions usually first appear as small white spots on the caudal fin and progresses towards the head. The caudal fin and anal fins may become severely eroded. As the disease progresses, the skin is often involved with numerous gray white ulcers. Gills are a common site of damage and may be the only affected area. The gill lesions are characterized by necrosis of the distal end of the gill filament that progresses basally to involve the entire filament.
- *Flexibacter columnaris* infections are frequently associated with stress conditions. Predisposing factors for Columnaris disease are high water temperature (25°C-32°C.), crowding, injury, and poor water quality (low oxygen and increased concentrations of free ammonia).
- *Flexibacter maritimus*: cause similar problems in salt-water environment.
- *Flexibacter psychrophilus* causes Cold Water Disease or Peduncle disease. Fish develop dark skin, hemorrhage at the base of fins, and anemia with pale gills with increase mucus. Hemorrhage into the muscles is common. Periostitis of cranial and vertebral bones is common in chronic cases. A chronic meningoen-cephalitis occasionally is observed with abnormal and erratic swimming.

BACTERIAL GILL DISEASE

- Bacterial gill disease is caused by a variety of bacteria. *Flexibacter columnaris*, *Flexibacter psychrophilus*, *Cytophagy psychrophila*and various species of *Flavobacterium* (all are gram negative rods) are the primary bacteria involved in this disease.

- Fry are the most susceptible to the disease, however, all ages may be affected. Clinically the fish become anorectic, and face the water current. Prominent hyperplasia (mucus and epithelial) of the gills is evident on gross and microscopic examination. Microscopically one observes proliferation of the epithelium that result in clubbing and fusion of the lamella. Necrosis of the gill lamella occurs in serious cases.
- Overcrowding, accumulation of metabolite waste products (particularly ammonia), organic matter in the water, and an increase in water temperature may all be predisposing factors.

CYTOPHAGA PSYCHROPHILA

- Gram negative filamentous bacteria
- Occurs primarily in rainbow trout fry. Fish develop abdominal distention, exophthalmus, increased pigmentation, lethargy, loss of balance, pale gills, and occasional cutaneous ulcers and necrosis of tail fins. Epidermal hyperemia and increase mucus secretions are common. Splenomegaly and hepatomegaly are common with multifocal necrosis of the liver spleen and kidney.
- Transmission is believed to be by direct contact with contaminated water and is an indication of poor water quality and overcrowding.

RENIBACTERIUM SALMONINARUM (BACTERIAL KIDNEY DISEASE)

- Gram positive nonmotile diplobacillus.
- This is a serious disease of salmonids. Brook trout are the most severely affected species.
- The disease follows a slow course with clinical signs not present until the fish is well grown. The fish may exhibit exophthalmus, skin darkening, and hemorrhage at the base of the fins. Cutaneous vesicles and ulcers may develop in mature trout "spawning rash". Abscesses, cavitation and contraction of muscles is occasionally observed. Splenomegaly and swelling of the kidney and liver with abundant ascites fluid is commonly observed. The large swollen kidney and spleen have numerous white nodules visible in the parenchyma. Numerous granulomas (containing gram positive bacteria) are observed in the kidney and may be also present in the spleen, heart and liver.
- Transmission of the disease is believed to be via direct contact with contaminated fish. It is believed that the organism enters through the epidermis and then becomes a systemic disease.

MYCOBACTERIUM SPECIES (TUBERCULOSIS)

- Gram positive, acid fast rods (*M. marinum*, *M. chelonei* and *M. fortuitum* are the most common *Mycobacterium* species involved.)
- All species of fish are affected. This disease affects both saltwater and freshwater aquariums as well as fish raised for food (up to 10 to 25 per cent of pen raised fish).
- Clinical signs of tuberculosis are quite variable. The most common signs are anorexia, emaciation, vertebral deformities, exophthalmus, and loss of normal colouration.
- Numerous variably sized granulomas are often observed in various organs throughout the body. Often numerous acid fast bacteria are observed in the granulomas.
- The aquatic environment is believed to be the source of initial infection with fish becoming infected by ingestion of bacterial contaminated feed or debris. Once an aquarium is infected with this disease, it is difficult to remove except by depopulation of the aquarium and disinfecting the tank. Remember this is a zoonotic disease (atypical mycobacteriosis).
- Atypical mycobacteriosis may manifest itself as a single cutaneous nodule on the hand or finger or may produce a regional granulomatous lymphadenitis of the lymphatics near the original nodule. Occasional local osteomyelitis and arthritis may also occur.

NOCARDIA SP

- Gram positive filamentous rod (weakly acid fast positive)
- The organism is a problem with mostly aquarium fish. However, it is occasionally observed in cultured salmonids.
- Clinically this is a chronic disease characterized by raised granulomatous masses in the mouth, jaw, gills and skin (The mouth and jaw are the most common sites). Dermal masses eventually ulcerate. Numerous white raised nodules (granulomas) are often observed in the viscera.
- The exact route of transmission is unknown. However, it is felt that entry through wounds and abrasions is the most common source of infection. (Ingestion of the bacteria has been known to cause the disease.)

FLAVOBACTERIUM SP

- Gram negative rods
- Usually a problem for individual fish. This disease is a cause of concern to primarily hobbyist and producers of ornamental fish. (Mollie granuloma, Mollie madness, Mollie popeye)

- Infected fish are usually emaciated and pale. Multifocal white nodules are observed in the visceral organs, the retina and choroid and the brain. These nodules may be cystic or mineralized. Histologically the nodules are granulomas with a caseous center, a thin peripheral rim of macrophages and lymphocytes and a fibrous capsule.(Must be differentiated from Mycobacterium)
- The mode of transmission is unknown.

EPITHELIOCYSTIS (CHLAMYDIAL INFECTION)

- Obligated intercellular parasite. Organisms stain red with Macchiavello stain.
- These organisms have been observed in many species of fresh water and marine fish. Mortality occurs most commonly in heavily infected juvenile fish.
- Clinically infected fish may be asymptomatic or show respiratory distress or excessive mucus secretions. Multiple white cysts are observed on the gill lamella and skin. Histologically, the cyst consists of distended epithelial cells with numerous basophilic organisms.
- The means of transmission is unknown.

DISEASES AND PARASITES OF BALTIC FISH

This will provide a brief description of the prevalence and geographical distribution of selected fish diseases and parasites in the Baltic Sea, based mainly on data from the past twenty years. Information is provided for the major Baltic Sea fish species on which most research and monitoring activities have been conducted, namely, flounder (Platichthys flesus), cod (Gadus morhua), herring (Clupea harengus) and, recently, Atlantic salmon (Salmo salar). However, other species, affected by significant diseases and/or parasites. In addition to the grossly visible fish diseases/parasites that have been recommended by ICES for fish diseases surveys and widely used for biological effects-monitoring purposes, other diseases/parasites that have previously received considerable attention due to their possible link to marine contamination and/or their suspected impact on mortality and fish-stock size are considered here.

The most current data on the prevalence and spatial distribution of diseases/parasites of flounder, cod and herring are those obtained during the BMB/ICES Workshop "Fish diseases and parasites in the Baltic Sea" which was held from 25 November to 8 December 1994 on board the rv "Walther Herwig III". Practical work was conducted on a transect from the Mecklenburg Bight to the western Gulf of Finland, representing the largest area in the Baltic Sea ever studied for this purpose in a narrow time-window and using identical methods. Although the results of the workshop have not yet been published, some of them have been included here. Additional information on diseases/parasites of the Baltic flounder was presented at the BMB/ICES symposium "Diseases and parasites of the flounder (Platichthys flesus) in the Baltic Sea".

FLOUNDER (PLATICHTHYS FLESUS)

Information on larger-scale geographical distributions of externally visible diseases of Baltic flounder used for monitoring purposes, including data on temporal trends, has been provided by different authors. Other published data cover more restricted areas, including the Kattegat and the Skagerrak, and certain time periods. A current review has been provided on the unique parasitic fauna of the Baltic flounder, which, due to the strong salinity gradient from the western to the eastern/northern parts of the Baltic Sea, consists of both marine and fresh-water species. Other publications were based on more restricted areas. Of these publications, only a few contain information on temporal trends.

The viral lymphocystis disease is by far the most prevalent externally visible disease of Baltic flounder. There is general consensus about the aetiology of lymphocystis, the infectious agent of which is a virus classified as belonging to the family of Iridoviridae. The prevalences recorded in November/December 1994 during the BMB/ICES Work-shop, according to single sampling sites, were in the range of 5–38 per cent in flounder 20 cm, with a decreasing trend from the western to the eastern stations.

The high prevalences, detected at the westernmost stations, were well in accordance with data from 1993 recorded in the same area. A clear increase in the prevalence of lymphocystis has occurred in the southwestern parts of the Baltic Sea, *i.e.,* southwest and southeast of Bornholm, during 1986–93, the reasons for which have not yet been elucidated. There is evidence that the prevalence of lymphocystis in Baltic flounder is influenced by both sex and size/age of the fish (males and intermediate size groups are more frequently affected than females and small/large size groups, respectively), and by seasonal effects. The prevalence of the bacterial skin-ulcer disease of flounder ranged from 0–12 per cent at the different workshop stations, with some indication of increasing prevalences from the western to the eastern sampling sites. Various bacteria considered to be involved in the aetiology of the ulcer disease of Baltic flounder have been isolated.

However, particularly 'atypical' Aeromonas salmonicida was consistently isolated from diseased Baltic Sea flounder, and it is therefore likely, that this bacterium is the main cause of the skin-ulcer disease. Acute as well as healed skin ulcers are more prevalent in male than in female flounder. Seasonal changes in the prevalence were reported. No temporal trends in the prevalence of acute/healing skin ulcers in flounder from the southwestern parts of the Baltic Sea, *i.e.,* southwest and southeast of Bornholm, were found in the period 1986–93.

Studies on the occurrence of neo-plastic liver lesions in Baltic flounder have only recently started. During the BMB/ICES Workshop in November/

December 1994, the prevalences of liver nodules >2 mm in diameter (which, according to ICES standard methodologies for fish disease surveys, is recorded as a macroscopic indicator of the occurrence of neo-plastic liver lesions) were found to be generally low (0-3 per cent), with a tendency for slightly increased prevalences at the easternmost stations These data are in accordance with a mean prevalence of 3 per cent in flounder of the same size group (>=20 cm) from Finnish coastal waters. However, for flounder >=30 cm, a prevalence of 10.1 per cent was calculated, which is very high compared to other Baltic Sea areas. Histological confirmation of the liver nodules collected during the BMB/ ICES Workshop showed, that tumours were rare and that the other nodules consisted either of unspecific storage cell changes or putative pre-neoplastic lesions, mainly clear cell foci or eosinophilic foci. Other externally visible flounder diseases, such as acute/healed fin rot/erosion and skeletal deformities, were only recorded at low prevalences (<1 per cent), without revealing any spatial trends.

COD (GADUS MORHUA)

Information published during the past two decades on prevalences and spatial/temporal trends of externally visible diseases and parasites of Baltic cod, including in the Kattegat and Skagerrak, are available from many sources. Parasitological data, mainly on parasitic helminths, were also presented.

The most prevalent externally visible disease of Baltic cod is the bacterial skin-ulcer disease (ulcus-syndrome). Although there is evidence that the conspicuous disease signs (open, red ulcers affecting the skin and, occasionally, even the underlying musculature) are caused by bacterial infections, the primary cause may be different. For example, Danish studies on ulcerated cod occurring at high prevalences (>40 per cent) around Bornholm in 1982 revealed, that these lesions were most likely primarily due to mechanical damage of the skin of specimens which escaped from fishing nets.

Thereafter, the open lesions were probably invaded by pathogenic bacteria, thus leading to the occurrence of the typical skin ulcers. However, there is also evidence from the literature that pollution might have been involved in the aetiology of the disease in cod from the Danish Belt Sea in the late 1970s. Prevalences in cod >=20 cm total length, recorded in November/December 1994 during the BMB/ICES Workshop, were in the range of 0.0–4.2 per cent in relation to single sampling sites, with the highest prevalences in Polish waters.

These results are well in accordance with data from the southwestern part of the Baltic Sea for the period 1980-88 and for December 1993, regarding both the range of prevalences recorded and the identification of regions with the highest prevalences. However, considerably higher prevalences have been found at certain sites, such as 22 per cent reported for 1977 from polluted sites in the Danish Belt Sea, 14.1 per cent for the Gdansk Bight in 1983 and 15.8 per cent for the Polish fishery zone in 1986. From the literature, there is no clear indication of consistent temporal trends in the disease. However, it appears that the prevalences generally were higher in the 1980s compared to the 1990s.

The second most common externally visible diseases of Baltic cod are skeletal deformities, such as vertebral compression, lordosis/scoliosis and deformation of the head skeleton, which have been known for a long time to occur occasionally in certain areas in the Baltic Sea at very high prevalences.

Factors involved in the aetiology of these lesions are manifold. Unfavourable hydrographic conditions during early ontogenesis, malnutrition, parasitic infestation, effects of heavy metals and differences in migratory behaviour between healthy and deformed fish are discussed as possible causes of elevated prevalences in wild fish. Significantly higher cadmium contents were detected in organs of cod with skeletal deformities compared to healthy cod. However, these data did not permit any conclusions about the cause-effect relationship between higher cadmium residues and the occurrence of skeletal deformities.

During the BMB/ICES Workshop, the prevalence of externally visible skeletal deformities recorded in cod 20 cm was 0.0–4.0 per cent, with the highest prevalence in the Gdansk Bight and the lowest prevalence at the western- and easternmost stations. These prevalences are in accordance with other published data for cod in the southwestern parts of the Baltic Sea. Prevalences of <1 per cent were reported in cod from the Polish fishery zone. However, from historic data, there is information, that skeletal deformities in Baltic cod may occur at much higher prevalences, *i.e.,* >50 per cent in the Sound and 75 per cent in the Gulf of Riga. From the literature, there is no information on consistent trends as regards spatial and temporal distribution patterns.

The third grossly visible disease, recommended for monitoring purposes in Baltic cod, is the X-cell disease (pseudobranchial pseudotumours) causing proliferations in the pseudobranches and adjacent tissue. The epidemiology and histopathology of this disease have been described and additional data were presented. Although the disease has been recorded in a large variety of fish species during the past ten years, and its histopathology has been described thoroughly, its aetiology has so far not been resolved conclusively. However, there are indications that the disease is caused by proliferative parasitic protozoans, possibly Amoebae.

During the BMB/ICES Workshop in November/December 1994, the X-cell disease was only recorded at the two westernmost stations, with a prevalence of <1 per cent in cod >=20 cm. These data again correspond to previously published information, indicating that the disease is very rare and restricted to the southwestern parts of the Baltic Sea. The infestation of Baltic cod with conspicuous externally visible parasites, the copepod Lernaeocera branchialis in the gill chamber and encysted metacercariae of the digenean

Cryptocotyle lingua in the skin, is restricted to the southwestern parts of the Baltic Sea. During the BMB/ICES Workshop, maximum prevalences in relation to sampling sites were 20.0 per cent and 2.9 per cent for Cryptocotyle lingua and Lernaeocera branchialis, respectively. Regarding the spatial distribution of cod infested by Lernaeocera branchialis, the workshop results confirm findings based on data from 1983-88. For cod from the southwestern Baltic Sea (ICES Sub-division 22), a prevalence of 4.9 per cent was calculated, with some annual fluctuations in the prevalence, without, however, revealing a temporal trend. New diseases of Baltic cod causing some concern are the occurrence of a yet unknown protistan endoparasite in the yolk of cod embryos and larvae, and certain indications of a possible occurrence of a M-74-like syndrome, similar to the one known to have a deleterious impact on reproduction of the Baltic stock of Atlantic salmon (Salmo salar).

HERRING (CLUPEA HARENGUS)

The diseases and parasites of Baltic herring, that have been the subject of most scientific activities during the past twenty years, are the infestation by larvae of the parasitic nematode Anisakis sp. and, since 1991, the epizootic caused by the parasitic fungus Ichthyophonus sp. Data on the prevalence and spatial distribution of Anisakis sp. in Baltic Sea herring have been provided, for example, by several authors. From these data, there is evidence that the infestation mainly affects the western spring-spawning herring stock which enters the Baltic Sea for spawning after leaving its feeding grounds in the Kattegat, Skagerrak and the North Sea. This migration to the Baltic Sea usually starts in late autumn and, having spawned, the herring leave the Baltic Sea in spring. Since the major spawning areas are located in the southwestern parts of the Baltic Sea, infested herring can be mainly found west of Bornholm. However, at least some of the western spring-spawners migrate further east and have been recorded off the Polish coast and the Latvian coast.

The infestation with larval Anisakis sp. is restricted to this particular herring stock, and specimens, belonging to the 'real' Baltic herring stocks, which stay in the Baltic Sea throughout their whole life, are infested only very sporadically. Therefore, it has been concluded that the infestation of herring takes place on feeding grounds outside the Baltic Sea by feeding on infested intermediate hosts of the parasite, probably euphausids.

Mean prevalences in herring in the size range 20–27 cm total length, sampled west of Bornholm in December 1987 and 1988, were in the range of 30–45 per cent, whereas prevalences in areas east of Bornholm were between 0.3 and 0.7 per cent. The same authors demonstrated a clear positive relationship between the length of the herring and both the prevalence and intensity (number of nematode larvae per infested herring) of the infestation in samples from the Kiel fishery market covering the period 1973–88. The smallest infested herring were 19 cm, a steep increase occurred in the size group 22–29 cm, and herring larger than 30 cm were infested to 100 per cent. Based on the same data set, an analysis of temporal trends in the prevalence was conducted. However, the results did not reveal a clear upward or downward trend. Parasitic nematode species in Baltic herring other than Anisakis sp. have been also reported.

The Ichthyophonus sp. epizootic in Baltic Sea herring was noted for the first time in summer 1991, when mass mortalities occurred at the Swedish west coast, causing great concern by the public, the fishery industry, and the scientific community as well. This concern was mainly due to the well-known effects of epizootics in the 1950s that affected herring stocks in North American Atlantic coastal waters. These epizootics caused a drastic stock reduction, followed by considerable economic losses for the fishing industry. From experimental studies, carried out following the first epizootics, summarized in, there was evidence that the infestation was lethal for herring, in contrast to many other fish species, within a relatively short period after infestation, thus explaining the massive stock reduction recorded.

Due to the fear in the Scandinavian countries, that the European herring stocks may experience a similar decline, studies were started nearly immediately after the observation of mortalities in 1991 in order to obtain baseline data on the spatial distribution of the epizootic and the prevalences in herring stocks in the Baltic Sea as well as in the North Sea.

For the southwestern Baltic Sea, it was demonstrated very quickly that herring infested by Ichthyophonus sp. belonged to the western spring-spawning stock, the same stock which is characterised by high prevalences of Anisakis sp. larvae. In areas, dominated by herring of the 'real' Baltic stocks, the infestation was at a low level, for example, since 1991 in herring of the Gulf of Finland and the Gulf of Riga. Mean prevalences of grossly visible disease signs in the heart of herring >=20 cm total length, recorded in December 1991 west of Bornholm, were 2.3 per cent and 5.3 per cent. However, the prevalences were considerably higher in single catches, revealing a patchy distribution of infested herring. In contrast, no infested herring were recorded east of Bornholm (ICES Sub-divisions 25 and 26).

In the following year, the prevalences had dropped to 0 per cent and 0.5 per cent. At present, there is a general consensus that the Ichthyophonus epizootic in Baltic Sea herring is over, and that the prevalences have approached natural background levels. There is evidence, that other Baltic fish species (sprat, cod) are infested at low prevalences.

However, there is no indication of increased mortalities in these species. Other significant diseases of Baltic herring include lymphocystis, and a bacterial infection by Pseudomonas anguilliseptica, associated with haemorrhagic eye lesions, possibly involved in the transmission of the infection, which has been known for some time to occur in cultured Baltic salmonids between trout mariculture facilities in Finnish waters. Additionally, the increased prevalence of the infestation of herring and sprat from the Gulf of Finland and the Gulf of Riga with the sporozoan parasite Eimeria sardinae has been observed.

ATLANTIC SALMON (SALMO SALAR)

Apart from the Ichthyophonus epizootic in herring, the most spectacular disease occurring in Baltic Sea fish species is the M–74 syndrome of Atlantic salmon, which continues to cause high mortalities in yolk-sac fry obtained from wild salmon and artificially reared salmon for re-stocking purposes within Swedish and Finnish compensatory stock-enhancement programmes. The syndrome has been known since 1974, but massive mortalities (>50 per cent) have only occurred since 1992. Whilst in previous years direct effects of environmental contaminants on the reproductive success of adult wild salmon were discussed as possible causes of the M–74 syndrome, current information indicates that a vitamin deficiency (vitamin B1, thiamine), due to the feeding of the adults on clupeids with high thiaminase contents, might be the main causal factor.

For example, experimental studies have shown, that the addition of thiamine to the water reduces both the behavioural M–74 characteristics and the mortality of salmon fry significantly. However, although this therapy seems to be promising for the enhancement programme, the wild Baltic salmon stock will probably still continue to suffer from M–74 and natural reproduction will be seriously endangered.

OTHER DISEASES IN OTHER FISH SPECIES

Some other significant diseases or parasites studied in different Baltic Sea fish species during previous years are:

- Externally visible diseases of dab (Limanda limanda) in the Kattegat and Skagerrak, and their association with oxygen deficiencies,
- High prevalences (>50 per cent) of skin ulcer disease in four-bearded rockling (Enchelyopus cimbrius) in deep-water regions off the Polish coast,
- The infestation of Baltic cod and turbot (Scophthalmus maximus) embryos and yolk-sac larvae with a yet unknown protistan endoparasite,
- Elevated prevalences of skeletal deformities in four-horned sculpin (Myoxocephalus quadricornis) from polluted Swedish coastal waters,
- Parasitic helminths in Salmo trutta,
- Other parasites,
- The infestation of Baltic eel (Anguilla anguilla) with the swimbladder nematode (Anguillicola crassus),

- A jaw erosion syndrome affecting smelt (Osmerus eperlanus) mainly in polluted areas off the Finnish west coast,
- Fin erosion of perch (Perca fluviatilis) and ruffe (Gymnocephalus cernua), and skeletal deformities in northern pike (Esox lucius) and perch in Swedish coastal waters, due to effluents from pulp mill industries,
- The eyefluke Diplostomum spp. in perch (Perca fluviatilis) and roach (Rutilus rutilus) from warm-water effluents along the Swedish coast, and
- Reproductive disorders in roach (Rutilus rutilus) in brackish waters on the Finnish coast, probably due to a myxosporidian infection (Pleistophora mirandellae).

IMPACT OF ANTHROPOGENIC ACTIVITIES

From a number of studies, carried out in the Baltic Sea, there is strong indication of a link between anthropogenic environmental changes, *e.g.*, industrial and urban pollution, eutrophication and thermal discharges, and the occurrence of elevated prevalences of certain fish diseases and parasites in certain areas. Some of these studies dealt with

- Increased prevalence of the ulcus-syndrome in cod from polluted areas in the Danish Belt Sea,
- Increased skeletal deformities in perch and pike in Swedish coastal areas affected by pulp-mill effluents,
- Increased prevalence of skeletal deformities in four-horned sculpin in polluted areas of the Gulf of Bothnia,
- The occurrence of fin erosion in perch and ruffe in Swedish coastal areas affected by pulp mill effluents,
- Increase in the prevalence of externally visible diseases of dab due to oxygen deficiency in the Kattegat,
- The occurrence of an elevated prevalence of a jaw-erosion syndrome in smelt on the Finnish west coast,
- The occurrence of liver neo-plasia in flounder from polluted areas in the Gulf of Finland,
- Changes in the parasite fauna of flounder in the Gdansk Bight due to effects of pollution on the abundance of intermediate and final parasite hosts, and
- Increased prevalences of the eel parasite Anguillicola crassus in waters affected by thermal discharges.

The results of these studies support the assumption, that changes in the prevalence or intensity of diseases and parasites in wild fish can be used as an indicator of biological effects of contaminants and other anthropogenic activities, and that studies of fish diseases/parasites in wild fish should, therefore, be included in Baltic Sea (and other) monitoring and assessment programmes on changes of the quality of the marine environment.

IMPACT OF FISH DISEASES AND PARASITES ON FISH STOCKS

There is little conclusive information regarding the impact of fish diseases or parasites on mortalities in Baltic Sea fish stocks. In only a few cases have mortalities, induced by specific diseases or environmental factors, been so obvious that the assumption seems justified that these conditions might have had a significant effect on stock size in the affected fish species.

Examples are mortalities in garfish at the south coast of Sweden due to gas super-saturation associated with thermal discharge effluents from a nuclear power plant, mortalities in perch (Perca fluviatilis) attributed to effects of pulp-mill effluents, and mortalities in western spring-spawning herring due to the Ichthyophonus sp. epidemic. The most recent case is the heavy mortalities in yolk-sac fry of the Baltic stock of Atlantic salmon (Salmo salar) due to the M-74 syndrome. The Ichthyophonus sp. epidemic in herring has so far been the only disease, affecting parts of the Baltic Sea, in which attempts have been made to estimate mortality due to the infestation and the resultant impact on the stock. However, attempts to quantify disease-induced mortalities in general suffer from a number of confounding factors, such as,

- Large fluctuations in fish stock sizes due to natural and anthropogenic causes other than diseases may mask and/or exceed disease-induced changes,
- Methods employed in fish-stock assessments do not permit a distinction to be made between mortality due to specific diseases, natural factors, or fishing effort,
- The prevalence of a disease, on which mortality estimates are based, only gives information at the time of sampling, and does not provide important information from the past (*e.g.,* number of fish that have already died) or for the future (number of fish that will become infected),
- The prevalence estimated from a sample may not reflect the true prevalence in a fish population or stock, since diseased fish may be over- or under-represented due to differences in the spatial distribution of infected and uninfected fish, and/or because the gear used selects for infected or uninfected fish, and
- The prevalence may not be an appropriate measure of mortality, at least as long as there is no clear evidence of how lethal a disease is under natural conditions and the length of the survival time of infected fish.

7

Fish Resources in Freshwater Sector

Surveys in Nepal have shown no fish records beyond an altitude of 1 650 masl and fisheries have not been noted above 1 800 masl. In the appended list the uppermost point on the main stem of the Ganges is the Alaknanda, 460-1 600 masl where the fish zone probably ends. Slightly below this is a sample from the upper Ganges in the Garwhal region (460-310 masl) above the transition zone at Rishikesh/Hardwar. The sample for the northern tributary of the Kosi (79-600 masl) takes into account both lowland and upland species for the river as a whole. The results of two-year surveys at Allahabad and Patna are included for the upper and middle plains. A comprehensive survey from the Padma in Bangladesh represents the delta and floodplain.

In total for the whole freshwater sector 161 species are recorded. Other species counts have included estuarine species or have been confined to one country of the Basin. River sectors will vary as to what proportion of these species they contain. Thus thc numbcr rccorded for the Kosi is 103 or 63 percent of the total. Numbers will also increase as further surveys are done.

The Alaknanda has the lowest number of species for any sector of the river. However, a total of 41 is still appreciable for a single cold, upland river and gives an indication as to how relatively rich the cold upland communities are. The community of the Alaknanda is characterised by a few specialised cyprinid types, specifically the snow trouts *Schizothorax/Schizothoraichthys spp*, the mahseers (*Tor spp*) and small *Garra spp,* together with some of the mountain loaches, *Noemacheilus spp* and the highly specialised sisorid torrent cat fishes, *Glyptothorax spp*.. A typical day's fishing is likely to produce representatives of each of these groups although the emphasis is always upon the snow trouts and mahseers, with regard to numbers.

The fish community of the upper Ganges is very similar to that of the Alaknanda, although a few lowland species begin to appear, such as *Mastacembelus* and *Channa* so that the final species total is a little higher at 54. Again, however, numerically the snow trout and mahseers would tend to dominate the fishery. The snow trout and mahseers are both migratory and it is essential to understand their movements in order to interpret their role in the fishery. The snow trout, *Schizothorax spp*, migrates upstream and is reported to spawn in March to June at water temperatures ranging from 14-21°C in the Himachal Pradesh. It is generally regarded as tolerating waters from 8°C to 22°C. Spent individuals and the presence of fry in October may suggest a longer or later spawning period in the Garhwal Himalaya. For the mahseers, upstream migration takes place at the beginning of the monsoon and they may spawn during the period of July to September. The common species, *Tor putitora* (Hamilton), could have three peaks between February and September.

The rivers and few lakes of the Ganges Basin in Nepal contain more than 130 species. The upland waters have a similar cold-water fish community to the upper waters of the main stem of the Ganges and Alaknanda in India. This does not extend into the Terrai, the lowland area of Nepal, beyond the transition zone, where the rivers are wider, warmer and meander more than those of the more torrential upper reaches, in particular the snow melt streams of the Himalayas. The lowland regions have a similar fauna to that of the other sections of the lowland Ganges of the plains.

The lowland sites at Allahabad, Patna and Bangladesh showed considerable similarities with communities dominated by cyprinids, particularly major carp species and catfishes. A distinction can be made between main channel migratory species, such as the major carps and the floodplain resident species that are often small and have accessory respiratory systems and prolific reproduction. In the delta region of Bangladesh, some from the estuary start to appear such as the scieanid, *Scieana coiter*, the mullets, *Rhinomugil corsula* and *Sicomugil cascasia*. Particularly significant is the anadromous *Tenualosa ilisha* or 'hilsa', which was still recorded as far up river as Allahabad in the 1993-1994 survey. It is perhaps significant that the highest individual total of species is for the Kosi River, which included both upland and lowland communities. The other northern tributaries are also quite rich in species, with 74 being recorded for the Karnali and 69 for the Mahakali.

FISHERIES IN THE BASIN AND COLD WATER UPLAND FISHERIES

The cold-water upland fisheries can be defined as those occurring in waters with temperatures up to 21°C, the limit of the snow trouts. Otherwise, they have been related to the temperature tolerance of introduced salmonids, *i.e.* 0-20°C. These fisheries are those dependent upon the typical fish communities of the Himalayan sector of the Basin. The approximate boundary in India is at Hardwar (230 masl), as the river leaves the Siwalik range and enters the plains and in Nepal where the northern tributaries enter the Terrai. There may be some overlap of species since the major carps, more typical of the lowland communities, can extend to 250-450 masl in Nepal. There are, for example, tributaries in the mountains, such as the Seti which arise below the snow line and which are relatively warm and in which snow trout seem to occur only seasonally.

The mountain fisheries have been very poorly documented. The steep gorges of the Himalayan regions of India and Nepal render fishing a difficult and hazardous operation. The variety of habitats and difficulty of the environments give rise to a variety of fishing techniques. The commonest is the cast net, where the rivers meander and also found here, in both India and Nepal, is a long-line technique which has a series of nylon constricting loops, which act as snares, rather than hooks which is particularly effective for snow trouts. This is variously called the "fase", "passo" or "gill net". Originally the snares were made of horsehair and dangled from a rod. In addition to these, the use of dynamite is common and also of electricity by using car batteries or connecting with insulated wires to overhead power lines. Traps are also common in some places.

There are reported to be very few professional fishers in the upland region but a widespread general participation in fishing activity. In the Kuman Himalayas of Uttar Pradesh, snow trout are estimated to provide 20-80 percent of the catch, with mahseers contributing 20-27 percent. There appear to be two peaks in the catch of snow trout; the first in June/July during the rising waters of the early rains and the second in September/October as the river waters begin to fall. The minimum catch rates are generally through the winter season. For mahseer, the peak landings occur during May/June and this coincides with upstream movement for spawning. It is considered that in the Himalayan reaches, the catches are related more directly to water temperature than to altitude. Both snow trout and mahseer may migrate downstream during cold spells, which inevitably leads to decline in the upstream landing.

Distribution of mountain fisheries in the Indian Basin is necessarily patchy owing to the steep inaccessible gorges through which the river runs in this region. In addition, however, the extreme sanctity of certain points on this river, which is central to the Hindu faith, means that fishing is often forbidden in such places. Examples of such points are the towns of Hardwar and Rishikesh where the River Ganges first meets the plains and Devprayag where the two main upstream branches unite. Here, vegetarianism is expected and fishing is totally prohibited on religious grounds. Similarly, much of the main channel from the plains up to its source is a route of pilgrimage where the consumption of flesh, fish or fowl is not encouraged. Markets are, therefore, very limited. A catch survey has been carried out on the Bhagirathi River, a headwater feeder tributary in the Garhwal Himalayas, close to the site of the Tehri Dam. Eight different methods of fishing were documented and 23 species of fish recorded. The most common were the snow trouts, *Schizothorax* (3 species) contributing between 61 and 74 percent of the catch over a year. The sites ranged from 1 855 masl to Tehri at 770 masl with seasonal temperatures kept between 10.2

and 19.4°C by snowmelt near the source. Surveys along a number of stretches of upland rivers in India and Nepal showed significant fishing activity along most of them. Estimates of catches at four points along the Alaknanda in the Garhwal Himalaya showed a range of between 1 035 to 2 475 kg km^{-1} $year^{-1}$ with an average around 1 650 kg km^{-1} $year^{-1}$. Alower tributary, the Nayer, produced 621 kg km^{-1} $year^{-1}$ whilst a tributary of the Bahgirathi yielded 2 250 kg km^{-1}. This last estimate reflects a genuine abundance of fish and not just fishers and markets. These, however, migrate in for a short period of the year in the pre-monsoon, March to June, to give a peak in fishing rather later than at most sites where fishing takes place throughout the low-water season, from October to March. This may indicate that the tributary is in an upper reach spawning area.

In Nepal, surveys have been carried out in the Seti, Trisuli, Narayani and Rapti Rivers of the Gandaki Basin and Sun Kosi and Indrawati Rivers of the Kosi Basin. All showed varied significant activity usually by part-time or occasional fishers for home consumption or a little extra money but some professional fishers had recently migrated in from the Terrai and India, even as far away as Bombay, to escape competition elsewhere. An estimate of catch rates of the Seti River (270 masl) gave 1 490 kg km^{-1} $year^{-1}$ composed of a mixture of warm and cold-water species. In considering the cold-water upland areas of the Ganges Basin, an average estimate of some 1.5 tonnes km^{-1} for annual fish production is indicated. The limits of the cold-water area can be defined at its lowest limit by this distinction of snow trout at around 180 masl but more realistically by the temperature less than 21°C throughout the year. The upper altitudinal limit is unlikely to extend much beyond 1 600 masl since most species of commercial importance do not extend up the rivers of the Himalaya much beyond this. At such altitudes the opportunities for fishing are also scarce and difficult. The upper limit for significant fishing activity may well be 1 200 m or less. Welcomme found the catch rates for African rivers to fall mainly within 1-15 tonnes km^{-1} $year^{-1}$. However, catch rates increased significantly downstream. Thus, for example, a river around 100 km from its source would yield in the order of 1 tonnes km^{-1} $year^{-1}$. The upland rivers surveyed in the Ganges Basin are this order of difference from the source and their yields are comparable. Since there are a number of dams for hydropower projects under planning in this region, such order of magnitude estimates are useful to enable a value to be put on the fish resources.

WARM WATER LOWLAND FISHERIES

The fisheries from Hardwar to West Begal are rather different in nature to those of the upland Himalayan region both with regard to the species taken and fishing activities. Surveys were initially conducted in 1957 by the Central Inland Capture Fisheries Research Institute, Barrackpore, (CIFRI) and regular updating of data between 1957 and 1981-82 showed no indications of any significant changes in fishing intensity in the middle reaches of the main channel and lower sections of the Yamuna.

The implication was, therefore, that any observed changes in catch rates found during coincidental fisheries surveys, represented changes in abundance of fish stocks concerned. However, a subsequent report of CIFRI indicated a perceptible rise in the occurrence of fishing villages, number of fishers and diversity of gears by the mid-eighties. There are 22 fish marketing centres on this stretch of the River Ganges, of which 5 are major and there are 4 centres on the Yamuna. The marketable surplus of fish for each part of the river is brought to these centres, which provided the focal point of the 22-year catch survey sequence carried out by CIFRI. Fishers can be categorised as "professional", "part-time" or otherwise. It is clear, however, that true professional fishers fall into a well-defined social category of sub-castes. This often renders their fishing villages distinctive and identifiable. There are no indications, however, of the extent of part-time or occasional fishing among essentially non-fishing groups, which is often a feature of floodplain fisheries elsewhere, including Bangladesh.

As with the upland areas of the Indian sector of the River Ganges, the religious influence on dietary habits along the river itself implies that local markets are unevenly distributed throughout the basin.

The major market within the basin is West Bengal in general and Calcutta in particular. The Bengali people of India (West Bengal) and Bangladesh (East Bengal) have a long tradition of eating fish and almost certainly create much of the demand throughout the lowland area of the basin. There are instances of catches on the western rim of the basin in Rajasthan being transported more than 1 500 km by train to Calcutta to reach a suitable market. The main gear types used in the lowland areas are seine or dragnets, gill nets, scoop nets, cast nets, long lines and traps. However, within these broad categories are a diversity of types and sizes, which are often designed to catch a particular range of fish species. Most fishery surveys so far conducted on the River Ganges, both in the Yamuna and the main channel have been based upon selected landing centres. The earliest surveys, between 1958-59 and 1965-66, were based on totals of daily arrivals of fish for the Yamuna at centres at Agra and Allahabad and for the main Ganges channel at centres downstream at (west to east) Kanpur, Varanasi, Buxar, Ballia, Patna and Bhagalpur. During this period, the migratory hilsa formed a major component of the catch from the middle and lower reaches of the main river, contributing 25-39 percent of the total catch between Varanasi and Ballia, just above Patna in Bihar. Hilsa was recorded as far upstream as Allahabad at the junction of the Yamuna River with the main channel, some 900 km from the Hooghly estuary and the Indian Ocean, but hilsa is rarely found penetrating upstream of the River Ganges as far as Kanpur, or upstream of the Yamuna as far as Agra. In the middle reaches of the Ganges at this time, the most important single group were the major carps (catla, mrigal, rui and calbasu). Together they constituted 53 percent of the catch at Agra, 45 percent at Kanpur and 38 percent at Allahabad, but declined somewhat towards the lower reaches, where they generally accounted for 19-26 percent at Patna and beyond. Amongst the major carps, mrigal (*Cirrhinus mrigala*) tended to predominate in the upper stations, with catla contributing a much smaller proportion. This proportion appeared to become more equal downstream. Since the 1958-66 period *L. calbasu* has become the commonest of the major carps around Allahabad rather than *C. mrigala*.

The total catches from each landing centre do not appear to show any consistent trends. It is possible that they vary with environmental and hydrological factors. There do, however, appear to be reduced catches of major carps and hilsa over time, particularly at Patna. Estimates of catches in the original 1957 survey estimated total annual catches from the rivers Yamuna and the Ganges stretch from Allahabad to Farakka at 770 tonnes and 275 tonnes respectively, which gave a consistent relative yield of 0.75 tonnes km^{-1} and 0.77 tonnes km^{-1} for the two stretches.

Yield from Allahabad has varied between 5.1-10.6 kg ha^{-1} and at Bhagalpur between 16.8 and 26.3 kg ha^{-1} and they show no apparent trend. Yield at Buxar does appear to have declined from 23.1 kg ha^{-1} in 1958-62 to 4.5 kg ha^{-1} by 1981-84. These yields are low compared to values achieved in the true floodplains of Bangladesh where values of 80-160 kg ha^{-1} have been recorded. They are also low on a worldwide scale where yield might typically fall between 40 and 80 kg ha^{-1}. These values for the River Ganges are, however, obtained solely from the commercial fishery and take no account of the subsistence fishery, although fish is not a favoured part of the diet in this region.

In addition to the fisheries of the main channel, there are also those of the northern tributaries, in particular the rivers Gandak, Buhri Gandak and the Sapta Kosi. All of these rivers meander through the alluvial plains in northern Bihar and, during the monsoons often produce large floodwater areas known as the North Bihar Wetlands.

Extensive fishing takes place in these floodplains but this is not well documented. In 1965-66 the oxbow lakes of the Burhi Gandak sub-basin alone covered an area of 36 000 ha which provided a fishery of 2 900 tonnes yr^{-1}. The natural flow of many of the Northern tributaries such as Kosi, Gandak, Rapti and Sarju, has, however, been affected by a number of hydraulic engineering schemes. For example, the construction of canals for water diversion and flood control along flood prone low-lying areas. It is reported that such schemes have greatly restricted access to breeding grounds for major carps and other species, not to mention the Gangetic dolphin, *Platanista gangetica.* Canal projects for water diversion and flood control schemes are regarded as factors largely responsible for diminished production. Nevertheless, these floodplains remain extensive and require assessment. In recent years, stock enhancement by the release of hatchery-reared fingerlings has been attempted. This fishery was reported to be widespread and to be jeopardising the natural recruitment of stock.

Further downstream the river spills out into the delta, which is characterised with a large floodplain and interaction with the estuarine zone. The floodplain is most extensive in Bangladesh and production from the rivers and their associated floodplains varied from 460 000 tonnes in 1983-84 to 561 824 tonnes in 1996-97. The largest single component of the inland fisheries in general is hilsa, which migrates up river from the estuary and the Bay of Bengal to spawn. It constitutes around 13 percent of all inland fisheries and 42 percent of river catches. Total riverine catches have been declining from 90 000 tonnes in 1983-84 to 84 463 tonnes in 1988-89 although there has been something of a resurgence to around 60 000 tonnes since 1996. Of this riverine total in Bangladesh, the Ganges (Padma) contributes around 4-5 percent but apparent declines have been even more marked, from 12 095 tonnes to 1 641 tonnes over the same period, but again with something of a resurgence after 1995.

The other constituents of the catch are categorised as major carps, catfishes, live fish (any other species with accessory respiratory organs) shrimp and miscellaneous species. The last tends to be the largest, containing as it does, largely small, floodplain dwelling species. The major carps generally provide a small percentage of the catch, being between 3-5 percent for all rivers but only 0.2-2.5 percent for the Ganges (Padma), tiny even compared to upstream areas such as Patna in India. If floodplain catches are included in Bangladesh, along with those from rivers, the major carps may constitute 6-10 percent. Overall catch per fishers is declining due partly to the growth in the population of fishers. As more people become landless, fishing becomes increasingly the only option. However, most people of the 80 million or so living on the floodplain fish at some time and at least 13 million people are part-time fishers.

The pattern of fishing along much of the Ganges is similar in that there is a major peak in the pre-monsoon season (May-July) and a second peak in the post-monsoon season (October-December). This largely coincides with the migratory movements of many fish species, particularly amongst the catfishes and cyprinids. Within these periods, peaks can be a little later at downstream sites. In fact, on the Yamuna the pre-monsoon peak can be as early as April. The earlier upstream trigger for the pre-monsoon peak could be the first impact of snowmelt water from the mountains. The largest single component of catches in the middle Ganges is the catfishes, which are mainly migratory. At the confluence of the Ganges with its major tributary, the Yamuna near Allahabad, a combination of catfishes and major carps (*Cirrhrus mrigala, Labeo rohita, Catla*

catla, Labeo calbasu) accounts for over 30 percent of the catches throughout the year. The same is also mainly true for the main stem of the Ganges at Allahabad except the contribution of major carps is less and other types predominate on occasion. This pattern is true of the high water season in the vicinity of Patna and other types become more prominent in the low water season. In the Ganges (Padma) section of the delta in Bangladesh by far the most dominant species of the catch is hilsa, which can be 45-47 percent of the catch although this shows considerable annual variation. Catfishes and major carps are much less prominent here.

MAJOR CARPS OF THE GANGES SYSTEM

In many ways, the major carps are key indicators of the Ganges system. They were originally a dominant group in the river and floodplain eco-system. They are amongst the most highly regarded of the fish species with respect to commercial value and also for aquaculture. In the first recorded survey of Gangetic fishes, they are reported as "abounding" and "very common" in the rivers and tanks of the system. Even at this time, *L. rohita* was reputed to be cultured. Historical data indicate that since the early sixties the proportion of major carps in the catches around Allahabad was some 43.5 percent. It fell through the seventies and eighties until most recently it reached only 20.5 percent. Similarly, around Patna the decline has been from around 27 percent to 4 percent of the catch. Traditionally the major carps were plentiful in Bangladesh but the proportion currently recorded is only around 6 percent. Unfortunately, there is no good historical data for comparison but they have been just a few percent of the catch since 1982.

The most plentiful location for major carps is around the Yamuna/Ganges confluence, where size-able individuals of 7-8 kg are not unusual. Fishing down of an ecological community tends to lead to the elimination of the larger species first and the selective market demand from Bengal and Calcutta must have enhanced this process. In addition, there is a considerable small-scale industry in trapping major carp larvae, which drift down the river after spawning to supply the large aquaculture industries of India and Bangladesh.

There are a large number of fry catching stations along the Ganges either side of the border and in India alone, in order to stock 1.6 million ha of ponds and tanks approximately 32 billion major carp seed can be required. A decade or so ago only 10 percent of this was available from hatcheries and whilst this has increased over time, the catching of wild fry still continues. The natural mortality rate of fry is, of course, very high but it has to be considered that entrapment on this scale may contribute to the decline of the species and, most importantly, the spawning stock. The major carps are given some protection, for example, the Fish Act of Bangladesh specifies a minimum size for capture but it is difficult to enforce over the delta.

Another fish that has declined markedly in some areas is hilsa, particularly above the Farakka Barrage in the Indian sector. At Allahabad, which is around the highest point this anadramous species reaches in its migration, the proportion in the catch has declined from around 10 percent in 1956-66 to 5 percent by 72-76 to less than 1 percent by 93-95. At Patna, hilsa has declined even more dramatically and most recently has fallen from 12 percent in 1952-66 to around 1 percent by 1993-95. Just above Farakka, the total annual catch fell from 19 tonnes before the Barrage was finished in 1972, to 1 tonne. The fish are most plentiful from December to April at this point.

In Bangladesh, the total catch of hilsa has oscillated between 97 000 tonnes and 71 370 tonnes over the period 1984-1997, with an average of 85 700 tonnes. This is the product of three major rivers and their combined estuary and its contribution to overall catch is around 13 percent. The Ganges alone showed a reduction in the Bangladesh fishery, from 4 193 tonnes in 1983-84, to 968 tonnes in 1988-89 and generally constituted around 40-50 percent of the catch.

Whilst fish are present throughout the year, the peak in the Ganges (Padma) itself from July to November with a peak of mature fish in September. The consenus in Bangladesh is that the hilsa stocks or fishery has shifted from inland to esturarine/coastal regions and that the catches are declining. However, like most of the riverine fisheries, they are diffuse and show considerable fluctuations so that keeping representative statistics is always a difficult task. There has been much conjecture whether the populations of hilsa that are found in Bangladesh and India are homogenous since this in an important point for their management. A recent genetic analysis of hilsa populations in Bangladesh has indicated that they belong to more than one gene pool.

Those species contributing most to the catch in lowland reaches are: the Schilbeids, *Ailia coila* (Hamilton), *Clupisoma garua* (Hamilton), the cyprinid *Oxygaster spp;* the catfishes, *Rita rita* (Hamilton), *Mystus* spp and *Aorichthys aor* (Hamilton); *Setipinna phasa* (Hamilton) and *Aspidoparia morar* (Hamilton). Despite the attention given to the major carps and hilsa, these species are now important components of catches in many areas and require more attention.

Prawns can also be a major element of the catch and, at Patna, for example, can amount to 25 percent the weight of the total catch. This is of a similar order to that which can be found downstream in the Ganges in Bangladesh. In addition, valuable *Macrobrachium* spp., the migrating freshwater prawn, can also be found throughout the delta and upstream as far as Patna. Prawns, however, are not taken in any numbers at Allahabad and it appears that the limit of these prawns lies between Varanassi and Allahabad. Where floodplains have been empoldered in Bangladesh it has been suggested that the relative increase of prawns in catches is an indicator of loss of biodiversity.

In the middle reaches of the Ganges between Allahabad and Patna, with its marked marginal floodplain, the floodplain resident species amount to between 1 and 5 percent by weight. On the floodplains of Bangladesh they constitute around 65 percent. These “black fishes” such as *Anabas spp, Mastacemblus spp and Channa spp* have a remarkably resilient life cycle. Each year, the floodplains drain down and most dry season refuges are drained or fished intensively yet each following year their numbers bounce back. They probably have extreme r-selected population characteristics.

As the fishing pressure builds up and more and more poor people enter the fishery, it is the remarkable characteristics of these small fishes that sustains the production and helps to keep poverty and malnutrition at bay. There are linkages between the warm water lowland river and the cold upland communities. Low numbers of the mountain migratory mahseer, *Tor tor*, appear in lowland catches at Allahabad almost exclusively during the winter period of January to March when water temperatures are between 17 and 22 °C.

They are also recorded at Patna. These individuals probably represent the extremity of the downstream migration of mahseer from the northern tributaries of the Gogra, Gandaki and Kosi from the Himalayas. The disappearance of the fish in March will mark the start of their upstream migration to spawn in the streams and tributaries of the mountains. The situation is probably complicated, however, by the existence of barrages across all three northern tributaries at the Indo-Nepal border. The opening of the gates causes fish to be swept downstream. There is also the possibility of these and other barrages causing isolated populations as they have with the Gangetic dolphin, *Platanista gangetica. Tor tor* does also occur in some of the southern tributaries, including the Tons, the Ven and the Paisuni, as they descend from the central shield.

There are also linkages of the middle reaches of the Ganges with the estuary in addition to that for hilsa. The giant river catfish, *Pangasius pangasius* is known to make long distance movements upstream from estuaries where the non-breeding adults tend to reside and feed. This has been recorded at sites on the Yamuna at Allahabad largely between December and March although not yet at Patna, en route for the estuary. It is quite plentiful in catches from the Ganges in Bangladesh where, in fact, it amounts to 8 percent of the annual catch. The species may be less prominent than in earlier times when a significant fishery for it occurred in the Gangetic estuarine areas during July and August. In the Mekong *P. pangasius* is recorded as migrating up to 1 000 km upstream from the estuary. Allahabad is some 1 200 km from the estuary.

FRESHWATER FISH

Freshwater fish are fish that spend some or all of their lives in fresh water, such as rivers and lakes, with a salinity of less than 0.05 per cent. These environments differ from marine conditions in many ways, the most obvious being the difference in levels of salinity. To survive fresh water, the fish need a range of physiological adaptations.

41.24 per cent of all known species of fish are found in fresh water. This is primarily due to the rapid speciation that the scattered habitats make possible. When dealing with ponds and lakes, one might use the same basic models of speciation as when studying island biogeography.

PHYSIOLOGY OF FRESHWATER FISH

Freshwater fish differ physiologically from salt water fish in several respects. Their gills must be able to diffuse dissolved gasses while keeping the salts in the body fluids inside. Their scales reduce water diffusion through the skin: freshwater fish that have lost too many scales will die. They also have well developed kidneys to reclaim salts from body fluids before excretion.

MIGRATING FISH

Many species of fish do reproduce in freshwater, but spend most of their adult lives in the sea. These are known as anadromous fish, and include, for instance, salmon, trout and three-spined stickleback. Some other kinds of fish are, on the contrary, born in salt water, but live most of or parts of their adult lives in fresh water; for instance the eels. These are known as catadromous fish.

Species migrating between marine and fresh waters need adaptations for both environments; when in salt water they need to keep the bodily salt concentration on a level lower than the surroundings, and vice versa. Many species solve this problem by associating different habitats with different stages of life. Both eels, anadromous salmoniform fish and the sea lamprey have different tolerances in salinity in different stages of their lives.

Status in North America

About four in ten North American freshwater fish are endangered, according to a pan-North American study, the main cause being human pollution. The number of fish species and subspecies to become endangered has risen from 40 to 61, since 1989.

MAJORITY OF FRESHWATER FISH PONDS

RENOVATION OF EXISTING PONDS

The majority of freshwater fish ponds in the Indian subcontinent are the dugout ponds of an undrainable nature which at times lack proper embankments. During the course of culture operations, such ponds receive huge amounts of feed, fertilizers and manures as critical inputs and sediment particles carried down by rain water from the catchment area.

A portion of the organic production in the pond also undergoes death and decay and gradually adds to the pond bottom sediment. Thus, with the advancement of time, a thick sediment layer is formed reducing the depth of the pond. They are quite rich in organic and inorganic nutrients, but due to slow bacterial action under prevailing anaerobic conditions the nutrients are almost locked up in the sediment and are not available for primary production. Further, the anaerobic decomposition of the organic matter accumulated in the sediment releases harmful gases and depletes dissolved oxygen level in the water. Thus, it becomes necessary to renovate the existing ponds periodically every 4–6 years by removing sediment from the pond bottom, redressing and repairing the dykes, etc., in order to make the ponds more suitable and to regain their fertility. For this, the following practical measures are recommended.

DEWEEDING

It has been observed that most of the rural ponds are not properly managed and become weed-infested in course of time. Before dewatering the pond, large floating weeds such as water hyacinth should be eradicated by pulling them out manually or mechanically. Otherwise, collection and removal of such weeds will require more labour and time. Other rooted emergent or submerged weeds can be taken care of only after draining the pond.

WHEN TO TAKE UP THE RENOVATION WORK

As soon as the water table of the area surrounding the pond goes down the renovation work can be initiated. Summer is the most suitable period for this Purpose as complete drying of the water body is possible. In this period pond renovation can be carried out efficiently and economically. Removal of slushy silt from the partially dried pond bottom is difficult, laborious and expensive.

DEWATERING AND DRYING

Dewatering of the existing pond is possible either by draining the water after cutting a portion of the embankment or by pumping out. If the water table in the surrounding area is high, there is considerable inflow of water from the pond bottom. This phenomenon of sub-surface secretion is called percolation. In case the rate of percolation is high, several furrows or ditches may be made towards the lowest contour point where a pit may be dug out to drain all the percolated wall. Periodical pumping of water from the pit facilitates keeping the bed dry.

DESILTING

After complete dewatering, the pond bed is allowed to dry and develop cracks in the silt mass. The texture of silt is different from that of the bottom hard soil and cracks quickly. At this stage dried silt is cut and removed manually or mechanically and heaped at a suitable place for its utilization in agricultural fields. Where complete drying is not possible due to high rate of percolation, walking platforms made up of bamboos or wooden planks may be put on the slushy bed to facilitate desilting work. In some larger ponds it becomes difficult to dry the central portion of the pond bottom as it is nearer to underground water table. In such cases the slushy and loose silt should be scrapped and spread to the sides with the help of wooden planks tied with ropes for pulling. This helps in drying the silt and easy removal thereafter.

CONTOURING

Where the bed is found to be uneven, contouring is necessary to estimate the amount of silt to be removed. Itis done by taking the level measurements at certain spots on the pond bed. It will also help in redesigning the pond taking into consideration the highest flood level and maximum rain water level.

MAINTENANCE OF DYKES

In general, rural ponds lack proper embankments. During high rainfall or peak irrigation periods in canal-irrigated areas such ponds get inundated with water from the neighbouring agricultural fields causing stocked fish to escape, predators and unwanted species to enter and at times results in mass fish kills due to pesticide pollution. Hence, provision of proper dykes is a must. Existing pond dykes should be repaired every year after the monsoon.

Rats and crabs cause great harm to pond dykes by making holes. Such holes allow serious leakage and if not checked immediately, may endanger the stability of the dykes. Periodically and especially at the time of renovation, such spots should be properly repaired by stuffing binding clay, claylime mixture or any other locally cheap cementing material. Due to poor consolidation, erosion from the top of the dyke during heavy rains usually results in grooving out of small channels. These areas should be covered with earth, levelled, thoroughly rammed and grass turfed. In relatively larger ponds, wave action due to wind also causes large-scale dyke erosion. By putting large floating aquatic plants such as water hyacinth along the sides of the dykes exposed to wave action during the windy season such erosion can be checked. Frequent erosion in steep dykes during heavy rain or wind can be avoided by strengthening the inner sides of the dykes with poles or bamboos or corrugated cement planks.

Most of the traditional pond dykes are below the required height; as a result, overflow of water occurs during heavy rains or flood. These dykes should be properly raised and the height may be kept at a minimum of one meter above the maximum water level recorded in that area. While raising the dykes, the top width may be kept at a minimum of 1.5 m with 2:1 slope (horizontal: vertical).

Cutting the dyke to allow water into the pond from the surrounding area without any secured screening is a normal practice, which however creates many management problems. The silt mass is very rich in organic and inorganic nutrients making it most suitable for application in agriculture and horticulture. Being non-cohesive and unstable, it is unsuitable for making dykes as it may be washed back in the pond.

RECLAMATION OF DERELICT WATER BODIES

Derelict waters in millions of hectares, lying unutilized, are common sights in most of the South Asian countries. Such untapped water bodies with potential for aquacultural production may be reclaimed and made suitable for fish culture by adopting more or less similar procedures.

In case of larger water areas, it would be better if they are connected temporarily to nearby natural or man-made drainage systems having relatively lower bed level for complete dewatering by gravity and making the entire area completely dry. However, if such topographic facilities are not available, heavy duty water pumps may be put into use for quicker dewatering.

In extensively large areas dewatering by draining or by pumping is not feasible. Moreover, the dry period of the year also may not last long enough to permit the work to be completed. It has been experienced that such areas can also be successfully reclaimed and renovated by partitioning into smaller units by raising cross bundhs, farm roads, etc. Each newly formed unit then can be dewatered, dried and desilted.

NON- FRESH WATER FISH CULTURE

The non-fresh water is a term used in a very broad sense and refers to all types of water that do not have the characteristics of the fresh water as described already. It may be saline, alkaline, brakish water, sea water, acidic, poorly oxygenated, muddy, sewage water, drainage from the residential areas or from industrial areas, or water in the marshy and swampy areas. It may be found in lagoons, esteries, brakish water lakes, canals, mangroves or inland ponds or wells with saline or brakish water.

There are people who have such types of water under their ownership or control. Several types of fishes can be reared in these types of waters and very good economic return can be obtained by them provided they have the know how. Fish rearing in such types of water may be termed as Non- Fresh water Fish Rearing. Some of the most important types of non-fresh water fish culture are briefly introduced here.

AIR BREATHING FISH CULTURE

From the name itself we can understand the nature of the fishes being reared in this system. These fishes can live by breathing the air directly. That means the water in which they live is unsuitable or is unable to provide enough oxygen to these fish because the water may not be really fresh. Such situation occurs in the nature due to many reasons as explained here.

Many low-lying areas where rainfall is fairly heavy and topography of the land is such that water logging occurs, get infested with various types of aquatic vegetation and become swamp. At times large waterlogged areas become choked with weeds which get decayed and the whole area becomes a swamp. In this swamp considerable quantities and qualities of organisms both of the plant and animal types grow and multiply. Various types of micro and macro-phyto and zooplankton (flora and fauna) and decaying organic matter are common in these swamps. Often the water of these swamps are not really fresh and very poor in the oxygen content.

The best way to use these types of swamps is to rear air breathing fishes such as giant murrel (*Channa marulius*), stripped murrel (*C. striatus*), spotted murrel (*C. punctatus*), walking fish or catfish (*Clarius batrachus*) singhi (*Heteropneustes tassilis*) and climbing perch (*Anaba testudineus*). All these are carnivorous as well as feeders of dead and decaying materials of plant and animal, origin. They also easily breed and multiply in these swampy water bodies.

Monoculture as well as polyculture of these air breathing fishes are done in many of the world where such natural lakes, water logged areas and swamps occur commonly. Efforts are being made under an All India Coordinated Research Project to develop suitable techniques for air-breathing fish culture which have given encouraging results. There may be enough natural feed generated in these water bodies under the natural conditions. However if possible supplementary feeding, should be given to augment the growth of the fishes.

SEWAGE WATER FISH CULTURE

In the present urbanised living conditions we generate large quantities of sewage water from the residential and industrial areas. Most of this can be utilised for agricultural and fishery purpose after proper treatment and dilution. The sewage water is treated and recycled in many parts of the world for a number of purposes.

The major steps involved in the treatment of the sewage are the following:

- Running down the sewage through a number of ponds,
- Filtration of sewage in two stages followed by sedimentation,
- Aeration of sewage and
- Dilution of sewage with fresh water (one part sewage with five parts of fresh water).

The sewage is made to stand in the ponds called oxidation ponds for about 10 days. During this time the heavier particles settle down in the form of sediment. Meantime due the action of aerobic microorganisms, there is break down of the organic matter resulting in the formation of inorganic nutrients. The aerobic decomposition improves the nutrition quality of the sewage water and algae and other microphytes grow and the water becomes suitable for fish culture. By growing water hyacinth, *Eicchornia* and other water plants in the oxidation ponds we can remove the toxic heavy metals from the water.

The total capacity of the oxidation ponds should be such that they should able to retain at least 1.0 to 12 days sewage. The ponds should not be more than 3-4 ft deep for the light to penetrate and the air to get mixed with for the oxidation process to happen. For the full mutilation of the treated sewage water the total capacity of the fish ponds should be equal to four to five time that of the sewage. The treated sewage water can tie considered equal to the total sewage let in for treatment minus the loss of water through evaporation. Fishes like silver carp, rohu, mrigal, common carp, grass carp, catla, fringe-lipped carp, etc., can be reared in the sewage fed fish ponds.

BRACKISH WATER FISH CULTURE

Slightly salty water is called brackish water. Such type of water is found in areas where the sea water get mixed with fresh water coming from the rivers and streams joining the sea (esturies) or fresh lake water get mixed up with sea water at the time of high tide. Brackish water is commonly observed in the water bodies situated along the sea shores. Certain fishes and prawns thrive well in the brackish water. Brakish water prawn culture is becoming very popular in India because prawns fetch very high prices. There are several other fishes that can be reared in the brackish water. But they are not becoming popular and commercial because their economic profits from them are not sufficiently attractive.

Besides various kinds of fishes and prawns several other economically beneficial organisms of both plant origin and animal origin can be cultured in brackish water. But except for the prawns, markets have not been developed significantly for the brackish water fishes. The scanty knowledge system and technology about rearing water organisms in the brackish water is also another reason for the poor development of the brackish water fish culture.

MARINE FISH CULTURE

When we hear about marine fish culture we may wonder how fishes are reared in the sea? Of course huge enclosed areas in the sea can be used for marine fish culture. All that required is to have a constant linkage and mixing of water within the enclosure and the water outside. Such systems of marine fish culture is still only in the conceptual level though Japanese are trying to do something in this line.

The Japanese breed and rear fishlings up to certain age and then they are let into the sea. By doing this they are ensuring survival of the maximum fishlings in the sea so that the harvestable population of fish in the sea is maintained optimum. Otherwise there is always very high mortality of fishlings in the nature and the fishes that grow up to harvestable age is very much reduced. Normally certain types of fishes are found to thrive well in certain part of the sea. In other words different types of fishes are seen to be thriving well in different parts of the sea or different sea. For example fishes commonly found in the West coast area are different from the East coast area. Again fishes that are found in the Orissa coast are different from that of in the Tamil Nadu coast. In the same way the fishes found in the Gujarat coast are different from that are found in the Karnataka or Kerala coast. Even in the same state the fishes in one coastal area will be different from the fishes of some other coastal area. For example the fishes in the southern parts of Kerala coast are different from those found in the Northern parts of Kerala; similarly the fishes in the sea of Cape Comerin area are different from those found in the Tuticorin or Chennai area. Even in different parts of the marine areas of the same state we find different types of fish. For example the fishes in the marine areas of the Malabar area is different from the fishes of the Cochin or Trivandrum areas.

Taking advantage of this phenomenon in the sea we can increase the fish production in the sea by several ways. The first method is to increase the survival rate of the frys and fingerlings of the fishes. This is done by breeding selected fishes to produce trys (md rearing the frys till they become fingerlings and then releasing them into the sea. By this the survival rate of the fishes in the sea is increased. The second method is by increasing the generation of the natural feed of marine flora and fauna or by supplying supplementary feed for the fishes of a particular area. Fishes will remain in those areas where abundant feed is available. By generating natural feed in a particular area or by providing supplementary feed or by both we can retain the fishes of an area to that place and harvest them when they are sufficiently grown. Obviously the marine cultivation of fishes is very expensive and probably only the government and the multinationals will be able to carry out such programmes. However it is good for the ordinary people to know that such possibilities are therein marine fish culture.

NON-FISH AQUACULTURE

Besides the above mentioned fish cultural practices for fishes the aquacultural practices include culture of several organisms other than the fishes. Though some of them are already being practised commercially they are yet to be widely accepted by the people as possible and profitable aquaculture practices. Already we have some knowledge about most of them so that anyone can start and experiment on any of them.

SHRIMPS, PRAWNS, CRAY FISH AND LOBSTERS

In the common parlance people seem to confuse between shrimps, prawns, crayfish and lobsters because externally they look much alike to an ordinary person. Actually they are different physically and genetically. To distinguish the differences between them one has to observe carefully the anatomical differences, Size wise shrimps are small while the prawns and the crayfish are bigger and the lobsters are the biggest. Shrimps have thin and transparent shells/coverings while the prawns, crayfish and lobsters have thick and coloured coverings/shells, There is a lot of variation in the colours and colour patterns among the prawns, crayfish and lobsters. The legs and antennae of the shrimps are very slender and tender while that of the prawns and crayfish are harder and stronger and that of the lobsters hardest.

The body of the shrimps is very smooth and that of the lobtsters most rough and spiny while the prawns and the crayfish range in between. The shrimps do not appear to have any pincers while the prawns and crayfish have their first pair of legs turned into pincers. The pincers of the crayfish are broader and shorter (like that of a scorpion) than that of the prawns which have long and narrow pincers. Whereas in the case of lobsters more than one legs are turned into pincers the first one being very prominent and terrifying.

Habitat-wise the shrimps and prawns grow in fresh and non- fresh waters, while the crayfish is only found in fresh water streams and rivers with plenty of sand, gravel and rocks and lobsters are found in the deep sea. After having described briefly the basic distinguishing characteristics between the shrimps, prawns, crayfish and lobsters we can now focus on their fresh water cultural aspects.

However the cultural aspects of the shrimps and prawns are more developed than all others. A lot more work needed be done to generate sufficient theoretical and practical information regarding their life cycle, habitat, growth and behaviour before we can start their commercial rearing. Such information is more available at present on the case of shrimps and prawns.Though there are many species of shrimps and prawns mainly two species are used for commercial culture: *Penaeus monodon* and *Penaeus indicts*. Both take about 15 to 20 days to go through the early stages (eggs, six nauplius stages, two protozoan stages, three mysis stages and five post larval stages and after that by 90 to 100 days to go through early juvenile, sub-adult and adult-immature stages. After this they are in the adult stage and reaches marketable size by 10 to 12 months age. Among the prawns culture of fresh water, giant prawns are more important commercially. The culture of cray fish and lobsters are still to be taken up in a commercial manner. Perhaps much research is needed to generate sufficient practical know-how regarding the culture of these two. However one can try to select some good breeding stocks and start rearing them.

The success depends on how good a pond or growing situation one has, how far one can ensure maximum survival of the young ones till they become adults and how well one can feed them with nutritious and balanced feed. For the first purpose, one should have a well planned pond or growing condition, for the second purpose, one should have the support of a very good hatchery either own or by some one reliable and for the third one should have a steady supply of proper feed. Shrimps and prawn culture is a highly complicated practice that any one who plans to go for it should have a thorough knowledge on the same. The shrimps and prawns can be cultured both in fresh and non-fresh water.

MOLLUCS, CLAM AND OYSTER CULTURE

Molluscs, clams and oysters are name applied to several species of bivalves. They can be cultured in their natural envious or under suitable artificial conditions. Clams among them are the most common and are two types: one having the soft and the other having hard shells. The soft shelled belong to the species Maya areneria and the hard shelled to Venus mercenaria. They burrow into the sand or mud. The soft shelled clam is characterised by a stretchable neck or siphon having two tubes: one for sucking in water with food materials and the other for expelling wastes. The hard shelled clam is strongly hinged, close fitting, connected by two powerful abductor muscles and stays in the mud or sand sheltered by plants or something. Some of the hard shelled clam grow up to a kilogram weight and may live up to 35 years. Both these type of clams are used for meat and for shell which is good source of calcium. The artificial culturing of clams is yet to be taken up in the commercial level though there is plenty of scope for the same. At present they are mostly harvested from the nature.

The female clams release millions of eggs of which very few get fertilized and of the hatched one (called veliger) only very few survive to adulthood in the natural conditions. Under artificial rearing conditions we can increase the survival rate and production tremendously. They can be cultured both in fresh and non-fresh water conditions.

FROG REARING

Frog meat is excellent from the point of view of digestibility and nutrition. It is highly valued in the foreign countries. In India people have so much cultural and religious inhibitions for eating frog meat. If they can get over this it will not only help them to overcome the nutritional deficiencies but also enhance their income. Frogs can be reared in simple and small scale ways at home or large and commercial level provided one knows at least the basic requirements of frog culture. However for large scale commercial scale rearing a thorough knowledge about the breeds, breeding and reproduction, life cycle, feeding, habita., rearing methods, pests and predators, etc., is essential.

Frog rearing has several advantages:

- It involves little capital investment
- Frog waste could be processed into a protein rich byproduct similar to fish protein concentrate and used as a nutritional supplement in fish and livestock feeds

- Frog skins could be tanned for the manufacture of leather goods and
- Adult frogs and their larval stages could effectively control disease-spreading insect. Thus frog rearing has very high economic potential which is still to be harnessed.

Three indigenous species: *Rana tigrina* (Indian bullfrog), R dactyla (Grecn frog) and R. Crassa (Jerdon's frog) are found to be very suitable for commercial rearing in our country. An exotic frog called *R. catesbiana* (North America bullfrog) was introduced into our country in 1968 by the Central Fishries Research Institute (CFRI), Cuttack. These four are being cultured in our country at present. However commercial culture is yet to become common.

CRAB CULTURE

Crabs are delicacies and very costly. Hence culturing them for home use or for commercial purpose is certainly beneficial for the family nutrition as well as for the high profitability. However crab culture is still to be developed in its theory and practice. One can find crabs almost at any place where there is water: in the sea, in the lakes, in rivers, streams, in ponds, in fresh water, in saline water, etc. Fresh and flowing water is very conducive to the crabs. Flowing condition of fresh water can be created artificially for the crab culture. They require highly oxygenated and bubling fresh water.

Crabs in nature breed and raise young ones and are very active during the rainy season when there is plenty of water flowing in the streams and rivers. Then they can be seen moving about on the rocks and edges of the streams and rivers. All crabs have a hard shell on the dorsal side which protects the internal organs. This shell at the back side continues to the ventral side and form like a flap which ends into a pointed excretory outlet. Observing the ventral side one can distinguish between the male and female. Those with narrow nap are male and those with broad flap are females. On the edges of the flap of the female there are hair like structures called appendages. At the time of spawning the egg mass is held by these appendages.

Hence at the time of spawning a sticky spongy mass is seen held between the nap and the body but extruding outward. The eggs are hatched in about two weeks. In the sea crabs the young ones are like a larvae with a segmented body and tail. But in the land and fresh water crabs the young ones are like tiny adults. At the initial stage the young ones are held between the flap and the body of the mother till they are able to manage themselves without the mother. Crabs breed during rainy season. Artificial breeding is not yet known though it should be possible. Practically very little information is available on crab culture. Yet they can be reared by breeding the selected males and females. Good care should be given to the young ones so that they survive till they are able to manage themselves. Crabs can be reared in small tanks with shallow but clear, well oxygenated water flowing between the rocks which provides hiding place for the crabs. The tank may be as small as 4x4x4 feet, length, width and height. The size of the tank may be bigger according the land availability, size of the operation, number of crabs reared, etc. Separate tanks for breeding stock, breeding and spawning, tanks for hatching, tanks for the young ones and tanks for the growers can be arranged. The requirement of tanks and other infrastructural facilities are arranged as per the need. Actually the reader himself has to experiment on the system of crab rearing.

Crabs are omnivorous. Hence all kinds of feed materials and kitchen waste can be fed to them. The feed can be plant and animal material which can be collected and preserved as crab feed. Crabs are nocturnal in their habits. Still much observation and studies are required to develop a theory and practice of crab culture.

PEARL CULTURE

Everyone is aware of what a pearl is and how valuable they are both in the national and world market. Pearls have been in usage for many years. They are concretion formed by a mollusc consisting of the same material called acre or mother-of-pearls as the molluscs shell. It is a highly valued gem- stone.

Pearls are characterised by their translucence and lustrons and a delicate play of surface colour called orient. More perfect in shape are the spherical or drop like, and the deeper its lusture and the greater its value in the market. Only those pearls produced by molluscs whose shells are lined with “acre” (as in salt water and fresh water clams) are really the pearls. Pearls from other mollusks are reddish or whitish, porcelaneous or lacking in pearly lusture. Jewellers commonly refer to salt water pearls as oriental pearls and to those produced by fresh water molluscs as fresh water pearls.

The shell secreting cells of the mollusc are located in the mantle or epitheliums of its body. When a foreign particle penetrates the mantle the cells around the particles begin to secrete shell substance and cover it layer by layer in concentric circles forming the actual pearl in a period of 2-3 years.

Depending on the location of the foreign body there is qualitative difference in the pearls formed. When the particles are attached to the muscles of the mollusc irregularly shaped pearls are usually formed. Such pearls are called baroque pearls. Pearls that are grown close to the shell of mollusk are mostly flat on one side and round on the other side. They are called blister pearls. The spherical type of pearls are formed when the particle is located neither in the muscle nor close to the shell but somewhere in between which is called technically the nacre or mother of pearls.

The colour of the pearls vary from white to black. But the rose coloured Indian pearls are valued most. The size and weight of the pearls vary much the weight vary from 12.5 to 465 mg per pearl. The finest oriental pearls are produced by *Pictada martensii* species of salt water mollusc mainly found in

Oman-Qatar areas of Persian Gulf, Manner areas between India and Sri Lanka, Indonesian islands and islands of South Pacific.

Pearling is a carefully fostered industry in central Europe. Mississippi river is famous for pearl production. Pearling has been going on in China since 1000 B.C. by intentionally inserting some foreign material into the molluscs. People in China used to catch molluscs, open them and insert into them mall mud pellets, tiny wood pieces, bone or small metal pieces and leave them to the river or sea bed and wait for 3-4 year to pick them up to collect pearls from them. They were mostly producing blister pearls.

In 1890 Makinoto Kokichyi of Japan proved that introduction of a small bead into the mollusc at the correct position is a sure procedure for producing the pearls artificially. Since then Japan has been in fore front in the production of pearls. There are more than 2140 pearl farms in Japan. Following the example of Japan Australia also has become one of the leading pearl producing countries in the world.

TURTLE REARING

Turtle is a collective name referring to *Chelonia* family. Turtles may be aquatic or terrestrial and the territorial turtles are referred as tortoise though in common parlance no distinction is made between the turtle and tortoise. Turtles are valued for their meat, egg and shell. Turtle meat is a delicacy; the eggs are big and nutritious and have medicinal value. The shell is very precious as they are very rare. The shells are used for making handicrafts. At present turtles are mostly caught from the rivers, sea and forest areas the demand for them do not match with the availability or supply. Hence attempts are already being made to rear them commercially. Turtles and tortoises can be easily reared by anyone though it is a long term investment.

Turtles are very slow growing but live for many years. They are very hardy and can withstand very long spell of dry and feed scarcity conditions. It can store water in the cloacal bladders like the camels storing water in their hump. It is an omnivorous though it prefers to be carnivorous. Hence feeding and watering turtles is not at all a problem for those who would like to rear them. Even if they are not fed for a number of days they will not die weekly or monthly feeding is enough. The length of the turtles vary from few cm to 3. 7 metre and can weigh from few hundred grams to 680 kilograms.

Turtles lay eggs which are as good as any other kind of eggs used for human food. A female turtle lays on an average 300 eggs per year. But all the eggs are laid at one time on the land preferably in the sand. After laying the eggs the mother turtle has no role to play in hatching and in bringing up the young ones. One mating may be sufficient for a female to lay fertile eggs for several years. The number of days taken for incubation depends on the temperature. The young one require practically no care either from the mother turtle nor from anyone. If they are provided sufficient feed and water and a rather congenial habitat they can be reared very successfully. The only negative point is that it will take many years to get some returns from the turtle farm. However the amount of money one gets per turtle is a justification enough for the undue delay of the returns.

No doubt we still lack sufficient scientific information about turtle and tortoise rearing under artificial conditions. Therefore one who rears the turtles and tortoises should collect as much information as possible before he starts the commercial rearing. After starting it he should go on acquiring information and knowledge both from outside as well as from his own experience. For this he should maintain records and accounts on various details observed during the turtle rearing.

Keeping constant contact with people who study and rear the turtles and arranging platforms for mutual sharing and learning one can perfect the method of rearing turtles.

CROCODILE REARING

Crocodiles are valued for eggs, meat and skin and has very high economic potential. They are reptiles belonging to the family Crocodilia and about 20 species of crocodiles have been reported so far. The term crocodile is a common name used for all the species in the Crocodilia family. Alligator is another term used for those crocodiles which have broad snout. Crocodiles are mostly found in the tropical areas of the world mainly in Africa, America, India, Sri Lanka and South East Asian countries. They are nocturnal in habit and they remain in the water most of the time though they may crawl over to the land periodically. Recently several crocodile farms have been started in many parts of the world. In India too there are a number of crocodile farms.

AQUATIC WEEDS

Various types of aquatic weeds are edible to human beings and animals. Some of them are important raw material for a number industries and pharmaceutical firms. They may be fresh water or non-fresh water like the sea weeds. It is an established fact that much more vegetation is growing in the aquatic-ecosystem than in the terrestrial ecosystem. Hence in the future man will be compelled to look into the depth of sea and other aquatic ecosystems to satisfy their ever increasing demand for food and raw materials for various types of industries.

Of course cultivation of aquatic weeds is still an idea yet to be experimented and standardised. But as long as man is able to fulfil his requirements on the land he will not try for aquatic weed culture. The reason for not starting such ventures so far is that it is very expensive as well as it requires high level technology which is yet to be evolved and standardised.

CONCLUSION

Land being the limiting production factor, being already occupied and cultivated beyond the sustainability level and the land degradation being a serious environmental threat aquaculture offers to humanity a much more productive and profitable enterprise. India having more than five thousand kilometres of coastal line, numerous lakes, rivers and reservoirs hold much greater chance for establishing successful aquaculture systems for the future.

FISHERIES SECTOR

Fisheries sector can play a vital role, as a potential source, in attaining nutritional security in India. The current production of fish in India forms only 71.0 per cent of the total potential and hence there is an ample scope of improvement and thus can be added up to the nutritional security.

It is estimated that globally, about a third of the fish catch is not utilised for human food consumption because of post harvest loss resulting from poor handling and preservation. In India, there is also the problem of under utilisation of by- catch due to the many species that are caught in the net. The cost effective and efficient utilisation of aquatic products demands proper processing and distribution. Demand for fish and fish related products are increasing day by day in our country and reduction in post harvest losses can make a major contribution to satisfying this demand, improving quality and quantity for consumers and increasing income for the producers.

HARVEST UTILISATION OF FISH CATCHES

Thus, improvement in the post harvest utilisation of fish catches can ensure further nutritional security among a wide range of people in our country. Viewing fish primarily as a source of protein has been the dominant perspective in studies on nutritional security. This view is primarily not in the right direction, since it fails to highlight the critical role of fish as a wholesome source of Poly Unsaturated Fatty Acids (PUFA's); minerals such as calcium, phosphorus, iron; vitamins like A, B1, B2, B12, D etc.; and trace elements such as iodine and zinc. These attributes makes fish a vital contributor to nutritional security of the most deprived and vulnerable populations. For them, easily digestible fish is indispensable; other natural animal or vegetable protein sources are poor substitutes on both nutritional as well as economic grounds.

INTEGRATED FISHERIES PROJECT (IFP)

Established as Indo Norwegian Project during 1952 this was renamed as Integrated Fisheries Project (IFP) in 1972. The Project is engaged in the development of technologies for harvesting and post-harvesting of marine fish resources. It has a well established Fishery complex consisting of a fishing fleet, a modern mechanical workshop and Slipway to slip vessels up to a displacement weight of 250 tonnes, an Ice cum freesing Plant, a well equipped processing unit for processing and marketing of diversified value added fish products, a research and development laboratory to carry out quality analysis of raw fish, finished products handled by the Project and testing and developing suitable packages for different value added products and Life Raft Servicing Station. The Institute has a unit at Vizag also.

Mandate of the Project

- Technology development and transfer to beneficiaries consisting of rural fishermen community, small scale industries and export processing houses through consultancy and job work.
- Value added product development by way of process and product diversification from all varieties of fish including low value and unconventional species.
- Imparting training in the field of Post Harvest Technology, Refrigeration Technology, Quality control and Value added Products.
- Providing consultancy and training for rural development programmes like supporting local fish farmers, self-help groups of fisher community and fishermen's co-operative societies functioning and Panchayati Raj Institutions. And also to Women empowerment programmes in processing and establishment of SSI units to self help groups.
- Popularisation and test marketing of value added products from all fish varieties including low value and unconventional species.
- Extension of the popularisation and test marketing of value added products to new areas and developing market in all states in a phased manner with added attention to rural areas enthusing entrepreneurs to enter into seafood processing industry.
- Function as a nodal agency on all matters associated with quality assurance, standardisation of fish products and safety of fish products.

BIOTECHNOLOGY IN FISHERIES AND AQUACULTURE

The fisheries and aquaculture industries in Asia contribute about 45 per cent of world fish production. These industries are significant contributors to the food supply, livelihood, foreign exchange earnings and socio-economic stability in rural areas of several Asian countries. At the global level fish production is stagnant, at around 100 million tonnes, or has even slightly declined in recent years. Overharvesting of the world's oceans is recognised as a global threat. To obviate this threat, the production of cultured fish must be accelerated. The ability to produce transgenic fish and shellfish in culture, which grow faster and larger with more efficient utilisation of nutrients, is of particular value to developing countries, not only as a source of food, but also as export products.Biotechnology offers great promises for fish disease control and feed production as well. Gynogenetic and polyploid progeny production and the use of growth hormones have significantly contributed to fish production. The application of hypophysation (injecting of pituitary gland extracts into mature fishes for the induction of spawning) has been widely practiced in Asia during the past two decades. The use of purified gonadotrophin hormone synthetic luteinising hormone-releasing hormone (LH-RH) has further improved induced spawning techniques.

In China, following detailed discussions and workshops in the 1980s, a policy and plan for aquaculture biotechnology were included in the Seventh Five-Year Plan (1985-90). In 1987, they were also listed in the "863 Programmes", the state development programmes on high technologies, and received great attention from the Ministry of Aquaculture. Fish cell culture, sex control, chromosome manipulation, and to some extent transgenic production, have been the main areas of work.

China's success in fish cell culture, of grass carp, was reported in 1979 by the Freshwater Fishery Research Institute of Zhejiang Province. Up to now, more than ten fish cell strains have been cultured for producing vaccines. Bioreactors for industrial fish cell culture are being developed. Seaweed cell culture in China was first reported in 1985 and is being developed for further breeding work. Diploid gynogenesis, coupled with sex control is being used for mass production of all female common and crucian carps. Although triploid hybrids between 4n common carp (male) and 2n grass carp (female) have been obtained, the work is confined to laboratories.

China was one of the pioneers in transplanting of fish cell nucleus. In the mid-1970s, the reciprocal transplant of nucleus was accomplished between common carp and crucian carp. Of the cell hybrid fishes, 30 grew to sexual maturity and produced F2 and F3 progenies. In 1984, the F3 progenies were mass produced and these showed stable heredity and had 30 per cent faster growth than their grandparents. A similar practice was carried out on grass carp and Megalobrama amblycephala; 26 of the hybrids grew well, matured sexually and were mass produced by aquaculturists. In 1988, live fries were produced from the fusion of blastulla cells and eggs in different fishes: Paramisgrunus dacryanus, Megalobrama amblycephala, grass carp, common carp and red crucian carp. This technique holds great promise for fish breeding.

In fishes, the two sexes differ in their productivity and body weight. For instance, in Tilapia males grow faster than the females, the converse of which is true for carps. Of the several methods of sex manipulation, through distant hybrids, hormone treatment, induced diploid gynogenesis, induced triploids, antoimmure castration, surgical castration, and gene technique, in China the first two are commonly used. Hybrid populations between Tilapia nilotica (female) and T. aurea (male) were 95 to 98 per cent male, and on an average yielded about 25 per cent higher than the higher yielding parent. Moreover, the hybrid fish could tolerate lower water temperatures, and could be harvested more easily. Such all-male populations are already being mass cultured in China, the Philippines, Thailand and other countries. Israel has made comprehensive use of this technique.

As regards the use of hormones, using steroid hormones, induced females of T. mossambicais when crossed with male T. nilotica, produced super males with a "yy" sex chromosome combination. The "super males" crossed with female T. nilotica produced 100 per cent male progenies which possessed the twin superiorities of being hybrid as well as male. The hybrids grew 38.5 per cent faster than T. nilotica and the mass production increased by 43.4 per cent. Although a siseable gain, the difficulty in identifying the "super male" fish at fry stage is a major constraint to widespread exploitation.

As regards genetic engineering, Chinese scientists have succeeded in identifying and isolating the gene controlling growth hormone (GH) from salmon, common carp, grass carp and silver carp. Transgenic carps carrying human growth hormone gene have been produced. Antifreeze gene has also been identified and used for improving the antifreeze ability of Tilapia. Successful cryopreservation of fish sperm, involving eight species has been established in China. India, with a coastline of 7 512 km has 2.02 million km^2 of Exclusive Economic Zones, 4.7 million hectares of identified freshwater areas, and 1.7 million hectares of brackish-water areas. Its annual production of fish is around 4 million tonnes, half of it from aquaculture, and there is ample scope for enhancing fish production in the country. To supplement the fish feed resources, the use of bacterial cells as larval fish feed and processed aquatic plants as grow-out feed has been tested with success in India.

In Japan, chromosomal manipulation and modern biotechnology are being widely applied to improved fish production. Gynogenesis, artificial sex reversal and induced polyploidy are being routinely used for increasing productivity as well as the quality of fish.

The growth hormone of salmon and yellowtail is being mass produced through transgenic bacteria and used as a growth promoter on other fish such as rainbow trout. In the field of transgenic fish, the introduction and manifestation of the crystalline genes of chickens into killifish embryos were successfully achieved in 1986 at Kyoto University. Other useful genes are being identified and introduced into commonly used fish species.

New vaccines are also being developed to treat fish diseases. As regards fish feed, the development of microparticulate diets for larval fish to replace live foods in hatcheries is a major achievement. Mass production of ayu and carp fry in Japan with such diet formulates has been successful.

Malaysia has a relatively long coastline, stretching for about 4 334 km and its marine resources contribute about 9.5 per cent of the total value added in the agricultural sector; production has been increasing at a high annual growth rate of about 8 per cent over the past decade.

Moreover, the industry employs about 120 000 fishermen. The country clearly sees the scope for the application of biotechnology in fish production through genetic improvement of cultured fish, disease resistance and improved growth rate. Yet there is a gap in absorption or diffusion of the proven technologies. Besides fish, marine algae are now recognised as important resources for the production of valuable chemicals in Malaysia and local species of marine macroalgae (seaweed) are being screened for valuable chemicals. Some of the species studied and their products include: Gracilaria changii for agar and Turbinaria conoides, Sargassum baccularia and Sargassum siliquosum for algiric acid and antimicrobial compounds.

Singapore considers its marine bioresources as one of the most important and the government is highly supportive of the marine biotechnology venture. The National University of Singapore (NUS) is playing a leading role in this direction. Its Bioprocessing Technology Unit, established in 1990, concentrates on two main areas: fermentation and cell culture; and the isolation, separation and production purification technology.

In addition, the Unit also supplies to specific users, especially synthesised antibodies for immunobiological assays and analyses, and custom-made digonucleotide primers for nucleic acid research. In 1992, the NUS and the Economic Development Board (EDB) established a Bioscience centre in the University, with the following objectives: (i) to provide a multiuser central facility for biotechnology, (ii) to serve as a vehicle for collaborating with industries and other institutions in Singapore or abroad, in areas of common interest, and (iii) to provide training in biotechnology.

The areas of research of the centre are: bioactive compounds from marine organisms; toxins and venoms research; plant bioactive products; and products from microorganisms. Other related new establishments are the Centre for Natural Product Research and the Centre for Medical Informatics. The Reef Ecology Study Team of the Department of Zoology in NUS is actively surveying the distribution of the various reef organisms and the Bioscience Centre is screening organisms for antifouling, antibacterial, antitumour, antiviral, antifungal, anti-inflammatory and insecticidal compounds. Antibacterial compounds are being isolated and characterised from horseshoe crabs. Biological properties and potential therapeutic application of toxins and other bioactive compounds in two marine species, namely the "Thunder Crab" (Lyphozozymus pictor) and the stonefish (Sysanceja horrida), have been studied.

In addition, a few bioactive compounds have been purified from five local sea anemone species. These include a cytolysin, a trypsin inhibitor and two putative neurotoxins. Transgenics are also being attempted in a few fish species such as Marble Goby, grouper and salmon. The Marble Goby growth hormone gene has been cloned. NUS scientists are now in the process of combining this gene with a heterologous promoter to make a gene construct for transgenesis. Aquaculturists have been advised of the applications of (i) thyroid hormones in enhancing embryo and fry development; and (ii) gonado-tropin releasing hormones to help induce yolk formation and spawning. The hormones are being encapsulated into synthetic capsules for commercial use. Immunologists are studying the immune responses in fish and are developing various disease control methods, including vaccination with attenuated disease agents to develop antibodies.

Singapore is one of the major exporters of tropical aquarium fishes in the world. The DAN fingerprinting technology is being used to identify proper breeder stocks to be used in breeding programmes to maintain the quality and health of the fishes. Aquaculture is most developed in Thailand. A Marine Biotechnology Unit (MBU) was established jointly by the National Centre for Genetic Engineering and Biotechnology and Aquatic Resources Research Institute of Chulalong Korn University in 1987. The Unit has been screening algae strains for feed purposes. Using cloned mitochondrial DNA, RFLP patterns of giant freshwater prawns (Macrobrachium rosenberghi) were studied for analysing variation patterns to design appropriate breeding plans. Studies are in progress to manipulate the Gonad Inhibiting Hormones (GIH) for regulating the growth, maturity and reproductive success of prawns.

To control the most common and yield-reducing disease, vibriosis, caused by the bacteria Vibrio anguillarum, of the widely cultured fish scabass, vaccines have been developed. Chromosome manipulation of oyster has also been standardised. Studies on the gametogenic cycle of Thai abalone (Haliotis ovina) are proving helpful for resource regulation and management, and for broadstock conditioning, induction of spawning, control of mating and seed production for land-based production. An outdoor mass culture of benthic diatom, Navicula sp., as a food source of abalone spot was also standardised recently.

Research on marine natural products in Thailand began a few years ago and provides valuable information on the structures and potential applications of the compounds and their derivatives from Thai sponges. Such information could be, apart from the bioactivities of the compounds that can possibly be applied further to pharmaceutical use, helpful in the chemotaxonomy of Thai sponges. The use of seaweeds as a source of phycocolloids is being promoted. The Biopolymer Research Unit (BU) of the Srinakarinwirot University, established in 1987, has developed a simple and low-cost technique for agar extraction from Gracelaria sp. seaweeds which could be applied at the village level. By developing and using chitin filter medium, the technique has improved the quality of the agar produced. The chitin could also be changed to chitosan, another valued product that is biodegradable and non-polluting and can be used as a binder in recycling paper. This technology changes the shrimp wastes into more value-added products. The Unit is currently operating a project entitled "Technology Development of Shrimp Shell Processing". Other work relates to the development of biomembranes, copolymer membrane and biobeads. Another value-added product is a fluorescence pigment of R-phycoerythrin for protein markers.

The Marine Biotechnology Centre at Burapha University is concentrating on population dynamic studies of phytoplankton and zooplankton and identification of new pharmaceuticals from marine organisms. From the various species screened, the centre found that 21 marine species had shown some degree of antimicrobial action.

Twenty-three extracts from seven species had shown positive results when subjected to haemolytic testing against erythrocytes of 21 species. It can be seen that the following biotechnology-related research work on marine organisms is in progress: studies on bioactive metabolites from Thai sponges, isolation of pure culture of some marine microalgae, isolation of pure culture of some marine bacteria, and the use of microalgae in biological control of marine animal diseases.

While considerable progress has been made in fish biotechnology in Asia, the following aspects need to be further strengthened:

- Genetic improvement of cultured fish for improved growth, disease resistance and adaptability to new farming systems.
- Development of low-cost but efficient grow-out diets for cultured fishes using locally available feedstuffs and microbiological processes.
- Utilisation of detailed and microbial feed sources for pond cultured fish.
- Production of vaccines and monoclonal antibodies for the prevention and control of bacterial and virus diseases.
- Development of drugs and other biotechnological products from marine organisms.
- Improved availability of mother stocks and seeds, especially of brackish water marine fish and shellfish.

8

Advantages of Integrated Fish Farming

Water is emerging as international challenge and its most efficient management as well as recycling has been given high priority in the plan of formulation. Recycling of crop residue as well as agricultural by products inclusion of nitrogen fixing legumes in rotation, bio-fertilizers, vermicultures, agro-forestry, nutrient solublising micro-organisms, efficient nutrient up taking plant varieties, etc., are being strategies in the research mandate. Improved efficiency of farm machinery, agro-input and resource conservation technologies of minimum tillage are being researched to minimize the cost of production. Integrated Fish Farming is one of the best examples of mixed farming.

This type of farming practices in different forms mostly in the East and South East Asian countries is one of the important ecological balanced sustainable technologies. The technology involves a combination of fish polyculture integrated with crop or live stock production. On farm waste recycling, an important component of integrated fish farming is highly advantageous to the farmers as it improves the economy of production and decrease the adverse environmental impact of farming. Integrated fish farming refers to the simultaneous culture of fish or shell fish along with other culture systems. It may also be defined as the sequential linkage between two or more culture practices. Generally integrated farming means the production or culture of two or more farming practices but when fish becomes its major component it is called as integrated fish farming. Fish culture can be integrated with several systems for efficient resource utilisation. The integration of aquaculture with livestock or crop farming provides quality protein food, resource utilisation, recycling of farm waste, employment generation and economic development. Integrated fish farming is well developed culture practice in China followed by Hungary, Germany and Malaysia. Our country, India, is organic-based and derives inputs from agriculture and animal husbandry.

INTEGRATED FISH FARMING

Integrated fish farming, an efficient method of combining fisheries, agriculture and livestock to increase the overall production and obtain maximum utilisation of resources is a traditional practice in China. High fish production has been achieved.

In order to transfer and adapt the Chinese technology in developing countries having different agro-climatic conditions, there is a need to establish through research a better understanding of the biological processes that are taking place in fish ponds under the system of integrated fish farming. The fish pond is often treated as a "black box". We stock fish; we add manures and grasses and in some cases chemical fertilizers or processed feeds. Via photosynthesis algae grow. In several months, if we have managed the pond well, marketable fish are harvested. What the actual sources of the fish growth were we can only estimate from analyses of the gut content. But such analyses reveal only the foods most recently consumed and almost always the major component is "unidentified organic matter".

A tracer is needed that will show incorporation of food into the fish's body. Radioactive tracers (14C:32P) are useable only in very small ponds or tanks. Even then the feeds must be artificially labelled with the radioactive isotope.

There is in nature a naturally occurring tracer that is present in all organic matter. It is the ratio of the 2 stable isotopes of carbon (13C: 12C). This ratio, reported as delta C, varies among plant species in a way dependent upon the photosynthetic pathway of the particular plant. The delta C of animal bodies is similar to the delta C of the foods they assimilated.

Hence if a sufficiently large range of delta C values exists among the available foods, it is often possible to estimate which foods or groups of foods were assimilated by an animal merely by comparing the delta C of that animal with the delta C of the available foods. Clearly there are limitations to the method. We are using one tracer in a multidimensional system. When several foods are available, it may be possible only to distinguish between 2 groups of foods, each group containing several possible foods with similar delta C values. Even with this limitation the delta C isotope method has given insights into complex food webs.

BIOLOGY OF MAJOR CULTIVATED FISHES

China has a vast area of water, with a distribution of inland rivers, lakes, reserviors and ponds throughout its territory, and hence it is rich in fishery resources. There is an ample variety of fishes, of which more than 50 per cent are carps. Up until now, there have been about 20 species cultured in ponds in integrated fish farms. The introduction here focuses on the four main well-known carps: Silver carp, Bighead, Grass carp and Black carp, and other good stocks---Common carp, Crucian carp, Chinese bream (Wuchang fish), Mud carp and Tilapia etc. Understanding the habits of fish, mastering the laws of their growth, development, propagation and feeding and satisfying their ecological requirements accordingly will be of great practical significance to the development of fishery production, to the application of farming techniques and to the increase of fish yield.

MORPHOLOGY AND SILVER CARP

Silver carp belong in taxonomy to Family Cyprinidae, Subfamily Hypophthalmichthyinae. Body: compressed Scales: small, Mouth: in front, with lower jaw slightly slanting upward. Eyes: comparatively small, situated below the horizontal axis of body. Gill membrane: unconnected to isthmus. Gill rakers: dense, interlaced and connected, covered with a sponge-like membraneous sieve. Abdominal keel: extending from the base of pectoral fins to the anus. Pectoral fin: its terminal tip does not exceed the base of ventral fin. Pharyngeal teeth: one row in 4/4, with fine lines and tiny grooves on surface. Intestinal length: 6-10 times that of body length. Colour of body: silvery white while alive; colour of dorsal, very dark brown. The largest body so far discovered is about 20 kg.

BIG HEAD

Bighead are similar to Silver carp in shape. They belong to the same genus Hypophthalmichthys. Head: bigger. Snout: short and blunt. Eyes: small, situated below the horizontal axis of body. Gill membrane: unconnected to isthmus. Gill rakers, dense and separated; without spongelike sieve. Abdominal keel: between the bases of ventral fins and the anus. Pectoral fin: the terminal tip reaches 1/3-2/5 of the base of ventral fin. Pharyngeal teeth: one row in 4/4, surface flat. Intestinal length: about 5 times that of body length. Colour of body: while alive, dorsal and upper sides, light black, scattered with irregular yellowish black spots; ventral surface, silvery white. The largest body so far found is about 40 kg.

GRASS CARP

Grass carp are larger-sise fish in sub-family Leuciscinae of family Cyprinidae. Body shape: almost cylindric, with flat head and round abdomen. Scales: big. Mouth: in front; lower jaw, shorter. Gill membrane: connected to isthmus. Gill raker: small and short, in scattered arrangement. Pharyngeal teeth: 2 rows in 2,5/4,2 compressed like combs. Intestinal length: 2.3-3.3 times that of body length. Colour of body: while alive, dorsal, grey; abdomen, light grey; sides, greenish yellow; fins, a lighter colour. The largest body so far found is about 35 kg.

BLACK CARP

Black carp are more close to Grass carp among Cyprinidae. Body shape: like Grass carp with a pointed head. Scales: big and circular. Mouth: arc-shaed in front.

Eyes: medium sise, situated in the middle part of head sides. Gill raker: short. Gill membrane: connected to the isthmus. Pharyngeal teeth: one row in 5/4, big, short and molar-like; surface smooth. Intestinal length: 1.2-2 times that of body length. Colour of body: while alive, greenish black; dorsal darker; abdomen light grey; Fins, black. The largest body so far discovered is about 70 kg.

CRUCIAN CARP

Crucian carp are very close to Common carp. Body: compressed and relatively thick. Abdomen: round. Head: small and short. Snout: blunt. Mouth: arc-shaped in front. Lip: thick without barbels. Pharyngeal teeth: compressed, one row in 4/4. Intestinal length: 2.7-3.2 times that of body length, some even reaching 5 times. Colour of body: silvery grey when alive; darker on dorsal and lighter on abdomen. The largest body found is about 1.5 kg. They have a wide distribution and a strong adaptability. They can live in different water body such as rivers, lakes, ponds and ditches with some variations and differentiations in characteristics.

Carassius auratus gibelio are sub-species of Crucian carp. Body: higher than usual Crucian carp. Abdomen: round. Colour of body: bluish grey with silvery white on abdomen. The largest body is about 3 kg. Japanese Crucian carp originated from Lake Pipa in Japan and was introduced into China in 1976. They grow faster than Carassius auratus gibelio. A large variety of golden fish are bred out through long period of artificial breeding. Chinese bream, or Wuchang fish (Megalobrama amblycephala) Chinese bream belong to subfamily Abramidinae. Body: high, compressed and lozenge-shaped.

Head: small and short Mouth: slanting. Abdominal keel: extending from the base of pelvic fin to the anus. Pharyngeal teeth: 3 rows arranged in 2,4,5/4,4,2. Intestinal length: 2.7 times that of body length. Colour of body: dark grey while alive, darker on dorsal; scale, dark grey in the middle and lighter on its edge. The largest body so far caught, is about 3 kg.

COMMON CARP

Body: compressed. Dorsal: projected in arch-shape. Abdomen: round. Mouth: slightly downwards with a long blunt snout and with two pairs of barbels on upper jaw; lower pair a little longer. Dorsal fin: long:

- *Scales:* Big and thick. Pharyngeal teeth: 3 rows in 1,1,3/3,1,1; teeth on inner sides, molar like. Intestinal length: 1.5-2 times that of body length.
- *Colour of body:* While alive, varying with different living conditions, usually dark grey or yellowish brown on dorsal; sides golden yellow; lower part of caudal fin, red. The largest body so far discovered is about 40 kg.

- China has a long history of culturing Common carp, which have a wide distribution and strong adaptability. There are a lot of morphological variations through artificial breeding and natural selections, such as Scale carp, Mirror carp, Wu Yuan red purse carp, Xing Guo red carp etc.

MUD CARP

Mud carp belong to family Cyprinidae, subfamily Barbinae, genus Cirrhina. Body: long and compressed. Abdomen: round and slightly flat. Snout: short, round and blunt. Mouth: inferior and transverse, with two pairs of barbels; snout barbels, strong and thick; jaw barbels, small and short:

- *Caudal fin:* Deeply separated with upper part a little longer than the lower one. Lateral line: from the upper part of the pectoral fin around the lateral line, there are 8-12 scales with dark dots at their bases which form lozenge-shaped spots.
- *Fins:* Dark-grey. Pharyngeal teeth: 3 rows in 2,4,5/5,4,2. Intestinal length: about 14 times that of body length. The largest body caught is about 4 kg.

TILAPIA

Tilapia belong to order Perciformes, family Cichlidae, genus Tilapia. This genus comprises more than 100 species including subspecies. At present, 15 of them are taken as cultured fishes all over-the world. In China, mainly Tilapia mossambica and T. nilotica etc. are reared.

Body of T. mossambica: short and compressed. Dorsal: a little higher. Shape: similar to Crucian carp. Mouth: bigger. Lip: thick, with lower jaw a little long than upper jaw. Scales: circular. Lateral line: disjointed. The intestinal length about 7 times that of body length. Colour of body: dark grey while alive; during spawning stage, body colour of male fish, dark green; edges of dorsal, anal and caudal fins, obvious red; female, greyish yellow. The largest body weight so far discovered is about 0.5 kg.

Colour of T. nilotica: changing with external conditions, light black; abdomen white, with 9 longitudinal black stripes on body surface, of which, 7 below dors; fins and 2 on the peduncle; caudal fin with 10 clear vertical black stripes for life. Scales: ctenoid. The largest body weight is 2.5 kg. Nuptial colour can be found on the male and the female of Tilapia at reproductive period. But their external genital organs are different in appearance. The male has two pores; anus in front and cloaca in the rear. The female, 3 pores, *i.e.*, anus in front, genital pore in the middle and excretory pore in the rear.

FEEDING HABITS OF FISH

Although Silver carp, Bighead, Grass carp, Black carp, Common carp and Mud carp, belong to Cyprinidae, they have formed their respective ways of food in-take and their respective food chains at different stages of the development, It is due to their long-term adaptations to ecological conditions, the restrictions of water body environment and the perfection of body structure as well as the development of foodintake and digestive organs along with their growth. The main natural food Silver carp and Bighead feed on are plankton. Silver carp mainly feed on zooplankton at larval stage, whereas their feeding turns to phytoplankton after grown-up. Bighead feed on zooplankton mainly all their life. The differentiation of feeding habits are caused by the structure and the density of their filtering organs gill rakers. The gill rakers of Silver carp and Bighead are situated in the operculum with 4 pairs on either side, and the 5th pair of gill arch which was specialised into inferior pharyngobranchial. The gill arch bone is the base to which gill rakers and gill filaments attach.

The gill rakers of Bighead are delicate and sabre-shaped, each consisting of a neck, a stem and a base. The neck is narrow and short. The stem is the principal part of the gill raker. The dorsal part of it is thicker, while the ventral part thinner. On either side, there is a row of wartlike protuberance, so to speak, lateral protuberance.

The lateral protuberance of a gill-raker is interwoven with the next one in serration. Occasionally there are opposite protuberances, their triangle-shaped bases cling to the gill arch bones. Besides, gill rakers can be divided into two kinds, broad and narrow ones. There exists one broad gill raker every 3-6 narrow gill rakers. The gill rakers of Silver carp are different from that of Bighead. The gill rakers are inter-connected by minute bony bridges, which are covered with spongy sieve membranes. The density of gill rakers is higher than that of Bighead's gill raker.

The newly hatched Silver carp and Bighead fry nourish themselves with egg yolk and begin to take in plankton in the water when their body length reaches 7-9 mm, 3-4 days after hatching. The food-filtering organs are imperfect with short and sparse gill rakers before the body length reaches 15 mm. At that time, both Silver carp and Bighead eat the same food.

The major groups of zooplankton that Silver carp and Bighead eat are rotifera, nauplius of copepods and tiny cladocera. The shape and structure of filtering organs of fry about 20-30 mm in body length, are generally the same as those of adult fish's. The fry of Silver carp will take in phytoplankton as its main foods, since it has nearly 200 gill rakers, 1 mm in length each, with minute bony bridges between them Sieve membranes covering the bridges form a fine. The gill rakers of Bighead fry, short and sparse, are separated with larger spaces and difficult to detain tiny phytoplankton. As a result, their main food changes from tiny zooplankton to all sorts of zooplankton.

Beside the filtering organs—gill rakers, Silver carp and Bighead have accessary organs—palatine folds, that is, inter-gill raker folds. Palatine folds, located at the apex of mouth cavity, consist of 9 vertical ridges of mucus membrane, four on either side and one in between. The middle ridge is very short like an inverted letter Y with the branched end backwards. Palatine folds act in coordination with gill rakers, to get the food through filtering. Under culture conditions, Silver carp and Bighead can also feed on commercial feeds such as cakes, brans, dregs and wastes.

FEEDING HABITS OF GRASS CARP AND BLACK CARP

The fry of both fishes under 15 mm in body length have the same feeding habits, mainly feeding on zooplankton. But the feeding habits of the fry above 20-30 mm in body length will differentiate. The fry of Grass carp start to take in tender aquatic plants, while the fry of Black carp eat Benthos such as snails and corbicula spp. etc. Grass carp are typical herbivorous species taking in all sorts of aquatic and land grasses, hence, the pharyngeal teeth are well developed, tough and strong (tooth formula: 2,5/4.2). The teeth are shaped like choppers with saw-toothed edges. Pharyngeal teeth at both sides are interlaced with each other.

They are against callous pad of the basioccipital, grinding food into pieces for digestion in intestines. Grass carp are voracious eaters, feeding amount usually could reach 40 per cent. But the plant cellulose could not be digested and utilised. Black carp are carnivorous fish, and usually feed on molluscs like snails, clams and corbicula spp. By using pharyngeal teeth and callous pad, they crush hard shells, then swallow the meat. Their pharyngeal teeth are strong and tough and molar-shaped (tooth formula: 4/5).

Under culture conditions, both fishes tend to be more or less omnivorous, feeding on oil seed cakes, brans, dregs and animal feeds like silkworm pupae, earthworm, animal entrails.

CHARACTERISTICS OF INTEGRATED FISH FARMING

The integrated fish farming practices have developed into a complicated structural network in line with the local conditions. China is a vast country with a large population and varied natural environments. The agricultural structure and the economic conditions of each locality are also different.

Therefore, various integrated fish farming systems in line with the local conditions have developed into a complicated structural network. The Pearl River Delta is located to the south of the Tropic of Cancer. Its annual solar irradiation is 110 kcal/cm2 but averaging 60 Kcal/cm2. Average temperature is about 22°C; 2-3 days of frost a year; more rain and high temperature in summer with maximum temperature of about 37°C and relative humidity 76-85 per cent; annual sunshine time between 2000 and 2500 hours. Such geographic and climatic conditions are very conducive to the cultivation of mulberry trees, sericulture and fish farming. Hence, the farmers in the Pearl River Delta through production practices have been able to take advantage of local natural resources by integrating mulberry cultivation and sericulture with fish farming, which leads to the establishment of a complete, scientific "mulberry plot-fish pond" man-made ecosystem. Even in the same geographical zone, the items of integration by various production units are different. Helei Fish Farm, Xinan Fish Farm, Helei First Fishery Brigade, Wangzhuang Fish Farm as well as the Municipal Fish Culture Farm in Wuxi practise different items of integration.. Liutan village has recently incorporated agriculture, sideline occupations, aquaculture and commerce into its integrated system. The integrated fish farm was established in 1980. The farm site was earlier a water-logged paddy field of 17.33 ha, subject to annual flooding and with low yield of agricultural crops. Based on the topography of the low land, the farmers restructured the land into fish ponds of 10.67 ha. in the winter of 1979 and the spring of 1980.

The farm consists of 15 grow-out ponds (8 ha), 11 fingerling ponds (2.67 ha). Apart from pig raising, green fodder planting is the major item of the integrated management. It has 1.33 ha of pond dykes for the cultivation of English rye grass (Lolium pereme), sow thistle (Lactuca indica), etc. They utilised water cane shoots field to cultivate duckweed with average yield of 37,500-45,000 kg/ha. With sufficient supply of green fodder, Grass carp and Wuchang fish (Megalobrama spp.) become the dominant cultured species, with the yield of 5250 kg/ha, that is 45 per cent of the total pond fish production. It indicates that the maximal efficiency of the integrated fish farming system can be obtained only through maximal utilisation of natural conditions and the agricultural characteristics of the regions concerned.

The socio-economic conditions should be taken into consideration in developing integrated fish farming. The fact is that the diversified economy develops in the harmonious interaction among the socioeconomic conditions, agricultural production, and natural conditions on the basis of regional climatical differences. Since the development of integrated fish farming is site-specific and the conditions of each site are different and complicated either from the macro or micro view points, the linkage between the trades of integrated fish farms in China become a complex matrix. Simple modele involving mono-integration of fish-cum-animal husbandry, fish-cum-poultry or fish-cum-crops are now getting fewer and fewer in China with the exception of small-scale individual farms.

UTILISING WASTES BY VARIOUS WAYS OF RECYCLING

The integrated system of fish farming is rather complicates involving various forms of integrations and methods in utilisation of organic wastes. The animal excreta alone can be effectively utilised through employing various methods and techniques.

- Fresh animal manure can be applied directly to the fish ponds. pigsties, poultry coops and pens for ducks and geese can be constructed on the dikes or above the ponds. Fresh manure thus enter the ponds directly, avoiding energy losses due to processing of manure and transportation. The feedstuff of livestock are not fully digested and then can be directly utilised by fish. Therefore, the number of animals should be compatible with unit water surface.

- The residues and liquid part after anaerobic fermentation to produce biogas are used for fertilising fish ponds. Compost after aerobic fermentation can also be used for fish culture.
- Animal manure can be used indirectly through one or two trophic levels in a food chain such as growing fodder crop to feed herbivorous fish, producing earthworms or other animal-feedstuff for carnivorous fish directly or used as part of the composition of pelleted feeds.
- Poultry manure can be used to feed pigs and pig manure can in turn be used as fertilizers for fish pond.

COLLOCATION OF FISH FARMING AND CROP CULTIVATION

The ingestive variation of fish is caused by the growth of fish and environmental conditions. Among the environmental conditions, the seasonal change of water temperature is the main factor. The production period, therefore, has to be collocated with this variation of fish ingestion so as to synchronise the daily production of fodder grass with the daily ingestion of fish. The period of the lowest ingestion amount of cultivated fish in Changjiang Drainage is between Feb. and Mar. and between Nov. and Dec. in a year. The peak is between Jun. and Sept. accounting for 50 per cent of the annual total amount.

The production mode of English Ryegrass and Sudan grass nowadays coincides with the demand of fish feeds. Ryegrass is sowed in Sept. every year and transplanted in Oct. and mowed in Dec. in Changjiang Drainage. It reaches the peak production between Apr. and May. The integrated fish farm can supply itself sufficiently by the production of Ryegrass. Sudan grass is sowed in mid Apr. and mowed for the first time when it grows to 50 cm high just before the withering of rye grass. It reaches the peak production between June and Sept. The daily output is about 100 kg/mu. Based on the experiments the annual production of 2 grasses can reach about 15,000 kg/mu if it's well managed. The other ways of collocation are as follows:

- To intercrop gramineous grasses: Ryegrass, Sudan grass and leguminous fodder grasses.

  The unit area output of two families of fodder grass can be increased and the quality can be improved.
- To adopt ensiling method if there is a surplus of ryegrass or to pelletise ryegrass with other materials, so as to be supplied during crop change in June as supplements.

- To adopt sowing and transplanting by stages and to mow the grass in turn.

In Changjiang Drainage the seeds of Sudan grass are sowed by stages in April ahead of the usual time and can be mowed in mid May. In order to maintain the fertility of the land, pond silt must be fully utilised with some additional organic fertilizers apart from planting leguminous grass, and at last, the grasses should be harvested with stubble remaining in the field.

THE RATIO OF WATER SURFACE AND CROP FIELD

The ratio of water surface and crop fields means the total area of crop fields collocated with one mu of water surface of fish farming. The following factors must be taken into consideration:

- Source of feeds and fertilizers and their prices.
- The abundance of land.
- The yield and the proportion of various spp.

STOCKING MODELS OF FISH IN FISH-CUM-CROP INTEGRATION

The main or only source of feeds and fertilizers is the pasture grasses cultivated on the farm. The spp. stocked should be grass carp and Wuchang fish megalobrama spp. as major spp. which occupy 60-70 per cent. Silver carp and Bighead as minor spp. which occupy about 20-30 per cent assorted with a few of omnivorous fish which occupy about 10 per cent. The omnivorous fish can not only utilise residues and detritus but also can clean the fish pond for herbivorous fish but the ratio should be limited within 10 per cent. In order to get natural food organism ready for Silver carp and Bighead after stocking, it is necessary to mow the grass and make a compost to fertilize the pond water or stock Silver carp and Bighead half a month later after stocking of Grass carp. If the farm produces more compost, the proportion of omnivorous fish may be increased a little. The use of pond silt in fish-cum-crop integration There are 2 methods to use pond silt in accordance with crop strains and cropping system:

- Pond silt is directly used as base manure for Ryegrass, etc. The silt should be harrowed and smoothed after it dries a little and then the seeds can be sowed. If it's a transplantation, there's no need to harrow. The seedlings could be interpolated, economising on much labour and time. If the silt is used as additional manure, it should be topdressed to the roots of the plant. In summer, silt will be bailed with water to the fields. This method is beneficial for the silt to release or diffuse nutrient elements and detritus. It also benefits increasing of dissolved oxygen in the bottom layer of water.
- Making compost with pond silt and grass

Usually, there's a surplus of pond silt in winter whereas there's a shortage of pond silt in summer. Therefore dig out a pit, 5 meters square with a depth of

1 m near the crop field and then put in pond silt and grass (straw manure and stable matted grass are better) to make compost and cover the pit with mud. After fermentation, the effectiveness of manure is increased. The compost is usually used as base manure, sometimes mixed with water as topdressing.

It's safer to use pond silt as manure. The applying amount is not necessarily limited, with an average rate of 5-15 tons/mu or even a thickness of 35 cm on the soil.

THE EFFECTS OF "ROTATION" OF FISH AND GRASS

The system of rotation of fish and grass can fully utilise the productivity of fish ponds to provide both green fodder crops for fish and green manure crops for fish ponds to propagate large amount of natural food organisms. According to the practices of Suzhou Municipal Fish Farm, the phytoplankton can reach 3×10^8 ind/1 at the peak time. The growth of summerlings can reach 1.8-2.5 mm/day in the initial month. If the yield of barnyard grass in a pond is 5000kg, 40kg of grass can be transformed into 1 kg of fingerlings averagely. It can save 0.5-0.8 kg of marketable feeds and reduce 10 per cent of the cost.

In this system, crops utilise the nutrients of pond silt, whereas crop nutrients, which return back to the pond after submergence, not only improve the water quality but also increase the soil fertility. Practices prove that the fish yield increases after submergence of crops, *e.g.*, Suzhou Municipal Fish Farm has adopted this method to nurture fingerlings since 1979. In 1982, the average yield increased from 150 kg/mu to 391 kg/mu, increasing by 1.6 times.

FISH FARMING INTEGRATED WITH AQUATIC PLANT CULTURE

In a network of rivers like lower reaches of Changjiang River, a fish farm is often near lakes, rivers or water-logging area or in the vicinity of inlet and outlet of irrigation canal. These water bodies are rich in nutrients, esp. effluents from cities and fish farms. In order to utilise these water resources, fish farmers in the southern part of China often culture aquatic plants in these water bodies. The principal aquatic plants are water hyacinth Eichhornia crassipes, water lettuce Pistia stratistes and water peanut or alligator weed Alternanthera philoxeroides, so-called three Ap's; the secondary are duckweed such as (Spirodela polyrhiza) and Wolffia arrhiza and Lemuna minor.

THE WAYS OF UTILISATION OF AQUATIC MACROPHYTES

The output of aquatic macrophytes is the highest among the green fodder crops for fish. The yield could be about 15 ton/mu, even above 25 ton/mu. The aquatic macrophytes grow too fast and it causes a lot of trouble in the Tropics and sub-Tropics. However, the nutrients of aquatic macrophytes are higher. Water hyacinth is called "King of Aquatic Plants". So far as protein produced from per unit area is concerned, it is 6-10 times that of soy bean. Aquatic macrophytes are easy to manage with less labour and lower cost. It's said that one labour can manage 50 mu of 3 aquatic plants and can produce 13.1 ton of crude protein in half a year. The cost of one ton of three aquatic plants (including wages) is only about 1 yuan.

MARINE FARMING: PERSPECTIVE ON ITS INEVITABILITY AND SUSTAINABILITY

Fish farming or aquaculture was defined by the Food and Agriculture Organisation of the U.N., (FAO) as "the farming of aquatic organisms, including fish, crustaceans, mollusks, and aquatic plants". Marine farming, or marine aquaculture, or mariculture can be defined as "farming of marine organisms". It also implies some sort of ownership of the cultivated stock, although not necessarily of the area over which the marine farm is anchored or staked. Sea or ocean ranching, therefore, doesn't fall under this definition, since the "seed" fish grown in hatcheries once released are not owned, until captured. Aquaculture, including marine farming, has become a mass provider of animal protein, employment option for poor farmers and displaced capture fishermen, solution for marginal lands and water resources, and as exporter - a foreign currency earner. With marine and inland capture fisheries unable to satisfy a growing demand for some popular fish species, such as for example, salmon, cod and shrimp, as well as trout, tilapia and carps, respectively, it has also become their complementary source.

Aquatic foods have high nutritional quality, contributing on the average 20 per cent or more of per capita animal protein intake for almost 3 billion people, mostly in developing countries. Fish is also the world's most widely traded foodstuff and a key source of export earnings for many countries with particular significance for small island states and, as far as fish farming goes, for countries in the South and Southeast Asia.

HISTORY

Aquaculture has been practiced by mankind since times immemorial. Five thousand years ago, Chinese villagers trapped carp in artificial lakes that formed when flooded rivers receded. Ancient practice of carp culture in China was described in the 5th century BC, while the Egyptians might've been cultivating fish a thousand years earlier. Also the ancient Romans grew oysters and, most probably, fish, already 2,000 years ago. Around 600 A.D., the Menehune of Hawaii built a huge fish pond on Kauai, as the legend goes, by erecting overnight a 900-foot-long wall out of lava rock.

Most of the ancient fish farming was based on capture of young stages and transferring them to ponds and sea enclosures to grow. This could be done, for example, by fencing off tidal areas towards ebb tide, which arrested fish movement seaward and facilitated their collection during the outgoing flow.

Another method, practiced till the present in some places, is letting fish enter open enclosures during seasonal floods to feed and grow there, and fencing them off before the water recedes. Fish are kept in those enclosures to grow, or collected and moved elsewhere. Such types of culture can be seen even today, for example, in Italy's "vallicultura" and in SE Asia.

All these and other early variants of fish farming have been of the extensive type. Extensive fish farming implies that fish are not crowded much beyond their population density in nature and are not or almost not artificially fed. Thus, extensive fish farming hardly affects natural habitats. Environmental problems appeared only with intensification of the production.

While the ancient fish farming was based on eggs/larvae/juveniles collected from nature, in a true full circle aquaculture they should be produced on the farming premises. First to close the growth circle was a German farmer in the 18th century who fertilized trout eggs with their sperm and hatched them in tanks/ponds. During most of the 20th century, marine fisheries and fish farming were developing in parallel as separate industries with little market interaction. By and large, each produced different species and had respective traditional consumers. But during recent decades, things have been changing on the fish market. Now many consumers buy fresh or smoked salmon, sea-bream, oysters, or frozen shrimp, many without knowing, and some without caring, whether they were caught in open sea by fishermen, or grown in ponds, mollusks farms, or floating cages. Presently, farming of some 15 species of marine finfish is in its starting phase or expanding, each according to the progress made by researchers and fish farmers.

Notwithstanding, capture fisheries and fish farming are inter-related and to a great extent overlapping in their ecology, economics and social impacts. Both interact in several manners and often co-exist in common ecosystems. This essay approaches marine farming development, recognising the fact that our whole civilization has been based on man-modified ecosystems both on land and in water, and that further modifications are required in view of the badly mishandled needs of the expanding human population and the sustained destitution of many.

STATISTICS

In 2007, the total world fisheries yield was over 140 million mt, of which some 90 million was produced by capture fisheries and over 50 million by aquaculture, most of it in the developing countries, with China leading with some 31 million mt (FAO, 2010). In 2006, the world consumed 110.4 million mt of fish, 51.7 million mt originating from aquaculture. The earth's population is forecast to reach 8.32 billion in 2030. If capture fisheries production (92 million mt in 2006) and the non-food uses of fish (33.3 million mt in 2006) remain constant, aquaculture needs to produce 80.5 million mt by 2030 in order to maintain the current per capita consumption of 16.7 kg. That is, 25 years from now, aquaculture will need to produce 28.8 million mt more per year than its current annual production (FAO, 2008).

THE RECENT DEVELOPMENT OF AQUACULTURE

During the last 4 decades, fish farming has expanded to meet the soaring global demand for seafood. Both on land and in the sea it has undergone tremendous quantitative development, and soon will be overtaking capture fishery in the global supply of food fis.

Consumption of fish, both wild and farm raised, has doubled since 1973, with most of this increase in developing countries. But as the demand for fish rises, wide populations of both marine and freshwater species are unable to produce significantly increased yields, because of stagnant or declining catches. The total marine fish yield has reached 90 million mt a year, a yield that after a period of rapid growth and despite increasing demand has remained mostly level for the last decade.

Since the later years of the 20th century, salmon has become the main finfish farmed in cold waters, milkfish, shrimp, and yellowtail - in South Asia's and the Far East's ponds, cages and lagoons, and seabream and seabass - in cage farms all over the Mediterranean. Atlantic salmon, a fish exotic in Chile and on the west coast of North America has been farmed there since the mid 1990s. A relatively late comer to the salmon industry already a decade ago Chile produced more than 100,000 mt/year, and earned in 2006 over US$2.2 billion. This followed a 15-year development during which production expanded by an incredible 2,200 per cent. Between 2003 and 2006 Chile's export earnings grew by an average 22 per cent per year, challenging Norway as the world's top salmon producer. Unfortunately, it has been suffering during the last couple of years from massive outbreaks of salmon disease that caused considerable decline in production and earnings. Cod farming, already beyond the R and D stage, has become a reality mainly in Norway, the UK and Denmark. Also farming of halibut and turbot is becoming commercial.

The tuna grow-out industry, pioneered in Australia, towards the end of the 20th century has expanded also in the Mediterranean and the Central Atlantic Ocean's coastal waters. The practice of tuna on-grow (fattening) in cages, however, cannot be considered a real farming. In fact, it consists of creaming off of young fish from the stock years before they had any chance of spawning, and fattening them for half-an-year, or so, before harvesting. This procedure must negatively affect wild stocks of the most sought after tuna species. In Japan, in a procedure that shouldn't affect wild tuna stocks, it is the fry that is caught to be fattened at a fish farm.

Recently, however, successes were reported of closing the whole life cycle of tunas, *i.e.*, holding breeding stock, making them spawn and fertilize the eggs, on-growing larvae into fingerlings, etc. This, if fully implemented could increase very much the production and relieve the pressure on the wild populations. The snag is that tuna are grown on other, forage fishes, and if pellets are used, these would contain high share of fishmeal produced of "industrial", as a rule, small pelagic fishes, of which several kilogrammes are needed to produce one kg of tuna.

THE DILEMMA OF GROWING DEMAND AND SUSTAINABILITY

Worldwide, both governments and international and regional organisations define their marine policies as aimed at achieving sustainability in aquatic ecosystems and, particularly with respect to aquatic life and fisheries resources. At the same time, it is widely recognised that the present production of fishery products from the wild and from the existing aquaculture would not be able to match the increasing food needs of the expanding human population.

The U.N., defines..."sustainable development" as development "that meets the needs of the present without compromising the needs of future generations... to be achieved through ...balance between environmental integrity, social development and economic development...". According to FAO, sustainability entails the notion of progressive development, which has no negative effect on the environment and on the future of the resource concerned..

But, "sustainable development" suffers from different, often incompatible interpretations by economists, sociologists, environmentalists, and various stakeholders. This argument ranges from the extreme "nature first" conservation approach to a "development and business first" approach. The former is about maintaining of or returning to marine ecosystems as close as possible to their "virgin" or pre-industrial state. The latter is about extraction of fishery resource in the most profitable way, now.

CONSTRAINTS

It is important to bear in mind the various constraints that may impede further development of marine farming. Although growing sea fish in floating cages may be, under some conditions, less costly than on land, the marine fish farming industry has been focusing on raising species, which when supplied from capture fisheries, fetch relatively high prices. While it indeed may serve as a mass protein provider, its product is intended only for those who can afford the price. Hence, repeating cases of salmon market gluts. They are good and popular fish, but many potential consumers can only afford to pay for them prices that the salmon producing-processing-marketing system cannot live with.

According to FAO, aquaculture would keep growing so that the 2010 world's total fish production may reach some 140 million mt. While the supplement must come from farming, some 30 million mt of marine fish landings would go for fishmeal needed to feed, apart from poultry and cattle husbandry, and inland aquaculture, all the predatory fishes that are grown in marine cages. This is a nagging problem, all the more that the feed alone may account for some 60 per cent of total production costs. Processing and marketing technologies are advancing, and no doubt, some of the today's "industrial" fish will be made fit for human consumption and fetch prices that would make their reduction to fishmeal uneconomic. Availability of fishmeal, therefore, may become a constraint; hence, quite appropriately, vegetable surrogate feeds are investigated and here and there already applied.

Species that feed at lower levels of the food pyramid, like, carp, milkfish, tilapia (Gur, 1997 and private communication) and gray mullets and, according to information from Israel, also gilthead seabream, can be grown on reduced fishmeal or vegetable diets. Nonetheless, fish farmers still prefer to use feeds that incorporate some fishmeal, lack of financial motivation being one reason, inertia-another. Tilapias are basically freshwater vegetarian fishes, widely cultured throughout the world, with some species showing euryhaline behaviour. Recently Malta University reported on trials aimed at growing tilapia both in sea cages and in tanks with sea water.

Other problems confronting the marine farming industry are environmental concerns, public resistance to genetic engineering, bioaccumulation of various chemical substances by fish grown in polluted waters, frequent outbreaks of stock-devastating diseases, and proliferation of parasites.

Outlook. While markets and consumers get the fish they need, fishing industry strategists and also many fishermen look with wary eye on the ongoing expansion of marine fish farming industry. Although farmed sea fish cannot be sold cheaply, their regular supply prevents wild-fish prices from going up, even off-season to compensate a fishery for poor landings. Together with reduced quotas and subsidies, and several impoverished stocks, this may lead to significantly unfavourable consequences, and even shrinking of the affected capture fisheries. On the other hand, an increase in landings of wild fish of farmed species or market-wise equivalent may affect prices of the farmed fish with negative economic consequences for the farmers.

With this bad news come also a bit better ones. Firstly, where this happens, marine aquaculture may represent a way out for investment capital off the capture industry, and a second line of defence to displaced fishermen by providing employment. Secondly, fish farmed in the sea might resist unfavourable environmental changes in water better than wild fish. This, because if the organisms that form the natural food base of the fish in the wild are seriously affected by such changes, the food base of the wild fish stock would be reduced.

Their displacement or disappearance may cause wild population's migration or starvation or both. Farmed fish are supplied with their food whatever is the temperature and salinity of the surrounding water and would suffer only at the extremes of their physiological survival range. All this may make redundant fishing capital and low-income fishing people consider, respectively, investment and employment in the marine farming industry, and in particular - in offshore cage farms, where seamanship, sea legs, boat-operation, and net-making and net-mending skills represent important advantages. According to FAO, the maximum wild-capture fisheries potential from the world's oceans must've been reached, thus almost any further growth in the world's fish supply will come from fish farming. The rising demand and technological developments that have been fueling the explosive growth of fish farming, have stimulated what is considered by many to be the most hopeful trend in the world's increasingly troubled food system, although targeting at the more affluent consumer. In any case, the mankind is consuming more and more seafood, not so much owing to increase of consumption per capita, but rather due to the continuing growth of the world's population. In this context both, in terms of demand and of supply, the share of Asian aquaculture is overwhelming.

The commonly proposed solution for the problem of satisfying the demand for fishery products is both to improve the management of exploited fish stocks, and to further the development of commercial fish farming - a process, which is already going on at accelerating pace. There is a continuum between open-access fishing and intensive aquaculture, along which fishing rights and property rights develop from vague to almost absolute, often within shared habitats. However, such developments represent a focus of an earnest dispute on a global scale. This, because they affect inter-related processes within the domain of marine ecology, of economics and of social systems of coastal communities and other people involved in fishing, fish farming and fish processing and marketing.

The spiraling rate of fish farming development, however, has produced also undesirable "side effects" that could have been mostly avoided, would the necessary attention be paid timely and adequate money and efforts duly invested. Notwithstanding, as long as it can produce fish at prices people are ready to pay, aquaculture will keep expanding, especially, if wild marine and freshwater yields won't grow, while demand increases.

FEED AND ENERGY

Presently, small, forage fish account for some 37 per cent of the world's sea fish yield, and 25-30 million mt of them are reduced into fishmeal and oil, of which close to half is used for poultry and cattle fodder. In 2006, aquaculture consumed approximately 3.06 million mt or 56 per cent of world fishmeal production and 0.78 million mt or 87 per cent of total fish oil production with over 50 per cent of fish oil going to salmon farming. Between 1992 and 2006 the content of fishmeal and fish oil used in fish feeds has tripled on the expense of the poultry sector, which gradually reduced its reliance on fishmeal. Besides fishmeal or fishmeal-based diets, an approximate 5 to 6 million mt of low-value/ trash fish are used as direct feed in aquaculture, and notably in tuna cage culture.

FAO doesn't expect any significant increase of fishmeal production, all the more that the fishmeal usage in animal production sector, particularly poultry, will continue to decrease in the coming years. Furthermore, it is expected that a proportion of fishmeal and fish oil used in fish feed will be replaced by vegetable-based protein and oil, and that feed management efficiency is going to be improved. Additionally, price level is bound to affect aquaculture production, especially, when the demand for aquaculture products is outstripping the supply, and fish prices soar so that even inefficient farms make money.

The expansion of salmon culture in three continents - Europe, North and South America - has resulted in increased demands for feed fishes. Recently, farming of cod - another piscivore - has become the focus for massive development efforts. The magnitude of the farming of piscivorous species competes with the previously predominant culture of tilapia, carp and catfish that utilises mainly vegetable or algae-based feeds. Apart from the tuna that's mainly fattened on small pelagics, predatory fish grown in ponds and cages are usually fed with mixed feeds with varying share of animal protein. Fishmeal is very concentrated (some 60 per cent of protein) and normally about 4.5 kg of raw fish are needed to produce 1 kg of fishmeal.

Piscivorous fishes such as salmon and trout must be fed with animal protein; hence fish farming industry has become a major consumer of fishmeal. However, the world resources of fish that can be economically utilised for reduction are finite and, with the right market conditions and appropriate technology, some of them could be used for human consumption and might increasingly leak away to canning, sushi-type and fresh-fish markets. Thus, the presently spiraling growth of aquaculture rather sooner than later must face fishmeal supply constraint.

Altogether, the use of forage fish for fish feed has become a worrying situation. The existing management efforts focus on groundfish and large pelagics, rather than on forage fish, and little is known about their role in the marine ecosystem both as grazers and as food for seabirds and marine mammals, and what the true relation between their natural and fishing mortality is. If and when the demand for forage fish by human food market increases, some of the fishmeal industry and, consequently, also the fish farming industry, may find themselves facing feed prices that may preclude feasible operation. Although raising seafood like oysters, clams, catfish, and tilapia is many times more efficient than cattle breeding, a growing scarcity of fish feed may jeopardise future expansion of farming piscivore fish, like salmon and cod.

If such shift occurs, one would expect increasing reduction of the fishmeal contents in the various feeds and pellets, improving feed-production and feeding-in-cage technology. Today, at a rather conservative feeding coefficient of, say,

4:1, with feed containing 25 per cent of fishmeal, 5 kg of raw fish is needed to produce 1 kg of farmed fish weight. Only with much higher and hardly practiced fishmeal content of 50 per cent, 10 kg of raw fish for 1 kg of farmed fish weight would be needed. Reduction of fishmeal content in the feed of some other fishes grown in cages that are feeding in wild on invertebrate fauna, like seabream, is also indicated, in view of satisfactory performance of vegetable proteins. Although replacement of fishmeal by vegetable (soy, etc.) meals depends on their respective prices, a steadily increasing amount of the food supply for farmed fish could be coming from soybeans and other vegetable products.

Additional options could be to amplify the preparation of feeds from non-food by-products, such as fishing by-catch and discards, fish-processing offal and fishmeal made of industrial non-food fishes, as already up to one-third of fishmeal is made from various fishery wastes. Another way is using a mixture of poultry by-products and vegetable oils, such as worked out by a Malaysian team headed by Rossita Shapawi. Claims that those are the fish-farming feed requirements that detract forage fishes from becoming food fish are misplaced, for comparable amounts of fishmeal and oil are going into margarine, cattle feed and chicken feed. Fish farms compete for access to that supply with other, non-fisheries industries, a competition that influences prices for both the fishermen, who catch the small forage fish and for the fishmeal-and-oil industry.

The very processing and transportation of the fishmeal and the forage fish, often overseas, require energy, which reduces the economic efficiency of the whole process. Thus, when the energy costs and other costs of contemporary fish farming in marine floating cages are examined, it turns out that *e.g.*, salmon aquaculture may be even less efficient than extremely inefficient high seas salmon trolling. On the other hand, the farmed fish consume far less wild fish protein per unit of weight growth than are consumed by wild fish, which must spend lots of energy to chase down their prey. For example, 10 kg of capelin produces some 4.6 kg of farmed salmon, while the same weight of capelin would only produce 2.0 kg of wild salmon.

Better utilisation of both the fish farming area and the energy in the feed would make the industry more environment friendly. But, to introduce and invest in innovative industry practices that may help to create a shift towards progressive fish farming, there'd also be a need for a fundamental change in public attitudes. This includes a willingness to prioritise fish that are lower on the food chain and sensitivity to environment friendly practices. But can consumers today be mobilised to modify the aquaculture industry as they pressured tuna fleets to adopt more dolphin-friendly practices in the 1980s?

PROBLEMS

In recent decades, marine farming of seaweeds, invertebrates and finfish has become a main player in national waters of many countries. Therefore, in coastal waters, whether those facing open sea or those in enclosed and semi-enclosed habitats, any fisheries management must cover both capture fisheries and marine fish farming, as it must take into account also all other major stakeholders and participants in activities that affect environment in the managed area.

The "integrated coastal zone management" (ICZM) is supposed to take care of such problematique. Born as a tool to prepare nations for a possible rise in the level of the sea, it is now being applied by governments to harmonise, with their own policies, the often-conflicting interests of the various stakeholders. By definition ICZM has to get involved, at least partly, in fisheries management. The level of its involvement depends on both, the local fisheries, socio-economic and physical conditions, and the respective government policy.

Coastal mariculture and in particular fish culture in floating cages, much because of its impact on coastal ecosystems and capture fisheries and on the socio-cultural fabric of fishing communities, have been under substantial pressure of criticizm on the part of environmentalist organisations and activists, of commercial and recreational fishermen and other concerned bodies and individuals, and of the ensuing restrictions and regulation. Some, even, insist that the salmon industry is clearly a net-loss proposition, whether viewed from the ecological, social or economic perspective. This criticizm cannot be waived aside as that of some of the extreme critics of capture fisheries. It must be seriously examined and considered with the view of finding solutions to the negative effects of the mariculture.

Parasites and diseases spreading in the densely stocked fish cages and coastal marine ponds often cause mass mortalities and great financial losses to the fish farming industry, while escapees from cages may carry them to the vulnerable wild populations. While sea cages protect farmed fish from predators, pathogens can move or be carried both ways.

A sea cage thus becomes an "unintended pathogen factory" or receptacle. According to some reports, each year around two million farmed fish escape in the Atlantic. Of fish farmed, unlike the quantitatively less important wild seabass and seabream, cod and to some degree salmon create large wild stocks of major commercial importance. Hence, the capture fishery is looking with a wary eye on the impact of infected runaway fish on their wild brethren, and on the possibility of interbreeding of farmed varieties with wild stocks. Also, sea-lice spreading from cages to wild fish may increase their lice burdens and cause wild fish to decline.

While fish infected in the cages have better chance to survive, owing to veterinarian care and various treatments, wild populations are more vulnerable. Massive infections of wild fish can be avoided only by ensuring that they do not share water with farmed fish, either by locating sea cages very far from wild fish migrational paths and feeding/spawning grounds, or through the use of closed-containment systems. Fish farms with tons of feed being released into the cages create algae-promoting conditions similar to pollution from cities and terrestrial farms. The situation is reversed with oyster farms, because oysters are filtering animals. These farms provide water-cleaning benefits and support coastal economies. They also make better oysters: a farmed oyster is plumper, sweeter and prettier than its wild cousin. Hence, farming planktivorous, herbivorous and omnivorous freshwater fish like grey mullet, tilapia, carp and catfish, and mollusks like oysters and mussels is environmentally sounder. But the money is in the piscivores, like tuna, salmon and cod. The need to feed them with small whole fish or fishmeal is putting pressure on populations of wild forage fishes, which makes the fish-farming industry competing with wild carnivores over their limited resources.

With time, more problems materialised that, while not markedly slowing down the development, produced negative effects. Such has been, among others, the denuding of mangrove areas by the expanding shrimp farming in Latin America and in the south and southwest Asia, which has allegedly affected the catches in the adjacent artisanal fisheries and their communities, and more recently, was blamed for at least part of the damage caused all over the Indian Ocean by the 2004 tsunami.

Poorly run land-based fish farms, floating fish cages, and feeding pens release into the environment unutilised protein, nutrients and fecal matter creating wasteful and often noxious pollution. According to some estimates, a fish farm with 200,000 salmon releases nutrients and fecal matter roughly equivalent to the raw sewage generated by 20,000 to 60,000 people and Scotland's salmon aquaculture industry produces the same amount of nitrogen waste as the untreated sewage of 3.2 million people - just over half the country's population. Residual feed and bio-products pollute protected waters causing increased turbidity, and over shallow bottom - desertification. Complaints on the part of bathers and the tourist industry have forced some cage farms in the Mediterranean and the Red Sea to transfer their operations ashore.

EFFECT OF FISH DISEASES AND OTHER ENVIRONMENTAL PROBLEMS ON CAGE FARMING

Concentration of fish farms both, land-based and marine, along coastline, especially in or near enclosed or semi enclosed marine areas as for example, Norwegian fiords, Scottish lochs, Southeast Asia, China and Japan coastlines, and North American estuaries, is allegedly harming the coastal marine habitats and spreading diseases and parasites to wild fish populations, of which salmon seems to be particularly hit.

Parasites are a serious problem associated with densely populated fish cages. Caligid crustaceans, such as sea lices Lepeophtheirus salmonis and Caligus spp, are parasitic copepods that attach themselves to fish, marking their hosts with ugly lesions that lessen their market value, stunt their growth and weaken their resistance to diseases. Found on wild fishes, they are now common among Atlantic salmon grown in cages in Norway, Scotland, Chile, and North America. But now there're serious concerns that cage farms of salmon set on the migrational routes of wild salmon increase the risk of infection of the latter by sea lice originating from the fish cages.

The most harmful disease, spreading over cage farms affected by sea lice, is the infectious salmon anemia, or ISA. A highly contagious virus, ISA can be lethal to fish although it does not affect humans. The ISA virus is fast to spread over whole regions causing heavy financial losses and reduction of salmon production. One consequence is operators having to shut farms and processing plants and axing jobs. Also, diseases may leak from marine cages and pens and spread to wild populations. ISA was first discovered in Norway in 1984. In mid-2007, it turned up in Chilean waters, and within 2 years devastated the country's farmed salmon industry, which was forced to curb production by half and shed up to 4,000 jobs. Another concern is the residual materials from the drugs used by fish farmers to fight parasites and diseases and the pesticides used in agriculture. Their amounts may be substantial in view that, apart from the residual veterinary products in the agricultural effluents flowing into the seas, the fish farming industry alone spends on drugs an estimated $1 billion a year. All those, including toxic substances affect inshore and coastal fish, including the farmed ones, in various ways, sometimes causing various distortions and growth arrest in juveniles growing in polluted waters.

Anthropogenic pollution and effluents affect both wild and cultured species inshore and in coastal waters. Serratia marcescens, bacteria commonly found in the guts of people and animals is killing off corals and can also kill fish.

Unpredictable and uncharacterised impact of climatic, weather, and tectonic events presents unquantifiable threats. The first decade of this century has seen unprecedented impacts on aquaculture in Aceh (Indonesia), Bangladesh, China and Myanmar, which have all suffered from severe natural disasters. On the other hand, fish farmed in the sea might resist environmental changes in water, including the effects of climate change, such as temperature variations, better than wild fish, which depend upon their natural forage organisms. Forage species, however, may be more sensitive to such changes than the fish themselves. Their scarcity or disappearance may cause their predators' migration, starvation or both. Farmed fish are supplied with their food whatever is the temperature and salinity of the surrounding water and would suffer only at the extremes of their physiological survival range.

AQUACULTURE AND THE CAPTURE FISHERIES

Allocation of marine areas for fish and shellfish farming had become a problem when farms were established within traditional fishing grounds. While fish cages shouldn't be and need not be placed over prime or traditional fishing grounds, not everywhere regulations prevent ill-conceived offshore aquaculture projects and provide for their removal.

The accelerated development of aquaculture is calling for specific regulation and for allocation of marine areas where fish farms can be established, which willy-nilly must affect some traditional and other fisheries, through redistribution of access to fishing grounds essential for setting-up of the fish-farms. Notwithstanding, some of the claims regarding displacement of fishing grounds by aquaculture seem exaggerated, at least when it comes to open sea. The area taken by fish farms over exploitable fishing grounds is significant fishing-wise in a relatively few cases.

Apart from complaining that marine fish farms are expanding over fishing grounds, many commercial fishermen, oppose fish farming in floating cages, because of the associated influx of nutrients into the environment and of biological effects of densely populated fish farms on the habitat and wild stocks through broadcasting of parasites and viral diseases over wild fish populations and possible genetic effects due to massive escapes of farmed fish into open sea. The possible effects of fish escapes from cages in areas where massive marine farming is practiced, as in the N. Atlantic, at both sides of the Pacific, in Chile's waters and in the Mediterranean..

All this taken into account, growth of supply of fish from marine and on-land farming is a must, as long as mankind keeps its excessive proliferation and the demand is growing, and properly managed fish farming can not only help feeding an expanding global population, but also relieve the pressure of fishing on wild fish populations.

AGRI-BASED FISH FARMING

PADDY-CUM-FISH CULTURE

In India, this farming is practised in the states of Bihar, West Bengal, Orissa and Assam where enough water is present in the paddy fields. The paddy fields retain water for 3-8 months in a year. The interest in this practice has declined in recent years due to the use of pesticides to protect high yielding varieties of paddy.

This practice can be done in following types of paddy plots-

- Perimeter type–paddy grows in the middle.
- Central pond type — paddy growing area is on the perimeter.
- Lateral trench system–trenches are provided on either one or both sides of the moderately sloping field.

The variety of rice used in this culture is Panidhan, Jalmagna, CR26077, Tulsi, etc., while the fish spp. are Indian major carps, Channa spp, Oreochromis mossambicus, Clarias batrachus, Anabas testudineus, silver carp, grass carp, common carp. The total production in such practice is approximately 90 quintal from 2 paddy crops while the fish production is about 1000 kg from 1 ha.

Horticulture-Cum-Fish Farming

The horticulture-cum-fish farming system includes the culture of fruits, vegetables and flowers on the embankment of the pond. The fruits and vegetables contain various nutritive elements and the Indian Council of Medical Research has recommended 85g of fruits and 300g of vegetables to consume daily. For horticulture crop production the inner and outer dykes of the pond and adjoining areas are used. The selection of plant is the main criteria for the success of this system. The plant should be dwarf, seasonal, evergreen, remunerative and less shady.

The fruit crops which can be used are Mango, Banana, Papaya, Coconut, Lime, etc., and the vegetables like Brinjal, Tomato,Cucumber,Gourds, Chilli,Carrot, Raddish, Turnip, Spinach, Peas, Cabbage, Cauliflower, Ladies finger can be grown according to their season throughout the year. The flower plantation on the embankment is also useful. We can use the plants like Rose, Jasmine, Gladiolus, Marigold and Chrysanthemum, etc., which provides additional income to the farmer and beauty to the farm. This system provides 20-25 per cent more return in comparison to aquaculture alone. The agri-based fish farming includes the mushroom fish system, sericulture-fish system, fodder crop integration, etc. Pond bundhs may also used for growing pulses and oil seed crops. Aquatic cash crop like Makhana (Euryale ferox) and Singhara (Trapa spp) integration can also be done along with air-breathing or carnivorous fishes.

LIVE-STOCK FISH FARMING

POULTRY-CUM-FISH FARMING

This system utilises poultry droppings of fully built- up poultry litter for fish culture. The fish production obtained is about 5000 kg/ha/yr. with 1250 kg chicken meat and 70000 no. of eggs. Approximately 500-600 no. of birds is reared in a 1 ha pond. The Rhode Island or Leghorn variety birds are more preferred over others. They require 0.3-0.4 square meterspace/bird. Hoppers are used to feed them and to minimise feed wastage. The poultry birds (layers) are fed with starter, grower, and brooder feed according to their age. In India it is practised in Andhra Pradesh, Bihar, Haryana, Kerala, West Bengal, Uttar Pradesh, Maharashtra, Orissa, and Tamilnadu.

Duck-Cum-Fish Culture

The duck are commonly called as biologicals aerator. They are reared on the dyke of the pond in a low-cost house. This farming is practised in Tamilnadu, Assam, Bihar, Andhra Pradesh, Tripura, Orissa, Karnataka, Kerala and Uttar Pradesh. The 'Indian runner' and 'Khaki campbell' varieties are found more suitable in this culture. About 300 no. of ducklings (some spp. are reared 450-500 in no.) are reared to fertilize the 1 ha. pond. The duck not only act as live aerator by splashing water with their webbed feet but also control the aquatic weed (Lemna, Azolla, etc.), aquatic insects, molluscs, tadpoles, etc. Each duckling require about 0.3-0.5 square meter area as living space. The total production from such type of culture is about 3500-5000 kg fish, 18000-18500 eggs and 600 kg of duck meat. The duck droppings are used as manure for primary production.

Pig-Cum-Fish Culture

This system has certain advantages over others. The 30-35 pig's waste may produce 1 tonne of Ammonium Sulphate and 40-45 pigs are adequate to fertilize 1 ha water area under polyculture. Each pig requires about 3-4 sq.m floor space. This system of integration is very common in China, Taiwan, Vietnam, Thailand, Malaysia, Hungary and some European countries. The White Yorkshire, Hampshire and Landrace are the popular breed of pig for integration with fish. Pigs need clean housing which should provide adequate protection from adverse climates. The pigs are fed on pig mash which is made up of rice bran, rice polish, wheat-bran, broken maize, ground-nut oil cake, fish- meal mineral mixture, salt, etc. The spoiled vegetables can also be mixed in it. This system provides about 3000-4000 kg/ha/yr fish, 4500 kg/yr pig meat and 800 no. of piglets every year.

Cattle-Cum-Fish Culture

It is a common practice all-over the world. The cow excreta is most abundant in terms of availability and a healthy cow may excrete over 4000-5000kg dung and 3500-4000 litre urine on an annual basis. The BOD of cow manure is lower than other livestock manure. About 5-6 cows can provide adequate manure for 1 ha pond in addition to 9000 kg milk and about 3000-4000 kg of fish annually. Cow-shed should be built close to fish pond to simplify handling of cow-manure.

Goat-Cum-Fish Integration

It is considered as poor man's cow and a goat's excreta is considered as a very good organic fertilizer. The goat excreta contains organic carbon-60 per cent, N-2.7 per cent, P-1.78 per cent, K-2.88 per cent and its urine is also equally rich in both N and P. At least 50-60 goats are essential to fertilize 1 ha pond. The goats should be provided with dry, safe, comfortable house protected from excessive heat. The goat breeds are Jamanapari, Beetal, Barbari for milk and Bengal, Sirihi, Deccani are used for meat purpose. Goats are selective feeders and consume Berseem, Napier grass, Cowpea Soybean, Mulberry, etc. This integration can provide 3500-4000 kg fish/ha/year without supplementary feeding and fertilizer.

Rabbit-Fish Integration

Rabbit meat is preferred by most of the health conscious consumers owing to its low fat in comparison to other meats. The important meat breeds are Soviet Chinchilla, Grey Giant, and White Giant, etc. Rabbits are reared in cage, hutch and floor system (floor should be cemented). Rabbit excreta contain organic carbon-50 per cent, N-2 per cent, P-1.33 per cent, and K-1.2 per cent. The rabbit excreta is high in nitrogen content and low in moisture, thus quality manure for sustained plankton production. It is estimated that excreta from 300 rabbits would be enough for 1 ha pond fertilization.

FRESHWATER PRAWN FARMING

The words 'prawn' and 'shrimp' are often used synonymously. Actual use is geographically dependent. Animals of the genus Macrobrachium are referred to as freshwater prawns in Australia and freshwater shrimp in the United States of America (USA). In its statistical data, FAO refers to the genus Macrobrachium as freshwater prawns but also uses the word prawn for many species of marine shrimp, including the banana prawn (Fenneropenaeus merguiensis), the giant tiger prawn (Penaeus monodon) and the kuruma prawn (Marsupenaeus japonicus) (FAO 2001).

Although several species of freshwater prawns are currently being cultured, the major commercial species (Macrobrachium rosenbergii), is indigenous to South and Southeast Asia, parts of Oceania and some Pacific islands. M. rosenbergii imported into many other tropical and subtropical areas of the world and is the species most favoured for farming purposes.

Modifications need to take account of the different environmental requirements of the other species, especially in the larval stages. The most commonly cultured species in India is Macrobrachium rosenbergii, a hardy species, by virtue of its ability to adapt to various types of fresh and brackish-water conditions.

The peak season is September to November and May to July. The breeding takes place in low saline waters which is also needed for larval and post larval development after incubation.

Breeding of M. rosenbergii takes place in estuaries. Though seed may be available in natural sources to a limited extent, for large scale culture there is a need to ensure regular supply of seed.

For ensuring availability of quality seed in predictable quantity freshwater prawn hatcheries should be encouraged, technology for which is already developed. Freshwater prawn hatcheries are coming up in many states.

IT IS A GOOD CANDIDATE SPECIES FOR EXPORT ORIENTED AQUACULTURE

Importance of Giant Freshwater Prawn (Scampi) (Macrobrachium rosenbergii)

- It is very tasty and it's protein is of very high quality.
- It's growth rate is fastest in comparison to other freshwater prawns.
- It is suitable for culture in tropical and sub-tropical regions.
- It can be cultured in freshwater or saline water (salinity less than 10 ppt).
- This can be cultured alone in monoculture or mixed culture with carp fishes.
- Compared to marine prawns it has better resistance against diseases and hardy.
- It's market rate is always higher compared to fishes.

Mature male prawns are considerably larger than the females and the second chelipeds are much larger and thicker. The head of the male is also proportionately larger, and the abdomen is narrower. The head of the mature female and its second walking legs are much smaller than the adult male. A ripe or 'ovigerous' female can easily be detected because the ovaries can be seen as large orange-coloured masses occupying a large portion of the dorsal and lateral parts of the cephalothorax.

During rainy season the mating (copulation) of adults results in the deposition of a gelatinous mass of semen on the underside of the thoracic region of the female's body (between the walking legs). Within a few hours of copulation, eggs are extruded through the gonopores and guided by the ovipositing setae (stiff hairs), at the base of the walking legs, into the brood chamber. During this process the semen attached to the exterior of the female's body fertilizes the eggs and kept aerated by vigourous movements of the swimmerets more than three weeks. Female prawns of M. rosenbergii have 80000 to 100000 eggs during one spawning. Incubation period range 18–23 days at 26–28 0C. Eggs are slightly elliptical with a long axis of 0.6–0.7 mm, and are bright orange in colour until 2-3 days before hatching.

Larva becomes grey-black till the yolk sac absorbed. After hatching, rapid movements of the abdominal appendages of the parent disperse the larvae. Larvae are planktonic and swim actively tail first upside down. Larvae require brackishwater for survival. The larvae go through 11 distinct stages before metamorphosing into post larvae. Stage I larvae (zoeae) are just under 2 mm long (from the tip of the rostrum to the tip of the telson). Larvae swim upside down by using their thoracic appendages and are positively attracted to light. By stage XI they are about 7.7 mm long. Newly metamorphosed post larvae (PL) are also about 7.7 mm long and are identified by their movement and swimming like adult prawns. They are translucent and have a light orange pink head. On completion of their larval life, freshwater prawns metamorphose into post larvae (PL). They show mainly crawling rather than free-swimming. Post larvae exhibit good tolerance to a wide range of salinities. Post larvae migrate upstream into freshwater conditions within 7–12 days after metamorphosis and swim against rapidly flowing currents and utilize larger pieces of organic material. Post larval freshwater prawns are omnivorous can also be cannibalistic in absence of food material.

The farming of the giant freshwater prawn Macrobrachium rosenbergii has been expanding in India recent years. Scampi/prawn farming gained momentum after the set-back in shrimp farming due to disease outbreaks and other factors. Hygiene becomes important factor in farming system. The existing culture system includes both monoculture and polyculture with Indian major carps in ponds.

The ideal size is 0.2 to 1 ha. and rectangular in shape with 1 to 1.5 m in depth The pond should be provided with inlet and outlet (guarded by screen to avoid the unwanted fish, larvae, eggs and escape of prawns) and connected to water supply and drainage system respectively. They exhibit territorial behaviour. To enhance the more surface for clinging, branches of trees, hanging nylon screens, hume pipes, etc., have been kept. To increase the dissolved oxygen in pond the aerators or regular exchange of water were the best method. The pond either new or old may be provided with 250 to 400 kg/ha lime and cattle dung 1000 to 1500 kg/ha. and some inorganic fertilizers (if necessary) for the production of plankters. When the water turns brown more water is filled up to 1.2 m depth.

Table. Water Quality Requirements in Pond for Culture of Prawn.

Factors	Level	Factors	Level
Temperature	25–32°C	Salinity	0–10 ppt
Total hardness	30–150 ppm	Transparency	25–40 cm
Alkalinity	20–60 ppm	Ammonia (ionised)	Less than 03 ppm
Nitrite	Less than 20 ppm	Nitrate	Less than 10 ppm
Oxygen	3–7 ppm	Free Carbon di-oxide	Less than 08 ppm

pH is very important factor. The pH difference between pond water and seed containing water causes heavy mortality. The About 10 per cent to 15 per cent of the total pond area can be covered with the additional substratum. Grow out stocking densities of range from 0.5–2.5 post larvae of prawn per m^2 in polyculture and 1–5 per m^2 in monoculture. The culture period is 6–8 months starting at the beginning of southwest monsoon (June-July, 27–30°C).

The scampi are fed with farm-made or commercially available feeds to get good growth of them. Diets with about 35–40 per cent protein and gross energy level of about 3.2 kcal/g diet and protein:energy ratio of about 125-130 mg protein/kcal are suitable for growth of M. rosenbergii.

Protein/starch ratio of 1:1 is known to be effective for better feed efficiency and growth rate. Dietary glucosamine (an amino sugar and intermediary between glucose and chitin) facilitates molting followed by enhanced growth with 30 per cent dietary fibre.

The prawn requires 60–150 mg vitamin C/kg diet. Levels of 60 mg ascorbic acid and 300 mg tocopherol per kg diet are considered sufficient for proper reproduction and offspring viability in prawn broodstock. Calcium concentration at 5 ppm and vitamix and mineral mix at 1 and 2 per cent of the feed respectively given for good results. So add these above ingredients in the pellets/feed to achieve good growth and survival.

Periodic harvesting has to remove marketable size 50 gm and above allowing the rest to grow further. The production levels comes to 2.0 to 2.5 tons/ha (depends upon stocking) in monoculture and 600 to 700 kg/ha in polyculture. The time of harvest depend upon growth rate and market size desired. In continuous culture cull harvesting is practiced. Cull harvesting ponds are not drained. Larger prawns are harvested by seining in batch culture, batch harvesting or drain harvesting is followed.

FRESH WATER PEARL PRODUCTION INTEGRATED WITH ORNAMENTAL FISHES

Integrated farming may be defined as a sequential linkage between two or more farming activities. The basic principles involved in integrated farming are the utilisation of the synergetic effect of inter-related farming activities and the conservation, including the full utilisation, of farm wastes. It is based on the concept that "There is no waste" and "waste is only a misplaced resource which can become a valuable material for another product".

Integration of fish-freshwater pearl mussel is practiced in Taiwan. It is not only an efficient way of recycling farm wastes but also produces high economic returns from ornamental fishes as well as from freshwater pearls. Fish excreta and other organic suspended materials are efficiently utilised by freshwater mussels hence, reduce water pollution and the waste becomes pearls. And also the freshwater pearl mussels can utilise the space in ornamental fish farm, without affecting the ornamental fishes.

FRESHWATER PEARLS

Pearls, especially those with a good lusture have been among man's favourite gems since ancient times. With the advance of scientific technology and the rising standard of living, pearls are now used in make-up and medicine. The result is that pearls have become even more precious, with the price rising remarkably.

Today there is a great demand for cultured freshwater pearls and China produces 95 per cent of freshwater pearls sold in the world market.

IMPORTANT CULTURE SPECIES OF FRESHWATER PEARL MUSSELS

Triangle sail mussel	-	Hyriopsis cumingii
Wrinkle comb mussel	-	Cristaria plicata
Indian Freshwater mussel	-	Lamellidlens marginalis
Freshwater pearl mussel	-	Margratifera margratifera

DISTRIBUTION OF FRESHWATER PEARL MUSSELS

Fresh water pearl mussels are lived in lakes, rivers, fish ponds and irrigation canals. Typically it occurs in flowing waters with slightly firm and mud or mud bottom. It also can live in areas that have slow currents.

FEEDING HABIT

Fresh water pearl mussels are filter feeders, removing phytoplankton and other suspended particulate matter from the water.

LIFE CYCLE

Mussels have a very unique life cycle. In order to maintain, mussel larvae (glochidia) need to attach to a fish and use some of the fish's energy to develop internal organs. They do parasitise the gills, fins or other external structures of fish, but usually don't hurt it. After a few weeks, the mussels drop off the fish and are now juveniles. Blue gill sunfish, Lepomis macrochirus, juveniles of salmonids and Oreochromics niloticus are the important host fishes of glochidia larvae. The juveniles can live by themselves in the substrate, eating algae and bacteria, and eventually grow until become adults.

FROM PEST TO PROFIT

In actual fact, fresh water mussels are really a nuisance to fish farmers when they invade their fish ponds. The adults compete with cultured fish for oxygen and freshwater plankton which comprises their food. Mussel attaches themselves to the gills causing young and weaker fish to die. But because the epithelium of the mantle margin of freshwater mussels recreate a substance called nacre, the utilisation of technology to implant pieces of the epithelium in these mussels can result in the production of pearl farmers have thus been able to take a and use it to create a profit — making industry.

SUITABLE SPECIES FOR POND CULTURE OF ORNAMENTAL FISHES

Among the various ornamental fishes the koi carp varieties like kohaku, snake, showa, Bekko, shusui, koromo and Tancho are the gold fish varieties like common gold fish, shubunkin, fan tail, comet, veiltail, telescope, Moor, oranda, lionhead and celestial are reared in the pond ecosystem. These fishes are omnivorous and hence they feeding variety of feed items and have no dietary preferences. In commercial culture they are fed with artificial pellet feeds and flakes.

INTEGRATED CULTURE METHOD

There are basically two methods of culturing pearls. One is scattering method another is net suspension method.

SCATTERING METHOD

It consists simply of distributing the mussels in the pond where the part of water is derived from the ornamental fish pond through the central drainage outlet. This water contains lot of suspended organic material, faeces of fishes and plankton, etc. This water mixed with adequate amount of pollution free aerated water in the freshwater mussel culture pond. The removal of suspended organic matter and algae through their filter feeding habit in the water derived from the ornamental fish farm.

Hence, the freshwater pearl mussels serve as biofilters or living filters. There by mussels reduce the utilisation of water and recycling the waste. Mussels are collected by the nylon net screen fixed to check the entry of invading menaces such as crabs, fishes, macro vegetation, etc., from the primary feeder canal. Since the seeds are collected from natural habitat it is impossible to segregate the sex. Because of this inconvenience, integration by this method additional requirement of land hence it is applicable where the abundant land facility exists.

NET SUSPENSION METHOD

Net suspension method uses stainless steel wire mesh baskets to suspend the mussels in the water column of ornamental fish farm. The stainless steel basket can be kept in the water for 2–3 years before deteriorating. The baskets are 40 × 60 cm in diameter. A piece of netting is used to divide the inside of the basket into two levels, from which the mussels are suspended. The net has a mesh size of 2–3 cm netting is also used to wrap the steel basket.

The baskets are then suspended at near bottom of pond, from the racks made from bamboo. The racks should be positioned in the central part of the pond, in case of fixed basket method and the pond designed in a manner to accumulate the wastes at the central position for efficient utilisation of wastes by the mussels through their filter feeding habit.

And if the organic load is very high the water should be drained out through the central drainage to another scattering method of mussel culture pond. The large fish ponds normally has the central parts as a waste/ arid area since, the feeding and other activities are predominantly prevailing in the sides and around the central part of the pond. Hence, the central portion is utilised for mussel culture which reduces the additional requirement of land and water. The racks can be of floating type which is used in large ponds and reservoirs where the racks float in the entire pond and utilise the plankton rather organic load except the suspended materials. In net suspension method hatchery raised monosex or triploid mussels are stocked to avoid unwanted reproduction in culture pond during culture period. The devoid of reproduction helps to prevent the culture fishes from glochidia infection and also considerably regress the energy wastage through reproduction. As this method needs additional cost for seed production or procurement of seeds, but is an effective method for places with land scarcity.

CAPTIVE BREEDING

Sex is separate. No sexual dimorphism. The matured conditioned males and females are kept in the same breeding tank and a slight rise in temperature of water by 3°C above the ambient temperature induces spawning of mussels (thermal shock). The sperms are shed into the supra-branchial chamber and are passed out through the out going water. These sperms are taken into the inhalant siphon of the female by chance. The ripe eggs fall from the ovaries into the mantle cavity and then pass into the cloaca through the supra- branchial chamber. The eggs are fertilized in the cloaca and the fertilized eggs pass into the space of the gill chamber where development takes place.

GLOCHIDIUM LARVAE

The zygote undergoes cleavage and develop first into a blastula and then into a gastrula. The gastrula finally develops into microscopic larvae called glochidium. It means "The point of an arrow". It lives in the water tubes of gills of female mussel. The size is about 0.1 to 0.5 mm wide. It is covered by a shell with incurved. The larvae feed on the mucus recreated by the gills of mother mussel. The fully matured larvae are passed out through the outgoing water. Then, they sink to the bottom of the pond. Further development takes place in a fish provided in the breeding tank. When a fish comes in contact with glochidium larvae, the larvae is attached to the fish and encysted by an over growth of the skin of the fish. The larval undergoes metamorphosis during its encysted ectoparasitic life. After metamorphosis the tiny young ones come out by the rupture of the cyst. It sinks to the bottom and developed into an adult. It is estimate that the survival rate from release of glochidia to juvenile settlement is well below 0.01 per cent in natural environment.

CULTURE OF GLOCHIDIA IN ARTIFICIAL MEDIA

The glochidia can be cultured in artificial medium at 23 ± 2°C temperature. This media contain a mixture of M 199, fish (Oreochromis niloticus) plasma as a protein source, and antibiotic or antimycotics at a ratio of 2.1:0.5. The duration of glochidia development until the juvenile stage is 9–10 days in this media.

After 1 month of controlled feeding with phytoplankton, the juveniles showed an elongate of shell with several growth lines. Survival from glochidia to juvenile stage is upto 85 ± 4 per cent in fish plasma. The transformation of glochidia to juvenile stage is upto 84 ± 3 per cent in plasma.

CULTURE OF JUVENILE MUSSELS

The juvenile mussels are cultured in a separate large tanks/ smaller size ponds until they reach the adult stage. The juveniles are provided with adequate amount of phytoplankton for its accelerated growth. The matured mussels are used for pearl production through implantation.

IMPLANTATION PROCEDURE

The mussels from which the epithelial implants will be taken are collected and put in buckets of clear water to flush them. First, the adductor muscle is cut so that the shell may be easily opened. A pair of scissors is then used to cut strips of epithelial lining between the inhalant siphon and the adductor muscle. The epithelial strips are placed on the hard wooden board and the connective tissue is cleaned off the back of the strips. They are then cut into 3–4 mm long and 0.5–1 mm thickness of prices. Healthy mussels are selected and put into a vise assembly that will force the valves open 1–1.5 cm apart, are made in the epithelium of the marginal zone. The previously cut epithelial pieces are then inserted into the holes, about 0.5.cm deep, making sure they are firmly in place. About 25–30 slices can be transplanted into a mussel of 10 cm in length.

CARE AND CULTURE OF OPERATED MUSSEL

Operated mussel can be held in net bags, net cages and folders. Operated mussels should be reared in the water bodies free from pollution and disease. The water should contain adequate phytoplankton for its growth. The ideal temperature range for culturing mussel is 20 –30°C. Temperature <10°C will prevent the mussel from secreting nacre. If oxygen level is too low (<3mg/l) mussels will easily die. With in 2–3 weeks after transplantation, the wounds resulting from transplantation would have healed, but the mussels will still be weak. It is therefore easy for bacteria and parasites to infect the mussels. Dead mussels should be quickly removed. In the presence of any dead mussels in pond, high mortality is observed through spreading of infection.

QUALITY OF PEARLS

In order to stimulate more rapid secretion of nacre, the mussels should be suspended 20–30 cm below the water surface. The culture period of freshwater pearl is 2–3 years. About 6 months before harvest, they are lowered to 80–100cm below the surface. Although during these last 6 months, the nacre will be secreted more slowly, the pearl will become denser and its colour lusture will improve. Culturing for more than 3 years, the pearls tend to become duller. Pearls cultured for just one year are small in number and size, asymmetrical and of bad quality.

LIMITATIONS

Even though fresh water pearl production along with ornamental fish culture has much of benefits, which has some limitations too.

While the mussels integrated with ornamental fishes, if it reproduces, the glochidia cause severe problems to ornamental fishes.

To overcome these problems, the possible ways are.

- Only one sex either male or female mussel used for pearl culture in the integration with ornamental fishes.
- Triploid mussels can be used for this integration. Triploid mussels being a sterile animal; they could not reproduce in their life. (In fresh water pearl mussels tetraploid and triploid are reported in wild conditions by several authors and triploid mussel production technology is also established.)

CONCLUSION

The culture of fresh water pearl mussels and ornamental fishes in the same pond improve the productivity and reduce the space requirement. It also minimizes the water requirement. The freshwater pearl mussels consume the excess amount of algae available in the fish pond and there by protect the pond from algal bloom formation. It reduces the feed cost of the freshwater mussels. And water exchange from ornamental fish farming is also minimized considerably by this integration which ultimately lowers the cost for power utilisation. Fresh water pearls produced through this implantation method utilise the pest (F/W pearl mussel) to make profit by recycling the organic waste. If the seeds collected from the primary feeder canal through the screen, it is advisable to go for scattering method of culture where no contact between fish and mussel. The scattering method is possible if the farm yard with adequate land facility. The net suspension method is advisable for monosex or triploid mussels which produced through captive breeding not by natural collection. Here seed cost is also included as additional while comparing with the other method. The farmers should earn additional income through the pearl production along with the ornamental fish production.

FISH FARMING WITH AGRICULTURE

Agri-based systems include rice-fish integration, horticulture-fish system, mushroom-fish system, seri-fish system. In this system, fish culture is integrated with agricultural crops such as rice, banana and coconut, thereby producing fish and agricultural crops under one interlinked system.

RICE-FISH CULTURE

In India, though six million hectares are under rice cultivation, only 0.03 per cent of this is now used for rice-fish culture. This type of fish culture has several advantages such as:

- Economical utilisation of land,
- Little extra labour,
- Savings on labour cost towards weeding and supplemental feeding,
- Enhanced rice yield, and
- Additional income and diversified harvest such as fish and rice from water, and onion, bean, and sweet potato through cultivation on bunds.

Considering these, it is imperative to expand fish culture in the rice fields of our country. The paddy fields retain water for 3-8 months in a year. The culture of fish in paddy fields, which remain flooded even after paddy harvest, serves an off-season occupation and additional income to the farmer. This system needs modification of rice fields, digging peripheral trenches, construction of dykes, pond refuge, sowing improved varieties of rice, manuring, stocking of fish at 10,000/ha and finally feeding of stocked fish with rice-bran and oilcakes at 2-3 per cent of body weight.

SIMULTANEOUS CULTURE

For simultaneous culture, rice fields of 0.1 ha area may be economical. Normally four rice plots of 250 m^2 (25 $\times$ 10 m) each may be formed in such an area. In each plot, a ditch of 0.75 m width and 0.5 m depth is dug. The dikes enclosing the rice plots may be 0.3 m high and 0.3 m wide and are strengthened by embedding straw.

The ditches have connections with the main supply or drain canal, on either side of which, the rice plots are located, through inlet-outlet structures of the dikes.

The depth and width of the supply or drain canal may be slightly smaller than that of the ditches. Suitable bamboo pipes and screens are placed in the inlet and outlet structures to avoid the entry of predatory fish and the escape of fish under culture. The ditches serve not only as a refuge when the fish are not foraging among rice plants, but also serve as capture channels in which the fish collect when water level goes down. The water depth of the rice plot may vary from 5 to 25 cm depending on the type of rice and size and species of fish to be cultured.

The fish species which could be cultured in rice fields must be capable of tolerating shallow water (15 cm), high temperatures (up to 35°C), low dissolved oxygen and high turbidity. Species such as Catla catla, Labeo rohita, Cirrhina mrigala, Cyprinus carpio, Chanos chanos, Oreochromis mossambicus, Anabas testudineus, Mugil spp., Clarias batrachus, C. macrocephalus, Lates calcarifer, Channa striatus and C. marulius have been widely cultured in rice fields.

SIMULTANEOUS CULTURE OF FRESH-WATER PRAWN AND RICE

Semi-intensive culture of Macrobrachium rosenbergii could be undertaken in rice fields. Unlike for fish-rice culture, bunds for fish-prawn culture are raised so as to enclose 12 cm of water for four months, the period of rice culture.

Further, inlets and outlets should be provided with extended screen, say, 0.3 m above water surface to prevent climbing and escape of prawns. One or two small sump pits (1 × 2 × 0.5 m) should also be constructed near the outlet for trapping prawns when water is drained at the time of harvesting. The stocking of juvenile prawns (2-3 cm sise) at the rate of 1,000/ha may be done after the rice seedlings are well rooted. No supplementary feeding of prawns is required in this system.

The simultaneous culture has the following advantages:

- Fish increases rice yield by 5 to 15 per cent, which is chiefly due to the indirect organic fertilization through the fish excrement and also the control of unwanted filamentous algae which may otherwise compete for the nutrients.
- Tilapia and common carp control the unwanted aquatic weeds which may otherwise reduce the rice yield up to 50 per cent.
- Insect pests of rice like stem borers are controlled by fish feeding on them like murrels and catfish.
- Fish feed on the aquatic intermediate hosts such as malaria causing mosquito larvae, thereby controlling water-borne diseases of human beings.
- Rice fields may also serve as fish nurseries to grow fry into fingerlings. The fingerlings, if and when produced in large quantities may either be sold or stocked in production ponds for obtaining better fish yield under composite fish culture.

Limitations in simultaneous culture: The simultaneous fish-rice culture may have some limitations, like:

- Use of agrochemicals is often not feasible,
- Maintaining high water level may not be always possible, considering the size and growth of fish,
- Fish like grass carp may feed on rice seedlings, and
- Fish like common carp and tilapia may uproot the rice seedlings. However, these constraints may be overcome through judicious management.

CULTURE PROCEDURE

Five days after transplanatation of rice, fish fry (1 cm) are stocked at the rate of 5,000/ha or fingerlings (8-10 cm) at the rate of 2,000/ha. The stocking density can, however, be doubled if supplemental feed is given daily, particularly if plankton is found depleted after 10 days of stocking fish. The plankton production in rice fields could, however, be increased if some amount of fertilizer more than what is required for rice fields is added. To control the menace of insects, the insecticide Furadon (Carbofuran) may be used at the rate of 1 kg/ha. The insecticide is mixed with basal fertilizers and applied once during the final harrowing. It may be stated that fish grown in insecticide-applied rice fields are safe for human consumption.

After a period of 10 weeks (if stocked with fry) or six weeks (if stocked with fingerlings), the rice fields are slowly drained off and the fish are harvested. The harvesting of fish may be done about a week before the harvest of rice. The growth rate of fish is also moderate in rice fields as the production of plankton, the fish food organisms, is rich. Individual growth of 60 g and a per hectare yield of 500 kg have been reported under the simultaneous culture practice.

ROTATIONAL CULTURE OF RICE AND FISH

Through this practice, fish and rice are cultivated alternately. The rice field is converted into a temporary fishpond after the harvest. This practice is favoured over the simultaneous culture practice as it permits the use of insecticides and herbicides for rice production. Further, a greater water depth (up to 60 cm) could be maintained throughout the fish culture period. One or two weeks after rice harvest, the field is prepared for fish culture. C. carpio is found suitable for this practice.

The stocking densities of fry (2-3 cm) or fingerlings (5-8 cm) for this pracitce could be 20,000/ha and 6,000/ha, respectively. The fry are harvested after 10 weeks, while the fingerlings after six weeks. The average growth of the individual fish under this system has been reported to be about 100 g and a fish yield of about 2,000 kg/ha is possible. Further, it has also been reported that fish yield could exceed the income from rice in the rotational culture.

PADDY CUM FISH CULTURE

Coastal saline soil extends from the main sea coast to a few or even 50 km at places interior to the main land. The ground water table under these soils is generally present at a shallow depth and contains high amount of soluble salts.

These salts accumulate on the surface of the soil due to capillary rise of saline groundwater during dry periods of the year rendering the soil highly saline. Almost the entire area of the rain fed coastal saline soil is mono cropped in nature. The major agricultural crop of kharif is rice, grown during monsoon period when soil salinity is low. During the rest of the year, the land usually remains fallow due to high salt content of the soil. The kharif paddy varieties widely used in such areas are Mahsuri, Sadamota, Kalomota, Talmugur, Damodar, Dasal, Getu, Nona-patnai, Jaya, Ratna, Pankaj, Patnai-23, Luni, Cuttackdhandi, Pokkali, Vytilla, Bilikagga, CSR-4, CSR-6, Matla, Hamilton,

Palman 579, BKN, RP-6, FR-46B, Arya, etc. Paddy cum brackish water fish/ shrimp culture aims at utilising the summer fallow period of the coastal saline soil through a short-term brackish water aquaculture without affecting the subsequent kharif paddy crop. This type of activity provides the farmers with a substantial subsidiary income during the fallow season.

In West Bengal, where the salinity is either low or lowered by fresh water discharge diluting the tidal water, the cultivation of fish is undertaken in paddy fields. In pokkali fields of Kerala, summer fallow months are utilized for brackish water aquaculture. The production of fish in such culture varies from 300 to 1000 kg/ha. The brackish water shrimp culture is introduced in a big way in such areas as the remuneration is very high. The species commonly cultured are Penaeus monodon, Penaeus indicus, Metapenaeus dobsonii and Metapenaeus monoceros.

TECHNICAL PARAMETERS

The coastal area is mostly low lying, the elevation varying usually between sea level and 8 m above the MSL. Fields having elevation between low and high tide levels are desirable for water exchange during brackish water aquaculture and also for frequent draining of monsoon water during desalination process.

The sluice in the embankment is essential for regulating the flow of tidal and drainage waters. The area having more than 1 m tidal amplitude is considered suitable for paddy cum shrimp culture.

SOIL QUALITY

Medium textured soils like silty clay or silty clay loam are most suitable for paddy cum fish/ shrimp culture.

WATER QUALITY

Heavy monsoon precipitation for the site is essential for desalination of the soil after brackish water aquaculture. Intake of brackish water must be suspended before the onset of monsoon. The cultured species is harvested and then the land is exposed to monsoon precipitation for the purpose of desalination.

POND CONSTRUCTION

The paddy plots should be renovated suitably for the purpose of paddy cum brackish water aquaculture. Construction of an earthen dyke surrounding the paddy plot is essential for retaining water and also for holding the fish and shrimp during aquaculture. The height of the dyke is required to be maintained between 50 and 100 cm depending upon the topography of the plot and tidal amplitude at the site. A perimeter canal is necessary on the inner periphery of the plot. For a one ha paddy plot, the width and depth of the canal may be about 2 m and 1 m respectively. The earth removed from excavating the canal may be utilised for constructing or strengthening the dyke.

In addition to the perimeter canal, two cross trenches of about 1 m width should also be constructed at both the directions. The bottom of the trenches should be above the perimeter canal so that during the course of desalination, entire water can be easily removed to the canal. The area covered by the perimeter canal and the trenches will be about 12 per cent of the total land area.

WATER SUPPLY AND DRAINAGE

The entry of tidal water during the culture is made through feeder canal and the flow of water into the field is regulated by a sluice gate fitted with wooden shutters and placed at about 30 cm height from the main plot.

During high tide, water is taken into the plot after sieving through velon nets and split bamboo mats to prevent entry of any kind of fish/ shrimp and other undesirable species, especially carnivores.

Another sluice is used for draining out water from the culture plot to the feeder canal at low tide periods for water exchange, desalination and drainage of excess water. On the entry and exit mouths of the slice gate, wooden shutters are provided to regulate the movement of water.

POND MANAGEMENT

The plots are prepared in two phases, once for brackish water aquaculture and again for paddy cultivation. For aquaculture crop, the plot is sun dried after the kharif harvest. If necessary, to rectify acidic soils, lime is applied depending on requirement of the soil. Usually no inorganic fertilization is done. However, urea may be used in extreme cases of nitrogen deficiency of soils @ 60 kg N/ ha. Some shade zones are provided over the perimeter canal with twigs, hay, palm leaves etc., so that during summer the shrimp can take shelter and also hide themselves from predation.

FISH-FARMING DEVELOPMENT

Fish-farming development goes back to the colonial period of Zambia but progress has been moderate for many years, notably because of lack in government support as economic conditions have reduced budget required for development programmes. Governement backing of fish-farming development has consisted in supplying of fingerlings and providing some technical advice. However the strong development of commercial fish-farming which has happened in the past 5-6 years in private farms and companies has been largely autonomous, with minimum governmental involvement except for supplying of fingerlings. A new fish-farming development project, to be implemented with cooperation of UNHCR (United Nations High Commission for Refugees) and the Zambian Catholic Secretariat consists in creating 380 rural fish-farming operations of approximately 1200 m2 each (2-3 ponds) in the Western province.

The project would be implemented over a period of three years and, if successful, would add some 45 ha of ponds to the existing fish-farming capacity. Since 1980, a FAO/UNDP project has been implemented in order to demonstrate the technical and economic feasibility of large scale fish culture. The general objectives of the project were:

- To increase the total production of fish in the country for additional annual protein for human consumption;
- To create employment;
- To substitute fish imports and have foreign currency.

Since its inception in 1980, the FAO/UNDP project has allowed the development and management for three government fish-farming stations at Chilanga, Mwekera and Chipata. Different data collected during development and operational phase have been collected and analysed during the present mission.

UNDP/FAO PROJECT

The UNDP/FAO project did realise different renovation and development activities at Chilanga, Mwekera and Chipata. At Chilanga following activities were carried on:

- Clearing and repairing of 17 cemented ponds;
- Construction of outlets for 13 ponds;
- Construction of duck houses (2) and fencing around ten 800 m^2 earthen ponds;
- Construction of fish feed store and incubator room;
- Renovation of ducks and ducklings sheds;
- Building of a harvesting pitch for Pond 8;
- Renovation and clearing of 19 ponds in C-pond complex including construction of two new monks and upgrading of six old ones;
- Construction of one pigsty and one duck-house later changed to a pigsty;
- Construction of improved type of duck house on the dyke between ponds (19 and 20);
- Construction of cropping pits;
- Construction of a whole new pond of 0.5 ha with monk and harvest pit in the second half of 1981.

At Mwekera, development work covered the construction of 16 ponds of 0.25 ha water area, with a maximum water depth of 1.3 m and 0.5 m freeboard and equipped with monk type outlets. Also included in the project was construction of four line feeder canal of 0.4 m × 0.6 m. In Chipata, project staff proceeded to the upgrading of the old pond networks (clearing and repairing of old ponds, construction of new inflow canals, deepening of canal between dam and road). Yet the major work consisted in the construction of 9 ponds of 0.5 ha. each to be located on the right bank of the Masupe river downstream from the existing complex.

POND CONSTRUCTION COST IN CHIPATA

Like for the farms of Chilanga and Mwekera, the UNDP/FAO project included different renovation activities which in Chipata were the following:

- Clearing and repairing of old ponds
- Installation of asbestos pipes for outlet
- Deepening of canal between the dam and the road and lining with three layers of bricks
- Installation of an additional siphon on the dam.

Those activities were carried by project staff.

In addition, construction of 9 ponds of 0.5 ha each was contracted out to Brunelli Construction at a cost of US$112,837.61. Those conditions were obtained on the ground that the contract would be paid in US dollars and taking into account the fact that the required equipment had already been brought to the area for implementation of another project.

Table. Construction costs in Chipata was broken down as follows:

		$
1.	Clearing and site preparation	10,497
2.	Construction on dikes and pond bottoms	46,279
3.	Excavation of drains	9,074
4.	Construction of outlets	9,599
5.	Construction of feeder canals	8,618
6.	Construction of inlets	2,518
7.	Dressing of dikes	11,534
8.	Contingencies (15 per cent)	14,178
	Total	112,838

Some problems were met namely that start of construction activities was delayed for two months since some villagers had planted maise on planned site, despite warnings from officials. Also contrary to what appeared on plans, Masupe river was flowing on portion of planned pond site. Therefore, the river had to be diverted, which involved more earthwork than initially planned. Construction work was completed between May 1983 and December 1983. In Kwacha, construction cost comes to K141,118 (average rate of exchange for 1983: $ 0.7996) which is equivalent to K31,360/ha. Applying the 1982 average rate of exchange the cost per ha would have been K26,906.

Construction costs in Chilanga, Mwekera and Chipata indicate the trends in pond development cost. All were machine-built, over a period of three years.

The first operation, at Chilanga concerned construction of a single 0.5 ha pond with special outlet structure, therefore, should have been relatively costly; yet the final cost came to K16,124/ha. The second operation in Mwekera concerned a 4 ha pond complex development with 0.25 ha ponds where cost per ha came to K19,970.

The last operation in Chipata involved 0.5 ha ponds on a development covering 4.5 ha; the cost per ha came to K31,360. The rise in cost comes mostly from the trend in rate of exchange of the K which went from $1.1516 on average in 1981 to $1.0773 in 1982 and $0.7796 in 1983. If the cost per ha is expressed in US$, the difference in cost of construction per ha between the three sites is much smaller:

Table. Pond Construction Costs Incurred Under UNDP/FAO Project

	CHILANGA	MWEKERA	CHIPATA
Year of construction	1981	1982	1983
Total pond area developed (ha)	0.5	4.0	4.5
pond size (ha)	0.5	0.25	0.5
Total cost	K8,062	US$86,053	US$112,838
Average rate of exchange ($/K)	1.1516	1.0773	0.7996
Total cost in K	8,062	79,878	141,180
Cost/ha in K	16,124	19,970	31,360
Cost/ha in $	18,568	21,514	25,075
Construction cost/ha, US$			
Chilanga	18,568		
Mwekera	21,514 (+16 %)		
Chipata	25,075 (+17%)		

POLYCULTURE OF CYPRINUS CARPIO AND TILAPIA

Experiments were made of raising tilapia in association with C. carpio of Japanese origin. Only daily growth rates have been kept. Records also show that carps naturally bred in the pond. However, incidence of poaching was high and otters, who prefer big size fish, took their toll. The problem of poaching and predators, added to problems of broodstock supply for this non-indigenous species, and product marketability, do not encourage further development of this type of culture.

Experiments at Chilanga showed that a pure strain of O. andersonii gave better growth rates than the original mixed stocked used before start of the project. Other experiments also show that bisex culture of O. andersonii give growth rates more or less similar to mono-sex culture.

POND CONSTRUCTION COST IN CHILANGA

The 0.5 ha pond built in Chilanga was completed during the last half of 1981, at a cost of K8,062.20 which is equivalent to K16,124 per ha. The total cost was broken down as follows:

	K
Earthwork (6,500 m3)	6,839.00
Monk	507.00
Sand (Transport)	80.00
Gravel (Transport)	54.00
Cement (7 Bags)	33.40
Labour (1,120 m.h)	548.80
Total	K8,062.20

The cost of K16,124/ha is considered as high as the harvest pit is seen as experimental. It was then expected that building a private fish-farm under normal circumstances would cost K10,000/ha.

POND CONSTRUCTION COST IN MWEKERA

Project included renovation of 34 ponds in 1982 and 1983, and construction of ten new monks. Each monk required 24 m-h and cost approximately K100. Work also included construction of one duck house, of 6 manuring cribs and the fencing of one pond.

The major development work consisted in building 16 ponds of 0.25 ha each, which can be filled to a maximum water depth of 1.3 m, freeboard being 0.5 m, equipped with monks and four line feeder canals of 0.4 × 0.6 m. Construction was started in June 1983 and was finished by November except for installation inlet pipes and construction of 8 monks.

The whole construction contract done by Brunelli Construction cost US $86,052.94 (equivalent to K79,878.34 at 1982 average exchange rate), which brings the cost per ha to US$21,513 or K19,970. The cost breakdown was as follows:

		$
1.	Clearing and site preparation	9,090
2.	Construction of dikes and pond bottoms	29,098
3.	Excavation of drains	4,411
4.	Construction of culverts	1,972
5.	Construction of feeder canals	8,628
6.	Construction of outlets	12,365
7.	Construction of inlets	3,417
8.	Dressing of dikes	5,848
9.	Contingencies (15%)	11,224
	Total	86,053

CHIPATA FISH-FARM

Before the management programme introduced by the UNDP/FAO project, ponds at Chipata station were drained every two-three years and production rates were low. Development programme at Chipata was started in May 1983 and completed in January 1984. Management programme was initiated, based on the use of maise bran, rejected maise and floor sweepings from the local mill (200 kg/day). New ponds were stocked with O. andersonii. One pond of the new complex was used for breeding purposes as the old part could not meet the requirements. Stocking density was $2.5/m^2$. Management options used were: duck-cum-fish, mill sweepings, mill sweepings and compost. Feed is given 5 days per week at the rate of 2 kg per breeding pond and 25 kg per production pond. Computation of yields is complicated by the fact that both stocking and harvesting operations were done in many sequences. During year 1984 which was the only full production year since completion of expansion, best results were obtained on Pond N° 1 where duck-cum-fish was applied and when yields one 140 days cycle were 6.444 T/ha/yr. In another experiment with ducks yields were only 1.355 T/ha/yr but with a low stocking density of 20 fingerlings/are. Mill sweepings and compost gave yields varying between 2.135 T/ha/yr to 4.433 T/ha/yr. Mill sweeping only gave yields of 1.614 T/ha/yr and 3.158 T/ha/yr.

Production results were impaired by difficulties in producing fingerlings in adequate quantities.

It must also be mentioned that ducks were fed with mill sweepings, and rejected maise as project budget could only cover the cost of the expert. Yet ducks fed on that diet could reach an average weight of 2.35 kg in 16 weeks.

MWEKERA FISH-FARM

In Mwekera fish-farming station, at the start of the project, existing ponds were upgraded and renovated. Some of them were stocked with O. andersonii broodstock in order to produce fingerlings for the new ponds, some with O. andersonii in mono-culture or with carp fingerlings, others with carp fingerlings only. All ponds were fertilized with chicken manure at a rate of 5-10 kg (dry) per day (5 days/week), except Pond N° 7 which was stocked with ducklings. Chicken manure was thus bought from Copperbelt Power Company at K2/50 kg or K0.04/kg. However information available is not sufficient to provide yields.

It was observed that the presence of ducks reduced predation by tadpoles and frogs. Ducks also clear aquatic weeds. The completion of the new pond complex at the beginning of 1984, allowed the implementation of a production programme. All ponds would be stocked with O. andersonii at $2.5/m^2$. Two ponds would be under fish-cum-pig culture; two under fish-cum-duck; two with inorganic fertilizers; two with feeding soyabean cake and maise bran; two would include polyculture with common carp ($1/10\ m^2$), using chicken manure and local feed; six would be fertilized with chicken manure of three possible types. So far only one production result has been fully recorded.

That was for Pond N° 7 ($2793\ m^2$) on which 150 ducks had been put. Production cycle started on February 2, 1983 with stocking of O. andersonii ($2.5/m^2$). On March 31st, 1983, 100 carps fingerlings were stocked. Initial stocking was 279 kg (40 g per fingerling). Production after 7 months was 1.634 T. This is equivalent to a yield of 8-9 T/ha/yr not counting months of June and

July, if the estimated weight of fish stocked is correct. One harvest was taking place during the mission on Pond 16 and the results were not available then.

FISH-FARM MANAGEMENT

The UNDP/FAO project also introduced new management techniques in the three government stations under project, once the renovation and development phase was completed. The results obtained will be used as reference when planning for fish-farming development and management. However only the Chilanga station has so far managed to produce production records which can be used as a basis for planning. In Mwekera, only very recent harvest yields have been recorded. In Chipata, difficulties like insufficient supplies of fingerlings have kept yields at a level which cannot be considered as a basis for planning.

During the years 1976-1979 before the UNDP/FAO project started at Chilanga, yields varied from 156 to 463 kg/ha/year. After the start of the project different management options were applied namely feed with fertilizers, pig cum-fish and duck-cum fish, stocking either with a mixture of O. andersonii, O. macrochir and T. rendalli or monoculture of O. andersonii or C. carpio.

FEED AND FERTILIZER

A first cycle started in February 1981 and ended in May-June 1981, was done on the 16 cemented ponds, stocked with the three mentioned species at a density of 3-4/m^2. Superphosphate (46 per cent P_2O_5) and Sodium nitrate (15 per cent N) was applied. Feed consisted in a mixture of maise bran and sunflower oil cake. Production cycle last 113 days for 10 ponds, 102 for 2, 74 for 3 and 70 for 1. Yields varied from 1.938 T/ha/yr to 4.932 T/ha/yr with an average of 4.640 T/ha/yr. A second experiment was made in 6 cemented ponds with the three species of fish stocked separately. Stocking density was lower at 2.5/m^2. The cycle last longer from August to January (275 days).

The same fertilizer mix was applied and a mix of 50 per cent maise bran, 50 per cent sunflower oil care was used to the amount of 69.25 kg/100 m^2 for the whole cycle. Yields were lower than in the first experiment ranging from 1.53 T/ha/yr to 2.11 T/ ha/yr. Food conversion ratios varied from 3.3:1 to 4.5:1.

A cycle period more than twice as long might explain the difference in yields, although this is not specified. The impact of change in stocking method is not mentioned either. Further experiments in the C-pond complex using maise bran (40 per cent) and sunflower oil cake (60 per cent) and a stocking density of 425 fingerlings per 100 m^2 gave yields of 3.62 T/ha on a basis of 365 days production per year and 3.02 T/ha on a basis of 304 growth days per year (taking into account the cold period of June and July where growth is almost nil). A lower stocking density of 200/m^2 could give comparable results like for pond C15 in 1983, when yields reached 2.88 T/ha/yr on a 304 days basis.

DUCK-CUM-FISH

Experiments were made in 1981 with Muscovy ducks stocked at a rate of 1000/ha. Each female gave 54 eggs/year out of which 90 per cent were fertilized. Natural incubation was used resulting in an average of 4 ducklings per female per year.

However the Muscovy ducks did not stay long enough in the water to produce adequate manuring. Therefore, this species was replaced by Peking ducks in March 1982. Natural incubation was replaced by artificial incubation using 2 incubators of 600 eggs capacity each. Peking ducks are transferred to fish ponds when they are three weeks old, the optimal stocking density is 500/ha. In the early trials, yields obtained with duck-cum-fish option averaged 5 tons/ha/yr, based on one year production. Project management has later realised yields of 7 T/ha/yr.

9

Wastewater in Aquaculture

AEROBIC MICROBIAL PROCESS IN AQUACULTUTRE

Generally, aerobic microbial processes yield compounds which can be beneficial, and are either not toxic or have lox toxicity levels in aquaculture ponds or tanks. Oxidation of organic matter to carbon dioxide, a process which is the main consumer of oxygen in aquaculture ponds or tanks.

Oxidation of ammonia to nitrate via nitrite, which also consumes large quantity of oxygen. xidation of reduced sulfur compounds (such as hydrogen sulfide and elemental sulfur) to sulfate, a process that generally has low oxygen demand in aquaculture.

Conversion of carbon dioxide to biomass by autotrophic bacteria (such as the nitrifying bacteria) with a relatively mall amount of biomass produced in aquaculture facilities, when compared to the conversion of carbon dioxide to biomass by algae. Conversion of carbon dioxide to biomass by algae depending on the availability of light. Excluding feeding, the photosynthetic process in aquaculture is the main input of carbon source and natural food for aquatic animals.

ANAEROBIC MICROBIAL PROCESSES IN AQUACULTURE

Microbial anaerobic processes, if not controlled, can produce compounds that are highly toxic to cultured animals.

These processes include:

Consumption of organic matter, without the utilization of free oxygen, resulting in products which are usually not fully oxidized (such as alcohols, organic acids). Reduction of nitrate and nitrite, which can yield either nitrogen gas or ammonia. In aquaculture, due to the toxicity of ammonia and nitrite, ammonia production is not welcomed, while nitrogen gas production is beneficial. However, in agriculture, the opposite is true - the conversion of nitrate and nitrite to nitrogen das result in a loss of fertilizers. Reduction of sulfur compounds to hydrogen sulfide as a final product, a compound, which is toxic to most animals at even very low concentrations.

FUNCTION OF ENZYMES

Enzymes are "biological catalysts." "Biological" means the substance in question is produced or is derived from some living organism. "Catalyst" denotes a substance that has the ability to increase the rate of a chemical reaction, and is not changed or destroyed by the chemical reaction that it accelerates.

Generally speaking, catalysts are specific in nature as to the type of reaction they can catalyze. Enzymes, as a subclass of catalysts, are very specific in nature. Each enzyme can act to catalyze only very select chemical reactions and only with very select substances.

An enzyme has been described as a "key" which can "unlock" complex compounds. An enzyme, as the key, must have a certain structure or multi-dimensional shape that matches a specific section of the "substrate" (a substrate is the compound or substance which undergoes the change). Once these two components come together, certain chemical bonds within the substrate molecule change much as a lock is released, and just like the key in this illustration, the enzyme is free to execute its duty once again.

Many chemical reactions do proceed but at such a slow rate that their progress would seem to be imperceptible at normally encountered environmental temperature. Consider for example, the oxidation of glucose or other sugars to useable energy by animals and plants. For a living organism to derive heat and other energy from sugar, the sugar must be oxidized (combined with oxygen) or metabolically "burned"

However, in a living system, the oxidation of sugar must meet an additional condition; that oxidation of sugar must proceed essentially at normal body temperature. Obviously, sugar surrounded by sufficient oxygen would not oxidize very rapidly at this temperature. In conjunction with a series of enzymes created by the living organism, however, this reaction does proceed quite rapidly at temperatures up to 100°F (38 °C). Therefore, enzymes allow the living organism to make use of the potential energy contained in sugar and other food substances.

Enzymes or biological catalysts allow reactions that are necessary to sustain life proceed relatively quickly at the normal environmental temperatures. Enzymes often increase the rate of a chemical reaction between 10 and 20 million times what the speed of reaction would be when left uncatalyzed (at a given temperature). Nutrients locked in certain organics are complex macromolecules, or in hard-to-digest matrices may be released or predigested by a high degree of heat or concentrated acid treatment. In an alternative manner, specific enzymes can promote the pre-digestion of certain complex nutrients and facilitate the release of highly digestible nutrients in organics during processing without the need of excessive heat or rigourous chemical treatment.

Naming of Enzymes

One researcher reports treating grain, sorghum or barley with the enzyme "gumase" while another reports the same with the enzyme "beta-glucanase" When methodologies are examined, it is discovered that both of these preparations are the same product. Unfortunately, this apparent contradiction in terms happens often. Enzymes have been named by several methods and this fact has been known to cause confusion in their classification. For example, common or "trivial" names of enzymes, generally contain a prefix representing the name of the substance or substrate upon which they act or affect, followed by the suffix "ase". The "ase" simply denotes or identifies that the substance is an enzyme. Examples of this system of nomenclature includes the enzyme that catalyzes the conversion of proteins into their component amino acids, the name of this enzyme is "protease" or "proteinase".

Another example is the enzyme that accelerates the breakdown of the two components of starch into sugars. The components of starch are known as "amylose" and "amylo-pectin", thus, the enzyme helping to break them down is called "amylase". Confusion may exist, however, when older names of enzymes are used. Included in these older terms are ficin, pepsin, bromelin and trypsin, which are older trivial names of individual types of protease preparations, the enzymes that accelerate digestion of proteins. There are also many sub- classes of enzymes. Amylases are a prime example; subclasses of amylase include: alpha-amylase, beta-amylase, and gluco-amylase, to name a few. All these enzymes do is accelerate the digestion of starch and are broadly classified as amylases, but their actions are all slightly different in nature.

To help sort this out, the International Union of Biochemistry in 1961 proposed a system for enzymes' classification and naming which is finding acceptance mainly in this discussion. One example of this system, however, is the term: "alpha 1, 4-glucan glucanohydrolase" which is a name for alpha-amylase. All these systems of nomenclature may become confusing to someone who has use for only a few types of enzymes or uses them for industrial or agricultural purposes. Therefore, the use of the more widely known terms such as "amylase" and "protease" are more or less universally in these fields. It should be remembered, however, that there are many types of enzymes that fit into these broad categories that may be more or less suitable for specific agriculturally related application. The final selection for a specific application should be made only after consulting a knowledgeable individual well versed in the technical aspects of the particular enzyme requirements and applicable characteristics.

WATER QUALITY MANAGEMENT

Water quality is a dynamic web of the physical, biological and chemical factors, which constitute the water environment and influences the production of fish and other aquatic environment. There are many water quality variables in pond fish culture. All other things being equal, a pond with good water quality will produce more and healthier fish than a pond with poor quality. Water quality determines to a great extent the success or failure of a fish cultural operation. Water quality parameters, which are of prime importance, are mainly temperature, turbidity, oxygen, CO_2, nitrogen, ammonia, pH, alkalinity, hardness, etc.

TEMPERATURE

The water temperature is considered to be one of the most important factors in aquatic environment because it affects all metabolic, physiological activities and life processes of different trophic levels of pond ecosystem. In addition, it also affects the speed of chemical changes in soil and water. Water temperature plays an important role in influencing the periodicity, occurrence and abundance of phytoplankton as it had a direct relationship with total plankton. Fishes are cold-blooded animal and dependent upon the water temperature in which they live. Every fish species has an ideal temperature range within which it grows quickly. The optimum temperature range for 'cold water' and 'warm water' fishes are 14-18°C and 24-30°C respectively. Water temperature can be adjusted to optimum level in controlled system such as hatcheries. It is difficult to adjust temperature in large water bodies. Operation of aerator during calm and warm afternoon helps to break thermal stratification of pond by mixing warm surface water with cool subsurface water.

TURBIDITY

The turbidity is a term that refers to the suspended solids particles, planktonic organism and humic substances produced through decomposition of organic matter. In aquaculture ponds, turbidity from planktonic organism is often desirable to an extent, where as that caused by suspended particles is undesirable. However, heavy blooms limit heat and light penetration, then reducing the effective volume of productive zone. Optimum Secchi-disc visibility of fish ponds is considered to be 30-40 cm. In ponds with Secchi-disc visibility of 10-20 cm, dissolved oxygen concentration may fall so low at night that fish are stressed or even killed. Turbidity due to suspended solids can be controlled by application of organic manure 500-1000 kg/ha or gypsum @ 250-500 kg/ha or alum @ 25-50 kg/ha.

DISSOLVED OXYGEN

Dissolved oxygen is one of the most important chemical parameters in aquaculture. Low dissolved oxygen levels are responsible for fish kills, either directly or indirectly. The concentration of dissolved oxygen in natural water is influenced by the relative rates of diffusion to and from the atmosphere, photosynthesis by aquatic plants and respiration by aquatic biological community. Dissolved oxygen along with the turbidity could provide information about the nature of an ecosystem better than any other chemical parameters. It was also observed that dissolved oxygen content of pond water in the range of 5 mg/litre to saturation level favour good growth of flora and fauna. Aeration is proven technique for improving dissolved oxygen availability in ponds. Several form of mechanical aeration are available to the fish farm *e.g.* Paddle wheel aerator, airlift pumps, air diffuses, agitators etc.

CARBON DIOXIDE (CO_2)

The primary sources of carbon dioxide in fish ponds are derived from respiration by fish and the microscopic plants and animals that comprise the fish pond biota. Decomposition of organic matter is also a major source of carbon dioxide in fish ponds. The fish producers are rightly concerned with maintaining adequate concentrations of dissolved oxygen. The problem with the potential toxicity of carbon dioxide can be related to the daily fluctuating pattern of dissolved oxygen and carbon dioxide concentrations. Carbon dioxide concentrations are highest when dissolved oxygen concentrations are lowest. Carbon dioxide concentrations are maximum during winter and minimum during summer. However, carbon dioxide is rarely a problem in winter because dissolved oxygen concentrations are usually well above saturation levels. Freshwater fish pond should contain a low concentration of free CO_2 (<3 mg/litre), although it can tolerate high concentrations of CO_2 Aeration and increasing of pH can control the high concentration of CO_2. Experiment have shown that 1.0 mg/litre of hydrated lime can remove 1.68 mg/litre of free CO_2.

AMMONIA

Ammonia is the first measurement to determine the health of biological converter. Fish are very sensitive to unionised ammonia and the optimum range is 0.02-0.05 mg/litre in the pond water. When ammonia accumulates to toxic levels, fish cannot extract energy from feed efficiently. If the ammonia concentration gets high enough, the fish will become lethargic and eventually fall into a coma and die. In properly managed fish ponds, ammonia seldom accumulates to lethal concentrations. However, ammonia can have so-called "sublethal" effects such as reduced growth, poor feed conversion, and reduced disease resistance at concentrations that are lower than lethal concentrations. The main source of ammonia in fish ponds is fish excretion. Protein in feed is the ultimate source of most ammonia in ponds where fish are fed. Another main source of ammonia in fish ponds is diffusion from the sediment. The decomposition of this organic matter produces ammonia, which diffuses from the sediment into the water. There are two main processes that result in the loss or transformation of ammonia. The most important is the uptake of ammonia by algae and other plants. Plants use the nitrogen as a nutrient for growth. The other important process of ammonia transformation in fish ponds isâ 'nitrification'. Bacteria oxidise ammonia in a two-step process, first to nitrite (NO_2) and then to nitrate (NO_3). Aeration can also reduce ammonia toxicity. Healthy phytoplankton removes ammonia from water. Formalin may also reduce the ammonia. Proper feeding management should be maintained in fish pond. Biological filters may be used to treat water for converting ammonia to nitrite and then to harmless nitrate through nitrification process.

NITRITE

Nitrite is the second chemical measurement made to determine the health of the biological converter. Nitrite should not be detectable in a pond with a properly functioning bio-converter. Nitrite is produced by the autotrophic Nitrosomonas bacteria combining oxygen and ammonia in the bio-converter and to a lesser degree on the walls of the ponds. Nitrite has been termed as the invisible killer. It can be deadly, particularly to the smaller fish, in concentration as low as 0.25 ppm. Effective removal of organic wastes, adequate aeration and correct application of fertilizers are the methods to prevent accumulation of nitrite to toxic levels in pond culture.

HYDROGEN SULPHIDE

Freshwater fish pond should be free from hydrogen sulphide. Fish lose their equilibrium and subjected to sub-lethal stress at concentration of 0.01 mg/litre of hydrogen sulphide. Frequent exchange of water can prevent building up of hydrogen sulphide. Further increasing water pH through liming can also reduce the hydrogen sulphide toxicity. Potassium permanganate (6.2 mg/litre) is also used to remove hydrogen sulphide from the water.

PH

pH is a measure of hydrogen ion concentration in water is acidic or basic. It has direct effects on fish growth and survival of food organisms. Hence, to achieve good fish production pH of the water should be monitored regularly to ensure its optimum range of 6.5-8.5. It also exerts considerable influence on toxicity of ammonia and hydrogen sulphide as well as solubility of nutrients and thereby water fertility. The generalised effects of pH on fish are presented in Table.

Table. Effects of pH on Fish.

pH	Effects
4.0	Acid death point
4.0-6.0	Slow growth rate
6.0-9.0	Best for growth
9.0-11.0	Slow growth, lethal to fish over long period of time
11^+	Alkaline death point

The best way to counter water pH problem is application of lime for increasing soil pH to greater then pH 6 and total alkalinity and total hardness to greater than 40 mg/litre as calcium carbonate. Calcium carbonate ($CaCO_3$), dolomite $CaMg(CO_3)$, calcium hydroxide (slaked lime)-$Ca(OH)_2$ and calcium oxide (quick lime)-CaO are the different lime material used. Lime should be carried out a few weeks before addition of fertilizer and stocking of fish. Agricultural gypsum ($CaSO_4$) is applied to correct the total hardness without affecting total alkalinity. It may be also applied to correct the alkaline pH.

ALKALINITY

Alkalinity is the capacity of water to neutralise acids without an increase in pH. Total alkalinity is the sum of the carbonate and bicarbonate alkalinities. Some water may contain only bicarbonate alkalinity and no carbonate alkalinity. The carbonate buffering system is important to the fish growth regardless of the production method used. In pond production, where photosynthesis is the primary natural source of oxygen, carbonate and bicarbonate are storage area for surplus carbon dioxide in the buffering system would never be limiting factor that could reduce photosynthesis, as in turn reduce oxygen production. On the other hand, by storing carbon dioxide the buffering system prevents wide daily fluctuations. Without a buffering system, free carbon dioxide will form large amount of weak acid (carbonic acid) that may potentially decrease the night time pH level to 4.5. During peak period of photosynthesis, most of the carbon dioxide will be consumed by the phytoplankton and as a result, drive the pH level above 10. Pond water with low alkalinity <20 mg/litre as $CaCO_3$ and >300 mg/litre is unproductive. The ideal range of total alkalinity for freshwater fish pond is 50-300 mg/litre as $CaCO_3$.

HARDNESS

Water hardness is similar to alkalinity but it represents several facts. It is important to fish culture and is commonly reported aspect of water quality. Hardness is the measure of calcium and magnesium, but other ions such as aluminium, iron, manganese, strontium, zinc and hydrogen ions are also covered. Calcium and magnesium are essential in the biological process of fish. Fish can absorb calcium and magnesium directly from the water or food. Hardness values are of at least 30 mg/litre should be maintained for optimum growth of aquatic organisms. Low hardness levels can be increased with the addition of agricultural lime.

NUTRIENTS

Nutrient a major constituent of protein occupies a predominant place in aquatic ecosystem. Though a relatively minor constituent, phosphorous is often considered to be the most critical single element in the maintenance of aquatic productivity. Dissolved inorganic nitrogen in the range of 0.2 to 0.5 mg/litre may be considered favourable for fish productivity and phosphorous fertility for aquatic productivity ranges from 0.05 to 2.0 mg/litre. In natural water, silicate remains in silicate form and is important structural constituent of diatoms. The nutrient status of both water and soil play the most important role in governing the production of plankton organism in fish pond. Nutrient can be increased in the ponds by adding inorganic and organic fertilizers in measured doses. However, increased levels of nutrient may be harmful; it can cause excessive plankton growth, algal bloom and oxygen depletion.

WASTEWATER TREATMENT

Wastewater is water that has been used and must be treated before it is released into another body of water, so that it does not cause further pollution of water sources. Wastewater comes from a variety of sources. Everything that you flush down your toilet or rinse down the drain is wastewater.

Rainwater and run-off, along with various pollutants, go down street gutters and eventually end up at a wastewater treatment facility. Wastewater can also come from agricultural and industrial sources. Some wastewaters are more difficult to treat than others; for example, industrial wastewater can be difficult to treat, whereas domestic wastewater is relatively easy to treat (though it is increasingly difficult to treat domestic waste, due to increased amounts of pharmaceuticals and personal care products that are found in domestic wastewater.

RESPONSIBILITY FOR MAKING SURE THAT WASTEWATER IS TREATED PROPERLY

Similar to drinking water provisions, the federal government has delegated responsibility for wastewater treatment to the provinces and territories. There are two federal acts, however, that may apply to wastewater. The Fisheries Act prohibits the release of harmful substances into waters that fish live in. The Canadian Environmental Protection Act governs the release of toxic substances into the environment and allows the federal government to develop regulations for the use of toxic substances.

Most provincial and territorial governments have legislation regarding wastewater treatment standards and requirements. Operators of wastewater treatment facilities must obtain permits or licenses from the provincial or territorial government, and these permits may also require additional treatments or limits on effluent discharges. For example, in British Columbia, all municipalities are required to have a Liquid Waste Management Plan; without an approved plan, discharges are illegal. Provincial and territorial governments generally assist municipal governments with funds to build and maintain infrastructure. Municipal governments directly oversee the wastewater treatment process, and are able to pass additional by-laws. For example, the

Regional Municipality of Ottawa-Carleton has developed a programme to eliminate toxic substances from the wastewater treatment system, requiring all industrial, institutional and commercial facilities to limit the amount of certain pollutants that are allowed into sewers.

Treatment of Wastewater, to Make it Safe for Discharge

There are several levels of wastewater treatment; these are primary, secondary and tertiary levels of treatment. Most municipal wastewater treatment facilities use primary and secondary levels of treatment, and some also use tertiary treatments. The type and order of treatment may vary from one treatment plant to another, but this diagram of the Ottawa-Carleton wastewater treatment plant illustrates the basic components.

The primary level of treatment uses screens and settling tanks to remove the majority of solids. This step is extremely important, because solids make up approximately 35% of the pollutants that must be removed. The screens usually have openings of about 10 millimetres, which is small enough to remove sticks, garbage and other large materials from the wastewater. This material is removed and disposed of at the landfill.

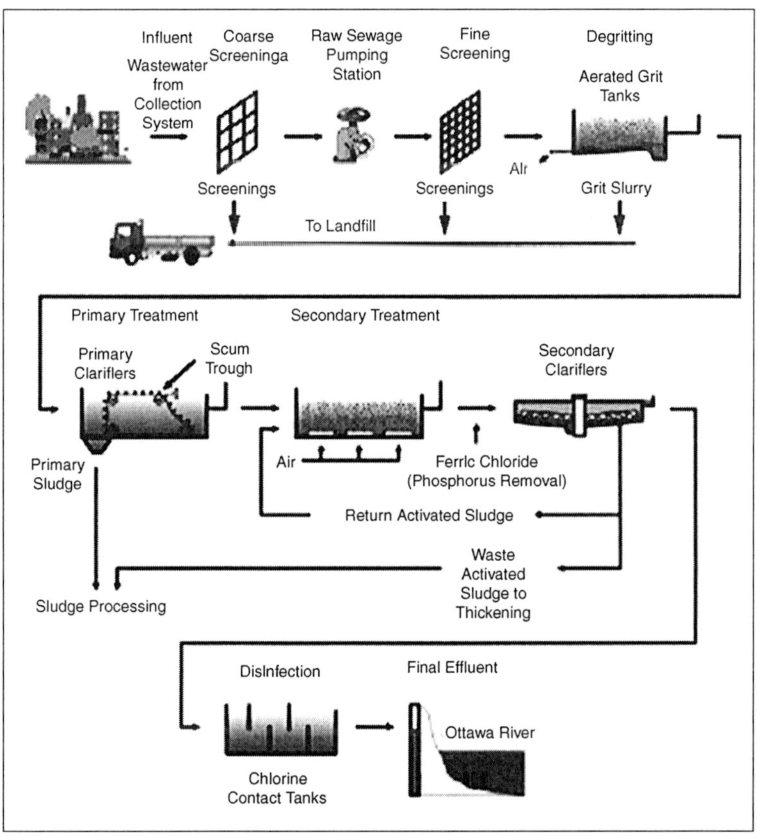

The water is then put into settling tanks (or clarifiers), where it sits for several hours, allowing the sludge to settle and a scum to form on the top. The scum is then skimmed off the top, the sludge is removed from the bottom, and the partially treated wastewater moves on to the secondary treatment level. The primary treatment generally removes up to 50 per cent of the Biological Oxygen Demand (BOD; these are substances that use up the oxygen in the water), around 90 per cent of suspended solids, and up to 55 per cent of fecal coliforms. While primary treatment removes a significant amount of harmful substances from wastewater, it is not enough to ensure that all harmful pollutants have been removed.

Secondary treatment of wastewater uses bacteria to digest the remaining pollutants. This is accomplished by forcefully mixing the wastewater with bacteria and oxygen. The oxygen helps the bacteria to digest the pollutants faster. The water is then taken to settling tanks where the sludge again settles, leaving the water 90 to 95 per cent free of pollutants. The picture below shows the settling tanks in the Winnipeg Wastewater Treatment Plant. Secondary treatment removes about 85 to 90 per cent of BOD and suspended solid, and about 90 to 99 per cent of coliform bacteria.

Some treatment plants follow this with a sand filter, to remove additional pollutants. The water is then disinfected with chlorine, ozone, or ultraviolet light, and then discharged.

The sludge that is removed from the settling tanks and the scum that is skimmed off the top during the primary steps are treated separately from the water. Anaerobic bacteria (anaerobic bacteria do not require oxygen) feed off of the sludge for 10 to 20 days at temperatures around 38 degrees Celsius.

This process decreases the odour and organic matter of the sludge, and creates a highly combustible gas of methane and carbon dioxide, which can be used as fuel to heat the treatment plant. Finally, the sludge is sent to a centrifuge, like the one shown in the picture below. A centrifuge is a machine that spins very quickly, forcing the liquid to separate from the solid. The liquid can then be processed with the wastewater and the solid is used as fertilizer on fields. Tertiary (or advanced) treatment removes dissolved substances, such as colour, metals, organic chemicals and nutrients like phosphorus and nitrogen. There are a number of physical, chemical and biological treatment processes that are used for tertiary treatment. One of the biological treatment processes is called Biological Nutrient Removal (BNR). This diagram shows the treatment steps that Saskatoon wastewater goes through.

In this treatment plant, wastewater first undergoes primary and secondary treatment. For the tertiary treatment, the BNR process occurs in the bioreactors. The BNR process uses bacteria in different conditions in several tanks, to digest the contaminants in the water. The three tanks have unique environments, with different amounts of oxygen. As the water has passes through the three tanks, the phosphorus is removed and the ammonia is broken down into nitrate and nitrogen gas, which other bacterial processes can not do. The BNR process can remove over 90 per cent of phosphates, while traditional processes remove much less than 90 per cent. The water spends approximately nine hours in the bioreactors, before entering the secondary clarifier, which is a settling tank, where the bacteria-laden sludge settles to the bottom of the tank.

Small Communities Treat Waste Ewater, to Make it Safe for Sischarge

In small communities, wastewater treatment facilities may consist of individual septic systems, simple collection systems that directly discharge effluent to surface waters, or municipal lagoons that are emptied annually. These facilities usually treat and disperse the waste as close as possible to its source, thus minimizing operational costs and maintenance requirements. The longer the waste can sit in a lagoon before being discharged, the less likely it will be to contaminate drinking water sources. Some communities store the waste in lagoons, but others release the waste directly into water sources.

Lagoons are reservoirs in the ground that store waste for a time until it is discharged, either to the soil or a water body. Shallow lagoons, that are less than 1.5 metres deep, are used for primary treatment, which allows the solid waste to settle to the bottom of the lagoon over a period of 6 to 20 days. Shallow lagoons, however, cannot effectively remove the majority of contaminants that pose problems for ground and surface waters. Deep lagoons, which are more than three metres deep, can provide long-term storage and treatment for six months to one year.

Many lagoons in small communities are emptied once per year. Rural communities often make use of surrounding land to dispose of wastewater. When the soil is adequate, and there are no water sources nearby, the bacteria in the soil can remove and break down the contaminants in wastewater. Due to the availability of land in many rural areas, this can be an effective method to treat wastewater. However, there are other communities that dispose of waste in a way that threatens the quality of the lake, river or groundwater source that provides drinking water.

The Environmental Protection Agency estimates that between 10 and 20 per cent of small community wastewater treatment facilities in the United States are not operating properly; state water quality agencies have identified malfunctioning wastewater treatment systems as the second greatest threat to water quality (after underground storage tanks). When the inadequate wastewater treatments are combined with ineffective drinking water treatment, the result is a serious contamination issue for a great number of rural communities.

Rural communities typically find it difficult to install and maintain wastewater treatment operations. And while many communities have inadequate methods of treating wastewater, there are some communities that are leading the way with innovative methods of treatment and water conservation measures. In several Arctic communities, including Iqaluit, Nunavut, the high cost of water has led to wastewater treatments that allow water to be reused. Wastewater is passed through a septic tank, filtered, and disinfected with ozone treatment; it is then reused for non-consumptive uses, such as toilets and laundry. These conservation measures allow them to reuse up to 55 per cent of wastewater, while decreasing pressure on wastewater treatment and storage processes. For more information about water conservation, including the ways in which rural and First Nations communities are leading efforts to reduce water use.

WORKING PROCESS OF SEPTIC SYSTEMS

There are many people living in rural areas that are not served by wastewater treatment plants. In fact, according to Environment Canada, as of 2000, only 57 per cent of Canadians were served by wastewater treatment plants, compared with 74 per cent of Americans, 86.5 per cent of Germans, and 99 per cent of Swedes. Many people in rural areas use septic systems to safely store waste. Wastewater travels through pipes, from the house to a buried septic tank. The diagram below illustrates the basic components of a septic system.

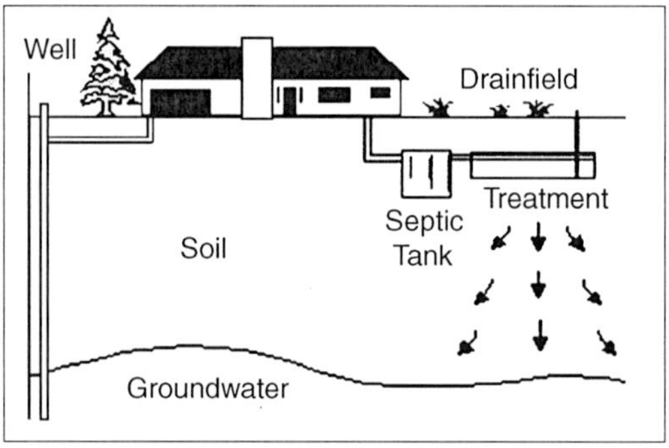

Fig. Septic Tank

The diagram below illustrates the tank in more detail. In the septic tank, the solids settle to the bottom and a scum forms on the top, similar to the process that occurs in settling tanks in municipal wastewater treatment plants.

Once separated, the water flows out to the drainfield, and screens and compartments keep the sludge and scum inside the tank, where bacteria begin to partially digest the sludge. When the partially treated wastewater enters the drainfield, it begins to infiltrate the soil and percolate downwards. So long as the soil is appropriate, the microbes in the soil digest the pollutants, removing the bacteria, viruses and excess nutrients by the time the water reaches the source.

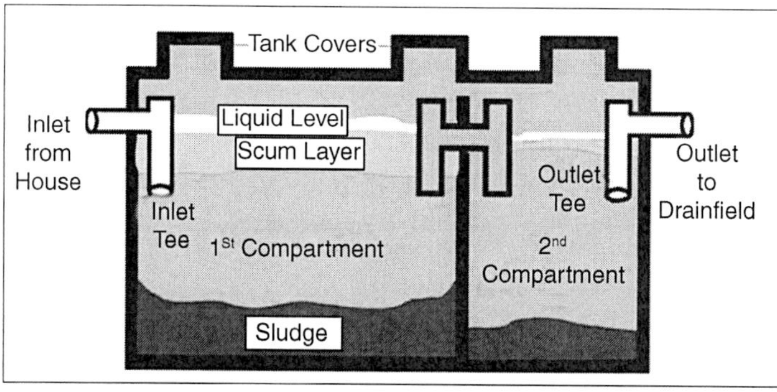

Fig. Inside of Septic System.

When the soil is not suitable, or there are nearby water sources, an alternative system may be used, so that water sources do not become contaminated. The alternative system may use sand, peat, or plastic instead of soil. Constructed wetlands, lagoons, aerators, or disinfection devices are also effective in treating the wastewater.

It is estimated that around half of all rural wells are contaminated, many from septic tanks. The United States Centers for Disease Control and Prevention suggests that wells should be at least 15 metres from septic tanks, but this distance also varies according to the type of soil.

In a recent study of groundwater sources in southeastern Michigan by the United States Geological Survey, 38 wells were tested between 1999 and 2001. Of the wells that were near sewerlines, viruses were detected in only two of the 18 wells. Of the 20 wells that were near septic systems, viruses were found in seven wells. This suggests that septic systems are a major cause of groundwater contamination. Previous studies of contaminated wells that were cited by the USGS study found coliforms in up to 80 per cent of the wells, as well as some with significant numbers of the E. coli bacterium.

If you are using a septic system, it is important to maintain it properly, as failure to do so could result in the leakage of pollutants into the soil or water sources. The United States Environmental Protection Agency (EPA) recommends that you have your septic system inspected at least once every three years, so that it can be checked for leaks and malfunctions, and also be pumped out when it gets full (typically once every three to five years).

Following some water conservation practices can greatly reduce pressure on your septic system.

Here are a few things that you can do to care for your septic system:

- Do not use your drain or toilet as a garbage disposal; avoid putting dental floss, diapers, coffee grounds and paper towel down the drain, as they can clog up your septic system.
- Spread your loads of laundry out over the week. When too much water is added to the septic tank, it does not have time to treat

wastes, and you could be flooding your drainfield with wastewater.

- Plant grass on your drainfield, but keep trees and shrubs away from it, because roots can clog the system and cause damage.
- Do not drive on your drainfield, because this can compact the soil and damage the septic system components.

NATURAL WAYS TO TREAT WASTEWATER

If nature itself can cleanse water, then imitating nature's processes may be the most effective and sustainable ways of treating wastewater. A great deal of water renewal occurs naturally in wetlands. Constructed wetlands consist of a lined cell, which the water flows into. Plants are planted in the cell and the roots filter the contaminants out of the water. Below is a diagram of a constructed wetland. Notice that many of the processes in a wetland are similar to the Biological Nutrient Removal process that was described above.

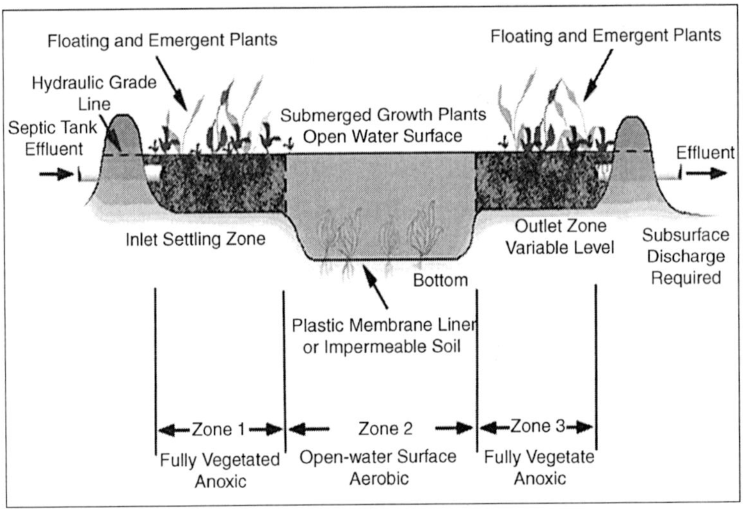

Fig. Constructed Wetland

Another natural method is called rapid infiltration, which is a process where a basin is filled with wastewater, which has already gone through a pre-treatment. The ground acts as a filter and removes the pollutants from the water. This method is similar to what happens in a septic system. A third "natural" process is overland flow, which is used in regions of nearly impermeable ground. The water flows down a sloped surface that is planted with thick grasses. Because the soil is highly impermeable, the water is forced through the vegetation, which effectively removes the pollutants.

Slow rate irrigation is a process that uses a portion of land, and allows the water to flow slowly enough that the land's capacity to infiltrate the water and remove the impurities is not overburdened. Silviculture is similar to slow rate irrigation, in that it uses a large amount of land to treat wastewater, by planting crops or trees that will flourish during the treatment process. Aquiculture uses aquatic plant and animal species to treat wastewater, similar to the constructed wetland process. There are also alternative separation systems that can conserve water. One such system separates blackwater (from toilets) from greywater (from showers and dishwashers), so that greywater can be minimally treated and used for watering the lawn. As well, there are incinerating, chemical, or composting toilets that release the waste when it is safe.

APPLICATION OF BIOLOGICAL PRINCIPLES IN WASTE WATER TREATMENT

Of the three aspects of biology outlined in this introduction, both taxonomy and physiology are necessary for a full appreciation of ecology. For those desirous of further study of any of these aspects of biology a list of appropriate references is given at the end of this chapter. In applying biological principles to waste water treatment, involving the controlled activities of populations of organisms, the ecological approach is probably the most rewarding and will be developed in subsequent sections.

The different aspects of ecology are all reflected in the several studies of the organisms found in sewage-treatment plants. Some resulted in mere systematic lists of organisms associated with different stages of the process and which, although useful as a basis for other workers, are of no practical value to the operator. Other observers have correlated the presence of organisms with different conditions within the plant and such organisms have then been used as "indicator organisms". For example, early in the history of activated sludge, different associations of protozoa were associated with different levels of sludge efficiency and microscopical examinations of the sludge to determine these associations were found to be of value in plant control. Probably because of the practical nature of the subject, early investigators enquired into the role of the different organisms in the purification process and thus the "synecological" aspect of the subject was introduced at an early stage. An outline of the historical development of our knowledge of the ecology of waste water treatment may be of interest.

HISTORICAL DEVELOPMENTS IN WASTE WATER ECOLOGY [H]

The discovery that micro-organisms were associated with water and putrefying liquids was made possible by the invention in 1675 of the compound microscope by Leuwenhoek. It was not until 1743, however, that Baker indicated the scavenging activities of protozoa and bacteria, and in 1839 Schwann and Schultze demonstrated that micro-organisms were the true agents of decompositio. Following his work, in the middle of the 19th century, on fermentation, Pasteur established the importance of micro-organisms in the process and distinguished between aerobic and anaerobic organisms for the first time. On the subject of organic wastes he declared "Dead matter which ferments and putrefies is not obedient, at any rate inclusively, to forces of a nature purely physical or chemical. It is life which rules over the work of death and the dissolution of animal and vegetable matter. This constant return to the atmospheric air and to the mineral kingdom of the constituents which vegetables and animals have borrowed from them is an act related to the development and multiplication of organized beings".

The setting up of the River Pollution Commissions of 1865 and 1868, as a result of the foul conditions of the rivers of this country, first initiated a scientific study into the problems of sewage treatment. At that time, the recognized method of disposal was by land treatment, but there appears to have been no appreciation of the role of microorganisms in the process in spite of the findings of earlier workers mentioned above. As a result of his investigations on the purification of sewage, Sir Edward Frankland in the second report of the Commission reported that the process was not merely mechanical filtration but involved chemical oxidation; the role of micro-organisms was apparently not appreciated.

He did appreciate, however, the need for adequate aeration and as a result of his experiments he did devise the "intermittent filtration" method using land. It was truly claimed "that Frankland's conclusions, based as they were on excellent experiments, have formed the foundation for all further progress relating to sewage purification up to the present time". Unfortunately, however, his mechanical-chemical concept of the process has persisted, although in a subconscious form, and still influences the design and operation of biological treatment plants; the term sewage "filter" reflects this attitude to the process!

Later work, however, by Schloesing and Muntz showed that nitrification was brought about by micro-organisms and they concluded that these were essential to the purification process. Warington showed that nitrification proceeded in two stages, each stage being the result of the activity of separate organisms. These were later isolated as *Nitrosomonas* and *Nitrobacter* by Winogradsky. For a more detailed history the reader is referred to Stanbridge.

The role of larger animals in the stabilization of organic matter was also reported by Dr. Sorby to the Royal Commission on the Metropolitan Sewage Discharge in 1883. He associated the disappearance of sedimentary faecal matter in the river Thames with the presence of certain crustacea and worms. Thus before the advent of the bacteria bed, which was evolved from soil and sand filters as a result of experiments at the Lawrence Experiment Station, Massachusetts, the role of both the micro-organisms and the macrofauna in sewage purification had been established. The results of the Lawrence experiments stimulated investigations of the principles involved in the bacteria bed method of treatment. In these, although the role of the micro-organisms was appreciated by most, and studies were carried out on the bacterial flora, the activity of the larger organisms, previously associated with purification, was at first overlooked, their presence, when observed, being regarded as incidental, as indeed it still is by some workers.

Johnson, in reviewing the early works, quoted Dunbar as first drawing attention to the function of higher animals and plants and states that later Höfer, in 1907, investigated their activities more closely. Dibdin in 1904 also observed the presence of large numbers of active insects and Annelid worms in his slate beds, and Fowler also reported on the importance of the higher forms of life in sewage purification. About the same time Harrison in his evidence to the *Royal Commission on Sewage Disposa* suggested that the seasonal discharge of solids from beds was probably due to the activity of the macrofauna. Work of a more truly ecological nature was carried out by Johnson when he studied the factors influencing the distribution of different species of macrofauna in bacteria beds at Wakefield. Parkinson and Bell demonstrated the useful activity of the springtail *Achorutes subviaticus* in controlling film accumulation.

Later, the environment of the bacteria bed, supporting a reduced number of species, attracted the attention of more academic workers as a habitat on which to study problems of the dynamics of populations. Notable among such workers were Dr. Lloyd and his succession of students at Leeds University who carried out a series of studies on insect and protozoan populations on sewage works in the West Riding; these are summarized by Lloyd. Nuisance arising from flies leaving the bacteria beds probably attracted attention to the macrofauna before their beneficial activities were fully realized. Later, this nuisance resulted in many investigations into methods of control using different chemicals.

Some such investigations were ecological in that they attempted to relate the populations to environmental conditions but most, although of practical value in assessing the effectiveness of different control measures, did not advance the knowledge of bacteria bed ecology. Another practical problem—the choking of the beds with accumulated film—has led to a series of ecological investigations both in this country. At Birmingham a study on the effect of insecticide treatment on the bacteria bed community and film accumulation has led to the two practical difficulties being studied as one ecological problem.

In the ecology of activated sludge both academic interest and practical problems have initiated ecological investigations. Ecological successions of different species of protozoa in the development of a sludge and the relative roles of protozoa and bacteria in the process have been studied by many workers. The development of filamentous growths associated with 'bulking' has also resulted in investigations being carried out.

The outcome of such ecological investigations usually results in the formulation of hypotheses which necessitate laboratory work for their proof or otherwise and much work being carried out at present by the Water Pollution

Research Laboratory and others will, it is hoped, assist in the solution of outstanding ecological problems.

ACTIVATED-SLUDGE AND BACTERIA-BED ENVIRONMENTS [H]

The treatment of waste waters by both methods involves similar biochemical processes the two differ in many respects. Firstly, whereas the activated sludge is truly an aquatic environment that of the bacteria bed has been likened to the wrack zone of the sea shore.

Also, whereas the fauna of activated sludge is normally restricted to microorganisms, the bacteria bed also supports higher forms of life such as oligochaete worms and insects. Associated with this difference in the fauna is the difference in the degree of control the operator has over the two biological systems. In the activated sludge process the amount of microbial mass is controlled by the withdrawal of excess sludge from the system; in the bacteria bed excess film is removed chiefly by biological agencies.

A fundamental difference in the ecology of the two systems is that in the bacteria bed a succession of communities becomes established at different levels of the bed and associated with the corresponding different degrees of purification; whereas in the activated-sludge process the same community within the floc is at one time associated with the untreated waste and at the other extreme with the purified effluent.

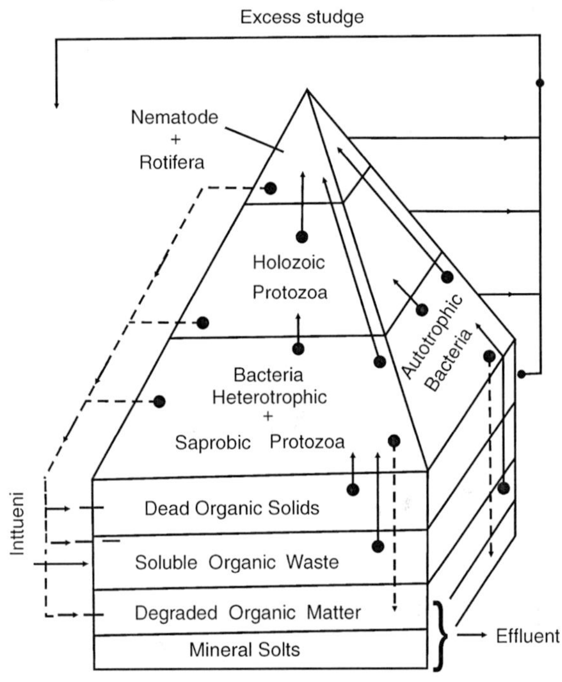

Fig. Diagrammatic Representation of the Main Food-links in the Purification of Organic Wastes by Activated Sludge and by Bacteria Beds.

It is of interest to note that many of the advantages and disadvantages of the two systems are attributable to these differences; fly nuisance and the choking of the beds being connected with film control by biological agencies; bulking of the sludge, with resultant settlement difficulties, and the difficulties associated with disposal of the surplus activated sludge are probably connected with its removal from the system as microbial flocs rather than as the faeces of the grazing fauna. Again, the relative sensitivity of activated sludge to toxic discharges may be associated with circulation of the sludge, whereas, in the more robust 5 bacteria beds such discharges are first taken by the surface growths. A highly nitrified effluent is more often associated with an efficient bacteria bed than with activated sludge and this may also be connected with the differences in the relative ecological systems. Nitrifying organisms are more effective in isolation from the other processes of purification, *e.g.* in the cleaner depths of the bacteria bed or in the cleaner secondary bed of the two-stage process. It may be therefore, that in the multipurpose floc of the activated sludge their activity is restricted. Also the length of life of a floc in the system is largely determined by the growth rate of the heterotrophic bacteria and may be such that the floc is discharged before the more slowly growing autotrophic nitrifying organisms become effectively established.

In nature, a succession of different ecological conditions and associated communities concerned with the breakdown of organic matter in waters has been described. A high concentration of complex decomposable organic matter is associated with the absence, or very low concentration, of oxygen—*Polysaprobic* condition. As purification proceeds and the organic matter is broken down first to aminoacids (*á-mesosaprobic*) and then to salts, the oxygen concentration increases until oxidation and mineralization is completed (*oligosaprobic*). Both the activated-sludge and the bacteria-bed environment differ from these systems in that, because of the aeration, high concentration of complex organic matter may be associated with fairly high oxygen concentrations. Obviously large numbers of organisms gain access to both activated sludge plants and bacteria beds; many find the environment inhospitable and never become established; others may persist but are not very successful, whilst the few species which find the habitat suitable, increase greatly and with reduced competition may become more abundant than in their natural habitat. In the following discussion on the ecologies of the two processes only those organisms considered to have a significant role in the community, *i.e.* those organisms which if removed from the community would appreciably upset its balance of populations.

IMPORTANCE OF HEALTH MANAGEMENT IN AQUACULTURE

Aquaculture is the farming of aquatic organisms including fish, molluscs, crustaceans and aquatic plants. Farming implies some sort of intervention in the rearing process to enhance production, such as regular stocking, feeding, protection from predators, etc. Aquaculture has a long history. In the People's Republic of China (PR China), common carp were raised for food in freshwater ponds as early as 1100 b.c. Other examples of early aquaculture practices include the Japanese culturing oysters for pearls; ancient Egyptians stocking ponds with fish; the Greeks and Romans raising eels; the Europeans cultivating oysters.

The aquaculture sector is highly diverse in terms of:

- Species- an estimated 230 species of fin fish, molluscs, crustaceans, aquatic plants, turtles, frogs, etc., are cultured.
- Culture systems- *e.g.*, water-based systems, such as cages and pens, bottom/pole/rack/raft/long-line systems for molluscs, inshore and off-shore; land- based systems such as rain-fed ponds; irrigated or flow-through systems, tanks and raceways; land/ water-based systems, such as sea ranching; recycling systems such as high control enclosed systems, more open pond-based recirculation; monoculture and polyculture systems; integrated farming systems, such as livestock-fish, integrated agriculture-aquaculture, livestock-aquaculture.
- Culture environment- *e.g.*, freshwater, brackish water, marine; inland, coastal and oceanic; temperate to tropical.
- Type of operation and scale- *e.g.*, small-scale backyard ponds and hatcheries to commercial operations; hatchery holding of broodstock and production of seed, nursing systems, grow-out.
- Intensity of practice- *e.g.*, extensive, semi-intensive, intensive.
- Type of management- from family to corporate ownership.

HEALTH AS A CONSTRAINT TO AQUACULTURE

The current trend in aquaculture development is towards increased intensification and commercialisation of aquatic production. Like other farming sectors, the likelihood of major disease problems occurring increases as aquaculture activities intensify and expand. Thus, the aquaculture industry has been overwhelmed with its share of diseases and problems caused by viruses, bacteria, fungi, parasites and other undiagnosed and emerging pathogens. Disease is now a primary constraint to the culture of many aquatic species, impeding both economic and social development in many countries.

This situation can be attributed to a variety of multi-faceted and highly interconnected factors such as the increased globalisation of trade in live aquatic animals and their products; the intensification of aquaculture through the translocation of brood stock, post larvae, fry and fingerlings; the development and expansion of the ornamental fish trade; the enhancement of marine and coastal areas through stocking aquatic animals raised in hatcheries; the misunderstanding and misuse of specific pathogen free (SPF) stocks (*e.g.* shrimps); unanticipated negative interactions between cultured and wild fish populations; poor or lack of effective biosecurity measures; slow awareness on emerging diseases; climate change; all other human mediated movements of aquaculture commodities. However, once a pathogen or disease agent is introduced and becomes established into the natural environment, there is little or no possibility for either treatment or eradication. While consequences of "trickle" infections from wild to cultured populations have predictable consequences due to accessible hosts under cultured conditions, the consequences of culture-borne transmission to wild stocks are harder to predict. Examples of infection of cultured stocks via wild stock reservoirs for shrimp diseases and for marine finfish disease. Koi herpes virus (KHV) has recently been introduced to Indonesia and Japan. In Japan, it has caused mass mortalities not only among farmed carp but also wild carp in many rivers and lakes.

Additional examples from Japan include the following:

- *Neo-heterobothrium hirame*, a monogenean parasite, the original host probably being southern flounder from the United States, is believed to have been the cause of a decline in the catch of olive flounder in some parts of Japan;
- White spot syndrome virus (WSSV) remains an important pathogen of farmed shrimp (*Penaeus monodon*) and has now been recovered from wild penaeid shrimps.

TRANSBOUNDARY AQUATIC ANIMAL DISEASES/ PATHOGENS

Aquaculture is faced with what is known as transboundary aquatic animal pathogens/diseases (TAAPs/TAADs), which are similar to the transboundary animal diseases or TADs in the livestock sector. TAADs are diseases that are highly contagious or transmissible, having the potential for very rapid spread irrespective of national borders and causing serious socio-economic and possibly health consequences. The Office International des Epizooties (OIE) currently lists 35 pathogens/ diseases of finfish, molluscs and crustaceans that fit three major criteria in terms of consequence, spread and diagnosis.

Criteria for urgent notification for the listed aquatic animal diseases are:

- First occurrence or re-occurrence of a disease in a country or zone of a country if the country or zone was previously considered to be free of that particular disease;
- Occurrence in a new host species;
- New pathogen strain or new disease manifestation;
- Potential for international spread of the disease;
- Zoonotic potential.

For non-listed diseases, the criteria for urgent notification is if there are findings in an emergency disease/pathogenic agent that are of epidemiological significance to other countries.

IMPACT OF TRANSBOUNDARY DISEASES IN AQUACULTURE

Infectious diseases are constraining the development and sustainability of the aquaculture sector through direct production losses and increased operating costs and indirectly, through restrictions on trade and impacts on biodiversity. Inadequate or poorly implemented biosecurity measures have led to significant losses due to aquatic animal diseases in many countries around the world.

The impacts of aquatic animal diseases on wild populations and biodiversity that can be measured in terms of:

- Impact on aquatic community structure through changes in predator and prey populations;
- Changes in host abundance (*e.g.* through altered genetic demands, altered host behaviour, increased mortality, decreased fecundity, increased susceptibility to predation);
- Reduction of intra-specific genetic variation;
- Local extirpation of susceptible components of aquatic communities;
- The possible extinctions of species.

The impacts of disease have been estimated in socio-economic terms (*e.g.* losses in production, income, employment, market access or market share, investment and consumer confidence; food shortages; industry failure or closure of business or industry). However, due to the frequency of occurrence and the magnitude of spread and effects, many countries are now providing some estimates of disease impacts.

Losses are expressed as monetary estimates (in many cases a scale of millions of US$), percentage decrease in production, export losses, unemployment, closure of aquaculture operations and lost consumer confidence. At the regional level, ADB/NACA reported that the minimum conservatively estimated lost farm production fish diseases (such as epizootic ulcerative syndrome (EUS) of fresh and brackish water fishes, penaeid shrimp diseases and a variety of other diseases causing losses in freshwater finfish pond culture and marine cage culture).

Bibliography

A.St.J. Macdonald: *Circumventing the Mahseer and Other Sporting Fish in India and Burma*, Natraj Publications, Delhi, 2001.

Ajit Kumar Roy: *Evaluation and Impact Assessment of Technologies* and Developmental Activities in Agriculture, Fisheries, and Allied *Fields*, New India Publishing Agency, Delhi, 2011.

Albert C L G Gunther and J Arthur Thomson: *Biology of World Fishes*, Arise Publishers, Delhi, 2012.

Andrew L. Winton and Kate Barber Winton: *Fish and Fish Products*, Agrobios Publications, Delhi, 2002.

Antonio Goncalves: *Beginning Java Ee6 Platform With Glassfish 3: From Novice To Professional*, Dreamtech Press, Delhi, 2010.

B L Kaul: *Advances in Fish and Wildlife Ecology and Biology: Vol: IV*, Daya Publications, Delhi, 2007.

B.L. Kaul: *Advances in Fish and Wildlife Ecology and Biology*: *Vol. 3*, Daya Publications, Delhi, 2004.

B.N. Pandey, Sunil P. Trivedi, Kamal Jaiswal and Navneet Kaur Sethi: *Fish and Fisheries*, Sarup Book Publishers, Delhi, 2009.

Bansi Lal Kaul: *Advances in Fish and Wildlife Ecology and Biology, Vol. II*, Daya Publications, Delhi, 1999.

Bubul Das and Devashish Kar: *Basic Limnology and Fish Biodiversity*, Manglam Publications, Delhi, 2011.

C. Van Duijn: *Diseases of Fishes*, Narendra Publications, Delhi, 2000. C.B.L. Srivastava: *Catfish Soft Anatomy*, Kitab Mahal Publications, Delhi, 2005.

Charls L. Cutting: *Fish*: *Processing and Preservation*, Agrobios Publications, Jaipur, 2002.

D.R. Khanna and P.R. Yadav: *Biology of Fishes*, Discovery Publications, Delhi, 2004.

D.V. Rao: *A Field Guide to Fishes (Chilika Lake, Orissa, East Coast of India)*, Akansha Publications, Delhi, 2009.

296 Fish Biology and Fisheries Devashish Kar: *Essentials of Fish Biology*, Dominant Publications, Delhi, 2013.

F.D. Ommanney: *A Draught of Fishes*, Arise Publishers, Delhi, 2012.

G.N. Chattopadhyay: *Chemical Analysis of Fish Pond Soil and Water*, Daya Publications, Delhi, 1998.

G.S. Sandhu: *An Introduction to Fishes*, Campus Books, Delhi, 2001.

G.V. Nikolsky: *Ecology of Fishes*, Allied Scientific, Delhi, 1999.

Gurdarshan Singh and H. Bhaskar: *An Introduction to Fishes*, Campus Books, Delhi, 2003.

H A Khan: *Catfishes Systematics, Biology and Farming*, Narendra Publications, Delhi, 2008.

Harish Lowe: *Beginner's Guide to Aquarium Fish and Fish Care*, Abhishek Press, Delhi, 2005.

Jagdish Ojha: *Biology of Hillstream Fishes*, Narendra Publications, Delhi, 2002.

K.C. Jayaram: *Catfishes of India*, Narendra Publications, Delhi, 2006.

K.P. Biswas: *Ecological and Fisheries Development in Wetlands: A Study of Chilka Lagoon*, Daya Publications, Delhi, 1995.

Kamal Maheshwari: *Fish and Fisheries*, Sonali Publications, Delhi, 2011.

Kamla Devi and D.V. Rao: *A Field Guide to the Fishes of Acanthuridae* (Surgeonfishes) and Siganidae (Rabbitfishes) of Andaman & *Nicobar Islands*, Zoological Survey of India, 2003.

M Sinha; Dhirendra Kumar and P K Katiha: *Eco-Friendly Management* of Resources for Doubling Fish Production - Strategies for Twenty *First Century*, Central Inland Capture Fisheries Research Institute, 2001.

Manas K Das and R K Das: *Fish and Prawn Diseases in India: Diagnosis and Control*, Inland Fisheries Society of India, 1997.

N B Marshall: *Fish: Life, Environment and Diversity*, Agrobios Publications, Jaipur, 2006.

N.K. Bose and Shambhu Dhir: *A Case Study on Intensification for Freshwater Fish Culture and Training*, Cyber Tech Publications, Delhi, 2011.

N.M. Chakrabarty, P.P. Chakraborty and S.C. Mondal: *Biology Breeding and Farming of Important Food Fishes*, Narendra Publications, Delhi, 2010.

Niranjan Sarangi and Ajit Kumar Roy: *Applied Bioinformatics Statistics and Economics in Fisheries Research*, New India Pub Agency, Delhi, 2008.

Index